OREGON'S LIVING LANDSCAPE

STRATEGIES AND OPPORTUNITIES TO CONSERVE BIODIVERSITY

A DEFENDERS OF WILDLIFE PUBLICATION

ABOUT THE OREGON BIODIVERSITY PROJECT

The Oregon Biodiversity Project is a collaborative effort involving dozens of public and private partners to develop a statewide strategy for conserving Oregon's biological diversity.

STEERING COMMITTEE

Daniel D. Heagerty (Chair)	David Evans and Associates
Thomas Imeson, Terry Flores	PacifiCorp
Catherine Macdonald	The Nature Conservancy of Oregon
Fred Otley	Cattle rancher
Howard Sohn	Sun Studs, Inc.
Sara Vickerman	Defenders of Wildlife

PRINCIPAL PARTNERS

Defenders of Wildlife is a national, non-profit organization headquartered in Washington, D.C. Its mission is to protect and restore native wild animals and plants in their natural communities. The West Coast Office emphasizes alternative approaches to environmental decision-making by facilitating partnerships among divergent interests seeking constructive solutions to environmental problems. Defenders invites you to visit its Web site at www.Defenders.org.

The Nature Conservancy is an international, non-profit organization headquartered in Arlington, Virginia. Its mission is to preserve plants, animals, and natural communities representing the diversity of life by protecting their habitats. The Nature Conservancy of Oregon maintains 53 nature preserves, encompassing more than 50,000 acres of some of the most biologically important habitats in Oregon. The Conservancy invites you to visit its Web site at www.tnc.org.

The mission of the *Oregon Natural Heritage Program* is to acquire, maintain, and distribute information on the organisms and ecosystems that constitute Oregon's natural heritage, and to ensure that the full range of Oregon's natural heritage resources is represented within a statewide system of recognized natural areas. The Heritage Program invites you to visit its Web site at www.abi.org/nhp/us/or.

Additional copies of *Oregon's Living Landscape*

can be obtained from the West Coast Office of Defenders of Wildlife. An order form for this publication and other associated products is at the back of the book.

Cover design: Ann Marra

Cover photo: Sycan River from *Oregon Rivers* by Larry N. Olson and John Daniel (Westcliffe Publishers 1997)

Background wrap-around image is a close-up of ponderosa pine bark by George Baetjer

Library of Congress Cataloging-in-Publication Data

Oregon's living landscape : strategies and opportunities to conserve biodiversity / Oregon Biodiversity Project .
p. cm.
"A Defenders of Wildlife publication."
Includes bibiographical references (p.)
and index.
ISBN 0-926549-01-4 (pbk. : alk. paper)
1. Biological diversity conservation--Oregon. 2. Endangered species--Oregon. 3. Endangered ecosystems--Oregon. I. Oregon Biodiversity Project. II. Defenders of Wildlife.
QH76.5.07078 1998
333.95'16'09795--dc21 98-15394
CIP

Contents

Foreword

The immensity and complexity of our biological systems are beyond our ability to fully comprehend. That we have not yet identified many of the plant and animal species living around us in Oregon should cause us all to wonder.

We do know that of the species we have identified in Oregon, more than 450 are listed as globally rare or sensitive, an alarming trend toward extinction. We also know that we have substantially reduced the populations of migratory birds — one of the most visible reminders of our rich wildlife heritage — to the point where several species are a fraction of their historic population. For most of these species, the problem is loss of habitat. The western meadowlark, our once-common state bird, is no longer seen or heard by most residents of Oregon, its native grassland habitats lost to changes in agricultural land use and increasing urbanization.

The Oregon Biodiversity Project was founded on a vision for Oregon's future — a vision that looks across the entire landscape, dropping the artificial lines imposed by humans and relying instead on the contours of biological form and function. To achieve that vision, Oregonians need a better understanding of the context for the biological landscapes of our state, and the challenges we face in trying to conserve biological resources while still meeting economic and social needs.

That was the starting point for the project's six-member steering committee, composed of representatives from two conservation organizations, executives from a large utility and an environmental engineering firm, a Roseburg timber company owner, and a Harney County rancher. We were attracted to the project because of the opportunities it offered to push discussion of the issues to a new level, beyond the rhetoric of choices limited to "salmon or jobs." We challenged each other on policy, science, and resource management issues. We agreed that there are many ways to practice good stewardship, and we concluded that we needed to give landowners greater incentives to participate actively in conservation. We came to see the Oregon Biodiversity Project as a framework for a larger set of values and a common understanding of the dynamic landscape in which we can all practice better stewardship. We proved, I believe, that a vision can be created that all Oregonians can share.

From the native pollinators that migrate here from Central America to the sandhill cranes overhead that thrill our school children, our biological resources are our "natural capital," providing basic goods and services to society. We must manage these resources just as we would manage our other capital assets. We are obligated to ensure that future generations have the opportunity to use and enjoy these resources. We have no greater right to this capital than the next generation.

Biological diversity must be a core value for Oregonians. It defines who we are and what we represent as a state. If we falter in the stewardship of our biological bank, we undermine not only this core value, but also our future economies and quality of life.

Daniel D. Heagerty

Chairman, Oregon Biodiversity Project Steering Committee

David Evans and Associates

Acknowledgments

Oregon's Living Landscape

This document is the product of the efforts of numerous individuals. Lori Kleifgen, who coordinated development of the Oregon Biodiversity Project's databases and created several of the key GIS coverages, was responsible for most of the GIS-based analysis that provided the foundation for the statewide overview and ecoregion assessments. Keith Hupperts stepped in to complete the GIS analysis and produced most of the final maps for the atlas. David Dobkin participated in the analysis for many of the ecoregions. Other individuals who helped with several ecoregions included Bruce Taylor, Jimmy Kagan, Cathy Macdonald, Dick Vander Schaaf, and Steve Caicco.

Bruce Taylor was primarily responsible for the document's text, which benefited from major contributions from Cathy Macdonald, Lori Kleifgen, Sara Vickerman, Wendy Hudson, Jimmy Kagan, and Dick Vander Schaaf. David Dobkin and Reed Noss each provided a detailed review of an initial draft of the entire document and Blair Csuti, Peter Brussard, and Bruce Marcot provided helpful comments on the biodiversity basics chapter. Numerous individuals, including David Perry, Reed Noss, Steve Caicco, Janet Ohmann, and Tony Svejcar, reviewed one or more of the ecoregion chapters. Pam Wiley helped out with detailed comments on the conservation strategy and suggestions that helped resolve several major editorial issues.

Wendy Hudson was responsible for overall editing and production coordination throughout the publication process, with assistance from Kassandra Stirling. The document was designed by Ann Marra and Judith Quinn. Processing of data for production of some of the final maps and graphics was done by Jon Bowers of Interrain Pacific.

A number of photographers generously shared their striking photographs of Oregon's habitats and wildlife, including Ed Alverson, George Baetjer, Darren Borgias, Beth Davidow/Visuals Unlimited, Robert Fields, Linda Hardie, Don Lawrence, Harold Malde, Geoff Pampush, and Alan St. John. Special thanks also go to the publication *Oregon Rivers* by Larry N. Olson and John

Daniel (Westcliffe Publishers). Stephen Anderson generously made available to the project The Nature Conservancy's extensive photo library.

Oregon Biodiversity Project

The Oregon Biodiversity Project is a true partnership. More than 50 cooperators contributed funding, personnel time, facilities, equipment, and other resources to the project. Space limitations make it impossible to list all the entities and individuals who have helped, but some played particularly important roles.

The Department of Defense's Legacy Program and the Department of the Interior's Gap Analysis Program (currently part of the U.S. Geologic Survey's Biological Resources Division) were early financial supporters. Foundation support included grants from the National Fish and Wildlife Foundation, Meyer Memorial Trust, Sequoia Foundation, Laird Norton Endowment Foundation, and the Weeden Foundation. Corporate contributors included PacifiCorp, Georgia Pacific, Starker Forests, Weyerhaeuser, Sun Studs, and Chevron Corporation. The U.S. Environmental Protection Agency contributed funding for this publication through a grant to the Oregon Department of Fish and Wildlife. The U.S. Fish and Wildlife Service provided additional financial support, and both The Nature Conservancy of Oregon and Defenders of Wildlife made substantial cash and in-kind contributions to the project.

Technical support in developing some of the project's database and graphics was provided by Interrain Pacific. Data developed for the Oregon Gap Analysis Project provided some key initial GIS coverages. The Oregon Natural Heritage Program made available its database on rare, threatened, and endangered species and provided data for the historic vegetation map. Numerous other sources contributed data that were incorporated into the Oregon Biodiversity Information System, including researchers associated with the Oregon State University, the Oregon Department of Fish and Wildlife, the Oregon Gap Analysis Program, the Biodiversity Research Consortium, and the Forest Service Global Change Program. Earth Design Consultants helped assemble the project's historic vegetation map. The regional office of the U.S. Fish and Wildlife Service made its geographic information system (GIS) work station available to project staff, and Environmental Systems Research Institute, Inc. contributed GIS software. CH2M Hill, David Evans and Associates, and Wildwood, Inc., contributed facilities and other support for project committee meetings.

The Nature Conservancy of Oregon and the Oregon Natural Heritage Program contributed substantial staff time to the project's biodiversity analysis and to the content development of this atlas. The High Desert Ecological Research Institute assisted with interpretation and analysis.

Special thanks go to all the members of the project's three committees:

PROJECT STAFF

Defenders of Wildlife

Sara Vickerman, *project director*

Bruce Taylor, *project manager*

Lori Kleifgen, *scientific and technical coordinator*

Wendy Hudson, *production coordinator*

Keith Hupperts, *GIS project manager*

Kassandra Stirling, *administrative support*

Pam Wiley, *consultant*

The Nature Conservancy

Cathy Macdonald

Dick Vander Schaaf

Oregon Natural Heritage Program

Jimmy Kagan

Eleanor Gaines

Oregon Gap Analysis Program

Blair Csuti

Tom O'Neil

Steering Committee

Dan Heagerty (chair), *David Evans and Associates (formerly with CH2M Hill)*

Thomas Imeson and Terry Flores, *PacifiCorp*

Catherine Macdonald, *The Nature Conservancy*

Fred Otley, *cattle rancher*

Howard Sohn, *Sun Studs, Inc.*

Sara Vickerman, *Defenders of Wildlife*

Science Committee

Duane Dippon, *Bureau of Land Management*

Craig Groves, *The Nature Conservancy*

Larry Irwin, *National Council for Air and Stream Improvement*

Willa Nehlsen, *U.S. Fish and Wildlife Service (formerly with Pacific Rivers Council)*

Reed Noss, *consultant*

Janet Ohmann, *U.S. Forest Service*

David Perry, *Oregon State University*

Jim Rochelle, *Weyerhaeuser Co.*

Mark Stern, *Oregon Natural Heritage Program*

Tony Svejcar, *U.S. Agricultural Research Service*

Implementation Committee

Ed Backus, *Interrain Pacific*

Hugh Black, *U.S. Forest Service*

Jim Brown, *Oregon Department of Forestry*

Paula Burgess, *Governor's Office, Natural Resource Policy*

Jody Calica, *Confederated Tribes of Warm Springs*

Martin Goebel, *Sustainable Northwest*

Steve Gordon, *Lane Council of Governments*

Bob Graham and Bianca Streif, *Natural Resources Conservation Service*

Mike Graybill, *South Slough National Estuarine Research Reserve*

Don Knowles, *Regional Ecosystem Office*

Sue Kupillas, *Jackson County Commissioner*

Bob Messinger, *Boise Cascade Corp.*

John Miller, *Wildwood, Inc.*

Geoff Pampush, *Oregon Trout*

Russell Peterson, *U.S. Fish and Wildlife Service*

Rudy Rosen, *Oregon Department of Fish and Wildlife*

Elaine Zielenski, *Bureau of Land Management*

List of Maps

Introduction

This publication is one of the primary products of the Oregon Biodiversity Project, a collaborative effort to develop a statewide strategy to conserve Oregon's natural biological diversity.

More than three years in the making, this document presents the results of the project's efforts to compile information for a "big picture" view of Oregon's biodiversity. It explains the ways we analyzed that information to assess conservation needs from a statewide and ecoregional perspective. It also outlines a long-term strategy for conserving Oregon's biological diversity, and highlights actions that landowners, resource managers and policy makers can take to help implement that strategy.

The resulting document is part atlas, part report; a mix of geography and conservation biology, technical analysis, and common-sense recommendations. Much of the information is not new. What is new is the way it has all been put together to place biodiversity conservation issues in a statewide perspective.

Many of these issues have been addressed in the past, but at a different scale — a single site, the range of a particular species, even a region encompassing multiple states. A statewide assessment makes sense for several reasons. While the boundaries of a state are entirely artificial in ecological terms, they do define the political arena in which many land and resource management policy decisions are made. Perhaps more important, state lines define an "Oregon" familiar to all and provide a context everyone can relate to.

Although much of the Oregon Biodiversity Project's analysis focuses on the state's 10 individual ecoregions (large areas with similar physical conditions and biological features), we have attempted to frame these assessments within a larger, statewide context. In doing so, we hope to encourage people to take a broader view of Oregon's ecosystems and their contributions to the state's biodiversity.

Running throughout the document is a strong conservation message. But the message is neither alarmist nor accusatory. The Oregon Biodiversity Project has been guided since its beginning by a belief that many of the conservation challenges the state faces can best be addressed through cooperative, non-adversarial efforts. Human uses of the land and other natural resources — the primary threats to Oregon's biological diversity — are a fact of life. "Either-or" choices between economic and ecological values are too simplistic to have much use in addressing the complexities of an issue as broad as conservation of biodiversity. We approached this project with the assumption that society needs and wants both a healthy economy and a healthy environment, and that the challenge is to find ways to reconcile those sometimes conflicting goals.

The issue is not whether a field of wheat or a conifer plantation is "better" or "worse" than a native grassland or forest, but whether we can continue to have both. *Native habitats are the primary focus of our concern in this book because they harbor many of the species most vulnerable to loss, and their degradation jeopardizes ecological processes that are critical to the health of Oregon's ecosystems.* With almost one-quarter of the state's native terrestrial vertebrate species considered "at risk" (sensitive, threatened, or endangered) (Marshall 1996), habitat issues clearly present the single, greatest challenge to conserving biodiversity.

Many of Oregon's native habitats have been reduced to a fraction of their historic extent, and most have been dramatically altered by human activities. The Willamette Valley's native grasslands, for example, have been reduced to less than one percent of their historic extent. Most of Oregon's forests are still "forest," but only a small fraction retain the biodiversity values of a forest shaped by natural patterns of disturbance, and many bear little resemblance to the forests encountered by nineteenth-century settlers.

Of those native habitats that do remain, the vast majority receive little or no formal protection, and very few are managed explicitly for biodiversity values. With the exception of a few types — including alpine habitats and, more recently, westside conifer forests — most native habitats lack the levels of protection many conservation biologists believe are necessary to ensure against progressive loss of biodiversity. But even lands that are "protected" by state and federal designations and other conservation-oriented management have not been immune to these threats, as managers of wildlife refuges battling invasive exotic plants can testify.

Strategies for conserving biological diversity at a statewide scale are untested and subject to considerable debate in the scientific community. The issue has yet to be given much serious consideration in the realm of public policy and day-to-day resource management. Clearly, we are a long way from being able to say how we as a society should manage our natural resources to ensure that our descendants enjoy an Oregon as rich in biological diversity as the one we inherited.

Nonetheless, resource management decisions are going to be made every day, with or without any blueprint for conserving biodiversity. We can't afford to wait to get all the answers. We need to begin now to establish a broader common vision for Oregon's future landscape.

This publication is envisioned as a first step in helping Oregonians to begin thinking about these issues. The data used by the Oregon Biodiversity Project to create an initial portrait of the state's biodiversity are imperfect. The conclusions we have drawn from our analyses can and should be debated. The recommendations we offer represent the thinking of people who have given considerable thought to these issues over the past few years, but they are far from the final word on the subject.

We hope our work will inspire others to take the next steps to begin translating conservation strategies into action on the ground, to collect better data, to refine analytical techniques, and to revise and improve upon our strategies over time.

ABOUT THE OREGON BIODIVERSITY PROJECT

The Oregon Biodiversity Project had its genesis among a small group of conservationists in the early 1990s. Frustrated with the state's continuing polarization and slow progress in dealing with individual endangered species, they were increasingly apprehensive about the absence of any concerted effort to address broader-scale concerns for Oregon's biodiversity. They were intrigued by the approach of the Oregon Gap Analysis Program (GAP), a promising joint federal-state effort to identify "gaps" in current protection for biodiversity. New computer technology, mapping based on satellite imagery, and the emerging science of conservation biology appeared to offer the tools needed for a more comprehensive, science-based approach to conservation issues.

The West Coast Office of Defenders of Wildlife and The Nature Conservancy of Oregon were both interested in pursuing this new approach. Defenders of Wildlife took the lead, laying the groundwork for a private sector-based initiative in late 1993. Defenders' original concept for the project was a fairly traditional one. It focused on convening a panel of scientists for an independent review of the results of the Oregon Gap Analysis Project. Defenders would coordinate the process and publish the scientific panel's findings and recommendations in the form of a statewide biodiversity conservation plan or strategy.

Although the underlying principles and goals remained much the same, the Oregon Biodiversity Project's approach and scope evolved dramatically after it was launched in early 1994. The original project steering committee — which included representatives of Defenders of Wildlife and The Nature Conservancy, and an executive with the CH2M Hill engineering firm — decided early on to seek involvement of a much broader range of interests. Leaders from the business community and Oregon's timber and cattle industries were recruited for the steering committee. An implementation committee was established to gain input from private land managers, local government and state and federal agencies.

The second significant change began in early 1995, when the project concluded that it needed additional data beyond those developed by the Gap Analysis Program. The project began a major effort to supplement GAP data with ecological and human-related data from a variety of other sources, eventually building one of the most comprehensive biodiversity databases ever developed in Oregon. The project also shifted away from its original focus on identifying potential biological reserves, adopting a broader approach that embraced an array of conservation options. The new direction placed a greater emphasis on voluntary actions and incentives. In 1998, Defenders of Wildlife published a companion document, *Stewardship Incentives* (Vickerman 1998), that describes more fully this aspect of the project's conservation strategy.

By 1996, the project had grown into a collaborative effort involving dozens of public and private cooperators. Funding support came from a variety of sources, including private foundations, federal agencies, and corporate contributors. Individual researchers and agencies contributed data. Input from project committees shaped the outlines of the biodiversity analysis and conservation strategy. The project's database was largely completed in 1996. The analysis and refinement of the conservation strategy continued into 1997.

PROJECT STRUCTURE

The project has been administered by Defenders of Wildlife's West Coast Office in Lake Oswego, Oregon, with a small core staff working closely with The Nature Conservancy of Oregon, the Oregon Natural Heritage Program, and other cooperators.

Project operations have been overseen by a six-member steering committee made up of conservation and industry leaders that has met regularly to address project management and policy issues. Two advisory panels helped shape the project's technical work and development of the conservation strategy. A science committee included leading scientists from federal and state agencies, universities, industry, and conservation organizations. An implementation committee included a diverse group of policy makers from all levels of government, and public- and private-sector resource managers and landowners.

OREGON BIODIVERSITY INFORMATION SYSTEM

One of the most important products of the Oregon Biodiversity Project is the computerized database created to support the project's biodiversity analysis. Called the Oregon Biodiversity Information System, this set of linked, electronic databases brings together an array of biodiversity-related data sets that have been compiled into consistent and compatible computerized formats. Most of this information is in GIS formats that allow data to be displayed in map form. The database has been organized to give users the option of manipulating data for a wide variety of purposes, and can be updated as improved information becomes available.

GIS technology essentially allows information compiled in digital form to be displayed "spatially" as points or lines on a map. Individual data sets transformed into GIS "coverages" or data layers can be combined or overlaid. GIS is particularly valuable as an analytical tool because it allows a user to integrate and quantify different kinds of data on a geographic basis. A data layer displaying the location of roads, for example, can be overlaid with other data layers — such as locations of rare species — to display the spatial relationships in map form. By breaking the map into units — watersheds, or a grid of one-kilometer squares, for example — the investigator can produce a variety of different analyses designed to answer specific questions about the information contained in the data layers.

Goals and Objectives

The Oregon Biodiversity Project's primary goal is to develop a pragmatic statewide strategy to conserve Oregon's native biodiversity. The strategy is intended to reduce the risk of future endangered species designations, and give landowners more flexibility in resource management decisions.

The project has also sought to establish a process to improve communication among diverse public and private interests and help people find common ground in resource management decisions.

The project's major objectives are to:

- Compile the best available information to identify habitats and species that may be at risk.
- Identify conservation opportunities where social and economic conditions are most favorable.
- Recommend management actions and policies to assure that representative examples of all of Oregon's habitats are maintained or restored to healthy condition.
- Engage a broad spectrum of interested parties in discussions about the future of Oregon's resources by providing high-quality, easy-to-use products.
- Identify incentives to encourage private landowners to participate in implementing the conservation strategy.
- Provide opportunities for citizens to help collect data on wildlife distributions, and to develop an informed and active constituency for biodiversity conservation.

The Oregon Biodiversity Information System is made up of hundreds of data layers organized into more than 50 different GIS coverages called "themes." Each one of these themes may include a number of different types of information, or "attributes." By linking these different layers through an integrated database, the system makes it possible for a computer user to click on a point on a map and bring up a table showing a variety of information associated with a particular location.

The data sets used in the Oregon Biodiversity Information System reflect the best information available in statewide coverages that could be compiled in consistent GIS formats. (In some cases, data sets with less than statewide coverage have been included to provide supplemental information.) Ecological data include current and historic vegetation; distribution maps for more than 400 terrestrial vertebrate species; hydrology; land forms; locations of rare, threatened, and endangered species; healthy salmon stocks; aquatic diversity areas; and a variety of other features. Human-related data include information on land use and ownership; roads; classification of lands for biodiversity management; population and demographics; socioeconomic information; and political attitudes, among other factors.

Data contained in the Oregon Biodiversity Information System are available to potential users in several forms, including a CD-ROM package, which can be ordered directly from Defenders of Wildlife (see back of publication for an order form).

HOW THIS DOCUMENT IS ORGANIZED

The document is divided into the following chapters:

Chapter 1, "Biodiversity Basics," provides a basic introduction to some of the major concepts and issues that will be addressed throughout the book.

Chapter 2, "A Strategy for Conserving Biodiversity," outlines basic principles of the project's conservation strategy and reviews incentives for improved stewardship. The conservation strategy is intended to provide an overall framework for a statewide approach to biodiversity conservation that could be implemented at different levels by public agencies, private interests, and individual land owners.

Chapter 3 provides a "Statewide Overview" of Oregon's biodiversity. It also describes the system developed by the project to assess and classify the state's current network of conservation lands, and includes background on the major sources of data used in the project's analyses.

Chapter 4, "Assessing Oregon's Ten Ecoregions," summarizes results of the project's biodiversity analysis for each of Oregon's ten ecoregions and highlights "conservation opportunity areas" in each region. Although all of the assessments address the same basic themes, the issues and conservation priorities vary significantly from ecoregion to ecoregion.

Chapter 5, The "Conclusion," summarizes conclusions drawn from the project's analyses and provides some broad recommendations for conservation action.

Biodiversity Basics

This section provides an introduction to some of the concepts that serve as the foundation for much of the analysis, as well as to recommendations outlined later in this publication. Concepts such as biodiversity, ecosystem management, and issues of scale have different meanings to different people. The purpose of this section is to explain in simple terms why these ideas are important from the standpoint of biodiversity conservation and to give readers a basic understanding of how these concepts have been interpreted and applied in the Oregon Biodiversity Project.

WHAT IS BIODIVERSITY AND WHY IS IT IMPORTANT TO CONSERVE?

Biodiversity (or biological diversity) is most simply defined as "the variety of life and its processes." One of the more widely accepted variations on this definition includes "the variety of living organisms, the genetic differences among them, the communities and ecosystems in which they occur, and the ecological and evolutionary processes that keep them functioning, yet ever changing and adapting" (Noss and Cooperrider 1994).

Mother lynx with kittens
Photographer, Cathy and Gordon Illg

Oregon's biodiversity is a product of thousands of microbial, plant, and animal species (including humans), all interacting with each other and with the physical environment. In a sense, biodiversity can be likened to the fabric of life, made up of thousands of individual threads woven into a complex tapestry laid across

Biodiversity Conservation: More than a numbers game

Conserving biodiversity is not the same thing as maximizing species diversity at the site level. In fact, actions that increase the number of species using a particular site might in the long run reduce overall biodiversity.

For example, a forest fragmented by clearcuts, which increase the amount of "edge" habitat, may support a greater number of species than an intact old growth forest. Although timber harvest within the old growth forest may increase the number of species using the area, it will further reduce a type of habitat that is already in short supply. It could also jeopardize the survival of some old growth-dependent species, ultimately leading to a loss of biodiversity at a broader geographic level.

the landscape. In Oregon, as elsewhere, that fabric has begun to fray with the wear and tear of human use. The loss of a single thread (a species or a habitat) may seem insignificant, but repeated many times over, may weaken the fabric until it rips under stress, leaving the tapestry in shreds and scraps that can never be put together again.

During the twentieth century, human alteration of the environment and resulting loss of biodiversity has accelerated dramatically worldwide. Biologist E. O. Wilson estimates that in tropical rain forests alone, roughly 140 species are either extinguished or condemned to extinction every day due to destruction of their habitat (Wilson 1992). In the United States and Canada, The Nature Conservancy has estimated that more than 200 full species of plants (plus many more varieties) and 71 species and subspecies of vertebrates have been lost since the beginning of European settlement (The Nature Conservancy 1992; Russell and Morse 1992). More than 750 species are listed as threatened or endangered under the federal Endangered Species Act, and more than 3,000 others are "species of concern."

Of course, ecosystem changes and the extinction and evolution of species have been occurring for millions of years. What is different now is the rate at which species are being lost, which E.O. Wilson estimates as 400 times greater than that experienced through recent geologic time and accelerating rapidly (Wilson 1992). The consequences of these changes are not fully understood. The potential impacts on the human condition, on the fabric of the earth's ecological systems, and on the process of evolution, are far from clear.

We do know, however, that biodiversity and healthy functioning ecosystems have substantial significance for our quality of life and the natural resource industries that provide the foundations for much of our economy. Biodiversity serves a number of human needs, supporting natural resource industries that produce commodities such as fiber, fuel, food, building materials, and medicine, as well as recreational uses such as wildlife viewing, fishing, hiking, and solitude. Healthy functioning ecosystems also provide essential "ecological services," such as water purification, flood control, and nutrient cycling that are critical to the sustainability of even the most human-dominated ecosystems.

From a strictly utilitarian standpoint, it could be argued that we don't need to conserve every single species just to maintain those basic ecosystem functions. But as Noss and Cooperrider (1994) point out, natural ecosystems have developed their functional relationships over thousands or millions of years, "whereas our experiments in manipulating ecosystems have been comparatively brief. Who knows when we may lose a species or set of relationships critical to ecosystem function?" It is this uncertainty that provides the most compelling single reason for doing what we can to conserve biodiversity. Given the human proclivity for tinkering with

Similarly, high species diversity does not necessarily translate into high priority for biodiversity conservation. A site that supports a large number of relatively common species may be less important from a conservation standpoint than one with a few rare or threatened species that may be able to survive nowhere else.

The Oregon Biodiversity Project has focused its assessments on conservation of biodiversity at the ecoregional and state level. Site-level biodiversity values are addressed in this document primarily in terms of their relationship to the broader ecological context.

ecosystems, it only seems prudent, as Aldo Leopold (1949) observed, that we should take care not to lose any of the pieces.

CAUSES OF THE LOSS OF BIODIVERSITY

Wildlife populations and the habitats or "communities" they occur in are typically in a constant state of flux. Their dynamics are related to changes in environmental conditions and in the landscape. Although subject to sharp and sometimes catastrophic changes due to natural disturbance, most ecosystems have developed through gradual changes, allowing time for species to adjust their ranges or adapt to new conditions. Human disturbances have disrupted this generally gradual pattern of change in biological communities. In the western United States, for example, more than a century of logging, road-building, clearing for agriculture, and urbanization have carved native ecosystems into fragments of varying sizes and shapes. Some of these fragments retain a semblance of ecological integrity, some are ecologically compromised, and some are merely relics (Grumbine 1992).

Today, the principal threats to biodiversity from human activities can be generally grouped into several broad but inter-related categories: habitat destruction, fragmentation, and degradation; introduction of non-native species; and exploitation and overharvest of natural resources (Meffe and Carroll 1997).

Loss of habitat is the major threat to the majority of vertebrates, invertebrates, plants, and fungi currently facing extinction. More than 95 percent of the species listed under the federal Endangered Species Act are threatened at least in part by habitat loss or degradation (Wilcove et al. 1993).

Habitats can be lost in a number of ways. The most obvious is conversion of ecosystems to accommodate human activities such as agricultural production or urban development (Noss et al. 1995). This type of ecosystem loss is readily visible and can be mapped and quantified by measuring the changes in a habitat's extent over time.

Some conservation biologists believe that habitat fragmentation — the breakup of extensive habitats into small, isolated fragments — is "the most serious threat to biodiversity and is the primary cause of the present extinction crisis" (Wilcox and Murphy 1985). These fragments are often isolated from each other and surrounded by a modified or degraded landscape. The result is a reduction in the total area of the habitat, less "core" habitat, and more "edge" habitat. These changes in the nature and configuration of the habitat may make it less suitable for many of the species that originally occupied the area. Habitat fragmentation can increase the vulnerability of resident wildlife to competition from and predation by more aggressive species and non-native pests. Fragmentation can also lead to changes in migration patterns of birds and native pollinators, resulting in population declines and impacts on plant species as well.

The Humble and the Ignored

Few people think of bees, moths, or hummingbirds when discussing biodiversity. But in the words of eminent biologist E.O. Wilson, it is the small creatures — "the humble and the ignored" — that are the true building blocks of life.

As pollinators, these small creatures perform a vital function. Pollination is essential to plant propagation, and is responsible for producing as much as a third of the food we eat every day. Yet we know almost nothing about the suite of pollinators that are so important to our survival.

While pollination has generally been taken for granted, serious problems have begun to surface. Traditionally, management emphasis has been on just one kind of pollinator — the European honeybee. Nationwide, managed honeybee colonies, as well as wild bee colonies, have declined drastically in the last decade, reducing the total number of bees available to pollinate food crops and native plants. Research is finding that the natural decline of pollinators may have serious consequences for the long-term viability of native plant communities.

Native pollinators migrate with the flowering of plants across the landscape. Pollinator corridors, from south and central America through North America, have been seriously fragmented. Natural habitats have been destroyed and broad stretches of migratory routes are subject to agricultural pesticide uses.

The challenge ahead is substantial. To stem the decline, researchers need to broaden the scope of their research beyond honeybees, gardeners and farmers need to reduce their reliance on pesticides, and society needs to understand more about the importance of biodiversity — from the smallest of creatures to the largest of habitats — and how to sustain that diversity.

Like the canary in the mine, the plight of nature's pollinators and their habitats is a wake-up call to society to appreciate the pivotal role these tiny creatures play in the wild and across the managed landscape.

Many factors influence the quality of habitat fragments and their ability to continue to support diverse populations of native plants and animals, including fragment size, surrounding land use, and corridors or connections to adjacent native habitats.

Habitat degradation is often less visible than loss or fragmentation of habitat. Impacts on biodiversity may involve more subtle, insidious changes in the structure, function, or composition of the system. Habitat degradation can be more difficult to estimate, monitor, or map than habitat loss. Activities that degrade habitat for one species may go unnoticed by another or may even be a habitat enhancement for another (Meffe and Carroll 1997). Soil erosion from disturbed areas, discharges from industrial sites, and municipal sewage treatment plants, and runoff from agricultural lands and highways degrade water quality and reduce aquatic diversity in many rivers and streams. Air pollution can deposit toxic substances that may degrade terrestrial habitats for years to come.

EXOTIC SPECIES: A DIFFERENT KIND OF THREAT

The spread of non-native or "exotic" species has emerged in recent years as one of the most serious threats to biodiversity, undermining the ecological integrity of many native habitats and pushing some rare species to the edge of extinction.

Of course, many of the plant and animal species introduced to Oregon over the years have provided humans with substantial benefit. Most of the state's crops and livestock are non-native species. Many have become such a part of our modern lives that we often forget their exotic origin and the impact they have had on the landscape. Two of Oregon's ten ecoregions — the Willamette Valley and the Columbia Basin — are dominated by non-native vegetation types, and most areas east of the Cascades have been modified by livestock grazing.

Knapweed removal,
Tom McCall/Rowena Preserve
Photographer, Linda M. Hardie

The greatest threats to biodiversity are posed by a relative handful of exotic species with invasive tendencies and provide no benefit to humans. Described by some as a form of biological pollution, these species have been introduced — sometimes by accident, but often with the best of intentions — into systems where they thrive at the expense of native species. With no natural competitors or predators, some introduced species simply out-compete native plants and animals for space, food, or water. Others, such as cheatgrass, which now dominates shrub steppe habitats in parts of eastern Oregon, can fundamentally alter natural fire regimes and other ecological processes, making it difficult or impossible for native species to survive.

Within their natural range, populations of most plants and animals are limited by competition, predation, and disease. Introduced to new areas outside their natural range, species may be freed from those constraints. Most introduced species confront the same kinds of biological and physical limitations in their new habitats, but those that have invasive tendencies and are not too limited by natural controls can spread rapidly, with dramatic, adverse ecological and economic impacts.

About 15 percent of the estimated 6,000-plus non-native plant and animal species in the United States cause severe economic or ecological impacts, according to the Congressional Office of Technology Assessment (1993). In one year alone, the European gypsy moth caused an estimated $764 million in losses in American forests, according to the U.S. Department of Agriculture. The zebra mussel, rapidly expanding from the Great Lakes through the Mississippi River system and now beginning to appear in California, could cause more than $5 billion in damages by the year 2002 (The Nature Conservancy 1996).

Impacts of non-native species on biodiversity are more difficult to quantify but are clearly substantial. Exotic species have been implicated in the decline of 42 percent of the species listed for protection under the federal Endangered Species Act. Introduced species were a contributing factor in the loss of more than two-thirds of the 40 North American freshwater fishes (including Oregon's Alvord cutthroat trout) that have become extinct over the past century (The Nature Conservancy 1996).

Invasive exotic species have also dramatically altered entire ecosystems. Cheatgrass and other exotics like yellow star-thistle have invaded eastern Oregon shrub steppe habitats, crowding out native plants and changing the natural fire regime. In addition to the ecosystem impacts, cheatgrass reduces the value of areas it invades for livestock grazing. European beachgrass, planted earlier this century to stabilize oceanfront dunes, has halted the inland movement of sand and transformed large expanses of shifting dunes into more stabilized habitats. The result has been the elimination of much of the historic habitat for two at-risk species that need open habitat and shifting sands, the western snowy plover

(Charadrius alexandrius) and the pink sand verbena *(Abronia umbellata* ssp. *Breviflora)*. Reed canary grass *(Phalaris arundinaceae)*, another introduced plant, now dominates large expanses of Oregon's remaining wetlands, crowding out native vegetation that provides essential habitat and food for migratory birds.

Once established, many exotic species are virtually impossible to eradicate. Biological controls may offer hope in some cases, but many of the invasive exotics now found in Oregon are probably here to stay. As a result, land managers struggle just to limit their further spread. The best option for combating invasive exotics is to prevent them from being introduced in the first place, and failing that, early detection and eradication before they become fully established. However, simply getting rid of an invasive exotic may not be enough. If no action is taken to restore native species and ecosystems and to prevent future introductions, native species and ecological communities will remain vulnerable to re-invasion or to other new pests.

TWO WAYS TO CONSTRUCT A CONSERVATION SAFETY NET

Any approach to conserving biodiversity presents immense challenges. But trying to inventory and manage thousands of individual species that may be vulnerable is, from a practical standpoint, clearly impossible.

An alternative strategy used by The Nature Conservancy and the state Natural Heritage Programs combines a "coarse filter" approach focused on protecting natural communities with a "fine filter" approach that addresses needs for individual rare, threatened, and endangered species. Ideally, these two approaches should be complementary, with the fine filter picking up those rare, threatened, and endangered species that might otherwise fall through the cracks of a coarse-filter conservation strategy. The Nature Conservancy estimates that a "coarse-filter" approach that adequately conserves examples of natural communities and their associated plant and animal species could protect 85-90 percent of all species, without the need for species-specific management.

A technique developed in the mid-1980s called "gap analysis" provided the basis for an ambitious attempt to use the coarse-filter approach to assess conservation needs on a large scale. Gap analysis, in its simplest form, is basically a technique for assessing how well existing conservation lands provide protection for biodiversity. By comparing the distribution of species, or vegetation types, for example, with a map of lands that are currently managed for conservation, it is possible to identify "gaps" in current protection for some elements of biodiversity.

Originally developed by researchers at the University of Idaho, gap analysis efforts have been expanded into a nationwide program currently administered by the U.S. Geological

Survey's Biological Resources Division in cooperation with individual states and a variety of federal, state, and private partners.

The Oregon Biodiversity Project was begun as an outgrowth of the Oregon Gap Analysis Program (GAP), and the GAP data sets provided the initial foundation for the project's efforts to develop a statewide biodiversity conservation strategy.

ISSUES OF SCALE: LOOKING AT THE BIG PICTURE

Biodiversity conservation priorities may vary significantly, depending on the scale of the assessment. At a local scale, for example, a small pristine marsh or a remnant stand of old growth forest may appear to be particularly significant due to its diverse plant communities or use by large numbers of wildlife species. However, looked at within the context of a larger landscape or ecoregion in a broad-scale analysis, that same site may not appear so special. It may turn out that a number of places with very similar qualities are already relatively well "protected" in wilderness areas, parks, or other special management areas. From the standpoint of conserving biodiversity on a broad scale, it may be more important to focus on an otherwise unremarkable site that happens to support a particular rare species found nowhere else in the ecoregion.

However, a species or habitat type that may be rare in one ecoregion may be quite abundant in another ecoregion. For example, the Columbia Basin Ecoregion has only about 25,000 acres of ponderosa pine woodlands — almost none of them managed for biodiversity values. Yet ponderosa pine woodlands occupy more than four million acres in the adjacent Blue Mountains Ecoregion. In this case, the "rarity" of ponderosa pine woodlands in the Columbia Basin is simply an artifact of the way the ecoregion boundaries were drawn. It may be more appropriate to address conservation needs for this vegetation type in other ecoregions where it is more abundant. However, examples of vegetation types on the edge of their natural range may in some cases have special significance for conservation because of the unique communities they support. In general, conservation biologists suggest that it is important to maintain examples of a community type throughout its range to maintain genetic variability not captured in the simple community classifications (Scott et al. 1997).

Because biodiversity conservation needs take on a very different complexion when viewed from a watershed, ecoregional, or continental perspective, conservation priorities need to be assessed at several scales.

The Oregon Biodiversity Project has focused on biodiversity conservation needs at the statewide scale, in part because it is this view that is so clearly missing in many of the current discussions about ecosystem management and watershed-level planning. Under Goal 5 of Oregon's statewide land use planning system, for example, local governments are required to protect significant wildlife habitats and natural areas, among other natural resource values. But few local planners have the information and tools needed to assess the significance of these resources outside a very local context.

However, in looking at biodiversity on a statewide scale, we have focused much of our analysis at the ecoregional level and have used watersheds at several different scales as the principal units of analysis.

The ten Oregon ecoregions that provide the framework for our analysis are based on geological and vegetational patterns and represent a synthesis of the classification systems developed by the U.S. Environmental Protection Agency and the U.S. Forest Service. These ecoregions are useful large units for analysis because their boundaries are based on physical features and conditions that often define distinctively different ecosystems. (A look at the vegetation map with superimposed ecoregion boundaries on page 45 reveals how closely the ecoregion lines mirror major vegetational patterns.) The ecoregions provide a coarse unit of analysis that nonetheless allows us to consider the very real differences between, say, the oak woodlands found in the Willamette Valley and those in the Klamath Mountains.

The watershed units used in our analysis are based on the hydrologic unit classification (HUC) system developed by the U.S. Geological Survey, which defines watersheds on a range of scales, from the basin level down to sub-basins, watersheds, subwatersheds, and even smaller units. The two units most commonly used in our analysis were the sub-basins (90 units within the state) and the watersheds (1,032 units). These units are particularly appropriate for data related to aquatic systems. However, watersheds are also useful for summarizing many other kinds of information because their boundaries are based on physical features that are directly related to some ecological processes that are otherwise difficult to map or quantify.

Computerized databases and geographic information systems (GIS) make it possible to summarize and display information about biodiversity at a variety of scales. Much of the data used in our analysis are relatively coarse (the smallest unit of classification in our basic vegetation map is 320 acres), so it is most useful in presenting a broad-scale, "big picture" view of Oregon's biodiversity. Although on-the-ground conservation activities will require more site-specific analysis and planning, this kind of broad-scale analysis can help landowners, resource managers, and policy makers focus their efforts on areas of greatest ecological significance.

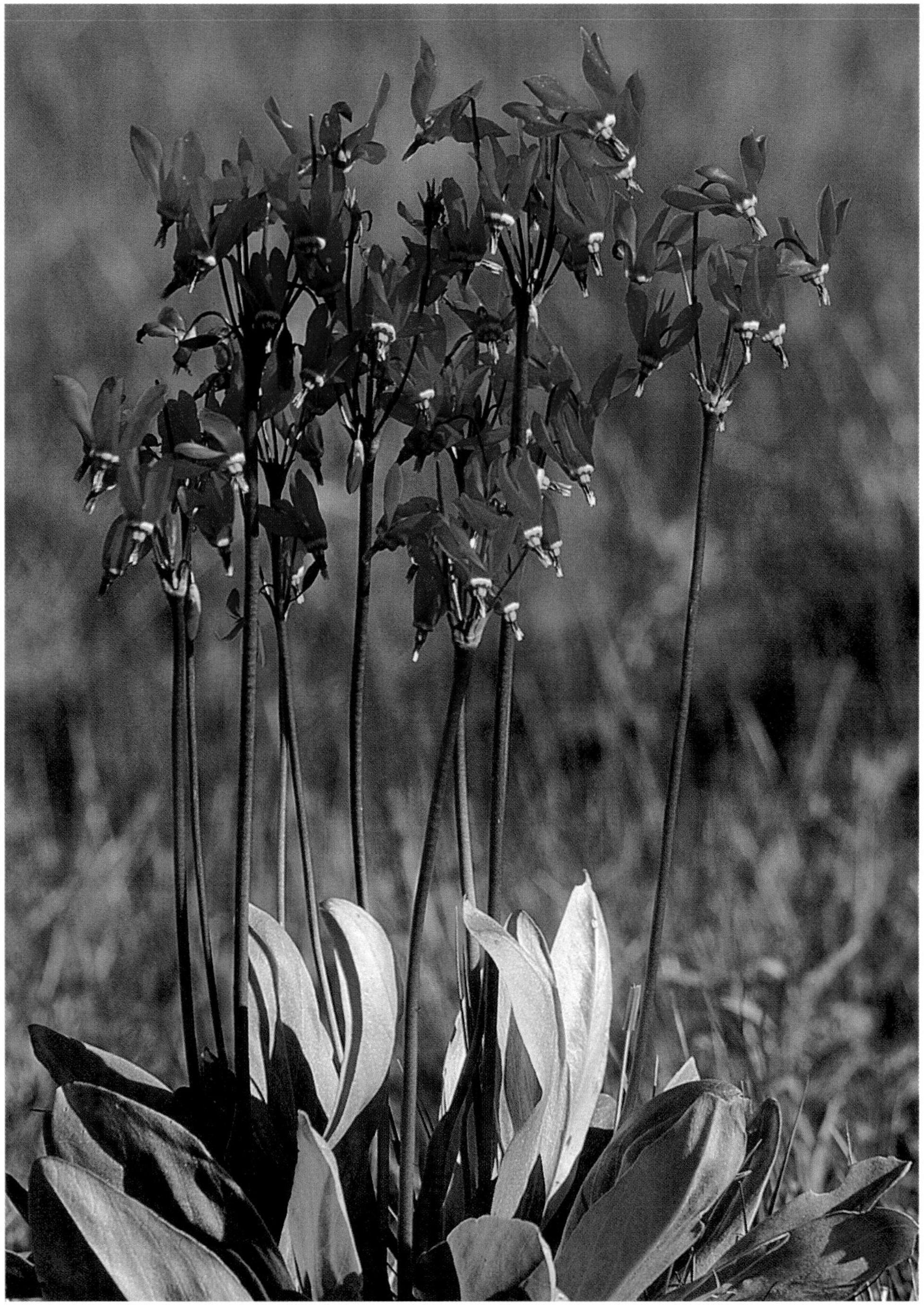

Conservation strategies look beyond species richness

Although locations with high levels of species richness might seem like natural candidates as priorities for biodiversity conservation efforts, that isn't always the case.

Sometimes, what appears to be a high level of species richness may be nothing more than an artifact of the mapping unit chosen for analysis. In the case of the maps on the following page, for example, hexagons are a useful unit of analysis because each unit contains the same area, but the lines bear no relationship to anything on the ground. One area may show up as being particularly rich in species simply because the hexagon falls on an area that contains a wide range of elevations and a variety of different habitat types. In reality, hexagons may provide only small pieces of the habitat needed by many of the species associated with it and may be largely irrelevant to their long-term survival.

Areas rich in species diversity may make important contributions to biological diversity on a broad scale. No single area or small group of areas, however, is likely to include sufficient habitat to support the full range of species and ecological processes that contribute to biodiversity at a statewide level. As a practical matter, there is often little correlation between areas of species richness for different taxonomic groups. A map of species richness for birds, for example, looks very different from a species richness map for reptiles. And some species may only be found in areas of low species richness, yet may still warrant special attention because of their limited distribution or small population size.

Conservation strategies, therefore, need to look beyond simple patterns of overall species richness to ensure that all species are represented in any identification of lands important for biodiversity.

Shooting star, Kingston Prairie
Photographer, Alan D. St. John

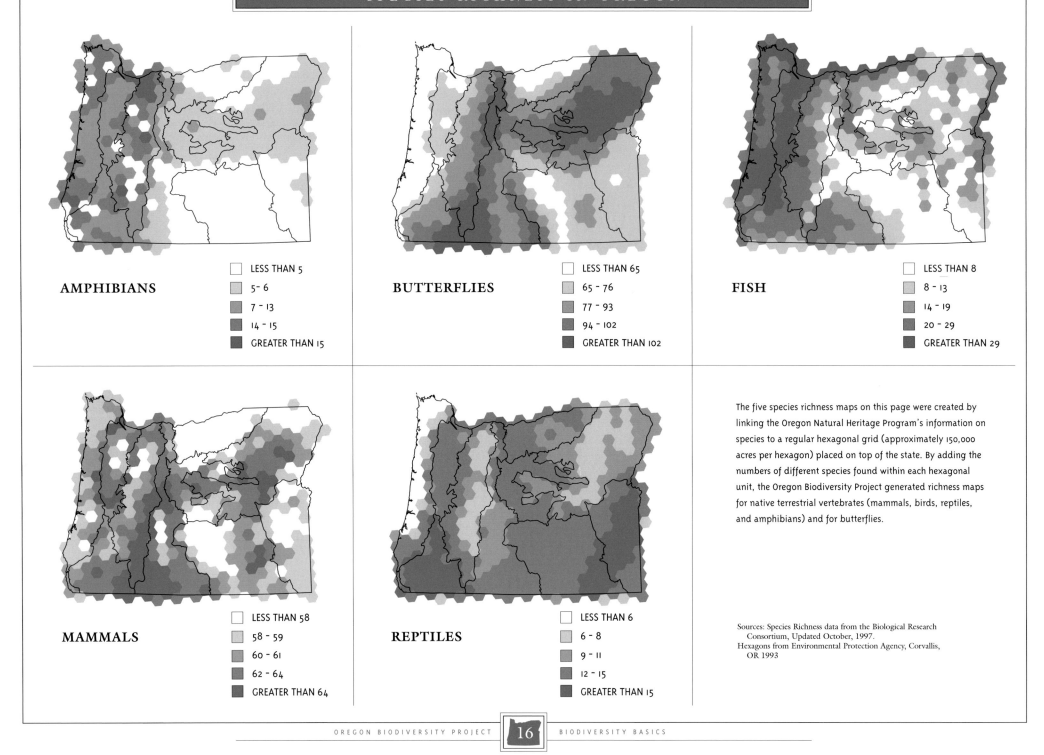

SPECIES RICHNESS IN OREGON

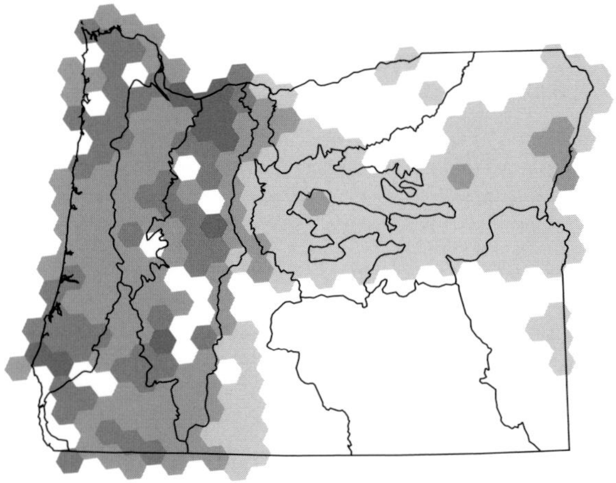

AMPHIBIANS

- LESS THAN 5
- 5 - 6
- 7 - 13
- 14 - 15
- GREATER THAN 15

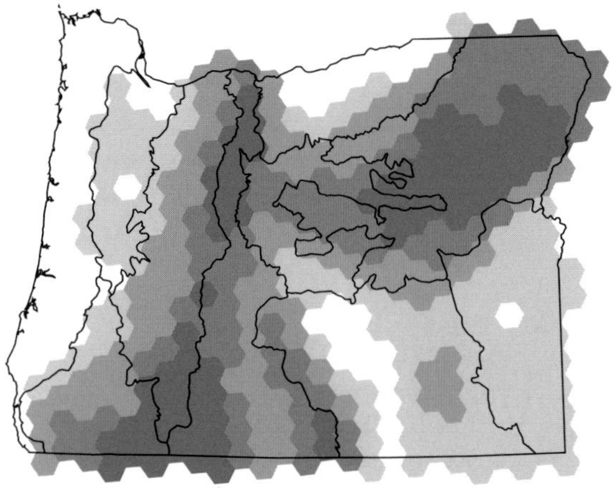

BUTTERFLIES

- LESS THAN 65
- 65 - 76
- 77 - 93
- 94 - 102
- GREATER THAN 102

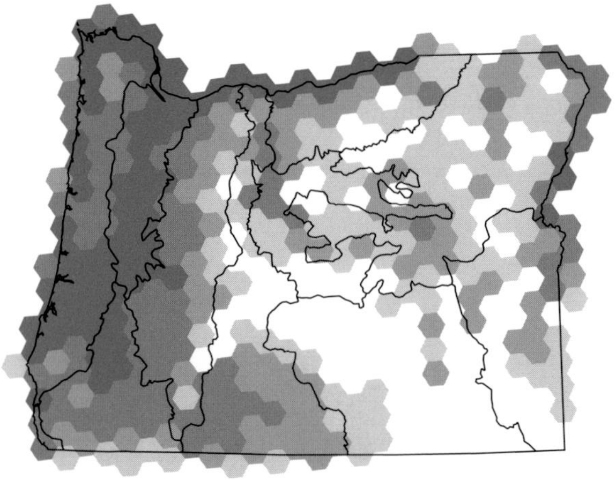

FISH

- LESS THAN 8
- 8 - 13
- 14 - 19
- 20 - 29
- GREATER THAN 29

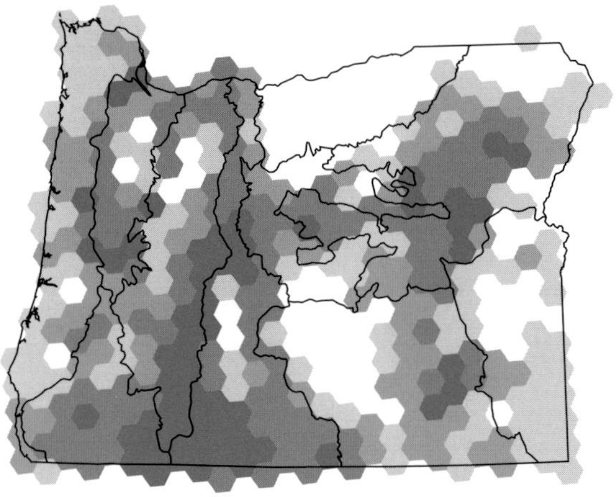

MAMMALS

- LESS THAN 58
- 58 - 59
- 60 - 61
- 62 - 64
- GREATER THAN 64

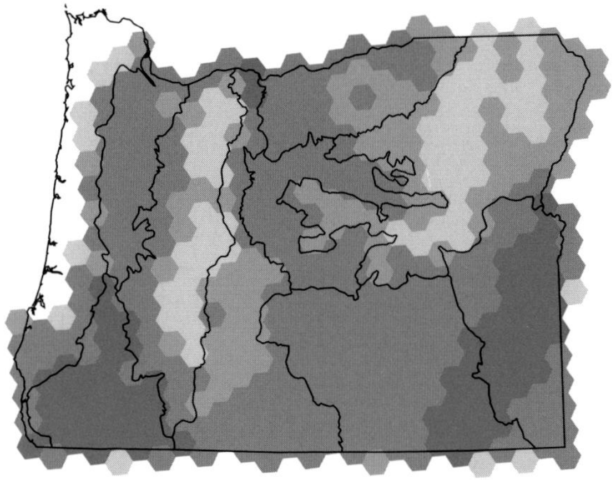

REPTILES

- LESS THAN 6
- 6 - 8
- 9 - 11
- 12 - 15
- GREATER THAN 15

The five species richness maps on this page were created by linking the Oregon Natural Heritage Program's information on species to a regular hexagonal grid (approximately 150,000 acres per hexagon) placed on top of the state. By adding the numbers of different species found within each hexagonal unit, the Oregon Biodiversity Project generated richness maps for native terrestrial vertebrates (mammals, birds, reptiles, and amphibians) and for butterflies.

Sources: Species Richness data from the Biological Research Consortium, Updated October, 1997.
Hexagons from Environmental Protection Agency, Corvallis, OR 1993

SPECIES RICHNESS: ONE DIMENSION OF BIODIVERSITY

Although scientists generally agree that biological diversity needs to be conserved at all levels of the biological hierarchy (genetic, species, community or ecosystem, landscape, and regional), the reality is that we know very little about the genetic level of diversity. And many researchers and resource managers have only recently begun to grapple with the problems involved in conservation at a landscape or regional level (the primary focus of this book), which requires a broad understanding of the patterns and distribution of biological diversity.

Most assessments of biodiversity are based on information gathered about individual species and individual places. But much of the world's biological diversity remains unknown to science. Our basic knowledge of the identity and distribution of species is still very sketchy for the vast majority of living organisms. Our fragmentary knowledge is particularly striking for entire groups of some organisms, such as insects, microfungi, and mollusks.

Nonetheless, assessments of species diversity remain one of the best-developed tools available for describing and quantifying biological diversity within a given area. Indices of species diversity provide useful tools for making ecological comparisons and identifying concerns important to biodiversity conservation.

At a very simplistic level, biodiversity can be measured or defined as the number of species found in a community or a particular location. This is known as species richness.

Recent efforts to map more accurately distributions of Oregon's terrestrial vertebrate species (Csuti et al. 1997) provide one basis for comparing relative levels of species richness across the state. Of the 641 terrestrial vertebrate species mapped, 425 breed in Oregon, 91 visit during winter or migration, 98 are occasional visitors, and 27 are introduced. The maps on the opposite page display general patterns of species richness for different taxonomic groups.

Although the information in these species richness maps is coarse (i.e., it cannot be broken down for analysis at a finer scale), it provides a broad-scale depiction of patterns in the distribution of different groups of species. When combined with information on other aspects of biodiversity — e.g., vegetation communities; aquatic habitats; locations of rare, threatened, and endangered species; roads; human population — a more holistic picture of the landscape begins to emerge.

TRACKING AND CLASSIFYING THE STATUS OF AT-RISK SPECIES

Because they represent the most vulnerable elements of biological diversity, species considered rare, threatened, or endangered require special consideration in any strategy for conserving biodiversity.

California mountain kingsnake, Siskiyou Mountains
Photographer, Alan D. St. John

In this document, the term "at-risk species" refers to species classified as "critically imperiled," "imperiled," or "vulnerable" at the global or state level under the Oregon Natural Heritage Program's global ranking system. (These include species with Heritage rankings of G1, G2 or G3 [global]; T1, T2, T3 [trinomial — a subspecies, variety, or recognized race], and S1 or S2 [state]. See below for an explanation of the Heritage rankings.)

These species are addressed in some detail in later chapters on the results of statewide and ecoregion analyses, so this section is intended mainly to provide background on the sources of data and terminology used in our analysis.

There are several major sources for information on rare, threatened, and endangered species in Oregon. The U.S. Fish and Wildlife Service and the National Marine Fisheries Service track the status of species listed or proposed for listing under the federal Endangered Species Act. They also maintain lists of species that are candidates for listing or are considered "species of concern."

The Oregon Department of Fish and Wildlife and Oregon Department of Agriculture maintain lists of animal and plant species listed under the Oregon Endangered Species Act. The Department of Fish and Wildlife also maintains a "sensitive species" list of native vertebrates likely to become threatened or endangered throughout all or a significant portion of their range in Oregon.

The broadest compendium of information on vulnerable elements of biodiversity is maintained by the Oregon Natural Heritage site-specific locations of rare, threatened, and endangered species. The program collects reports of species observations from a wide variety of sources and maintains a computerized database with location information on all state-listed and federal-listed species, as well as others believed to be rare, threatened, endangered, or otherwise vulnerable in Oregon.

The Oregon Biodiversity Project relied heavily on the Heritage Program database for many of its analyses. Heritage Program data are particularly useful because they provide site-specific information on individual observations of individual species. In addition, the Heritage Program's global ranking system often provides a more representative picture of the status of species than the state and federal endangered species lists. These latter lists have lagged behind scientific knowledge due to the cumbersome nature of the process involved in listing a species under the Endangered Species Act. (One-third of the 2,400 plant species ranked as "imperiled" or "critically imperiled" at the global level under the Heritage system have never even been formally considered as candidates for listing under the federal Endangered Species Act.)

The Natural Heritage Program's ranking system is used in Heritage Programs or Conservation Data Centers in all 50 states and a number of other countries. The system ranks species on a scale of 1 to 5, primarily based on the number of known occurrences, but also including threats, sensitivity, area occupied, and other biological factors. These rankings also reflect the status of species on a state level (S-rank), national level (N-rank), range-wide or global level (G-rank), and a "trinomial" level (T-rank) for a subspecies, variety, or recognized race.

In general, species with a rank of G1, G2 or G3 are biologically qualified for listing as endangered or threatened under the federal Endangered Species Act, subject to additional questions about the degree of threat. For example:

- Species with a G1 rank are "critically imperiled" throughout their range and typically have fewer than six worldwide occurrences or fewer than 1,000 individuals.
- Species with a G2 rank are "imperiled" throughout their range and typically have between six and 20 occurrences, or fewer than 3,000 individuals.
- Species with a G3 rank are "vulnerable" throughout their range and typically have fewer than 100 occurrences, or fewer than 10,000 individuals.

By way of example, the northern spotted owl, listed as "threatened" under the federal Endangered Species Act, is classified as a G3S3 or "vulnerable" species at both the global (G) and state (S) levels under the Heritage ranking system. The shortnose sucker *(Chasmistes brevirostris)* and Lost River sucker *(Deltistes luxatus)*—two endangered fish found only in Klamath County, Oregon, and parts of adjacent northern California—are ranked G1S1, or "critically imperiled" at both the global and state levels, under the Heritage system. Other species, such as the American white pelican *(Pelecanus erythrorhynchos)* (G3S1) are considered "vulnerable" at the global level, but breeding populations found in southeastern Oregon are classified as "critically imperiled" at the state level.

THE COMPLEX DYNAMICS OF ECOLOGICAL PROCESSES

Some elements of biodiversity, such as species and vegetation communities, can be quantified and mapped in a fairly straightforward way because their occurrence and distribution are relatively predictable or stable over time.

In contrast, the ecological processes that play a critical role in maintaining biodiversity do not lend themselves to the same kinds of portrayal and spatial analysis. Six major categories of interrelated ecological processes play a key role in biodiversity: energy flows, nutrient cycles, hydrologic cycles, disturbance regimes, equilibrium processes, and feedback effects (Noss and Cooperrider 1994). Although scientists have been able to quantify some aspects of these processes, they are processes —inherently dynamic and not easily reduced to simple maps and graphics like species distributions, land ownership, and some of the other factors that affect biodiversity. In that sense, ecosystem processes are much like the wind — we can see the results of their influences, but the processes themselves remain largely invisible in the GIS-based data sets available for analysis.

This inability to incorporate dynamic and temporal factors, such as disturbance and plant succession, into our analysis is one of the fundamental weaknesses of the Oregon Biodiversity Project's somewhat two-dimensional portrayal of the state's biodiversity. Recognizing the limitations of computer-based analyses, we have attempted to address the role of ecological processes in a more qualitative fashion by discussing it at appropriate points throughout this document. We may not be able to quantify their role, but we can and will emphasize the point that conserving ecosystem processes is an essential part of conserving biodiversity.

Many of the ecosystem processes that shape biodiversity have already been significantly altered or disrupted in Oregon, with far-reaching consequences for the state's native species. Dams, diversions, and drainage systems have dramatically altered hydrologic processes in many areas.

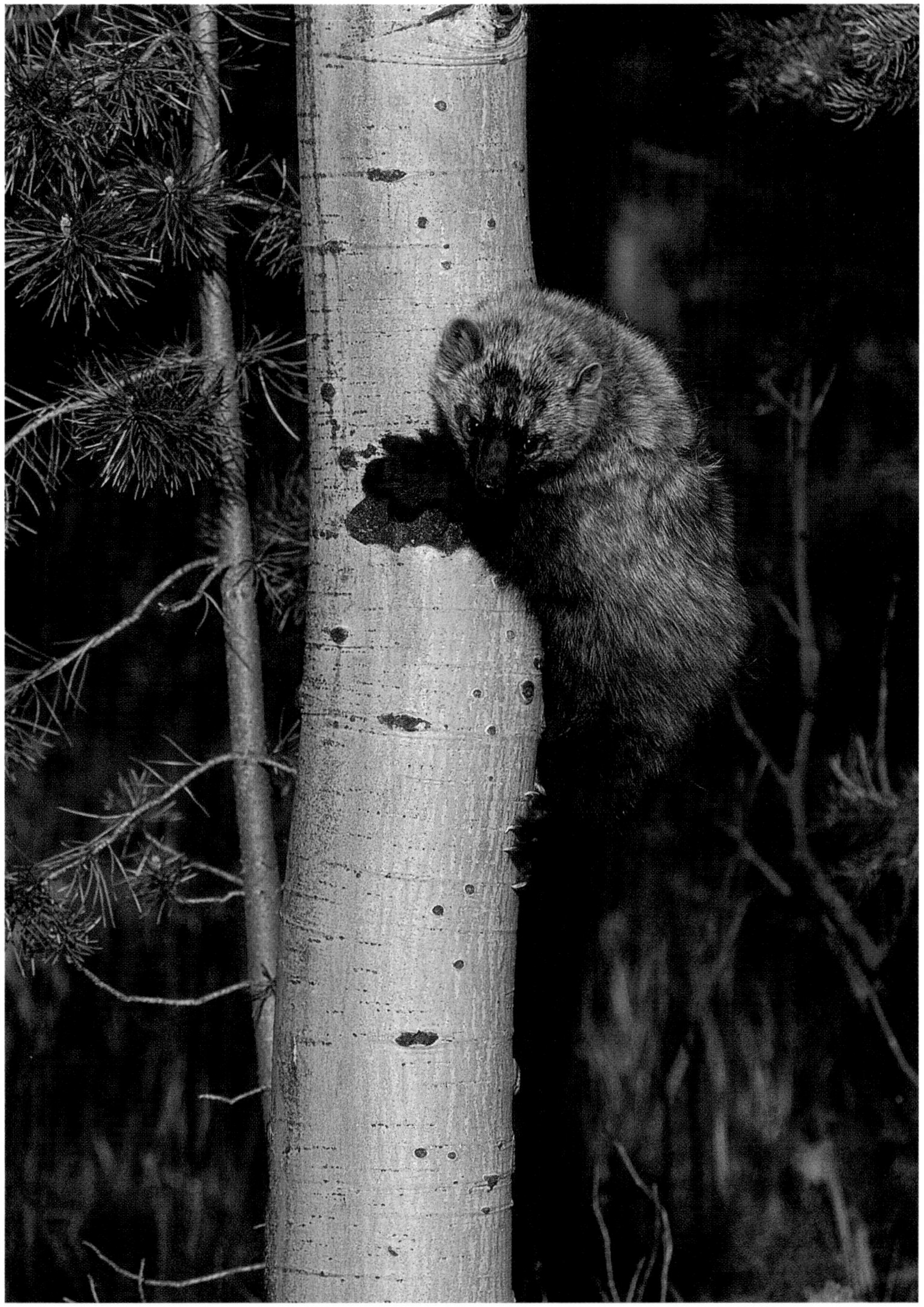

Nutrient and energy cycling processes have been disrupted or changed, with consequences that are not always obvious or expected. Decomposing salmon carcasses and decaying chunks of large wood once provided a major source of minerals and nutrients in Oregon's streams. Declining salmon populations and the removal of snags and downed logs along many streams have altered nutrient and energy cycling processes in these aquatic ecosystems and reduced their capacity to support larger salmon runs in the future.

Disturbance regimes — the frequency and pattern of events such as fires, floods, windstorms, and landslides — have been modified by human influences. Fire suppression, for example, has resulted in major changes in vegetation, with mixed conifer and true fir forests replacing the more fire-tolerant ponderosa pines that historically dominated much of eastern Oregon's forests. Subject in the past to regular, low-intensity fires that swept through the understory and prevented buildup of high levels of fuel, these forests are now vulnerable to high-intensity fires that have the potential to fundamentally alter entire ecosystems.

Unfortunately, re-establishing natural disturbance patterns is not a simple matter in landscapes that are missing some of their original components or support large human populations. Re-establishing historic fire patterns in the Willamette Valley, for example, is not a realistic option. In areas like the Blue Mountains,

Fisher
Photographer, Richard Day, Daybreak Imagery

measures taken to reduce the threat of fire (such as large-scale salvage logging) may reduce the immediate fire risk to remaining old growth forests, but at the expense of impacts on other critical habitats for fish and wildlife. "Finding balance between these potentially conflicting goals is the central challenge, both ecologically and politically," according to forest ecologist David Perry (1995).

ECOSYSTEM MANAGEMENT: A FRAMEWORK FOR ACTION

The fact that ecosystem management has been defined many times in many ways hasn't seemed to hinder widespread acceptance of the concept. Although arguments will continue over what exactly ecosystem management is, recent years have already seen a fundamental shift in the way natural resource issues are framed for debate and decisions. And because of that change, biodiversity concerns have been elevated to the point where they are now on the table as a resource management issue, rather than being the exclusive province of scientists and conservationists.

For example, decision-making about management of national forests in the past typically started with the question of how many board feet of timber harvest the land could be expected to produce. Under ecosystem management, timber production may still be one of the goals, but managers are also expected to address how it relates to other ecological and human values and how it affects the function of the ecosystem as a whole.

"One of the main distinctions of ecosystem management," according to the scientists charged with developing a new framework for management of federal lands east of the Cascades, "is that it concentrates on overall ecosystem health and productivity through an understanding of how different parts of the ecosystem function with each other, rather than on achieving a set of outputs" (ICBEMP 1996).

Ecosystem management recognizes humans as legitimate components of ecosystems, but as forest ecologist David Perry has noted, it also requires a "recognition of the unique power of humankind and the responsibilities inherent in that power" (Perry 1995).

To the extent that it is actually implemented, ecosystem management can and should be the vehicle for addressing many of the biodiversity conservation needs that are highlighted in this document. Under ecosystem management, actions to conserve endangered species and habitats need to be implemented in the same way as timber management and grazing strategies — with full consideration for other ecosystem functions and relationships and human values. By making biodiversity a basic element in the equation for land managers, ecosystem management sets the stage for a much more proactive approach to conservation, and a substantially reduced risk of additional threatened and endangered species in the future.

EMPLOYING A BROAD RANGE OF CONSERVATION TOOLS

Virtually all biodiversity conservation comes down to land management and land use. The tools available for conservation are essentially the same ones used in development — land acquisitions, exchanges, easements, and management agreements; zoning and planning designations; regulations; tax incentives; technical assistance; and cost-sharing. Many of these tools are addressed in a separate publication produced by the Oregon Biodiversity Project, *Stewardship Incentives* (Vickerman 1998).

In the long run, the best way to conserve biodiversity is to change the way people think about the natural world and the ways in which we live our lives and manage our natural resources. In the short run, however, biodiversity conservation will be achieved only through on-the-ground action to protect and restore habitats, species, and ecosystem processes.

Two of the traditional mainstays of environmental protection — regulatory systems and government land acquisitions — can play an important role in biodiversity conservation, but also have serious drawbacks or weaknesses. Regulations provide a useful base for resource protection across the board, but cannot usually be tailored to address site-specific conservation needs. (Regulations also tend to be more effective in discouraging negative activities and less effective in encouraging positive actions.) Governments will never be able to afford to purchase all the lands important for biodiversity; even if that were possible, public ownership is no guarantee that lands will be managed for conservation purposes.

As a result, conservation of biodiversity will depend heavily upon voluntary actions by private and public landowners and resource managers. They first need to understand why their and or other resources are important for biodiversity. Ecological inventories and assessments thus become an important conservation tool. Seeing how a particular site's biodiversity values fit into a larger context is a key step toward ecosystem management. Some landowners or resource managers may be willing to implement conservation measures on that basis alone. Others will need some economic or other incentives. Conservation incentives and elimination of existing disincentives may prove to be the most important tools for protecting and restoring biodiversity.

The statewide and ecoregional analyses found in the following chapters identify a number of conservation needs and priorities, including some geographic areas that appear to offer good opportunities for conservation action. The most appropriate conservation tools will vary with the situation in any particular area. There is no "one-size-fits-all" solution.

To be effective, conservation strategies will have to be tailored to meet local needs and ecological requirements. In that respect, the best conservation tools for biodiversity may be creative thinking and an open mind.

A Strategy For Conserving Biodiversity

What is lacking in conservation biology are tested strategies and tactics for conserving biodiversity at various scales of space and time... We cannot turn to model regions or societies... and say, "This is the way to conserve biodiversity within a sustainable society." We are groping in the dark.

— Noss and Cooperrider, *Saving Nature's Legacy* (1994)

Scientists will be testing and refining strategies to conserve biodiversity for years to come. But landowners, resource managers, and policy makers must make decisions that affect biodiversity every day — with or without the benefit of a statewide conservation strategy. Clearly, we can't afford to wait for science to give us all the answers. But neither can we afford to rush blindly ahead, squandering limited conservation resources (funding, personnel, landowner and public support) on actions that don't pay off with long-term benefits for biodiversity.

There is no single, simple recipe for biodiversity conservation and no unanimity on how a conservation strategy should be implemented. But a handful of consistent themes have emerged from research in the field of conservation biology and the discussions engendered by the Oregon Biodiversity Project that, taken together, may provide some useful guidance for our efforts.

These themes involve the need to look at biodiversity from a broader perspective, including the role of lands managed for commodity production and other purposes; recognition of human needs and uses; the importance of providing tools and incentives for voluntary conservation action; and the value of a network of public and private conservation lands committed to long-term management for biodiversity values.

The conservation strategy outlined in this chapter is based on these themes, melding some basic tenets of conservation biology with practical suggestions for translating these ideas into action.

The first two elements of the strategy focus on the "where" of biodiversity conservation, using a dual approach that takes into consideration both individual areas and the landscape as a whole. Some places have special significance for biodiversity; we need to make sure that we recognize them and address them appropriately. But biodiversity is too complex and dynamic to be dealt with only in discrete pieces — we need to do a better job of managing for biodiversity across the entire landscape.

The other major elements of this strategy focus on the "how" of biodiversity conservation: identifying conservation opportunities; providing tools and incentives for voluntary conservation action; developing partnerships; coordinating data collection and management; promoting public education and outreach; and improving the conservation strategy over time.

PROMOTE MORE BIODIVERSITY-FRIENDLY MANAGEMENT

Maintaining biodiversity means more than just identifying a few "hotspots" for species richness or rare or endangered species, and setting aside some additional lands for protection.

Most biodiversity conservation strategies have been built around the concept of a system of "reserves" set aside for protection of certain species, habitats, or ecosystems. But all reserves are vulnerable to outside forces, and no reserve can maintain its biodiversity for long unless it contains many millions of acres (Noss and Cooperrider 1994). As a result, most conservation biologists agree that we also need to do a better job of managing the "semi-natural matrix (multiple-use public and private lands)" (Noss and Cooperrider 1994), which makes up the bulk of Oregon's landscape.

That means conservation efforts will need to involve a broad range of land uses and management practices on both public and private ownerships. All of us — government and private landowners, producers and consumers, urban and rural residents alike — share some responsibility for our culture's impacts on biodiversity, and we can all play some role in conservation. Although reserves and other "protected" areas provide an essential foundation for biodiversity conservation, an effective strategy also needs to include a broader vision for management of the state's natural resources.

Sycan Marsh
Photographer, Alan D. St. John

Oregon's working landscape is made up of millions of acres of forests, farms, rangelands, and urbanized areas. On the Oregon Biodiversity Project's 10-point scale for rating biodiversity management (see pages 38-39) these lands fall into the 3 to 7 range. Most are managed for commodity production. Individually, these lands may appear to have little ecological importance. From a statewide perspective, however, they collectively support a significant portion of Oregon's overall biological diversity — including much of the state's wildlife and a wide variety of "common" species that have adapted to, or coexist with, various human uses. Activities on these lands also affect larger ecosystem processes (hydrology, nutrient cycling, fire, and other disturbances) that transcend traditional boundaries of ownership and resource management.

A growing population can only increase the demands placed on these lands for economic) food and fiber) and ecological (clean air and water) goods and services. But hundreds of opportunities exist to enhance biodiversity values while managing lands to meet human needs.

Relatively marginal changes in land management — restoring wetlands and riparian corridors, changes in timing of grazing, control of invasive exotic plants, planting of native species, implementation of habitat conservation plans — can provide significant benefits for biodiversity.

The goal is not to make these lands rate a 9 on the 10-point scale for biodiversity management, but rather to move them up the scale wherever possible, from a 3 to a 5, or a 4 to a 6. We don't need to transform every rye grass field into a native prairie, or grow every conifer plantation into an old growth forest. But we do need to maintain basic ecosystem functions and processes to keep "common species" common and reduce the risk of additional endangered species in the future.

The Oregon Biodiversity Project has taken some first steps in creating a context for understanding how these lands managed for human needs fit into the bigger picture of Oregon's biological diversity. A companion publication produced by the project, *Stewardship Incentives* (Vickerman 1998), highlights some relatively simple actions landowners and resource managers can take to benefit biodiversity. But in the long run, this element of the conservation strategy will require not just individual actions, but a broader change in the way we as Oregonians think about managing our natural resources. Emerging concepts of "sustainable development" and "ecosystem management" may offer the best avenues toward this vision for Oregon's future.

EXPAND THE EXISTING NETWORK OF CONSERVATION LANDS

Although minor changes in management of multiple-use and commodity production lands can help conserve biological diversity, the most certain way to ensure that species, habitats, and ecosystem processes are maintained over time is to devote some portion of the landscape to those specific purposes. Oregon's existing parks, wildernesses, and other "protected" areas provide a solid foundation for building the network of conservation lands needed to help ensure the long-term conservation of the state's natural biodiversity.

This network of conservation lands does not have to be limited to traditional forms such as national parks, wildlife refuges, or private preserves. Nor do these lands need to be managed to the exclusion of human uses. The key lies in the emphasis on biodiversity values, not as a collateral or subsidiary benefit, but as a primary goal for managing the land. Many of these areas are likely to be public lands, but voluntary management by private landowners can provide the same benefits. Ideally, all of the lands in this conservation network would rate a 10 on the 10-point scale for biodiversity management. In reality, Oregonians will be doing well if we can patch together a system of 7s, 8s and 9s that can be improved over time.

For purposes of this conservation strategy, additions to the existing network should address three major priorities: Statewide representation of all native land cover types; site protection for species known to be sensitive or at-risk; and habitat needs of potentially vulnerable species.

Represent all native land cover types

The network of conservation lands should ultimately encompass the full spectrum of the state's species, habitats, and ecosystems. Because so little is known about most of Oregon's biodiversity, it will never be possible to conserve each element of biodiversity on an individual basis. But it is possible to conserve a host of biodiversity values that are not well documented or understood simply by maintaining healthy, functioning and sustainable examples of the ecosystems that support them.

In practice, vegetation may provide the simplest surrogate for the bulk of biodiversity (Noss and Cooperrider 1994). By protecting adequate areas of juniper woodlands, for example, we are presumably conserving a suite of plant and animal species associated with this habitat, as well as the underlying physical variables that allow juniper woodlands to persist. Although this "coarse-filter" approach — based on conservation of vegetation communities rather than species — may be inadequate for some at-risk and endemic species, it appears to offer the simplest and best technique for ensuring that our network of conservation lands encompasses the broad range of Oregon's biological diversity.

The Oregon Biodiversity Project's statewide vegetation analyses, summarized in Chapter 3, found that well over one-third of the state's native vegetation types have less than five percent of their distribution within the existing network of conservation lands. Although there is no consensus in the scientific community on how much of each of these "under-represented" vegetation types needs to be protected (most conservation biologists would argue that five percent is inadequate), simple prudence dictates that at least some should be managed for conservation purposes. The statewide overview in Chapter 3 identifies a half-dozen general vegetation types that should be priorities because of their substantial decline from historic levels, and the ecoregional assessments highlight priority types for each ecoregion.

Protect species known to be at-risk

The "coarse-filter" approach described above can be used to help conserve a substantial portion of Oregon's biological diversity, but some elements of biodiversity require more site-specific consideration. Narrow endemics (species native to a restricted area that have a limited distribution) and species that are already threatened or endangered have to be protected *where they are* to prevent loss of biodiversity. Protection of several large blocks of a particular vegetation type may help conserve the vast majority of species that use that habitat, but could miss entirely some species found only in one area or that occupy a specialized ecological niche. A "fine-filter" approach, focused on conservation needs of particular at-risk species, is an essential complement to the broader-scale strategy based on conservation of larger communities.

American beaver
Photographer, Beth Davidow
Visuals Unlimited

The Oregon Natural Heritage Program tracks the locations and status of rare, threatened, and endangered species, and a variety of conservation efforts are already under way as a result of listing some of these individual species under the Endangered Species Act. Incorporating these efforts into broader conservation strategies — targeting protection of "under-represented" vegetation types to areas that also offer opportunities to conserve sensitive species — can help ensure more efficient allocation of conservation resources.

Address habitat needs of potentially vulnerable species

Some wildlife species are not currently rare or endangered but may be vulnerable to future loss because of their large home ranges or specialized habitat requirements. Although many of these species will benefit from more general efforts to improve management for biodiversity across the landscape, they deserve special consideration in selecting and designing management strategies for additions to the existing network of conservation lands. (The "aquatic diversity areas" designated by the American Fisheries Society represent a useful first attempt to identify broad areas important for vulnerable aquatic species. These are discussed further in Chapter 3.)

Although this kind of analysis was beyond the scope of the Oregon Biodiversity Project, vertebrate species distribution maps developed for the Oregon Gap Analysis Project provide a tool for assessing the extent to which habitats for individual species are represented within the existing network of conservation lands. Together with other data compiled for this project, these distribution maps could provide a useful framework for addressing the needs of potentially vulnerable species in conservation planning at the regional and local levels.

FOCUS CONSERVATION ACTIONS ON BEST OPPORTUNITIES

Because there will never be enough financial resources to address all biodiversity conservation needs, investments in conservation need to be as effective and efficient as possible. In general, that means directing conservation actions to areas that provide the best opportunities to maximize biodiversity values, minimize resource conflicts, and avoid future threats. Although these principles may appear little more than truisms, they raise some important issues.

To the extent that agencies and organizations are able to pursue more strategic — as opposed to opportunistic — approaches to biodiversity

Spotted Frog, Davis Lake
Photographer, Alan D. St. John

conservation, it makes sense to direct efforts to areas where multiple objectives can be satisfied. In looking for areas to fill in gaps in the existing conservation network's representation of major vegetation types, it may be possible to target lands that also offer opportunities to benefit at-risk species or address aquatic conservation needs.

In general, conservation strategies should follow "the path of least resistance." Given the option — and in many cases there are a number of options, or places, to address individual conservation needs — biodiversity conservation efforts should be targeted to areas that are the least vulnerable to current and future threats. This is just the opposite of the more traditional approach, which has typically focused on the most vulnerable sites. Although there may be compelling local reasons for protecting sites near growing urban areas, from a statewide standpoint it makes more sense to invest limited conservation resources in lands likely to be less vulnerable to the long-term impacts of development and population growth. Conservation is also usually cheaper in these areas because land values are lower.

Pragmatic considerations suggest a similar strategy in political terms. Although adversarial and regulatory approaches have produced some notable environmental gains, biodiversity conservation efforts will increasingly depend on cooperation and support from landowners, resource managers, and local communities. Conservation resources should be targeted to areas where existing patterns of land ownership and management and community attitudes provide the greatest opportunities for success.

The databases compiled for the Oregon Biodiversity Project include a wealth of information — roads, population, land ownership, and biodiversity management — that can be used to help identify potential opportunity areas for conservation action. "Reserve selection"-type analyses that attempt to optimize choices for additions to the conservation network are beyond the scope of this project. However, each of the ecoregion chapters highlights several areas that appear to offer good opportunities to address high-priority conservation needs.

PROVIDE CONSERVATION TOOLS AND INCENTIVES

Few landowners and resource managers are opposed to the goal of conserving biodiversity, but most have little knowledge of what they can do to help. The first step for most is gaining a better understanding of what role their land plays in supporting biodiversity. Some will be willing to take action on their own to improve management for biodiversity values. Many others will need encouragement and assistance. The best way to do that is not through sweeping new regulatory measures, but with a system of financial and other incentives.

The Oregon Biodiversity Project's products provide some of the tools (databases, GIS coverages, analysis, and interpretation) landowners

Incentives for Improved Stewardship

The primary focus of this document is on specific places or habitat types within each ecoregion where opportunities exist to protect or restore the natural values that contribute to the state's biological diversity. However, the Oregon Biodiversity Project's conservation strategy also emphasizes the importance of improved stewardship across the entire landscape, and the need for incentives to encourage landowners to manage their lands in ways that contribute to biodiversity conservation.

The Oregon Biodiversity Project's *Stewardship Incentives* (Vickerman 1998) reviews stewardship issues for a broad range of land uses and highlights a variety of incentives that now exist or could be implemented to address biodiversity concerns on lands not managed primarily for conservation purposes. For ordering information, see the back of this book.

and resource managers need to be able to address biodiversity conservation needs. A number of existing and potential incentives for biodiversity conservation could be implemented through existing programs.

Incentives can be broadly defined and include such concepts as market-based incentives, direct financial assistance and tax relief, regulatory relief, educational programs and technical support, reliable and useful information for cooperative planning, and public recognition and personal benefits.

In considering options for encouraging more "biodiversity-friendly" land and resource management, it is important to clarify the purpose for which incentives would be offered. What activities are to be encouraged (or discouraged) with incentives? It is also important to define the target audiences for incentive programs, and to match incentives with their intended recipients.

To be effective, incentive programs should meet broad conservation needs and not focus too narrowly on certain species or management activities. They should be cost-effective since financial resource funds are limited; they should be easy to understand, administer, and implement, otherwise people are unlikely to use them. They need to be acceptable to landowners; and, finally, they should offer a range of flexible options to meet a variety of needs.

DEVELOP COOPERATIVE PARTNERSHIPS

No single government agency or private organization has the necessary authority or financial resources to take on the task of conserving Oregon's biological diversity on its own. Implementation of a statewide biodiversity conservation strategy will require the cooperative efforts of a wide range of agencies, landowners, and private organizations.

Partnerships and cooperative arrangements can be used to leverage individual partners' limited resources, build bridges between different interests, and expand conservation efforts across traditional lines of ownership and jurisdiction. They can reduce duplication of effort, increase sharing of information, and promote more efficient allocation of resources to conservation priorities. Partnerships are rarely easy, particularly for those accustomed to doing things their own way. But with limited budgets and increasing pressure for "ecosystem management," cooperative efforts are likely to be the primary vehicle for biodiversity conservation in the years ahead.

Some examples of successful cooperative conservation efforts are mentioned throughout this book, but dozens of other entities — ranging from government agencies and private conservation groups to watershed councils, soil and water conservation districts, and "joint venture" organizations — could play a similar role.

COORDINATE DATA COLLECTION AND MANAGEMENT

One of the biggest problems for biodiversity conservation lies in the purely human challenge of collecting, managing, and interpreting the masses of data needed to understand the issues. Better coordination of these efforts is clearly needed. Government agencies, academic institutions, and private organizations have collected mountains of potentially useful information. But variations in data quality and documentation, scale, and format can make it next to impossible to integrate this information for analysis and planning — even if it is all gathered together in one place. In reality, much of the relevant information about biodiversity is scattered in bits and pieces among dozens of agencies and institutions.

To be used and useful, data need to be compiled in consistent and compatible formats, with clear documentation of sources and quality. Data need to be accessible to a wide range of users and updated on a regular basis. But for many users, simply having access to raw data is not enough. They may also need or want analysis and interpretation to help them make sense of the information for planning and policy purposes.

The Oregon Biodiversity Information System, discussed in the Introduction to this atlas, for the first time collects into a single package some of the most important data sets for assessing biodiversity conservation needs at the statewide level. But as a snapshot in time, this database has limited value. Its greater potential lies in its value as a framework for building a comprehensive set of linked databases that can be expanded, improved, and updated as better information becomes available. Making this system work will require a long-term commitment to coordination by all the agencies and organizations that share responsibility for developing and maintaining information about Oregon's biodiversity.

EXPAND PUBLIC AWARENESS AND UNDERSTANDING

No biodiversity conservation strategy will succeed without broad public support. Right now, there are few clearly defined "constituencies" for biodiversity. But there is a large reservoir of potential support among Oregonians who value things associated with biodiversity: healthy populations of fish and wildlife, outdoor recreation, open spaces and natural areas, clean air and water, and economic opportunities unencumbered by the uncertainties of endangered species designations. The only way to connect these interests with biodiversity is through education to improve public awareness and understanding of Oregon's biological resources and the ecosystems that sustain them. A number of these efforts are under way; others can be adapted to include recognition of biodiversity needs. For purposes of this strategy, the key lies in ensuring that some form of public education and outreach is built into all conservation efforts.

Boy scouts planting native grasses
Photographer, Darren Borgias

The Oregon Biodiversity Project is a first attempt to paint the "big picture" of the state's biological diversity for a wide range of audiences. This document and other products of the project can help communicate the importance of some of the issues we confront. But the most effective way to ensure the active support of Oregonians for biodiversity conservation is to give them a meaningful role in conservation. Watershed councils give citizens an opportunity to participate in planning for the long-term health of their local ecosystems. Many community and conservation organizations offer opportunities for volunteers to assist with habitat restoration and improvement efforts.

APPLY PRINCIPLES OF ADAPTIVE MANAGEMENT

The final element of this conservation strategy reinforces several points emphasized throughout this document: *Our current understanding of Oregon's biodiversity is far from perfect. Ecosystems are dynamic, not static. The Oregon Biodiversity Project's analyses are only a first step toward making sense of the available information. This conservation strategy is largely untested.* And perhaps most important, *conservation is a process, not a product.*

All of this dictates an adaptive approach to management for biodiversity conservation. Oregon's conservation strategy needs to be a dynamic one that can evolve over time as we test different tactics, evaluate the results, and revise our thinking.

The strategy outlined in this chapter, and the databases developed to support it, can provide a framework for statewide efforts to conserve Oregon's biological diversity. But the only way to make it work is to put it into action — to apply our knowledge to real-world conservation problems, honestly evaluate our successes and failures, and adjust our course accordingly.

Statewide Overview

This chapter provides a statewide context for the more in-depth look at biodiversity issues in Chapter 4, Assessing Oregon's Ten Ecoregions. The broad overview in this chapter includes a review and analysis of statewide data on vegetation (current and historic), aquatic ecosystems, at-risk species, human population and development, and land ownership and administration. The data discussed in these sections provided the basis for much of the analysis summarized in the ecoregion assessments that follow in Chapter 4.

This chapter also introduces a key measuring stick — a biodiversity management rating system — used in many of the Oregon Biodiversity Project's statewide and ecoregional analyses. This classification system was used to rate lands on a ten-point scale in terms of their contributions, under current management, to long-term conservation of native biological diversity. The rating system is based on the concept that land management should be viewed on a continuum — taking into account variations in management objectives, resource values, and long-term security — rather than simply dividing lands into "protected" and "unprotected" categories.

The Oregon Biodiversity Project developed this rating system primarily to identify those lands at the upper end of the scale that effectively constitute the state's current conservation network. However, the criteria used in the ratings could be applied to any piece of land, regardless of ownership. As such, the classification system provides a conceptual framework for assessing management for biodiversity across the entire landscape and could eventually be used as a yardstick to measure progress toward conservation goals in the future.

BIODIVERSITY MANAGEMENT IN OREGON

A broad range of land uses and ownerships contributes to biodiversity conservation in Oregon. Public lands, wilderness areas, wildlife refuges, and other special management areas provide a relatively high level of protection for some elements of biodiversity. Most "multiple use" public lands recognize biodiversity as one of many resource values. Private forest and rangelands provide important habitat for many plant and animal species, and play a critical role in maintaining overall ecosystem functions and processes. Even lands that are intensively managed for agriculture and other intensive human uses contribute to biodiversity conservation by providing seasonal habitats, supporting common species, or serving as buffers against more intensive development.

Overall, however, only a small portion of Oregon's landscape is devoted to management that focuses on long-term protection of biodiversity. Taken together, these areas comprise an informal "network of conservation lands" that provides a critical foundation for building a statewide biodiversity conservation strategy.

For the Oregon Biodiversity Project's purposes, the current conservation network includes only those lands rated 8-10 on the project's 10-point rating scale for biodiversity management (see sidebar), nearly 10 percent of the state's total area. (The project did not attempt to assign ratings to private lands other than those managed by The Nature Conservancy. As a result, the map on page 40 showing biodiversity management status of various lands in Oregon tells only part of the story. However, most private and tribal lands, like most public lands, are not managed for long-term biodiversity conservation.)

The components of this existing network of conservation lands range in size from sites of a few acres or less to wilderness areas with more than 350,000 acres. These conservation lands are unevenly distributed across the state and fall far short of representing the full range of Oregon's native habitats.

Current management for biodiversity is heavily skewed toward westside forests and alpine habitats, largely as a result of the President's Northwest Forest Plan and past congressional wilderness designations. In the three westside ecoregions with extensive federal forests (Coast Range, Klamath Mountains, West Cascades), about 25 percent of all lands receive high ratings (categories 8-10) for biodiversity management under the Oregon Biodiversity Project's classification system.

The picture in the Willamette Valley and east of the Cascades is far different. The Willamette Valley and the Columbia Basin, both almost entirely in private ownership, have less than two percent of their area in categories 8-10. Eastside

Biodiversity management ratings

Any assessment of biodiversity conservation needs requires some kind of evaluation of what is already protected, which in turn, opens up a host of questions: Is biodiversity "protected" in wilderness areas? What about a multiple-use wildlife refuge or a heavily used state park? The answer is rarely as simple as "protected" or "unprotected" — more often, it is somewhere in between.

For its assessment, the Oregon Biodiversity Project developed a new classification to reflect better the range of protection for biodiversity provided by different kinds of land management. Using this system, most public lands were rated on a scale of 1-10, with 10 providing the highest contributions to biodiversity conservation. Private lands, with the exception of The Nature Conservancy's preserves, were not rated due to lack of information. The ratings are based on a structured subjective evaluation of:

Management objectives. Lands where biodiversity conservation or protection of natural values is the primary management objective are rated at the higher end of the scale.

Security. Lands formally designated for long-term protection of natural values are eligible for a high rating. Lands subject to zoning or other land use designations intended to maintain natural values or natural resource-dependent uses are in the middle range.

Biodiversity values. Lands deemed to be of critical value to biodiversity conservation are rated high. Other lands that provide quality habitat for native fish and wildlife, or that make important contributions to ecosystem functions, fall in the upper-middle range of the scale.

Size. Larger blocks of land managed as a unit receive a higher rating than smaller blocks with the same management objectives, security, and biodiversity values.

Most federal and state lands in Oregon were rated in the middle (4-6) of the 10-point scale. Wilderness areas, some large national and state parks, and some wildlife areas and refuges were rated at the upper end of the scale (7-10), as were most federal lands designated as research natural areas or areas of critical environmental concern and most of The Nature Conservancy's preserves. For the Oregon Biodiversity Project's analyses, only lands rated 8-10 were considered part of the current conservation network.

How the ratings were developed. The Oregon Biodiversity Project asked state and federal land management agencies and The Nature Conservancy to assess their land ownerships and provide recommendations for rating individual properties or classes of land under a common management designation. Because few individuals have detailed knowledge of all areas under their agency's jurisdiction, recommendations were also solicited from other experts both within and outside each agency. Most of the ratings represent a synthesis of several assessments, with project staff assigning the final numbers.

ecoregions with large federal ownerships are not dramatically different, with figures ranging from two to seven percent.

Some habitat types, such as subalpine and alpine meadows (more than 90 percent in categories 8-10 statewide), are quite well represented in the existing network of conservation lands. Others, such as big sagebrush-bunchgrass (1.8 percent), Oregon white-oak woodlands (3.1 percent), and bitterbrush steppe (0.1 percent), have little — if any — of their limited distribution in areas managed for long-term biodiversity conservation. (See page 212 for a statewide summary by vegetation type.)

Much of the existing network of conservation lands is in federal ownership. National forest wilderness areas and Crater Lake National Park encompass some of the largest remaining blocks of native habitats, mainly high-elevation forests and mountain peaks in the West Cascades, Klamath Mountains, and Blue Mountains ecoregions. The system of late-successional reserves established under the Northwest Forest Plan includes a substantial portion of the remaining low- to mid-elevation mature and old growth forests in the Coast Range, Klamath Mountains, and West Cascades ecoregions.

Special congressional designations help protect biodiversity values in the Columbia River Gorge and some of the canyonlands of eastern Oregon, including Hells Canyon and areas along the Deschutes, John Day, Owyhee, and other "wild and scenic" rivers. Some of the largest remnants of the state's diverse wetland systems are protected in national wildlife refuges and BLM special management areas in the Coast Range, East Cascades, and Basin and Range ecoregions. Hart Mountain National Wildlife Refuge and BLM special management areas in the Owyhee Uplands ecoregion encompass large blocks of sagebrush and shrub-steppe habitat. In addition, federal agencies have set aside several hundred smaller areas across the state as "research natural areas," "areas of critical environmental concern," and other special management designations — all intended to protect biodiversity values.

The largest blocks of state lands where management focuses on biodiversity values are found in some of the larger state parks and a few state wildlife areas. State parks are particularly significant on the coast, where they encompass some of the largest remaining areas of undeveloped shoreline and headland habitat.

The Nature Conservancy has more than 50 preserves in Oregon, many of them established to protect key elements of biodiversity, such as rare or vulnerable habitats and species. Although most preserves are less than 1,000 acres in size, the largest — Sycan Marsh — includes more than 20,000 acres of wetlands in the headwaters of the Klamath Basin.

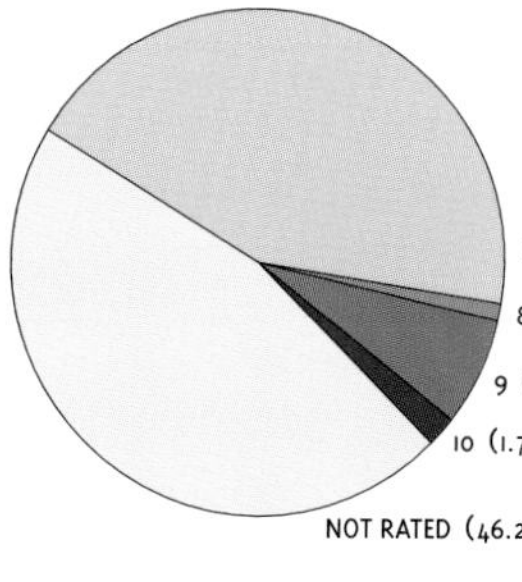

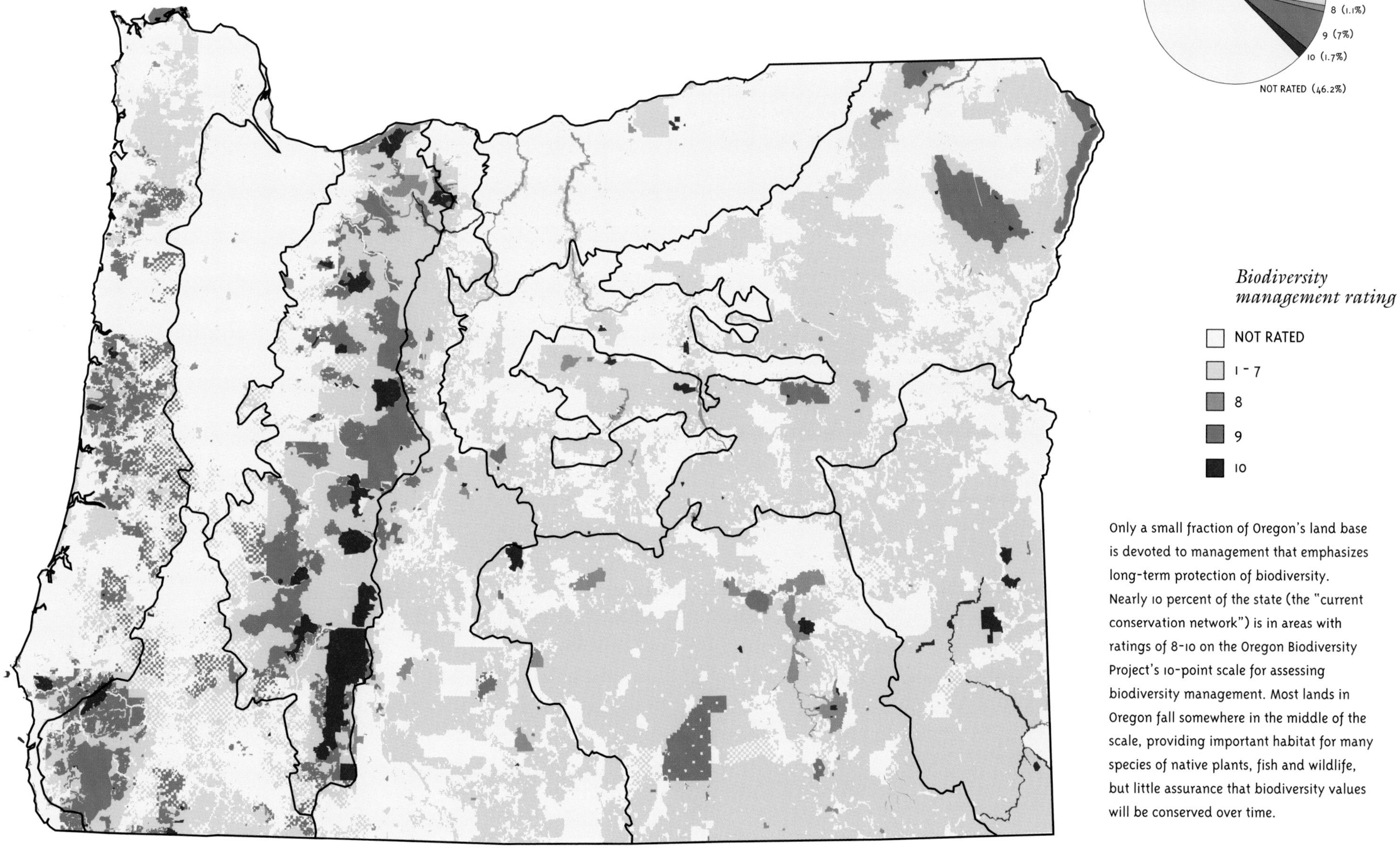

Only a small fraction of Oregon's land base is devoted to management that emphasizes long-term protection of biodiversity. Nearly 10 percent of the state (the "current conservation network") is in areas with ratings of 8-10 on the Oregon Biodiversity Project's 10-point scale for assessing biodiversity management. Most lands in Oregon fall somewhere in the middle of the scale, providing important habitat for many species of native plants, fish and wildlife, but little assurance that biodiversity values will be conserved over time.

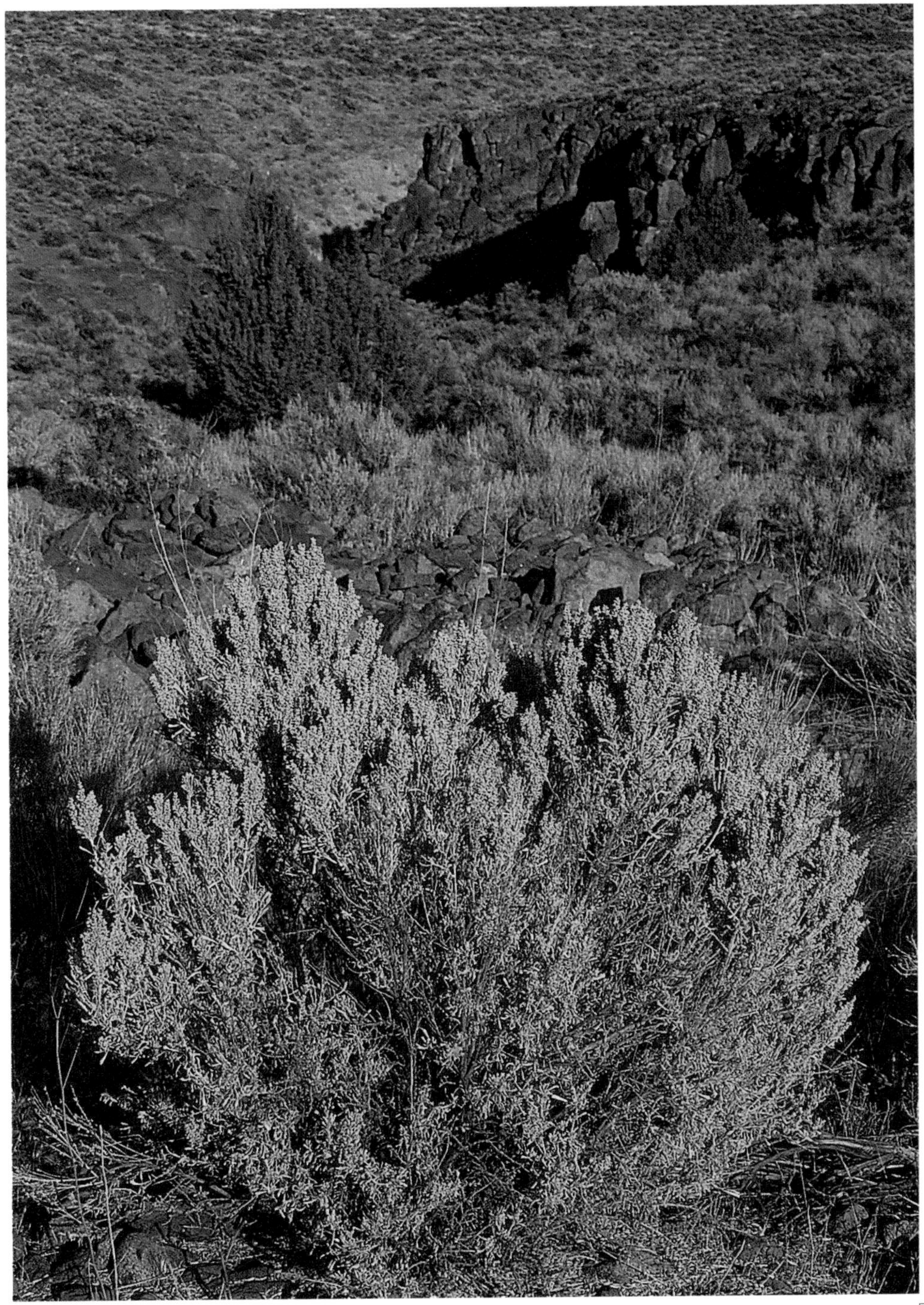

Big Sagebrush, Warner Valley
Photographer, Alan D. St. John

VEGETATION

Oregon's vegetation is highly diverse, ranging from lush coastal forests and alpine meadows to arid grasslands and the sagebrush steppe of the high desert. This vegetational diversity is in large measure a result of physical factors related to the state's climate, geology, geography, and topography.

Oregon is a "crossroads" for plants from many regions, with numerous species at or near the edge of their range. Plants typically found in the Arctic dominate the high Cascades. Coastal Alaskan plants such as Sitka spruce dominate the north Coast Range, while the southern coast has a redwood belt that spills over from California. The Wallowa Mountains are the western edge of the Rocky Mountains, and are home to many species common to central Colorado. Southeastern Oregon is the edge of the Great Basin, and is characterized by plants found in the cool deserts of Nevada and Utah. In the Klamath Mountains, the flora of the Sierra Nevada, the Cascades, and the Great Basin come together to form unique combinations. A two-mile stretch of the Siskiyou Crest in southwestern Oregon supports plant communities as varied as old growth Douglas fir forest, alpine meadows, western juniper steppe, Jeffrey pine savannas, red fir forests, and rigid sagebrush steppe.

Vegetation as a surrogate for biodiversity

Vegetation is a function of the same biological and physical factors that have shaped the state's overall biological diversity. It is also relatively

Current Vegetation

The current vegetation map used by the Oregon Biodiversity Project is based on the digital map developed for the Oregon Gap Analysis Program (GAP) (Kagan and Caicco 1992). This map was developed through interpretation of satellite photos (1:250,000 scale). The smallest polygon or unit of classification in this map is 320 acres; most polygons are much larger.

The GAP map includes 133 primary vegetation types. These types are vegetation "alliances" — groups of habitat types that have the same dominant species (ponderosa pine), and basic structure (woodland). Many polygons were labeled as mosaics of two of these primary types. In addition to identifying vegetation types, the map also labeled forest types with a "fragmentation" modifier (based on evidence of fragmentation from logging). An "L" is used for low fragmentation (up to one-third harvested), an "M" for moderate fragmentation (one-third to two-thirds harvested), and an "H" for high fragmentation (more than two-thirds harvested, with remnant small patches of forest).

easy to describe, classify, and map. As such, it provides a useful, if simplistic, "surrogate" for habitats and the myriad components of terrestrial biodiversity that are little known, poorly understood, or difficult to quantify.

The Oregon Biodiversity Project has used vegetation data as a "coarse filter" to help assess the broad distribution and status of Oregon's biological diversity. However, vegetation maps are only a static representation of one aspect of the state's complex and dynamic ecosystems. Vegetation types and conditions change over time due to a variety of factors, some related to natural processes, others to human activities. Any depiction of vegetation is really only a snapshot in time, and interpretations are limited by the quality of the data.

Historic changes in vegetation

Looking at historic vegetation patterns and the changes that have occurred over time provide a useful perspective on the significance of the patterns apparent in a current vegetation map.

To establish a historical context for its vegetation analyses, the Oregon Biodiversity Project developed a "historic" vegetation map of the state based on information derived from a number of sources (see box accompanying historic vegetation map for a detailed discussion). This map has limited utility as a representation of the vegetation that existed in any specific place at a particular time. However, a comparison of the relative amounts and general distribution of vegetation types in the historic and current vegetation maps reveals significant changes since the advent of European settlement.

The most obvious changes are in the many areas that no longer have native vegetation, but have been entirely converted to human uses. These include lands currently mapped as urban areas, farmlands, large reservoirs, and recent clearcuts, as well as grasslands or shrublands dominated by exotic plants.

Some habitats and ecoregions have been much more impacted by human uses than others. The ecoregions showing the most dramatic changes are the Willamette Valley and the Columbia Basin. The Willamette Valley has been converted to agriculture and urban development in many areas, and the native prairies and oak savannas that once dominated the landscape have been reduced to a few small fragments. In the Columbia Basin, low-elevation native prairies dominated by bluebunch wheatgrass and Idaho fescue have also largely been converted to agriculture. Similar changes are apparent in virtually all of the interior valley bottoms, which were historically dominated by prairies and gallery riparian forests and woodlands.

Some other changes are not as obvious. Ponderosa pine habitats were historically widespread in the Klamath Mountains, East Cascades, and Blue Mountains. A combination of logging and fire suppression have greatly

The scale of the current vegetation map limited mapping of linear features, precluding identification of riparian habitats along any but the largest rivers. The other major scale limitation affected forest mapping, especially in southwestern Oregon, which has a very high diversity of native forest vegetation types that could not be mapped at this scale and were thus lumped in very general categories such as "mixed conifer."

Timber harvest. More than three-quarters of the lands mapped as forests show evidence of recent timber harvest. About 32.5% are classified as "high" fragmentation (more than two-thirds of the area harvested). Only 21.4% of forests show little or no evidence of timber harvest.

Non-native habitats. Farmland and developed pastures account for about 6.8 million acres, or 11% of the state. About 2.8 million acres (4.5%) are dominated by exotic species such as cheatgrass. Urban, industrial, and residential lands occupy 435,000 acres (0.7%).

Historic Vegetation

The Oregon Biodiversity Project's historic vegetation map was created using expert judgment to incorporate and interpret data from three main sources.

One was a historic vegetation map developed by the federal government's Interior Columbia River Basin Ecosystem Management Project for most of Oregon east of the Cascade Mountains crest. The second was a forest vegetation type map by H.J. Andrews et al. (1936) of the U.S. Forest Service, and based on detailed survey data from the 1920s and early 1930s. The third source was the Oregon Natural Heritage Program, which provided maps for the Willamette, Umpqua, Rogue, and Illinois river valleys and the Columbia Basin. These maps were based on General Land Office plat maps for the periods 1850-1870, and on notes from the original surveyors.

reduced the extent and changed the character of most of these forests. Old growth Douglas-fir forests were the dominant vegetation in the Coast Range, Klamath Mountains, and West Cascades ecoregions. Although the distribution of these forests has not changed dramatically, old growth habitats have been reduced to a small fraction of their historic extent.

Direct comparison of statewide acreage figures derived from historic and current vegetation maps can be misleading, and is not even possible in many cases due to differences in the classifications used in the two maps. However, analysis of past and current vegetation patterns can help frame issues for biodiversity conservation efforts in Oregon.

Conversion to non-native cover types

Overall, grasslands, prairies, bottomland hardwood forests, and wetlands have probably experienced the greatest habitat losses. These losses are due to conversion to non-native land cover types, primarily those associated with urbanization, agriculture, and invasion by exotic plant species (see adjacent sidebar). Currently, these non-native land cover types are found on more than 16 percent of the state's landscape.

Modification of native vegetation types

The vast majority of Oregon's historic forests and shrub steppe are still dominated by native trees and shrubs, but most have been modified to at least some degree as a result of human activities. Forests in most areas show evidence of recent timber harvest, and are classified in the current vegetation map as "high," "moderate," or "low" fragmentation based on the extent of harvest apparent in 1988 satellite photos. (Fragmentation in this case refers only to the extent of recent harvest apparent within an area mapped as an individual polygon or discrete unit of vegetation; it does not reflect either natural or other human-related forms of habitat fragmentation.) Although these forestlands are still dominated by native species and may eventually have the potential to regain many of their original characteristics, they currently provide habitats very different from those historically found in unharvested native forests.

The adjacent sidebar summarizes harvest-related fragmentation of mapped vegetation polygons. The numbers reflect only readily apparent harvest (e.g., a 30-year-old clearcut that now supports a conifer plantation would probably not be identified as "fragmented"), so the extent of past timber harvests is understated.

Many rangelands show similar evidence of modification related to livestock grazing and other human uses. The presence of exotic plant species as a subdominant component of native shrub steppe vegetation types is one indicator of these impacts.

Other vegetation changes

In many areas, major vegetation changes have occurred as a result of changes in historic patterns

The historic vegetation map has a number of weaknesses. The Columbia River Basin portions are uneven in quality, with good information for public lands, but patchy information for private lands in the valley bottoms, where much of the landscape has been converted to non-native habitats. The map grossly underestimates the amount of wetlands that formerly occurred in the eastern Oregon valleys, especially the Silvies Valley, the Klamath Basin, and the Powder River Valley. The mosaic of shrubsteppe in southeastern Oregon is not well mapped. Mapping of forested areas appears to be good, although Andrews' original classification (lumping all true firs into one category, for example), limits the accuracy of interpretations. Finally, the scale of this map limits the detail that can be shown.

HISTORIC VEGETATION

Forest and woodlands

- DOUGLAS FIR
- PACIFIC SILVER FIR • MOUNTAIN HEMLOCK
- SHASTA FIR • WHITE FIR
- SUBALPINE FIR
- SITKA SPRUCE • WESTERN HEMLOCK
- WESTERN RED CEDAR
- SHORE PINE
- JEFFREY PINE
- LODGEPOLE PINE
- MIXED CONIFER
- PORT ORFORD CEDAR
- COASTAL REDWOOD
- BOTTOM LAND HARDWOODS
- OAK • MADRONE
- OAK SAVANNA
- PONDEROSA PINE
- WHITEBARK PINE
- GRAND FIR
- ASPEN
- WESTERN JUNIPER
- WESTERN JUNIPER • SAGEBRUSH

— ECOREGIONS

Shrublands

- MOUNTAIN MAHOGANY
- MOUNTAIN SHRUB
- ANTELOPE BITTERBRUSH
- BIG SAGEBRUSH
- MOUNTAIN BIG SAGEBRUSH
- LOW SAGEBRUSH
- LOW & RIGID SAGE
- SALT DESERT SCRUB

Grasslands

- FESCUE • BUNCHGRASS
- AGROPYRON WHEATGRASS
- PRAIRIE

Wetlands

- WETLANDS
- OPEN WATER

Sparsely vegetated

- ALPINE TUNDRA • BARREN
- DUNES

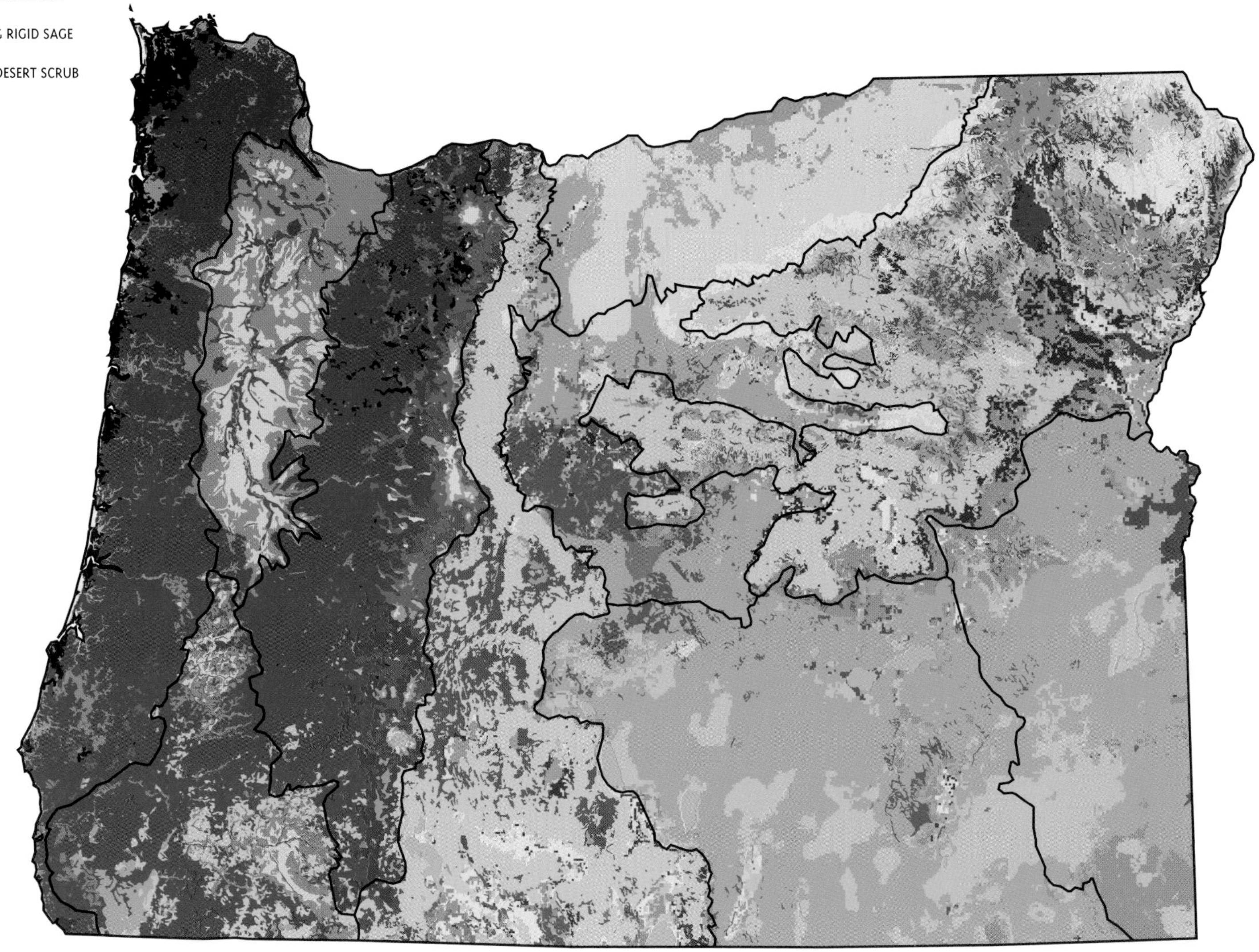

CURRENT VEGETATION

Forest and woodlands

- COASTAL REDWOOD
- SITKA SPRUCE • WESTERN HEMLOCK
- DOUGLAS FIR
- DOUGLAS FIR • TANOAK • PACIFIC MADRONE
- MOUNTAIN HEMLOCK
- MOUNTAIN HEMLOCK • RED FIR
- WESTERN LARCH • DOUGLAS FIR • TRUE FIR
- WHITE FIR • DOUGLAS FIR • INCENSE CEDAR
- WHITE FIR • GRAND FIR
- RED FIR FORESTS
- SUBALPINE FIR • ENGELMANN SPRUCE
- JEFFREY PINE
- PONDEROSA PINE • DOUGLAS FIR
- PONDEROSA PINE
- PONDEROSA • WESTERN JUNIPER
- LODGEPOLE PINE
- BIGLEAF MAPLE • RED ALDER • DOUGLAS FIR
- OREGON WHITE OAK • CALIFORNIA BLACK OAK • MADRONE
- OREGON WHITE OAK • CALIFORNIA BLACK OAK
- OREGON WHITE OAK • DOUGLAS FIR
- OREGON WHITE OAK • PONDEROSA
- ASPEN
- ASPEN • SERVICEBERRY • BITTERCHERRY SNOWBRUSH
- WESTERN JUNIPER
- WILLOW RIPARIAN WOODLAND
- COTTONWOOD RIPARIAN WOODLAND

— ECOREGIONS

Shrublands

- BUCKBRUSH • MANZANITA CHAPARRAL
- BIG SAGEBRUSH
- MOUNTAIN BIG SAGEBRUSH
- MIXED SAGEBRUSH
- LOW SAGEBRUSH
- BITTERBRUSH
- SALT DESERT SCRUB
- SALTSAGE • BUDSAGE
- SHADSCALE
- SPINY HOPSAGE • SHADSCALE • BLACK GREASEWOOD
- WINTERFAT
- MOUNTAIN MAHOGANY
- MOUNTAIN SNOWBERRY

Grasslands

- BLUEBUNCH WHEATGRASS
- BLUEBUNCH WHEATGRASS • CHEATGRASS
- IDAHO FESCUE
- TUFTED HAIRGRASS MEADOWS

Wetlands

- HARDSTEM BULRUSH • CATTAIL • BURREED MARSH
- REED CANARY GRASS WETLAND
- MONTANE SEDGE MEADOWS & WETLANDS
- COASTAL SALTMARSH
- SHORELINE COMMUNITIES
- OPEN WATER

Sparsely vegetated

- BARE PLAYA
- INLAND SAND DUNES
- LAVA FIELDS
- ALPINE FELL FIELDS

Human modified

- BRUSHFIELDS & RECENT CLEARCUTS
- EXOTIC GRASSLANDS
- RURAL PASTURE WITH REMNANT BOTTOMLAND
- AGRICULTURE
- URBAN • INDUSTRIAL

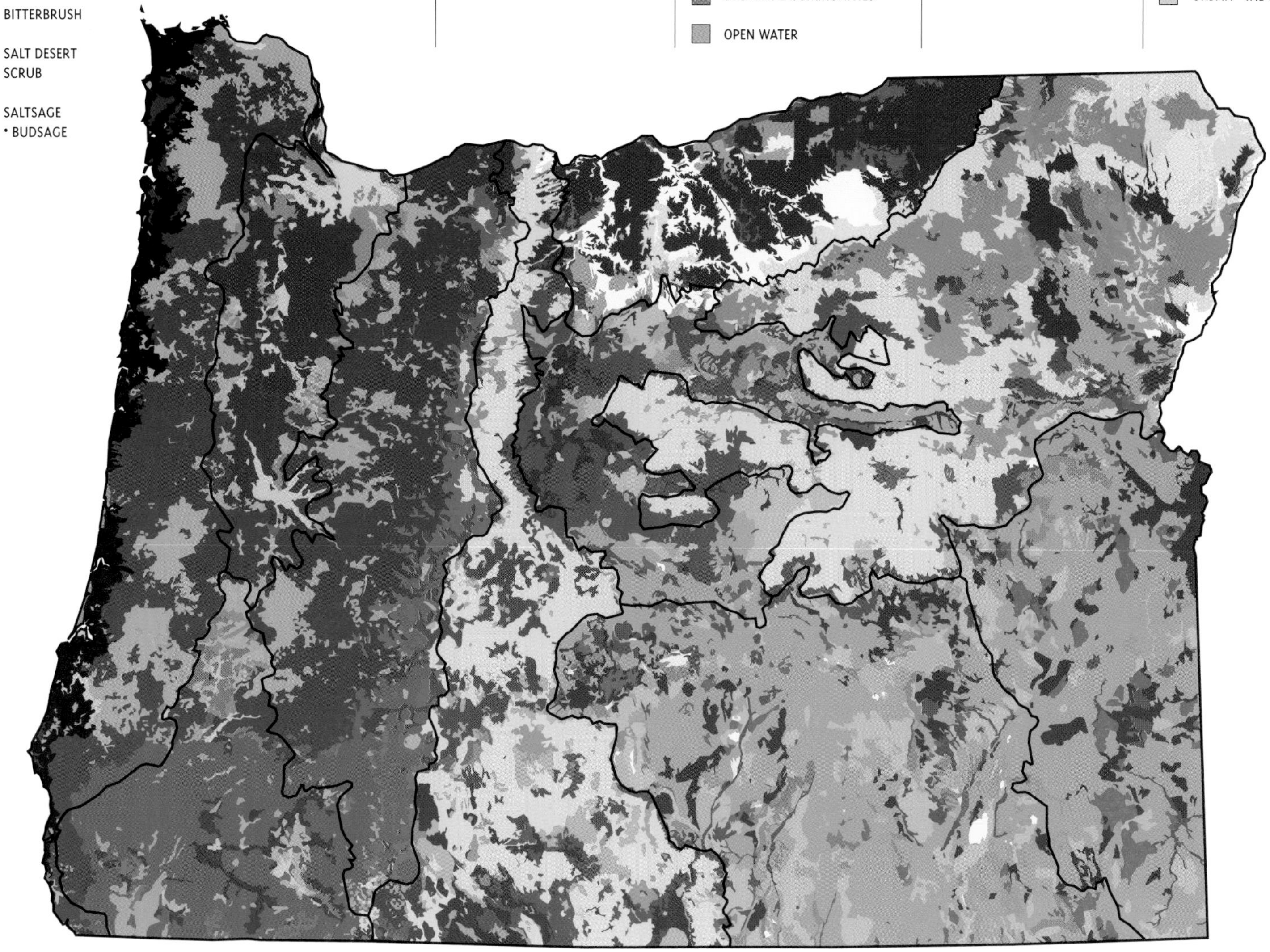

Data from Actual Oregon Vegetation (Kagan and Caicco 1992)

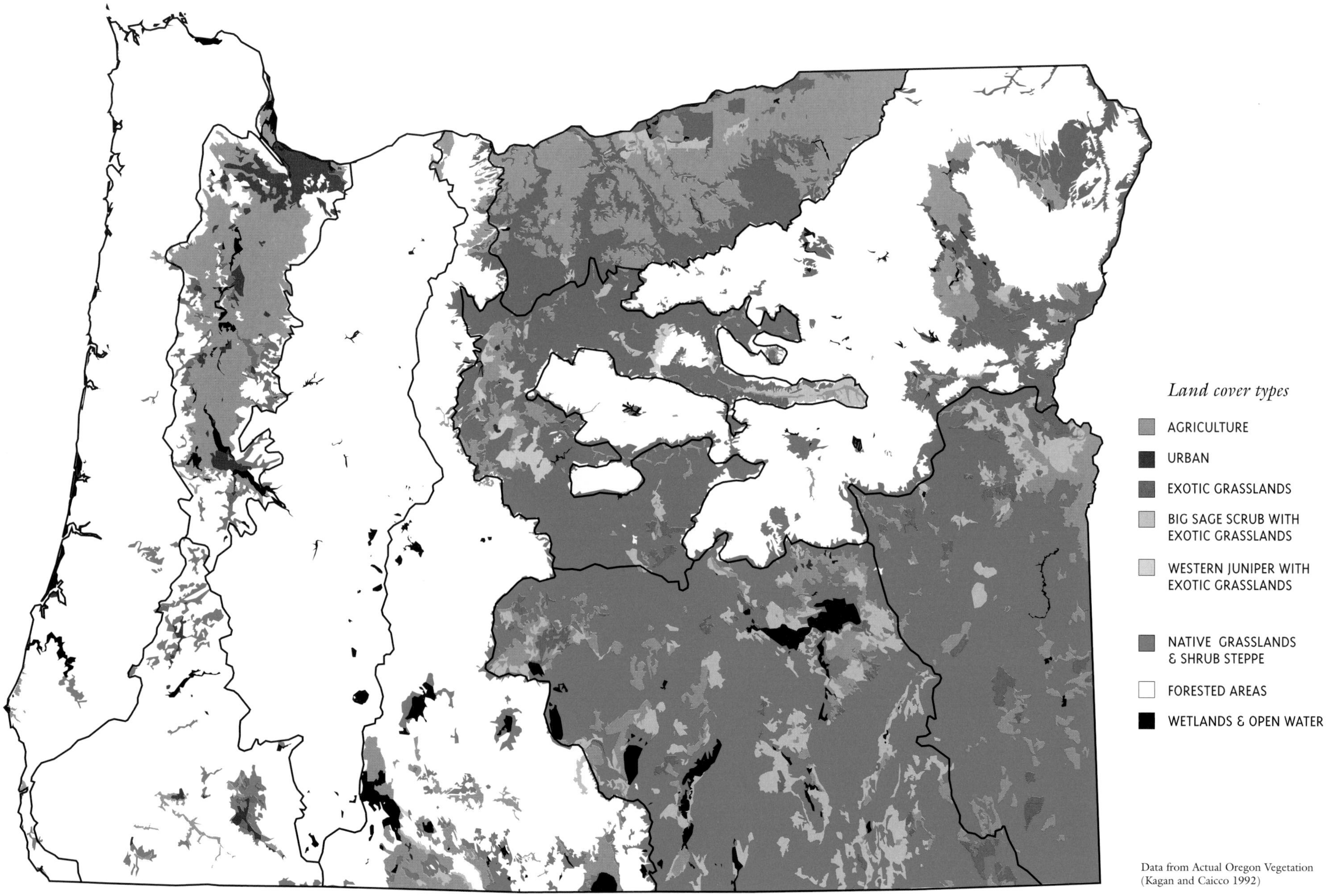

Data from Actual Oregon Vegetation (Kagan and Caicco 1992)

FORESTS MODIFIED BY RECENT TIMBER HARVEST

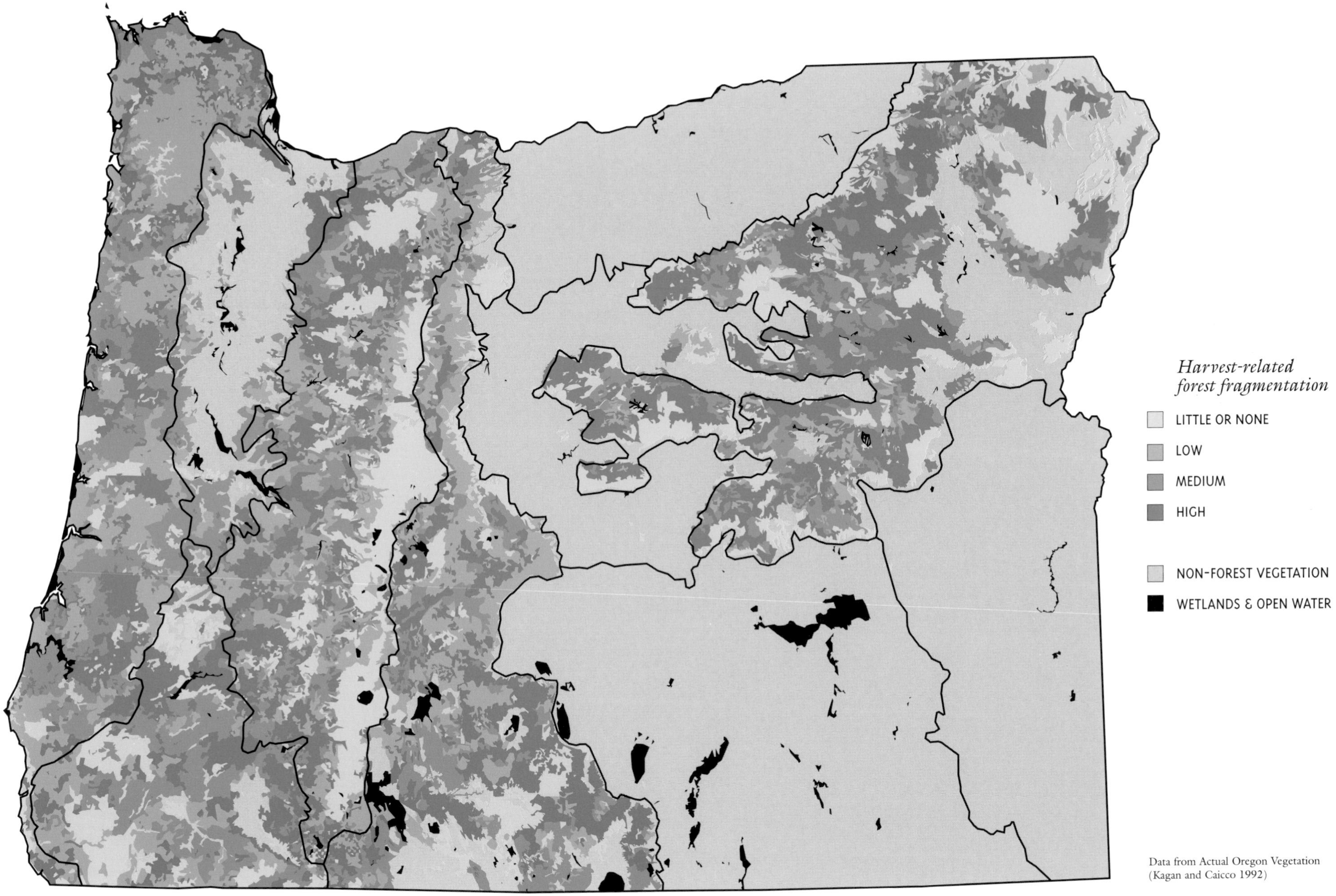

Data from Actual Oregon Vegetation (Kagan and Caicco 1992)

of disturbance and succession. Fire suppression has been a major factor in altering the composition, structure, and distribution of vegetation types in forests and rangelands across the state.

Western juniper, for example, has expanded dramatically in the current vegetation map, more than doubling its historic distribution in the ecoregions east of the Cascades. Although there is evidence that juniper distributions have varied widely over the centuries as a result of climatic variations, there is little doubt that livestock grazing and fire suppression have contributed significantly to the recent expansion of this vegetation type. Paradoxically, this increase has been accompanied by substantial losses of "old growth" juniper in the Lava Plains Ecoregion primarily due to the effects of urbanization and agricultural development.

In the Willamette Valley, areas that were historically mapped as oak savanna (grasslands with widely scattered oaks), grew into oak woodlands as a result of grazing and fire suppression. Now, many of the remaining oak woodlands have developed into closed canopy forests or have been overtaken by conifers. These lands are still covered with "native" vegetation types, but the habitats they provide are very different from those of 150 years ago.

Identification of conservation priorities

The Oregon Biodiversity Project used historic and current vegetation data to help identify general habitat types that should be considered priorities for conservation based on major declines in distribution.

For some vegetation types, these losses or changes were significant primarily at the ecoregion level, and they are therefore discussed in Chapter 4, "Assessing Oregon's Ten Ecoregions." However, a handful of general habitat types have been identified as statewide conservation priorities because of their widespread declines and significance in multiple ecoregions. These include:

Oak savanna and woodlands. Declines of 50-95 percent in all ecoregions where these vegetation types were historically common.

Wetlands. Poorly mapped, but major declines in all ecoregions; most remaining wetlands have been modified or degraded.

Riparian. Poorly mapped, but widespread losses and degradation.

Bottomland hardwood forests. Declines of 50-95 percent in most ecoregions.

Old growth conifer forests. Current and historic vegetation maps don't indicate successional status, but available evidence suggests declines of more than 50 percent among common forest types in all forested ecoregions.

Native grasslands and prairies. Declines of 50-98 percent for most types in all ecoregions where native grasslands and prairies were formerly abundant.

AQUATIC ECOSYSTEMS

Aquatic ecosystems are critical elements of Oregon's biodiversity, but they also present unique problems for a broad-scale assessment like the one undertaken by the Oregon Biodiversity Project. Most freshwater aquatic habitats are linear in nature (such as rivers and streams), or are too small (most wetlands and riparian habitats) to show up well in coarse-scale mapping. The marine ecosystem off Oregon's coast was beyond the scope of our terrestrial-based analysis.

Physical features aside, few aspects of Oregon's aquatic ecosystems have been mapped and quantified on a statewide basis, and fewer still have been put into digital GIS format. Statewide data related to aquatic species are primarily limited to fish distributions and locations of at-risk species. Water quality data are incomplete and focus more on physical parameters than on ecological functions.

With such limited information, few attempts have been made to address aquatic biodiversity

Steelhead, North Fork
Salmonberry River
Photographer, Robert Fields

The percentage of stream miles within a watershed that are designated as core area habitat varies widely. Watersheds with the highest densities of core area habitat are found in headwaters systems that provide spawning habitat for both coho salmon and steelhead.

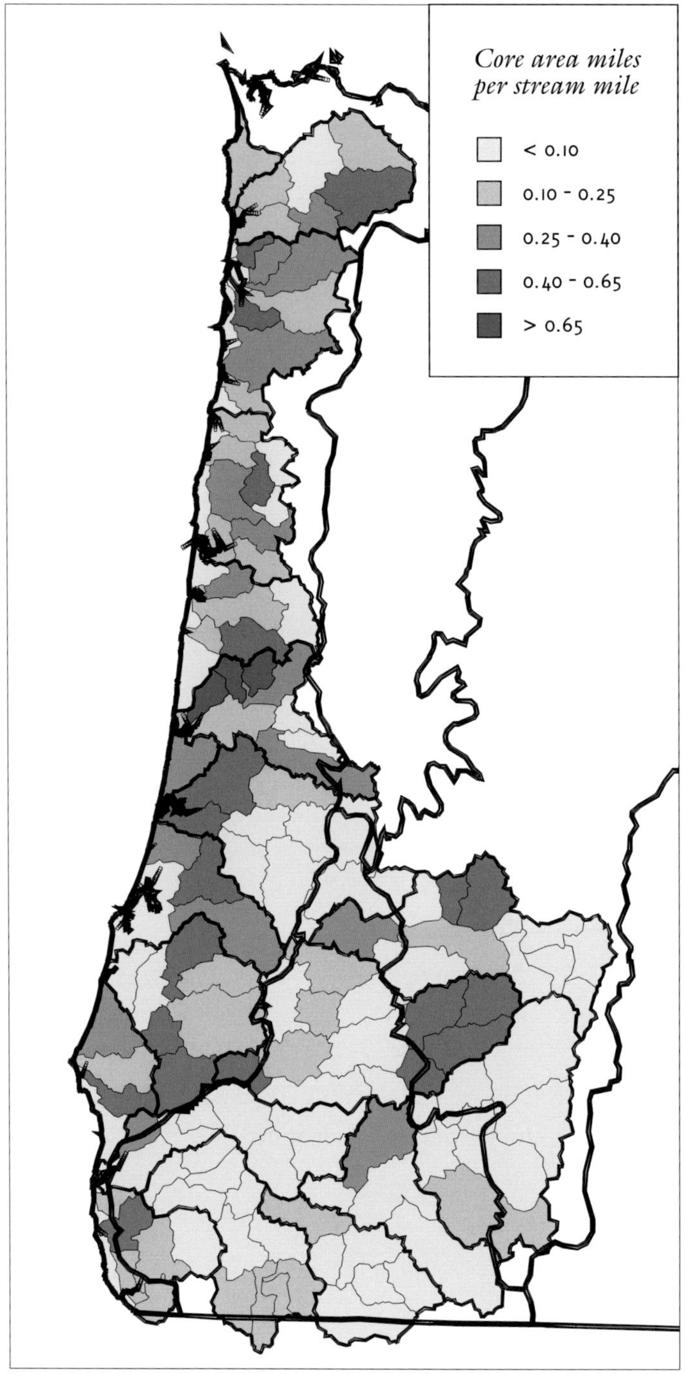

Data from State of Oregon 1997

conservation in Oregon on a broad scale; most conservation efforts have been directed at specific species or habitats. As a result, the Oregon Biodiversity Project's assessment of aquatic biodiversity has necessarily been limited in scope, and is, therefore, incomplete. (For example, it ignores almost completely the incredibly rich storehouse of biodiversity found in Oregon's marine and estuarine ecosystems.)

To some extent, we have attempted to compensate for these weaknesses by incorporating consideration of aquatic habitats into the more qualitative aspects of our assessment. For example, although it was not possible to quantify historic losses or current distribution of wetland and riparian habitats, ample evidence exists that these habitat types — which are critically important for biodiversity at many levels — have experienced dramatic declines statewide. On that basis, the project has identified wetland and riparian habitats as priorities for conservation statewide.

Sources of aquatic resource data

Several major sources of aquatic resource data were used in assessing Oregon's conservation needs at the statewide and ecoregional levels. The state's Oregon Coastal Salmon Restoration Initiative (1996) identified core areas and habitat data for coastal salmon. The Oregon chapter of the American Fisheries Society identified key aquatic diversity areas and aquatic corridors (Bottom et al. 1993). The Wilderness Society (1993) summarized data on the status of various salmon stocks. A report produced for Oregon Trout (Huntington et al. 1996) mapped the distribution of remaining healthy stocks of anadromous salmonids. In several eastside ecoregions, the analysis also used a GIS data layer put together by conservation interests that used information from BLM inventories to delineate potential federal wild and scenic river segments for a proposed Oregon High Desert Protection Act.

Much of the aquatic resources data focus on salmonids, which are considered broadly representative of the aquatic biota. The status of salmonids can, therefore, be viewed as a general indication of aquatic ecosystem health, and the problems affecting these fish are probably similar to those facing many other aquatic species (ICBEMP 1997b).

Salmon core areas. The Oregon Coastal Salmon Restoration Initiative identified "core areas" for coastal salmonid habitat. Core areas are defined as reaches or watersheds that are judged to be of critical importance to sustain salmon populations in individual basins. Ideally, they contain the resources and habitats necessary for the persistence of each population. Additionally, they will be a major source for seeding new habitats as restoration programs are implemented (State of Oregon 1997).

Core areas have only been designated west of the Cascade crest. The majority of key stream reaches (66 percent) are in the Coast Range Ecoregion, with the balance in the Klamath

AQUATIC DIVERSITY AREAS

REFERENCE WATERSHED

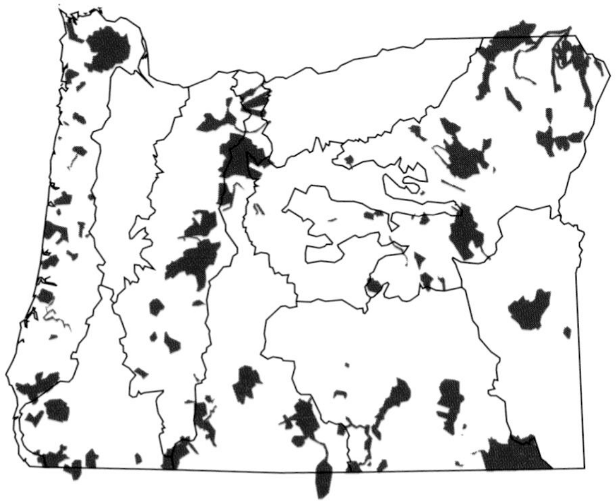

GENETIC REFUGES

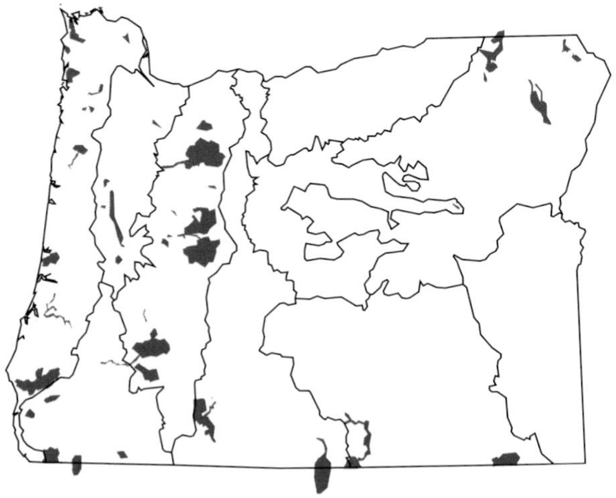

CENTERS OF SPECIES RICHNESS

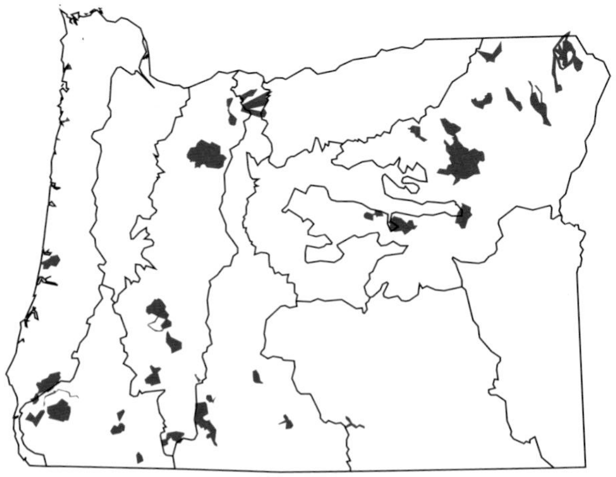

ECOLOGICAL FUNCTIONS

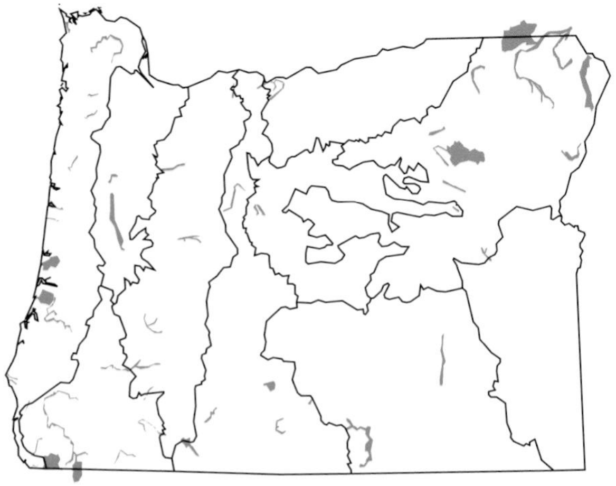

CONNECTING CORRIDOR

Aquatic diversity areas mapped by a subcommittee of the Oregon Chapter of the American Fisheries Society (Bottom et al. 1993) represent one of the few attempts to identify target areas for aquatic biodiversity conservation. Most aquatic diversity areas are found in mountainous areas where habitats have been less affected by human activities. Some lowland aquatic systems remain centers of species richness and provide important genetic refuges, despite habitat degradation.

Data from Oregon Critical Watersheds Database (Bottom et al. 1993)

STATUS OF SALMONIDS

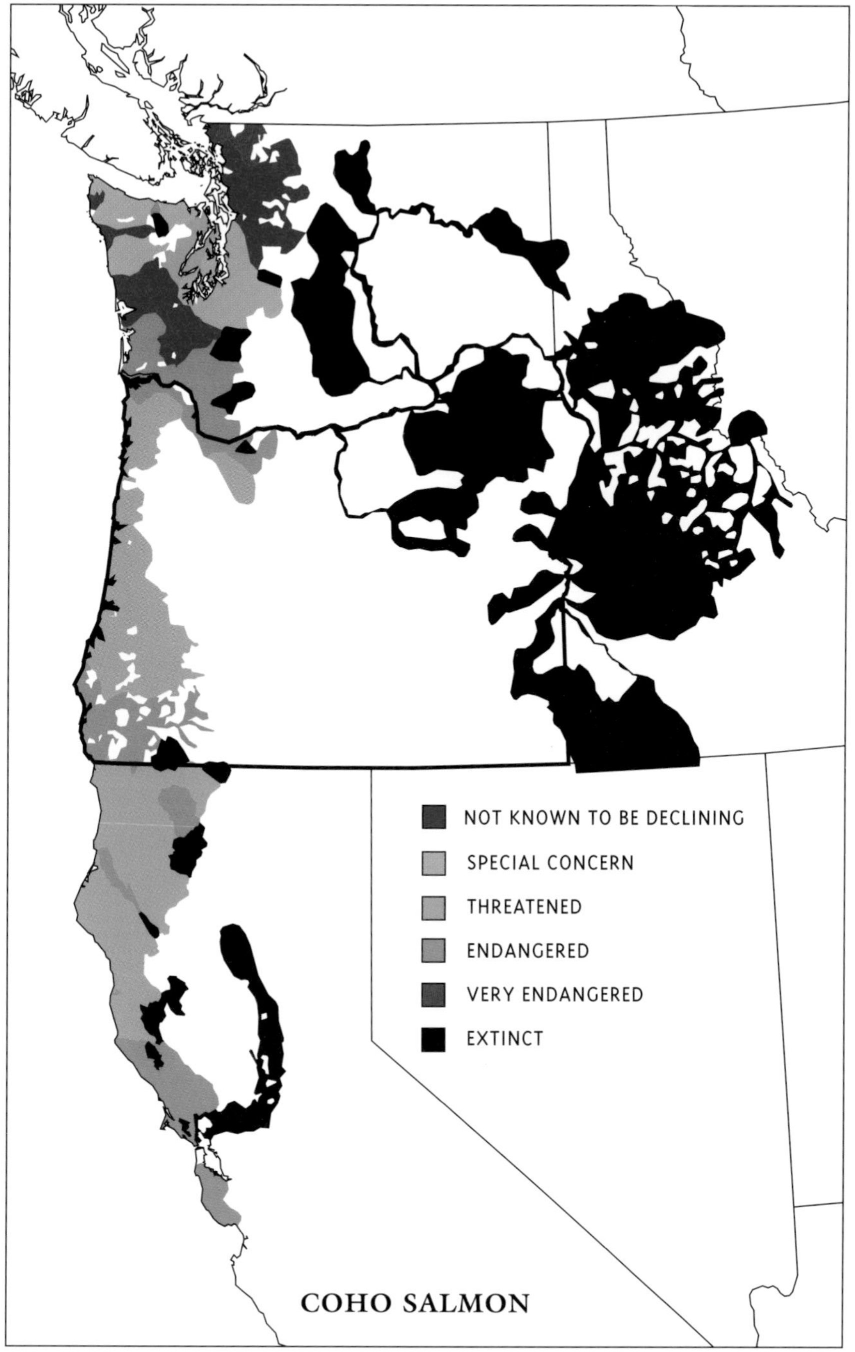

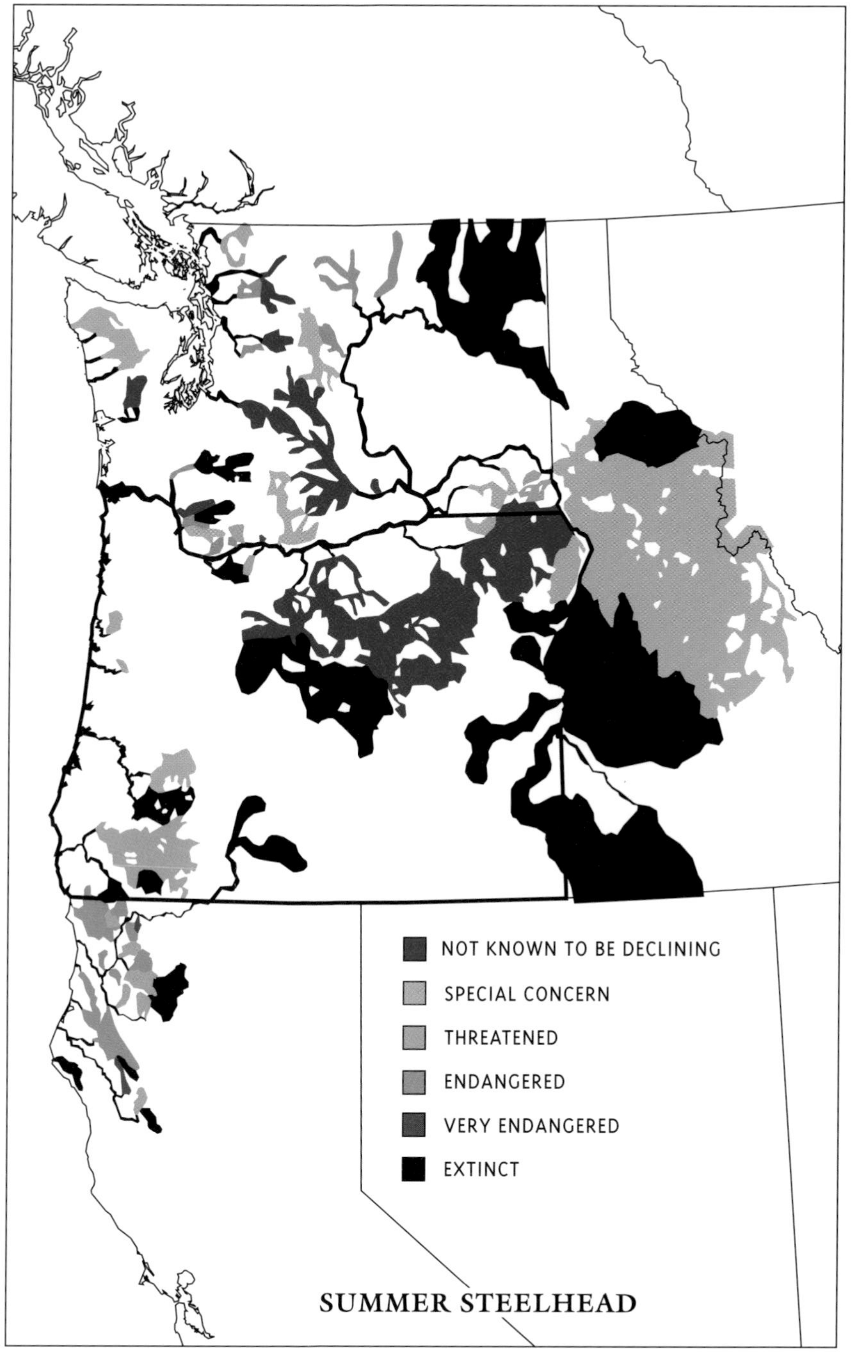

Data from Pacific Salmon and Federal Lands, A Regional Analysis (The Wilderness Society 1993)

Mountains (just under 18 percent), the West Cascades (15 percent), and the Willamette Valley (one percent). In general, core areas have a relatively even north-south distribution. However, the percentage of anadromous habitat identified as core areas varies substantially between basins, ranging from 19 percent in the Lower Rogue basin, to as high as 85 percent in the Siltcoos basin.

Almost 24 percent of salmon core areas are in areas with biodiversity management ratings of 8-10.

Ownership of the landscapes in which core area habitats are found is highly fragmented. More than half (53 percent) the core areas are on private forested land, with the percentage roughly split between industrial and non-industrial ownerships. About 25 percent are on national forest land, and approximately 10 percent each on BLM and state lands. The rest are on private, non-forested lands and other miscellaneous landowner categories.

Aquatic Diversity Areas. The watershed classification subcommittee of the Oregon chapter of the American Fisheries Society has recommended protection for more than 3.3 million hectares in watersheds the group designated as "aquatic diversity areas" (Bottom et al. 1993). The areas selected by the subcommittee were intended to represent Oregon's best remaining aquatic habitats, as well at-risk fish species. An additional 500,000 hectares were recommended for protection because of their importance as connecting corridors.

These aquatic diversity areas are generally limited to small streams, excluding for the most part lakes, wetlands, and large rivers. Because of historic patterns of land use and habitat modification, the network of aquatic diversity areas does not truly represent the full diversity of Oregon's native aquatic ecosystems.

Despite these limitations, the American Fisheries Society's recommendations represent one of the few attempts to analyze and synthesize information about a broad range of aquatic species for biodiversity conservation purposes. The Oregon Biodiversity Project used the American Fisheries Society's data extensively in its ecoregional assessments, giving substantial weight to aquatic diversity areas that meet one or more of five ecological criteria used in the designations. These include areas designated for their ecological functions (downstream water quality), or for their value as reference watersheds (areas with the highest ecological integrity), genetic refuges, centers of species richness, or connecting corridors.

Although every major drainage basin in the state contains aquatic diversity areas, they are unevenly distributed. Two ecoregions — the Columbia Basin and the Lava Plains — are almost completely devoid of habitats deemed eligible for the designation. And many of the lowlands that historically supported the state's richest and most productive aquatic habitats have been modified and degraded. As a result, a high proportion of the aquatic diversity areas are found in high-elevation and mountainous areas that provide the last remaining refuge for many native cold-water fishes.

Only about 15 percent of the areas identified by the American Fisheries Society as aquatic diversity areas are on lands rated 8-10 on the biodiversity management scale. Many of the aquatic diversity areas face threats from introduced exotic fish species, grazing, timber harvest, and other human activities. The U.S. Forest Service manages less than 25 percent of the land in eastern Oregon, but its lands contain almost 50 percent of the aquatic diversity areas in those regions. According to the Interior Columbia Basin Ecosystem Management Project (1996), many of the "unprotected" aquatic diversity areas contain "significant patches of late succession/old growth forests or roadless regions that are vulnerable to future logging and road building."

Status of salmon. Maps developed by The Wilderness Society (1993) display the historic distribution and current status (extinct, endangered, threatened, special concern, or not known to be declining) of anadromous fish species. The maps reflect a broad pattern of decline and extinction of Pacific salmon populations along the entire coast of California, Oregon, and Washington.

All anadromous salmonid species in Oregon have been extirpated from at least portions of their original range, and some have been reduced to a small fraction of their historic distribution. At least some populations of all species are considered at high risk of extinction (Nehlsen et al. 1991). Remaining "healthy stocks" (defined as being at least one-third as abundant as expected in the absence of human impacts) in Oregon include 20 populations of fall chinook and eight of winter steelhead, all found in coastal river systems. Also included are six stocks of summer steelhead, all but one of them in the John Day River system (Huntington et al. 1996).

AT-RISK SPECIES

Any strategy for conserving biodiversity requires some kind of assessment of the most vulnerable elements of biological diversity — those plant and animal species considered rare, threatened, or endangered. While many state and federal agencies maintain information on these vulnerable elements of biodiversity, the broadest compendium in Oregon is maintained by the Oregon Natural Heritage Program. (For a more complete discussion of the Heritage Program and its database, refer to Chapter 1, Biodiversity Basics.)

Because the Heritage Program's database provides site-specific information on rare, threatened, and endangered species, the Oregon Biodiversity Project relied heavily on it for many of the project's analyses. The Oregon Natural Heritage Program database contains records on more than 400 plant and animal species considered by the project to be "at-risk" because of their classification as "vulnerable," "imperiled," or "critically imperiled" at the state or global level. (See pages 18-20 for a more detailed description.)

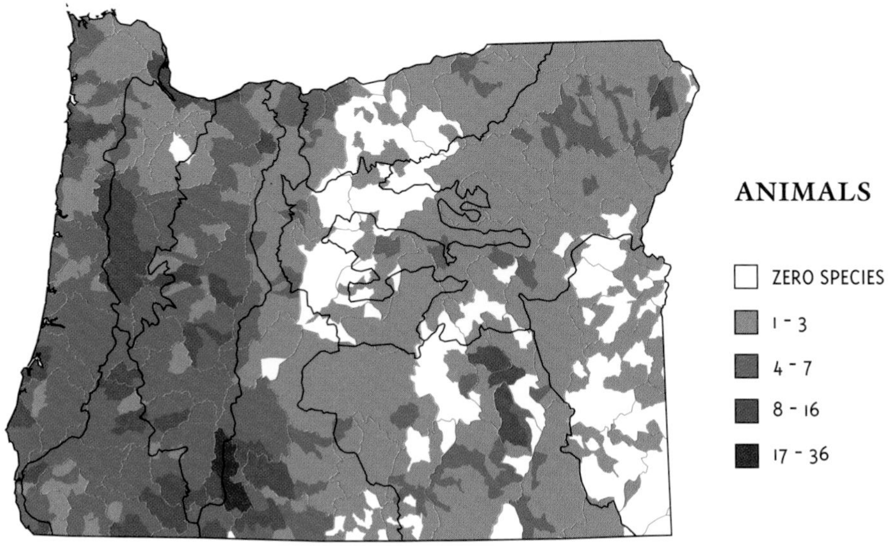

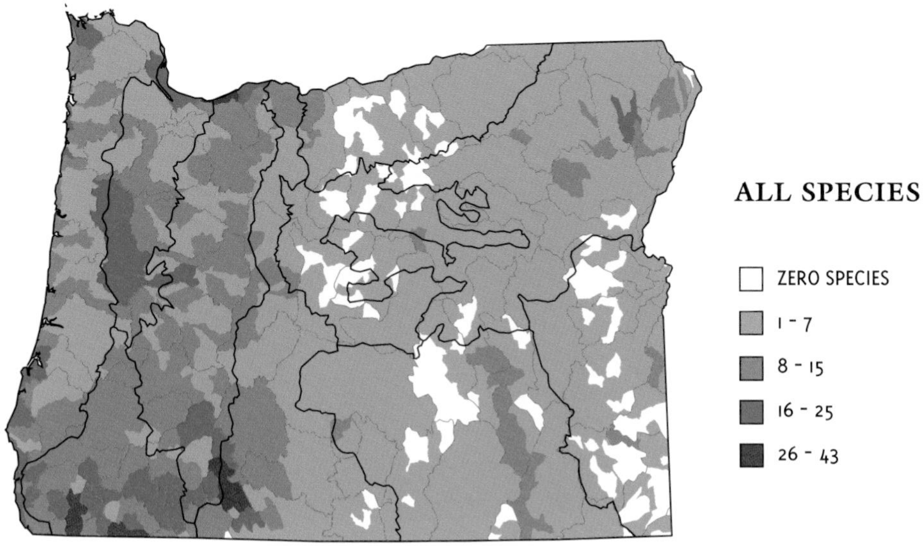

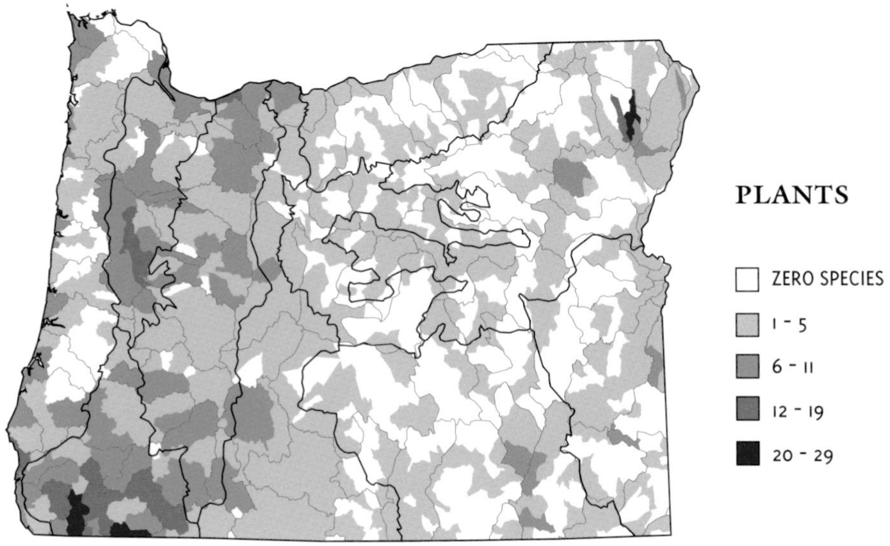

Distribution of at-risk species varies significantly between plants and animals. Overall, the largest clusters of at-risk species are found in the Klamath Basin, the Siskiyou and Wallowa mountains, along the west side of the Willamette Valley, in the Columbia River Gorge and the bottomlands downstream from Portland, and at a few locations on the coast. Not all of the state has been well inventoried, so the absence of at-risk species in some areas may be due to a lack of information.

Data from the Oregon Natural Heritage Program.

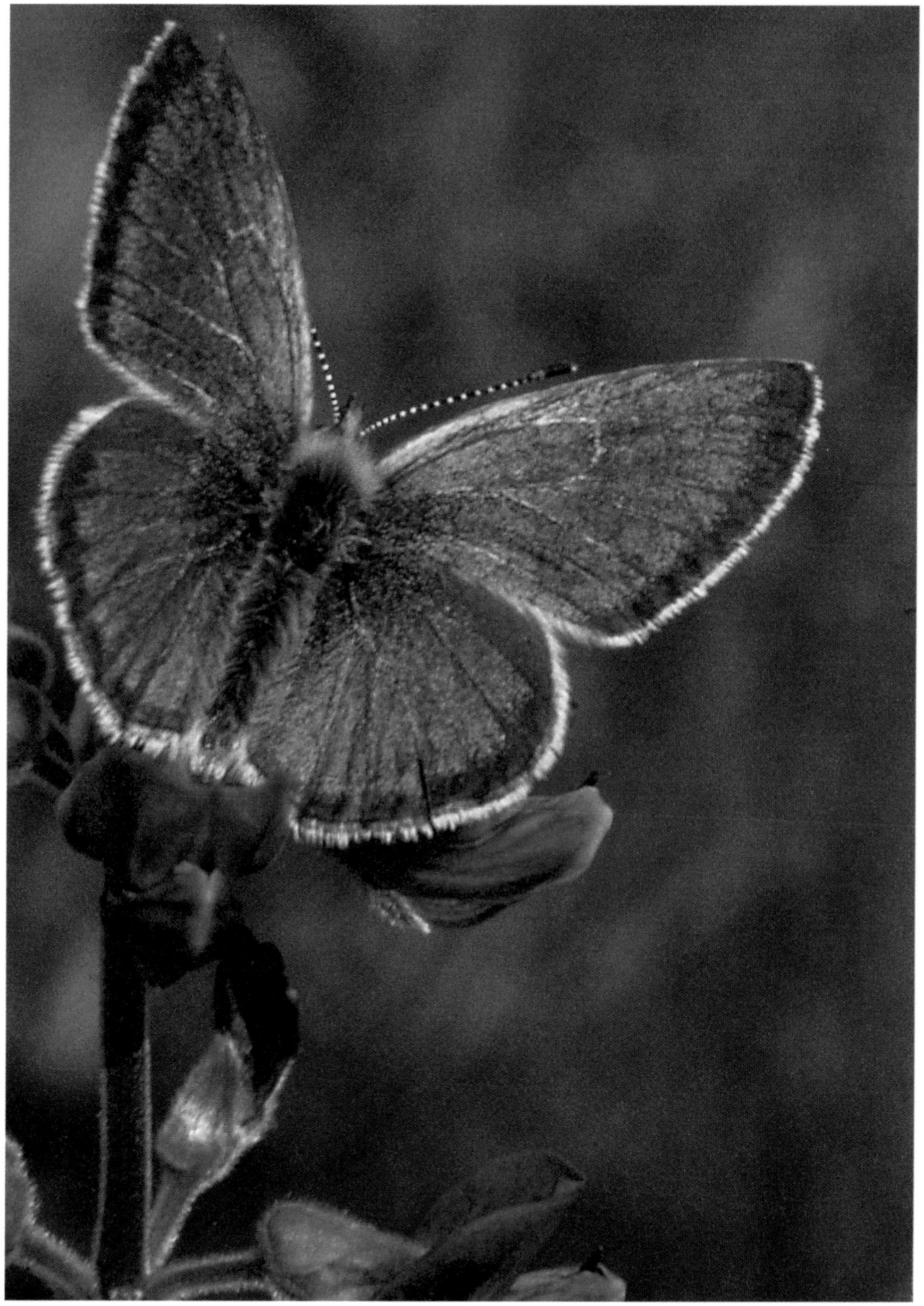

Of the 400-plus species in these categories, almost 5 percent (19 species) have already been extirpated from Oregon or their entire range; 25 percent could be considered "protected" either due to lack of threats or implementation of significant conservation efforts; and 22 percent need further survey or taxonomic review to determine their status. That leaves about 200 species, or nearly half the total, which are highly vulnerable to future extinction. It is these highly vulnerable species that are the subject of most of the analysis and discussion of "at-risk species" throughout this document. Each of these groupings — extirpated, protected, further review, and highly vulnerable — is examined briefly below.

Extirpated species

Plant and animal species have been extirpated in every ecoregion in the state. Eleven extirpated species are animals. They have been lost due to a variety of factors including hunting and predator control (gray wolf, grizzly bear, California condor), habitat loss (Columbia River tiger beetle, yellow-billed cuckoo, Clatsop philocasan caddisfly, valley silverspot butterfly, Willamette calliope fritillary butterfly, Columbian sharptail grouse), introduction of non-native species (Alvord cutthroat), and poisoning (Miller Lake lamprey). In most cases, more than one factor has been responsible for their demise.

Habitat loss — conversion of native habitats for agriculture, residential, and industrial uses —

Fender's blue butterfly
Photographer, Alan D. St. John

has been the primary cause of plant species extirpations. Howellia *(Howellia aquatilis)*, for example, formerly occurred in oxbow lakes, ponds, and wetland habitats throughout much of the Willamette Valley. It was lost due to conversion of habitat for agriculture and a variety of urban land uses. Remaining populations in Washington are threatened by an aggressive non-native plant species, reed canary grass *(Phalaris arundinaceae)*. The introduction of non-native species — both plant and animal — is a serious problem for at-risk native species.

As with animals, more than one factor is frequently responsible for the demise of plants. Malheur wire lettuce *(Stephanomeria malheurensis)*, for example, is teetering on the brink of extinction despite efforts to protect it, due to introduction of non-native species and habitat alteration from past livestock grazing.

"Protected" species

Of the approximately 100 species that may be considered "protected" due to lack of threats, the majority are plant species that occur on cliffs or at high elevations in Oregon's mountain ranges. Examples include species like Saddle Mountain saxifrage *(Saxifraga hitchcockiana)* found on peaks in the Coast Range; Hazel's prickly-phlox *(Leptodactylon pungens)* from Hells Canyon; and Steen's Mountain paintbrush *(Castilleja pilosa* var. *steensensis)* found on its namesake in southeastern Oregon. While human activities have occasionally threatened these cliff or mountain-top species (e.g., blasting for development or quarries, development of communications facilities, etc.), most can be considered protected due to the lack of threats to their habitat.

By contrast, very few "protected" species are animals. Animals' ability to move is an advantage in the face of localized habitat alterations. However, their generally lower reproduction rates, and their inability to remain dormant until conditions are more favorable (at least among vertebrates), increase animals' vulnerability to threats. In addition, many animal species need both large habitat areas and localized or specialized habitats during some portion of their life cycle, making them more vulnerable to habitat loss.

A handful of "protected" at-risk species owe their status to deliberate conservation efforts to halt and reverse population declines. Species such as the bald eagle *(Haliaeetus leucocephalus)*, Columbian white-tailed deer *(Odocoileus virginianus leucurus)*, and peregrine falcon *(Falco peregrinus)* all provide examples of successful conservation strategies.

Species in need of further review

Despite a long history of inventory and documentation of species' distributions and abundance, we still know little or nothing about the vast majority of Oregon's species.

Comprehensive surveys for invertebrate and non-vascular plant species have only recently begun, and less than half the state's invertebrates have even been named and described.

The higher-order plants and animals that need more survey and information before adequate conservation strategies can be designed are generally those that are very small, have very brief emergent phases, are secretive in habit, or are difficult to identify. The spotted bat *(Euderma maculatum)*, for example, is only known from mummified specimens found in a few caves — however, experts think that it still occurs in Oregon. Other species, such as American pillwort *(Pilularia americana)*, are so small that the specimens are generally acquired from accidental inclusions in collections of other plant species. And finally, some regions of the state have been studied more intensively. One of the least studied areas is the Owyhee Uplands Ecoregion.

Highly vulnerable species

The same factors that pushed 19 other species to extinction currently threaten this group of species. While better information about the status and distribution of species and more careful consideration of how current or proposed actions might affect them can help reduce the risks, these species remain highly vulnerable.

The diversity of this group of at-risk species is indicative of the variety of causes of their decline and the complexity of solutions needed to protect them. Some, such as the Hutton tui chub *(Gila bicolor* ssp.*)*, have always had limited and isolated habitats, and can only be addressed on a site-specific basis. Others, like the Snake River fall chinook salmon *(Oncorhynchus tshawytscha)*, were once so widespread that they remain important cultural symbols of an entire region (in this case, the Blue Mountains Ecoregion). Some of the species within this group are beginning the long road to recovery. Some can be protected with relatively simple and inexpensive fixes. Others, such as salmon, may require society to confront difficult conflicts between established human uses and ecological values.

The ecoregion assessments contained in Chapter 4 examine in more detail the distribution of these at-risk species, their relationship to the larger landscape, and potential opportunities to address their needs in conjunction with broader conservation strategies.

HUMAN POPULATION AND DEVELOPMENT

Historically, where humans have gathered, landscapes have been altered — sometimes irrevocably. Human settlement patterns tend to occur in areas conducive to natural resource exploitation (e.g., fertile valleys for farming or lowland forest for timber harvest), which typically support some of the most biologically diverse habitats. Increases in human population often come at

POPULATION DENSITY BY WATERSHED

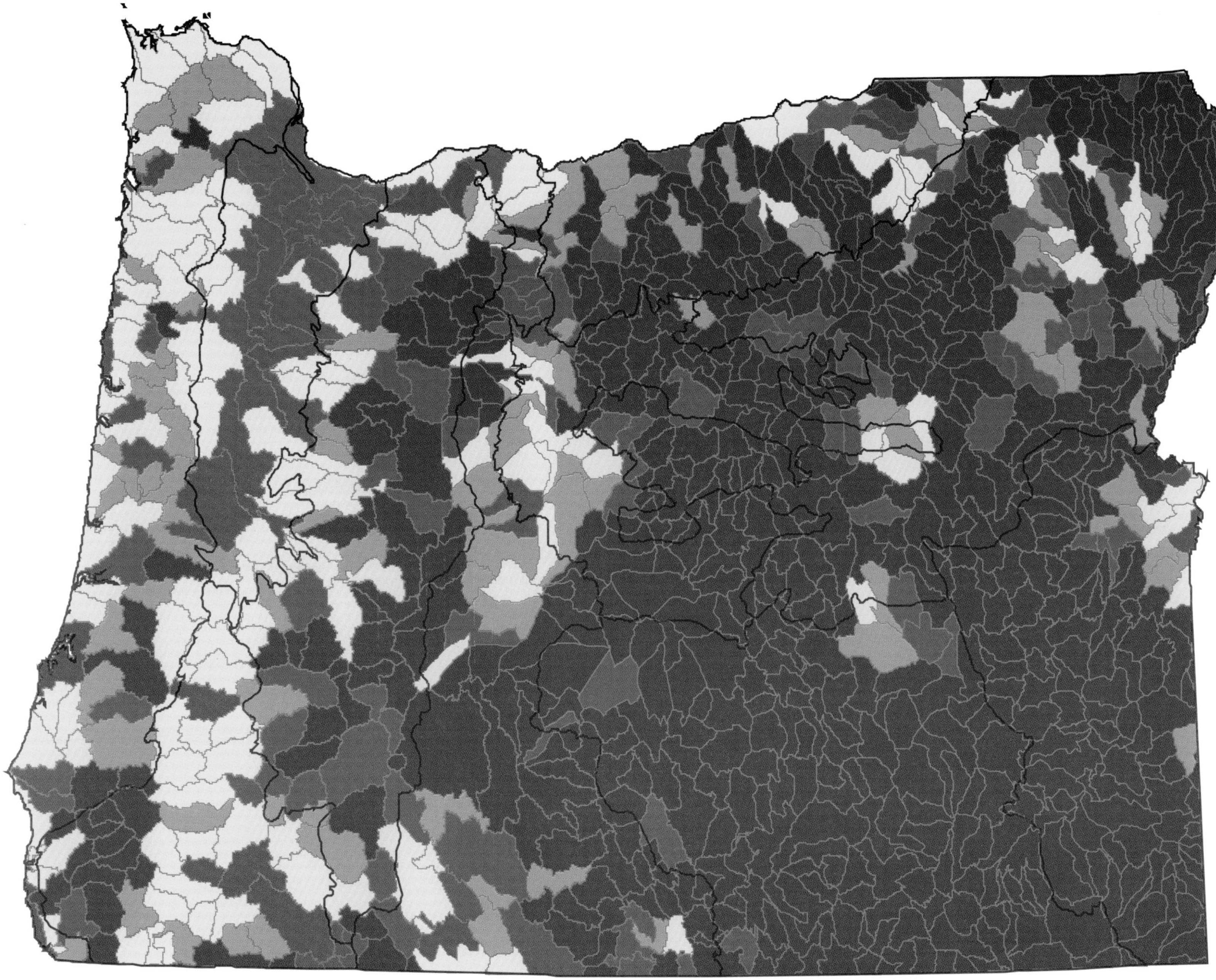

Population data from
U.S. Census Bureau 1995

ROAD DENSITY BY WATERSHED

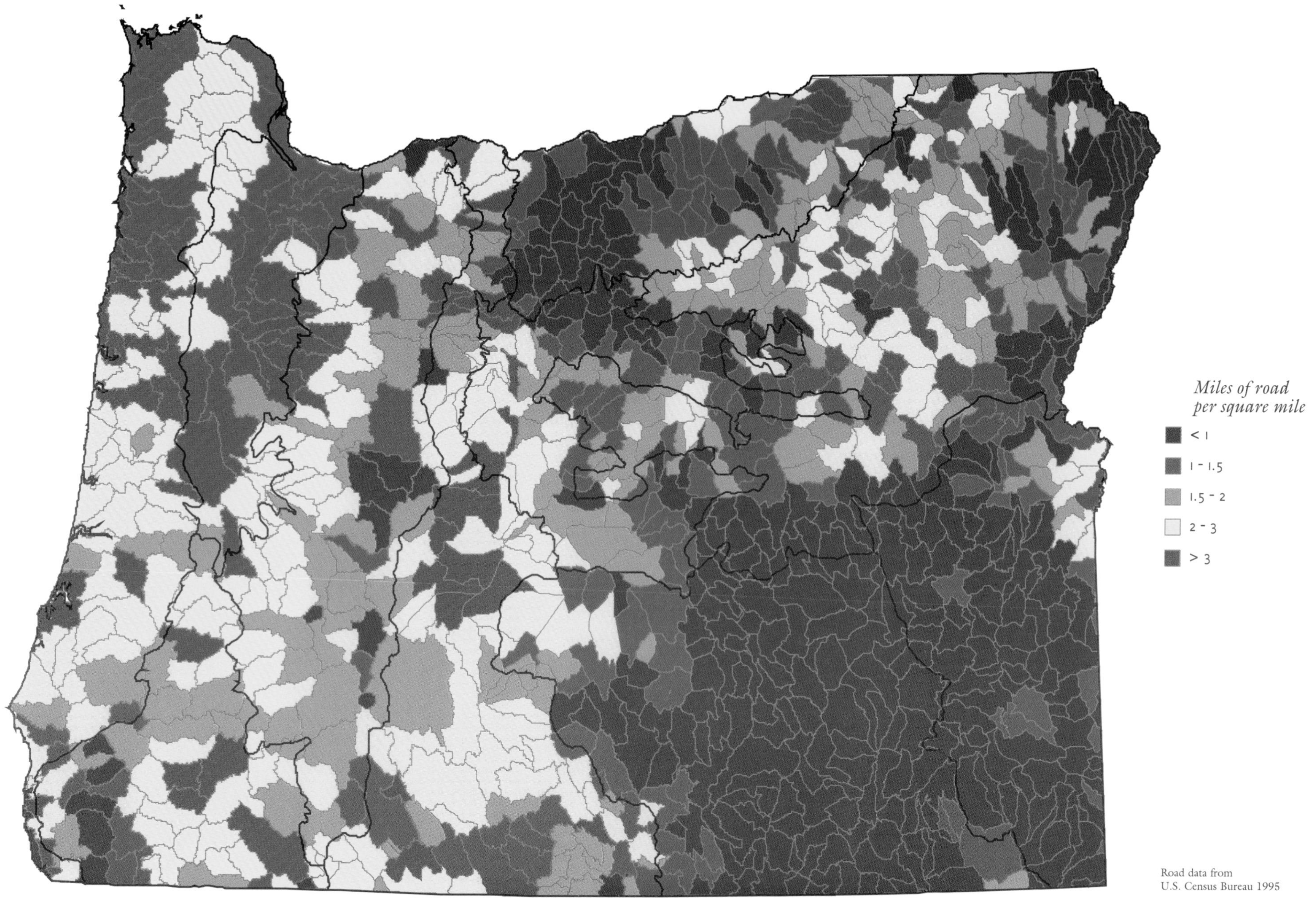

the expense of biodiversity by way of habitat loss, fragmentation, and degradation. A larger population requires more food, converts more land for housing and roads, and generates more waste, among other impacts.

As is usually the case, early settlement patterns in Oregon followed the network of river and transportation corridors, with the Willamette and Columbia rivers shaping the early development of roads and cities. Today, Oregon's population is concentrated along the Interstate 5 transportation corridor, which includes six metropolitan areas (Portland, Salem, Albany, Eugene, Roseburg, and Medford).

Population density in Oregon ranges from fewer than three people to more than 1,400 people per square mile. Seven of the 17 counties east of the Cascades average fewer than three people per square mile. In contrast, the highest concentration of people occurs in the Portland metropolitan area, in Multnomah (1,424 people per square mile) and Washington (427 people per square mile) counties.

Although population density is one reflection of potential impacts on biodiversity, the effects of human development often extend far beyond the immediate locales where people live. Roads are another indicator of the extent and intensity of human activities on the landscape, and the degree to which native habitats may be vulnerable to human-related fragmentation and disturbance. Some of the highest road densities in Oregon are found in watersheds where extensive road systems have been developed for timber harvest.

LAND OWNERSHIP AND ADMINISTRATION

Oregon's biodiversity bears the imprint of patterns of land ownership and administration developed over two hundred years. These patterns have had profound impacts on management of the state's natural resources in the past and will be key factors in shaping conservation strategies for the future.

More than half the state is administered by the federal government, with most of these lands managed under the jurisdiction of the U.S. Forest Service and the Bureau of Land Management. That gives these two agencies a preeminent role in resource management (and by extension, biodiversity conservation) for much of the state.

The same broad forces (endangered species, forest health, declining fish populations) that are driving the current shift toward "ecosystem management" on federal lands are also spurring state and private land managers to adopt new approaches in many areas. Nonetheless, differences in patterns of land ownership will continue to shape the impacts of these broad changes on biodiversity conservation efforts at the ecoregional level.

Large state forests and timber industry ownerships in the Coast Range, Klamath Mountains, and West Cascades ecoregions offer opportunities for development of large-scale habitat conservation plans that could complement the federal agencies' ecosystem management strategies.

In the Willamette Valley and the Columbia Basin ecoregions, most lands are in private ownership, and the majority have already been converted to non-native habitats. In the Willamette Valley, where there are few large ownerships of any kind, conservation efforts are more likely to focus on habitat restoration through cooperative efforts involving both public and private land managers. In the Columbia Basin, much of the focus will likely be on a few public ownerships (the U.S. Navy's Boardman Bombing Range, the state's Boeing-lease property) that harbor some of the last remnants of the region's native habitats.

In ecoregions east of the Cascades, the federal government is by far the largest land manager. But private lands play a disproportionately large role in eastside biodiversity issues because their owners typically control most of the water rights and critical historic wetland and riparian habitats of these largely arid regions.

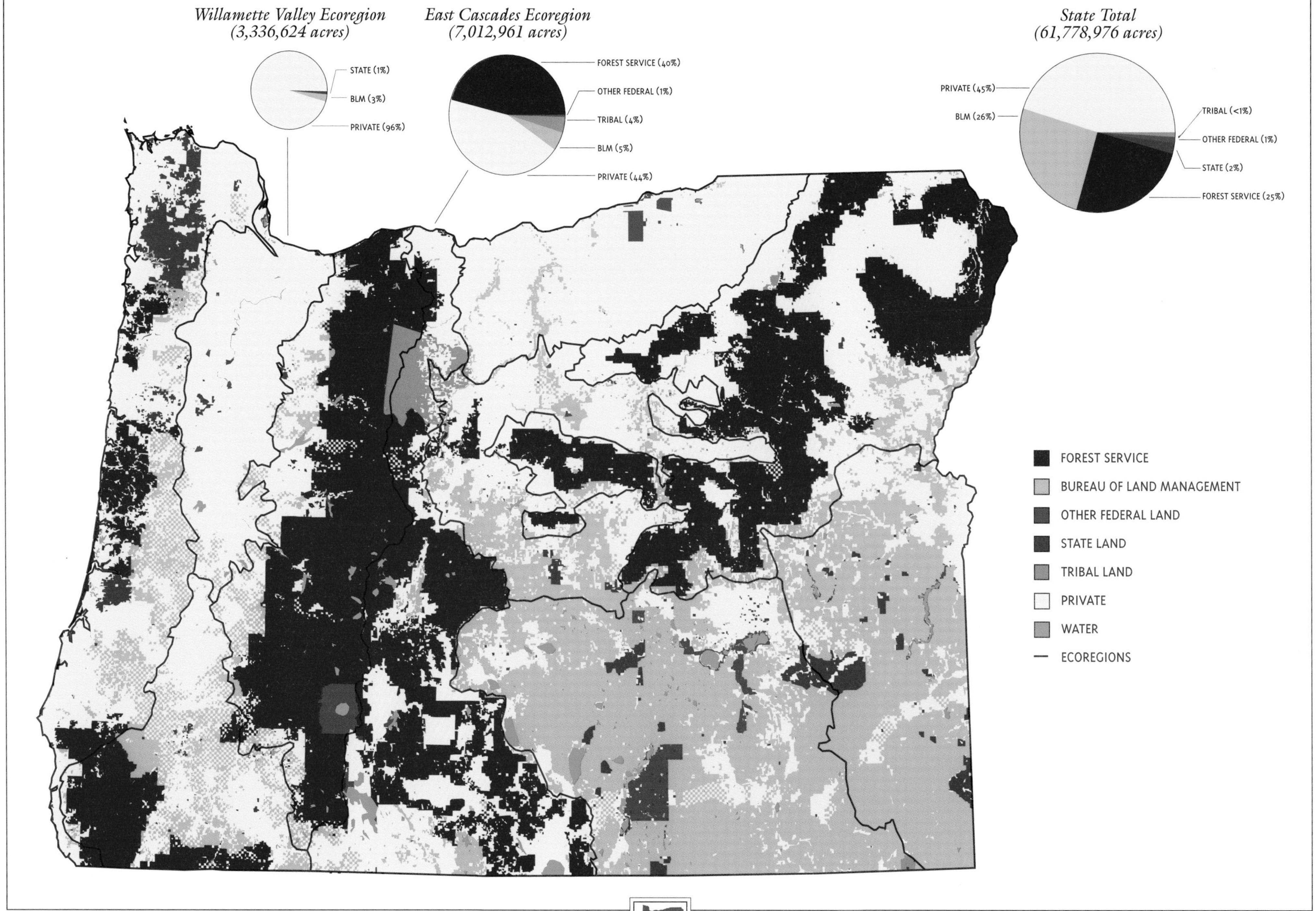
Willamette Valley Ecoregion
(3,336,624 acres)
STATE (1%)
BLM (3%)
PRIVATE (96%)
East Cascades Ecoregion
(7,012,961 acres)
FOREST SERVICE (40%)
OTHER FEDERAL (1%)
TRIBAL (4%)
BLM (5%)
PRIVATE (44%)
State Total
(61,778,976 acres)
PRIVATE (45%)
BLM (26%)
TRIBAL (<1%)
OTHER FEDERAL (1%)
STATE (2%)
FOREST SERVICE (25%)
FOREST SERVICE
BUREAU OF LAND MANAGEMENT
OTHER FEDERAL LAND
STATE LAND
TRIBAL LAND
PRIVATE
WATER
ECOREGIONS

Assessing Oregon's Ten Ecoregions

The discussions in this chapter summarize the Oregon Biodiversity Project's assessments of the state's ten ecoregions. As noted earlier, ecoregions were used as units for the analysis because their boundaries are based on physical features and conditions that often define very different ecosystems. All of the ecoregion assessments are based in part on the statewide data sets reviewed in the previous chapter. They also incorporate information from a variety of other sources that help to portray influences on biodiversity and conservation challenges at the ecoregion level. Although each ecoregion discussion follows a similar format, the types of information presented, level of detail, and amount of emphasis on different issues vary with the "story" that emerges from the analysis.

Each ecoregion discussion begins with a brief **overview.** A section on **vegetation analysis** identifies vegetation types and habitats that warrant special consideration in broad-scale or "coarse-filter" conservation efforts. All ecoregion discussions include a brief look at some of the **at-risk species** in the ecoregion that need to be addressed primarily at the site level through "fine-filter" conservation strategies. Some ecoregion discussions include a separate look at **aquatic species** where available data provided an additional dimension to the assessment of broad-scale biodiversity conservation needs. The **current conservation network** and **patterns of land ownership** are among the human dimensions of the landscape included to help round out the picture. A **summary of conservation issues** is provided for each ecoregion, followed by a description of a number of landscape-scale **conservation opportunity areas** that, based on the broad-scale analysis, appear to offer opportunities to address multiple conservation objectives.

CONSERVATION OPPORTUNITY AREAS

The Oregon Biodiversity Project's identification of conservation opportunity areas is based on the premise that targeted investments in conservation and ecosystem management can help build an expanded framework for future efforts to conserve Oregon's biological diversity. *The project's selection of these areas does not mean that they are the most important places for biodiversity, nor should it be inferred that they are the only areas deserving of conservation attention.* Their significance lies instead in the opportunities they offer to address conservation priorities that emerged from the project's statewide and ecoregional analyses.

Some of the landscapes identified as conservation opportunity areas contain clusters of at-risk species or vegetation types that are not well represented in the current conservation network. Others include watersheds deemed important for aquatic diversity, or roadless areas relatively unaffected by human development. Some could serve as linkages between existing conservation lands. Others could help fill in some of the gaps in the current conservation network. Conservation opportunity areas are not limited to potential reserves (although in some cases that might be an appropriate management strategy), and they are not necessarily areas with exceptional biological diversity at the local level. Most contain a mix of public and private ownerships. Most of these lands are not currently managed primarily for biodiversity values, although many are adjacent to, or include portions of, existing conservation lands.

The boundaries of these conservation opportunity areas are generalized and intended only as a first-cut attempt at broad-scale conservation planning. They can be used to direct more site-specific assessment of these landscapes to develop specific management strategies. Conserving Oregon's biodiversity will ultimately require thoughtful management of all of Oregon's natural resources. However, the conservation opportunity areas highlighted for each ecoregion in the following pages provide a promising starting point for a more strategic statewide approach to conservation.

METHODOLOGY

The Oregon Biodiversity Project experimented with several different approaches to selecting conservation opportunity areas. Analysts tested alternative methodologies that relied solely on computer-generated selections in two ecoregions (Klamath Mountains, Blue Mountains). Both approaches produced useful results but also had some shortcomings, due primarily to weaknesses in the data and the volume and complexity of the computerized analysis required to

Commonly used terms

Many of the concepts and sources of data used in the ecoregional assessments are discussed in the two preceding chapters, "Biodiversity Basics" and "Statewide Overview." A few of the more commonly used terms are reviewed briefly on the facing page.

Aquatic diversity areas. Areas identified by the Oregon Chapter of the American Fisheries Society (Bottom et al. 1993) as having particular significance for conservation of aquatic biodiversity. As used in this document, this includes areas designated based on five criteria: reference watersheds, genetic refuges, centers of species richness, ecological function, and connecting corridors. (See "*Statewide Overview,*" pages 54-55.)

At-risk species. In this document, the term "at-risk species" refers to individual species designated as critically imperiled, imperiled, or vulnerable at the global or state level under the global ranking system used by the Oregon Natural Heritage Program. These include species with Heritage rankings of G1, G2 or G3 (global); T1, T2, T3 (trinomial — a subspecies, variety, or recognized race), and S1 or S2 (state). (See "*Biodiversity Basics,*" pages 17-20.)

identify candidate areas. Based on those experiences, the project developed a hybrid approach that used GIS analysis as an initial screen to identify areas that were then evaluated for suitability based on best professional judgment of the analysts.

The first step in the selection process for conservation opportunity areas was an analysis that involved overlaying a number of GIS data layers. These overlays were used to identify gaps in the existing conservation network, assess changes in historic vegetation patterns, and display sites or areas already identified as having significant biodiversity values. Data layers used in this step included:

- existing vegetation
- historical vegetation
- aquatic diversity areas
- at-risk plant and animal species
- salmon core areas
- wilderness study areas
- existing conservation network

Analysts then evaluated landscapes for their potential to address ecoregional and statewide conservation priorities, looking for areas with:

- large blocks of native habitat
- vegetation types or habitats that have experienced major declines from historic levels
- vegetation types that are not well represented in the current conservation network
- at-risk species
- potential to complement or connect elements of the existing network of conservation lands.

The final step involved a subjective assessment of opportunities to enhance management for biodiversity within areas that appeared to have potential to address conservation priorities. Factors considered in selection decisions included land ownership, current management, existing and potential programs to implement conservation actions, pending public policy decisions, and potential future threats.

In practice, the relative importance of different factors and the quality of the data varied significantly from ecoregion to ecoregion. Unique features of the selection process are discussed in the conservation opportunity areas section of each ecoregion chapter.

Biodiversity management ratings. The project rated most public lands on a scale of 1-10, based on their contributions to long-term conservation of biodiversity under current management. (See "*Statewide Overview,*" pages 38-39.)

Current conservation network. In this section, this generally refers to lands with biodiversity management ratings of 8-10. (See "*Statewide Overview,*" pages 38-39.)

CONSERVATION OPPORTUNITY AREAS

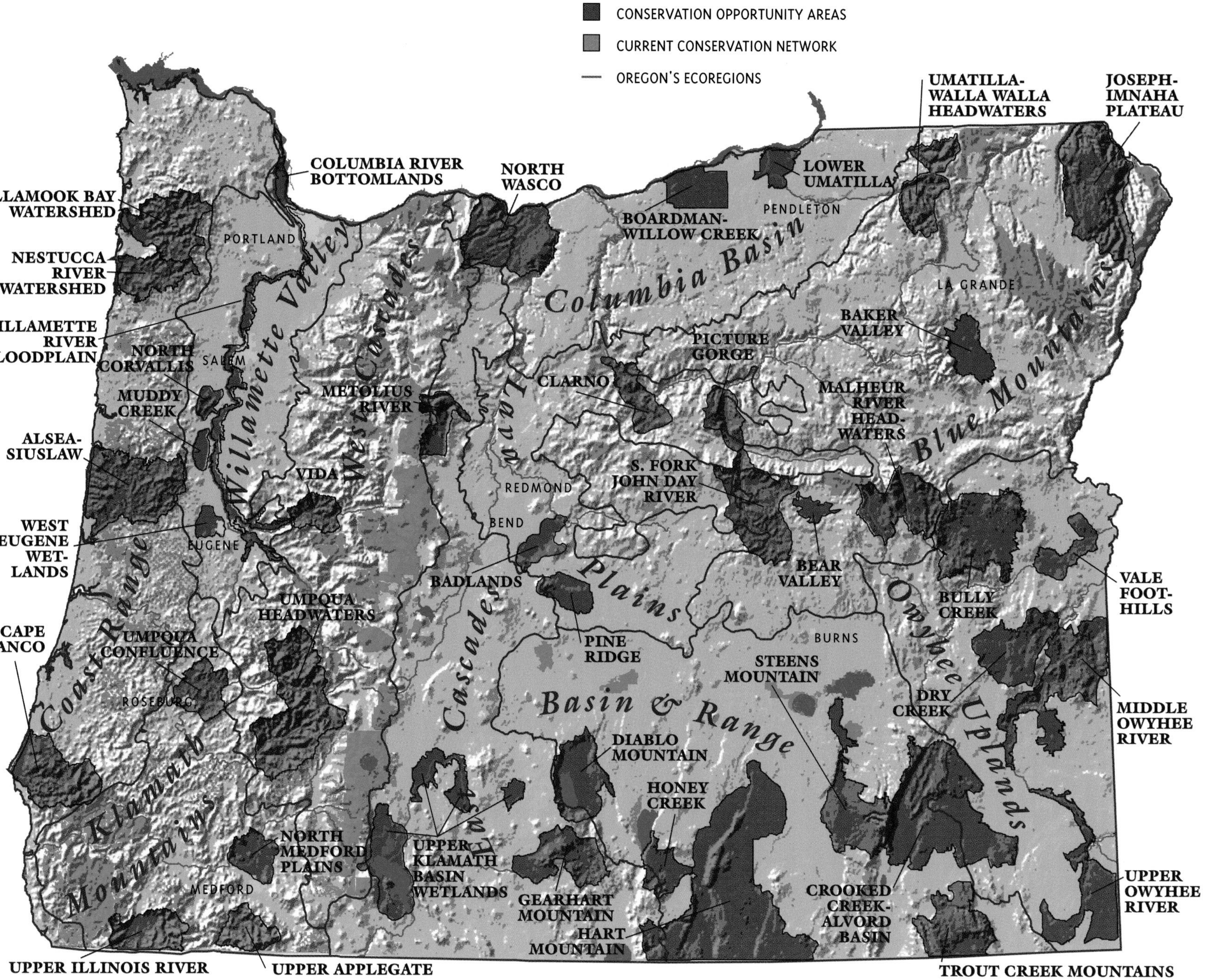

The Oregon Biodiversity Project identified a handful of areas in each of the state's 10 ecoregions where targeted conservation efforts could help address biodiversity needs at the state and ecoregional levels. Not just a compilation of ecologically significant sites, these areas were also chosen because of their prospects for successful conservation action, based on current ownership, management policies and other factors.

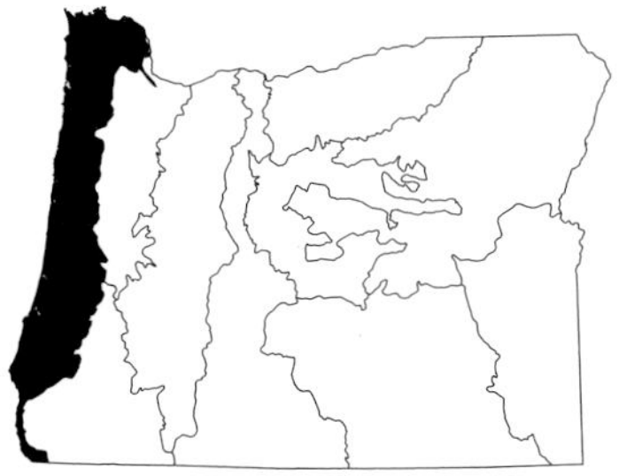

Coast Range Ecoregion

The Coast Range Ecoregion extends the length of Oregon's coast, from the Columbia River south to the California border. The ecoregion extends inland to the edge of the Willamette Valley, and further south, to the Klamath Mountains.

Elevations in the Coast Range rarely exceed 2,500 feet, but the terrain is rough and cut by numerous rivers and streams. The area's maritime climate is generally moderate, with mild, dry summers and cool, wet winters. Annual precipitation along the coast averages 60 to 80 inches and exceeds 100 inches in some inland areas. Vegetation is dominated by forests of Sitka spruce, western hemlock, Douglas-fir, and in disturbed areas, alder. Lodgepole pine (commonly referred to as shore-pine in this area) is common along the coast.

The character of the coast varies dramatically from north to south. The northern half is marked by a number of headlands and steep cliffs separated by stretches of relatively flat coastal plain and estuaries. Large sand dune systems dominate the landscape immediately south of the Columbia River's mouth, north of Sand Lake in Tillamook County, and from Heceta Head to Coos Bay. In many areas, freshwater lakes are scattered among the dunes behind the beaches. A broad marine terrace marked by shallow lakes and meandering streams extends from the Coquille River Valley south to Port Orford. Along many stretches in southern Curry County, mountains rise precipitously from the ocean's edge.

CURRENT CONSERVATION NETWORK & LAND OWNERSHIP

More than a quarter of the ecoregion is in biodiversity management categories 8-10.

The system of late-successional reserves established under the federal government's Northwest Forest Plan accounts for most of this area. Together with several small national forest wilderness areas, these reserves provide substantial protection for forest habitats in the southern and central portions of the Coast Range. Forests on the northern end of the ecoregion are largely unrepresented in the current conservation network.

National wildlife refuges and South Slough National Estuarine Research Reserve in Coos Bay encompass more than 40,000 acres around coastal estuaries. Coastal headland habitats receive some protection under the management of the Oregon Parks and Recreation Department, The Nature Conservancy and the U.S. Forest Service. The Forest Service's Oregon Dunes National Recreation Area and BLM's New River holdings both include areas managed specifically to conserve biodiversity values.

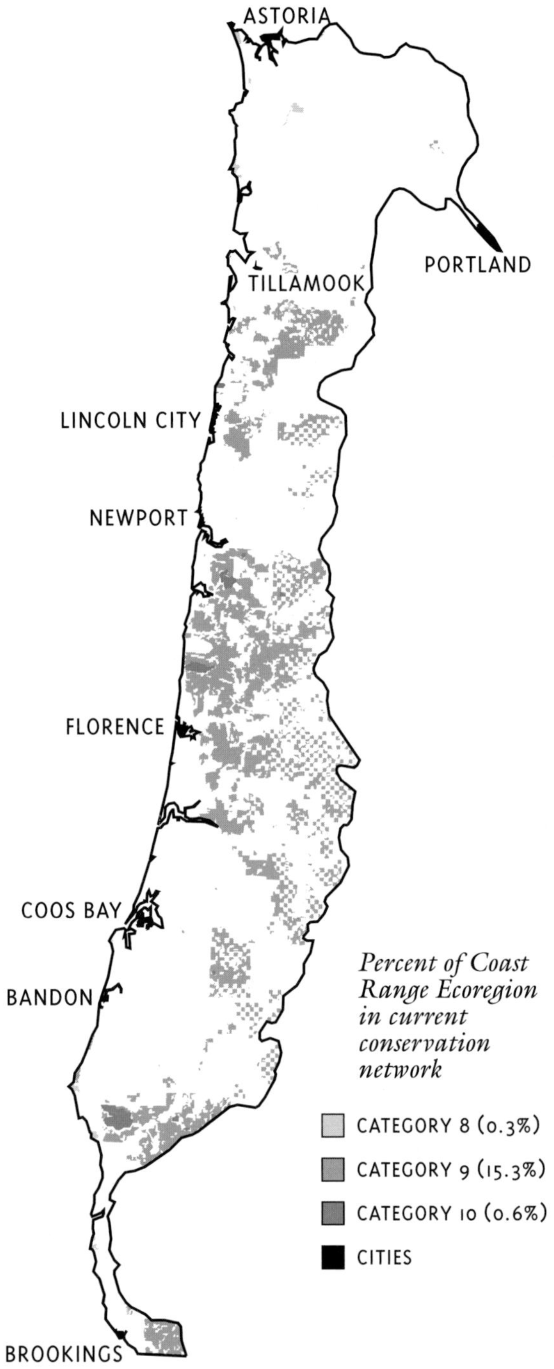

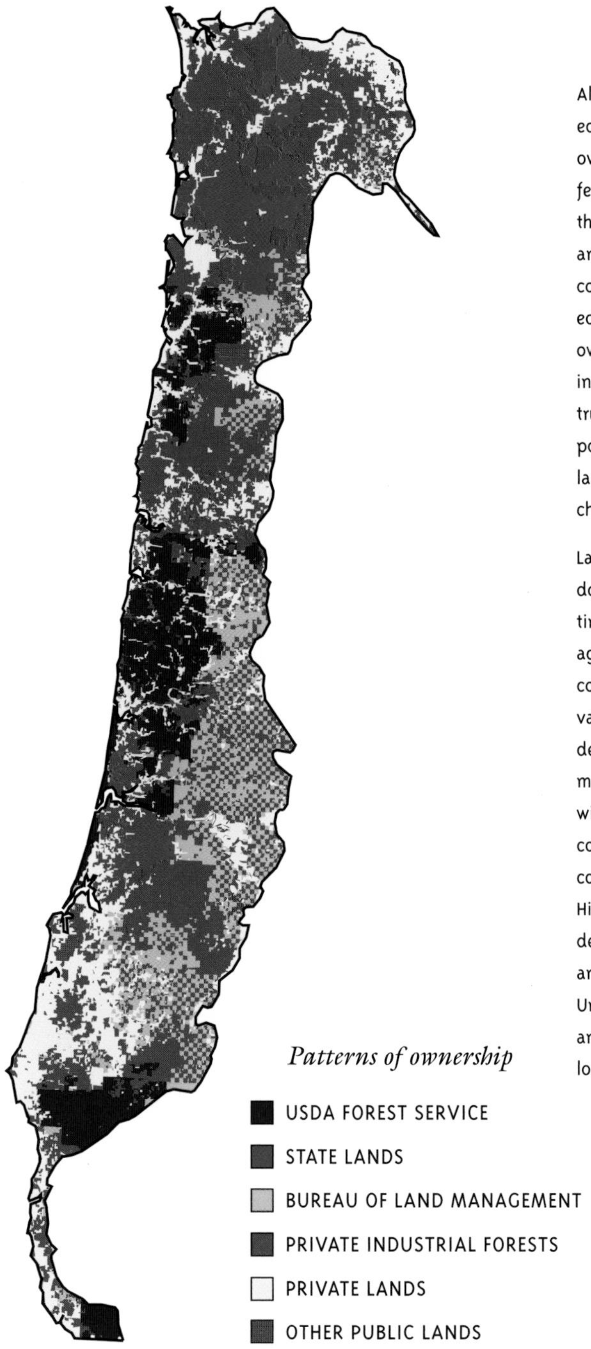

Almost 40 percent of the ecoregion is in public ownership, primarily state and federal forests. Although just three federal and state agencies and a handful of timber companies manage most of the ecoregion's forestlands, ownership is highly fragmented in many areas. This is especially true in the central and southern portion of the ecoregion where land ownership resembles a checkerboard.

Land use in the ecoregion is dominated by commercial timber production, with agriculture largely confined to coastal lowlands and river valleys. Residential development is widespread in many areas of the coastal strip, with commercial development concentrated in coastal communities along U.S. Highway 101. Heavy industrial development is limited to a few areas around Coos Bay, on the Umpqua estuary at Reedsport and Gardiner, and along the lower Yaquina River.

Data from Sollins 1994

Human population is concentrated in numerous small towns, most within a few miles of the coast. Forest products, tourism, and fisheries are the mainstays of the local economy.

VEGETATION ANALYSIS

Although more than a century of timber harvests and a number of large fires have eliminated most of the region's old growth forests, the distribution of major forest vegetation types in the Coast Range has not changed significantly from historic patterns.

Sitka spruce forests still dominate the coastal rain forests in a narrow zone that is generally only a few miles wide, except where it extends up river valleys. The wet and mild climate of this narrow zone limits the frequency and intensity of naturally occurring fires in these areas.

The western hemlock zone inland from the Sitka spruce belt is the most extensive vegetation zone in western Oregon. According to Agee (1993), the dominance of Douglas-fir in the western hemlock zone at the time of European settlement

Sitka spruce forest,
Oswald West State Park
Photographer, Larry N. Olson

was largely due to a long history of disturbance, primarily by fire. Douglas-fir plantations and second-growth now dominate.

Lands historically mapped as Douglas-fir forests are still predominantly classified as western hemlock-Douglas-fir. However, the red alder-big leaf maple-Douglas-fir type (often found in areas of past timber harvest and other disturbances) now covers more than 20 percent of the ecoregion.

Although the distribution of vegetation types has changed very little over the past century, the loss of **old growth forests** has had profound impacts on the ecoregion's biological diversity. Old growth forests currently account for only about six percent of the total landscape in the Coast Range (USDA/USDI 1994). Little old growth habitat remains on private lands. Federal lands contain most of the remaining late-successional forests, but they are highly fragmented in terms of habitat values and management. The current management direction for federal forest lands in the ecoregion places much of the remaining old growth habitat off-limits to logging and is eventually intended to restore a significant portion of federal lands — mostly along the central coast — to late-successional forests. However, three-quarters of the ecoregion is in state and private ownership and most private forest lands are currently managed on relatively short rotations, which will preclude future development of late successional habitats over vast portions of the ecoregion.

Western hemlock-Douglas-fir forest, which covers more than one third of the ecoregion, is relatively well represented (26 percent) on lands currently in biodiversity management categories 8-10. Less well represented is Sitka spruce forest, with eight percent in categories 8-10. About nine percent of the red alder-bigleaf maple-Douglas-fir type is in categories 8-10, much of it in second-growth on lands previously harvested.

Although conservation needs for old growth and late-successional forests have received considerable attention, a number of other less widely distributed habitat types in the Coast Range Ecoregion deserve consideration as conservation priorities.

Oak woodland communities in the Coast Range Ecoregion are not well represented in the current conservation network. Oak woodlands may be subject to less development pressure here than in some other areas of the state, but are threatened where the Coast Range abuts population centers in the Willamette Valley.

Sand dune ecosystems have been altered dramatically due to stabilization of foredunes through the introduction and spread of European beachgrass *(Ammophila arenaria)*. In some areas, deflation plain wetlands inland from the foredunes are rapidly being colonized by shorepine communities, with shorepines eventually being overtaken by other conifers. Residential development and off-road vehicle use pose threats to stabilized sand dune systems.

Some of the most important conservation priorities in the Coast Range Ecoregion center on aquatic habitats. The ecoregion's **estuaries** provide critical habitat for a wide variety of fish and wildlife, ranging from young salmon, crab, and other marine species to marine mammals, waterfowl, and shorebirds.

Estuarine habitats have been reduced and degraded by a variety of forms of human development. Conversion of tidal wetlands to pasture and other uses has resulted in substantial losses of salt marsh and tidal swamp habitats.

Similar losses have occurred in the ecoregion's river valleys, where **floodplain wetlands** and backwater sloughs and swamps formerly provided abundant, essential rearing habitat for juvenile salmon.

In-stream and riparian habitats have been reduced and degraded by a variety of human activities. Although the federal government's Northwest Forest Plan and the state's Coastal Salmon Restoration Initiative hold promise for improvement of aquatic habitats in this ecoregion, the remaining challenges are substantial.

Exotic plant species pose a serious problem in a number of areas. As noted above, European beachgrass has disrupted natural ecological processes in sand dune communities. Scotch broom *(Cytisus scoparius)* and gorse *(Ulex europaeus)* are widespread in many areas, and spartina *(Spartina patens* and *S. alterniflora)* could pose serious threats to the biodiversity of estuaries. Himalayan and evergreen blackberry *(Rubus discolor* and *R. laciniatus)* have displaced native vegetation over large areas in the interior valleys, especially in riparian areas.

AT-RISK SPECIES

Three at-risk species — northern spotted owl *(Strix occidentalis caurina)*, marbled murrelet *(Brachyramphus marmoratus)*, and coho salmon *(Oncorhynchus kisutch)* — have had a profound impact on resource use and local economies in the Coast Range in recent years. Although the coastal forests and rivers and streams that support these three species have received considerable attention, the majority of the ecoregion's at-risk species occur in non-forested habitats. The sweeping protection efforts undertaken on behalf of the owl, murrelet, and salmon have not had a major impact on these other at-risk species.

Native grassland and wetland habitats once occupied most of the ecoregion's marine terrace, estuaries, and headlands (Ripley 1983). Several species and the grassland ecosystems themselves are now among the rarest in Oregon. The Oregon silverspot butterfly *(Speyeria zerene hippolyta)*, originally thought to have occurred almost continuously from Florence to the southern Washington coast, is now found at only five locations. The butterfly's total population is less than 5,000; protection and management of habitats on the Clatsop Plains, where development pressure is strong, is critical to the species' recovery. Another grassland species, the

Butterfly depends on vanishing coastal grasslands

The larvae of the Oregon silverspot butterfly (*Speyeria zerene hippolyta*) feed exclusively on the common blue violet (*Viola adunca*), which does best in the early successional stages of coastal grassland habitats. These grasslands have been significantly reduced due to the combined effects of agricultural development, urbanization, and fire suppression. Historically maintained by periodic fires, these habitats are subject to rapid successional changes in the coast's mild climate and ample rainfall.

Maintaining the silverspot butterfly requires active management of its grassland habitat. Federal and state agencies and The Nature Conservancy have expanded efforts to protect and recover remaining populations. Four of the five populations in Oregon are being managed for the persistence of the species. The Oregon Military Department has taken some steps to protect the fifth population on its lands on the Clatsop Plains north of Gearhart, but a great deal more work will be needed to secure and recover this population and the species as a whole.

Cascade Head catchfly *(Silene douglasii* var. *oraria)* is one of Oregon's rarest plants. Known only from two sites in the world, 99 percent of the world's population occurs at Cascade Head, where The Nature Conservancy and the U.S. Forest Service have protected its habitat from development and recreational impacts.

Grasslands are also found on many coastal peaks and higher elevation ridges. Coastal "balds," like mountaintops in other ecoregions, host a number of plant species that are either endemic to the region or far outside their normal range, forming what are called "disjunct distributions." Several of these plant species — Saddle Mountain saxifrage *(Saxifraga hitchcockiana)*, queen-of-the-forest *(Filipendula occidentalis)*, and frigid shootingstar *(Dodecatheon austrofrigidum)* — occur on Saddle Mountain, Onion Peak, Sugarloaf Mountain, and Blue Lake Lookout in the northern portion of the Coast Range. Coast Range fawn-lily *(Erythronium elegans)* is found on the grasslands of Mount Hebo, and further south, on Fanno Ridge.

Upper Nestucca River
Photographer, Larry N. Olson

COHO & CHUM SALMON STATUS

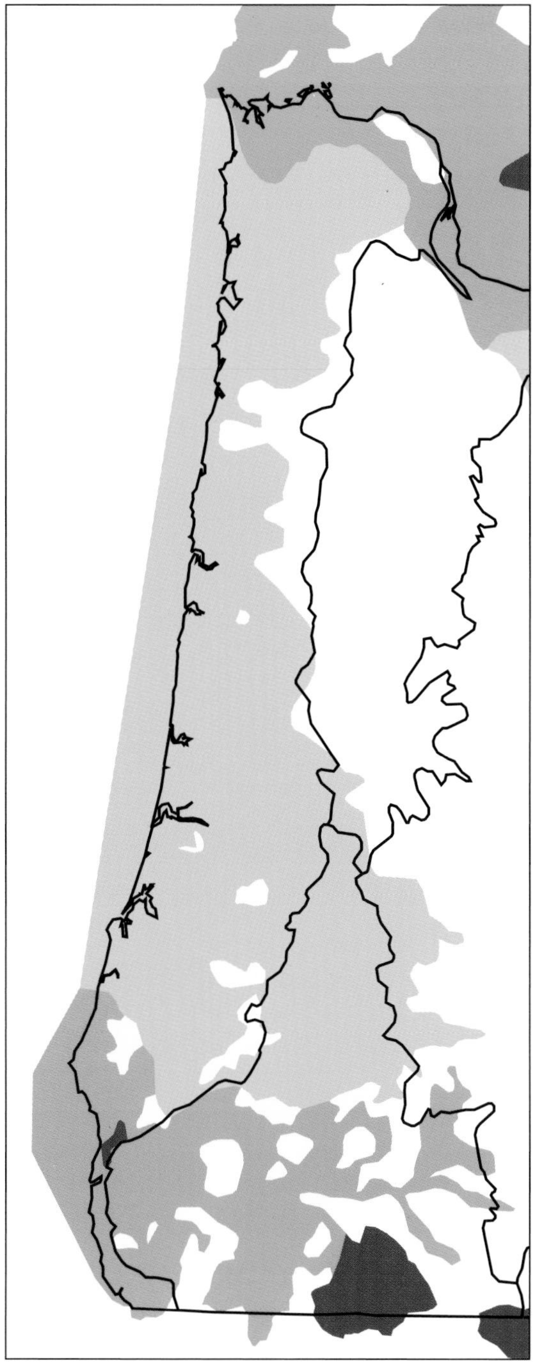

Coho salmon

- EXTINCT
- ENDANGERED
- THREATENED

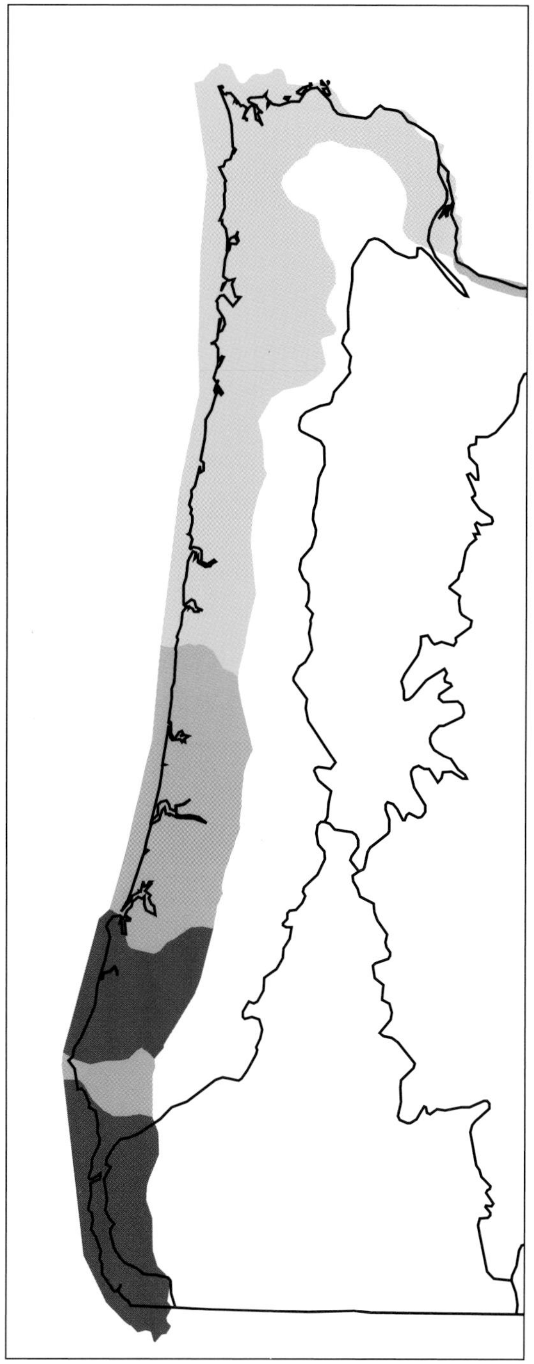

Chum salmon

- EXTINCT
- ENDANGERED
- THREATENED

Chum and colo salmon were historically among the most abundant salmonids in the Coast Range. Both species are heavily dependent on lowland habitats that have been most impacted by human settlement and development. Both coho and chum have been extirpated from portions of their historic range in Oregon, and populations of most remaining stocks have declined to a small fraction of their historic abundance.

Data from Pacific Salmon and Federal Lands, A Regional Analysis (The Wilderness Society 1993)

Two rare species of note — pink sandverbena *(Abronia umbellata* ssp. *breviflora)* and western snowy plover *(Charadrius alexandrinus nivosus)* — inhabit the foredune strand along the region's beaches. Moving sand, winter storms, and concentrated recreational use make this one of the harshest of coastal habitats. Once found all along the Oregon coast, these two species are now limited to a few isolated beaches in southern Oregon. Pink sandverbena — a plant historically found in coastal dune habitats from Point Reyes, California to Vancouver Island, British Columbia — is now restricted to seven sites in northern California and three sites in southern Oregon. Coastal breeding populations of the western snowy plover also have declined dramatically all along the Pacific coast, dropping to a few dozen known breeding sites. Fewer than ten of the bird's breeding sites are known to remain in Oregon. The decline of both of these species is largely linked to dune stabilization efforts that have led to widespread loss and degradation of open dune strand habitats.

Coastal wetlands support some of the Coast Range Ecoregion's at-risk species, including the Aleutian Canada goose *(Branta canadensis leucopareia)*. Most of this goose's remaining winter sites are in California, but many stop on the southern Oregon coast during migration. A disjunct wintering population uses offshore rocks, as well as wetlands and dairy pastures in Tillamook County. The ochyra moss *(Limbella freyi)* is only found in the shrub-dominated wetlands of Sutton Lake in Lane County. The Western bog lily *(Lilium occidentale)* occurs in association with the California pitcher plant *(Darlingtonia californica)* in boggy habitats along the southern Oregon coast and in grasslands along the northern California coast. Most of the 24 remaining lily populations are extremely small and are declining as the wetlands fill in with silt and peat.

AQUATIC SPECIES ANALYSIS

Although public attention has focused on coho salmon, the decline of Coast Range salmon stocks is emblematic of the deterioration of aquatic ecosystems and loss of biodiversity throughout the region.

Adverse ocean habitat conditions undoubtedly have contributed to the depressed status of most salmonids in recent years, but the stocks and species in the greatest trouble are those that spend a longer portion of their lives in freshwater habitats — chum and coho salmon, winter steelhead, and sea-run cutthroat trout. These fish provide a useful barometer of the health of the ecoregion's aquatic systems.

The Coast Range was historically one of the most productive areas in the nation for salmon and still supports a high diversity of native species and populations of anadromous fish. Most of these fish populations have declined dramatically in recent decades, and some are on the verge of extirpation from significant parts of their ranges (Nehlsen et al. 1991).

Chum salmon are almost gone from the ecoregion, lingering on with small remnant populations in Tillamook Bay and a handful of other systems. Coho stocks are severely depressed everywhere and nearly extirpated south of Cape Blanco. Winter steelhead and sea-run cutthroat trout populations are candidates for protection under the federal Endangered Species Act. Fall chinook salmon populations are relatively strong north of Cape Blanco, but spring chinook and fall chinook stocks south of Cape Blanco are all depressed significantly below historic levels (Huntington et al. 1996).

The threat of Endangered Species Act listings has sparked a concerted state effort to restore Coast Range fish populations under the umbrella of the Oregon Coastal Salmon Restoration Initiative. However, historic habitat losses and the relative ecological poverty of most aquatic systems in the region may limit recovery of many salmon populations.

Data compiled for an aquatic conservation strategy for the northern portion of the Coast Range illustrate some of the historic trends and the magnitude of the losses in aquatic ecosystem productivity (Huntington 1997). Tillamook Bay's watershed was historically one of the state's most productive, with an estimated 1,000 adult salmon per square mile. Current production is a small fraction of that level. Chum salmon, historically the most abundant species in the basin, have declined from an estimated 600,000 in the 1940s to fewer than 2,000 today. Coho salmon have declined from approximately 150,000 in the 1930s to fewer than 1,000. By contrast, fall chinook salmon, historically a relatively minor component of the watershed's overall production, are relatively healthy with populations estimated at about two-thirds their historic levels.

The picture that emerges from the analysis of Tillamook Bay watershed is probably generally applicable to aquatic systems throughout the Coast Range. Most striking is the impact of habitat loss and degradation in the lower watershed. The low-gradient streams, forested swamps, and sloughs and channels historically found in the bottomlands surrounding the bay were critical to chum and coho salmon populations that once accounted for the vast majority of the basin's fish production. In contrast, the upper watershed areas that currently support some of the ecoregion's strongest runs of chinook salmon were historically some of the least productive habitats in the basin. The fact that these areas are now viewed as "strongholds" for native salmonids is testimony to the magnitude of the decline of the basin's aquatic ecosystems.

The widespread destruction and degradation of aquatic systems in the Coast Range has left few large areas with high-quality habitats for salmon and other native species. Most watersheds still

Coast Range Ecoregion

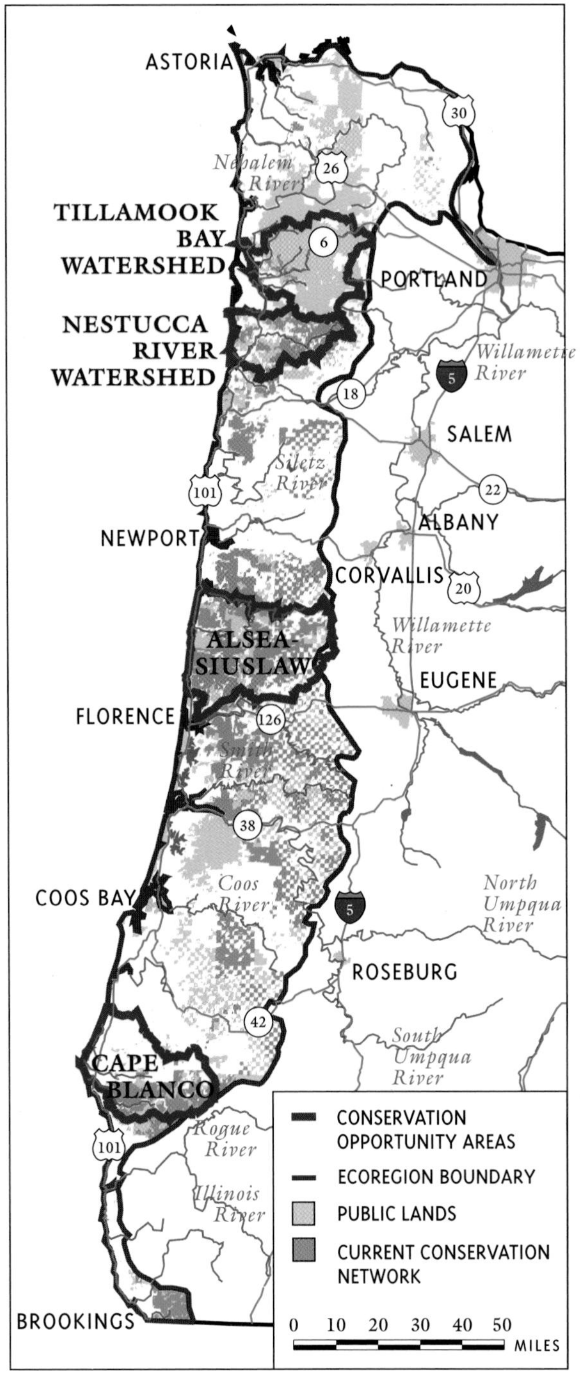

All four conservation opportunity areas provide critical habitat for Coast Range salmon populations. Other key features include some unique coastal habitats, important estuaries, and a large block of state-owned forests in an area dominated by industrial timberlands.

provide important habitat for salmonids, but they tend to be fragmented and degraded.

Salmon Core Areas. Two-thirds of the river miles deemed critical as core areas for coastal salmon recovery under the Oregon Coastal Salmon Restoration Initiative are found in the Coast Range. The highest density of core area habitats is found in the Siltcoos, Sixes, Tillamook, and Coquille basins. The Siuslaw basin, although only average in core area density, has the most core area habitat of any basin in the Coast Range, with a total of 281 river miles.

Aquatic Diversity Areas. Aquatic diversity areas identified by the American Fisheries Society (Bottom et al. 1993) are scattered throughout the Coast Range. The largest areas identified as important genetic refuges are in the Nehalem Basin and in the Elk and Upper Coquille river watersheds. The latter two areas were also recognized for their high species richness and value as reference watersheds (relatively high ecological integrity). Tenmile Lake, Siltcoos River and Nehalem River watersheds provide some of the most important corridor functions.

Overall, Siltcoos Lake and Succor Creek (headwaters of South Fork Coquille) watersheds rank among the most significant in the ecoregion, meeting four of the American Fisheries Society's five criteria for aquatic diversity area designations (Bottom et al. 1993).

SUMMARY OF CONSERVATION ISSUES

Major issues for biodiversity conservation in the Coast Range include:

- Few large blocks of old growth forest remain. High timber harvest levels over the past several decades have left vast expanses of forest in early-successional stages.
- Many of the federal lands designated as late-successional reserves are currently not late-successional habitat; others are relatively small "checkerboards" of forests embedded in a matrix of private industrial timber lands.
- Outside of late-successional reserves on federal lands, few lands in the ecoregion are managed with a strong emphasis on biodiversity.
- Land ownership is highly fragmented. The checkerboard pattern of BLM and private ownership along the southern and eastern edges of the ecoregion presents particular problems for coordinated, broad-scale land management.
- Many of the native habitats along the shoreline and in coastal plains have already been altered or converted to human use. Development pressure is likely to increase. These areas support a number of habitat specialists, including at-risk species that cannot be addressed adequately in a broad-scale analysis.

- Logging and disease have eliminated much of the ecoregion's Port Orford cedar; remaining patches are at extreme risk due to the water-borne pathogen, *Phytopthera lateralis.*

- Marine habitats and their contributions to biodiversity are often not included in traditional terrestrial-based conservation strategies, and marine and terrestrial systems have not been integrated in broad-scale biodiversity analyses.

- The decline of coastal salmon populations is emblematic of broader problems with aquatic ecosystems. Conservation efforts will need to look beyond recovery of coastal coho salmon populations to restoration of more natural ecosystem functions and processes.

- Exotic species have already had a major impact on some coastal ecosystems; if left unchecked, they could help push a number of native species to extinction.

- Although federal lands are managed under a comprehensive strategy, the northern portion of the ecoregion is almost entirely in state and private ownership, and future management direction for the large state forests has yet to be established. This northern part of the ecoregion represents a major 'gap' in the current conservation network.

CONSERVATION OPPORTUNITY AREAS

The Oregon Biodiversity Project identified four areas in the Coast Range Ecoregion that appear to offer good opportunities to address biodiversity conservation needs.

Importance for aquatic diversity and core areas for salmonid habitat figured prominently in the selection of all four areas, but especially so in the Alsea-Siuslaw and Nestucca River areas. At-risk species and unique coastal habitats also contributed to selection of the Cape Blanco and the inclusion of Sand Lake in the Nestucca River area. The young forests of the Tillamook Burn stand out as a large block of habitat that has largely escaped fragmentation by recent timber harvest in an area where the current conservation network is particularly weak.

The four selections described below encompass a number of key areas identified in an earlier assessment of the ecoregion's biodiversity conservation priorities (Noss 1992). The Noss assessment ranked sites based on judgments about their relative importance for a number of criteria, including at-risk species, old growth forests, spotted owls, landscape connectivity, and watershed values.

At-risk plants

Abronia umbellata ssp. *breviflora*, pink sandverbena

Arctostaphylos hispidula, hairy manzanita

Bensoniella oregona, bensonia

Brodiaea terrestris, dwarf broadiaea

Bryoria pseudocapillaris, lichen

Cicendia quadrangularis, microcala

Eriophorum chamissonis, russet cotton-grass

Iliamna latibracteata, California globe-mallow

Lasthenia macrantha ssp. *prisca*, large-flowered goldfields

Lilium occidentale, western lily

Microseris bidelovii, coast microseris

Phacelia argentea, silvery phacelia

Sidalcea malviflora ssp. *breviflora*, coast checker bloom

Triteleia hendersonii var. *leachiae*, Leach's brodiaea

At-risk animals

Ascaphus truei, tailed frog

Brachyramphus marmoratus, marbled murrelet

Branta canadensis leucopareia, Aleutian Canada goose

Charadrius alexandrinus nivosus, western snowy plover

Clemmys marmorata marmorata, northwest pond turtle

Oncorhynchus clarki clarki, coastal cutthroat trout

Oncorhynchus kisutch ssp., coho salmon

Oncorhynchus mykiss ssp., winter steelhead

Plethodon elongatus, Del Norte salamander

Rana aurora, northern red-legged frog

Strix occidentalis caurina, northern spotted owl

1. Cape Blanco area

This area in Coos and Curry counties extends from Bandon State Park south to Port Orford, extending inland to the headwaters of the South Fork Coquille River adjacent to the Wild Rogue Wilderness.

This area has high value for both aquatic and terrestrial biodiversity. Priority habitats found here include native sand dune systems, estuaries, and headlands, and further inland, old growth conifer forests. In addition to a cluster of aquatic diversity areas, it also contains core areas for coho salmon, fall chinook, and winter steelhead. The area provides habitat for more than 25 at-risk species, including birds, fish, amphibians, reptiles, and plants. Rare vegetation communities found in this area include Port Orford cedar forests and unique "pygmy shore pine" forests.

The U. S. Forest Service administers much of this area's inland forests, including a large portion in late-successional reserve designation. Three large state parks and the BLM's New River Area of Critical Environmental Concern encompass most of the shoreline area, with ranches and cranberry bogs occupying most of the rest of the lowlands.

2. Alsea-Siuslaw area

This area includes the coast between Waldport and Florence, extending inland to the crest of the Coast Range.

This area is particularly significant for its fish habitat values, encompassing 12 aquatic diversity areas and one of the highest concentrations of salmon core areas in the state. It also includes two small wilderness areas (virtually the only roadless areas left on the central and northern coast) and offers opportunities for long-term restoration of Coast Range forest habitats on a large scale.

Ownership in this area is predominantly federal, and most of this is in late-successional reserves. The U.S. Forest Service has been acquiring private lands in this area for their importance as fish habitat.

At-risk plants

Abronia umbellata ssp. *breviflora*, pink sandverbena

Anemone oregana var. *felix*, bog anemone

Cimicifuga elata, tall bugbane

Microseris bidelovii, coast microseris

Plantago macrocarpa, North Pacific plantain

Pseudocyphellaria mougeotiana, lichen

Utricularia gibba, humped bladder-wort

At-risk animals

Ascaphus truei, tailed frog

Brachyramphus marmoratus, marbled murrelet

Ceraclea vertreesi, Vertrees's ceraclean caddisfly

Corynorhinus townsendii, Townsend's big-eared bat

Eumetopias jubatus, northern sea lion

Incisalia polia obscura, hoary elfin butterfly

Oncorhynchus clarki clarki, coastal cutthroat trout

Oncorhynchus kisutch ssp., coho salmon

Oncorhynchus mykiss ssp., winter steelhead

Pelecanus occidentalis, brown pelican

Plebejus saepiolus insulanus, insular blue butterfly

Rana aurora, northern red-legged frog

Speyeria zerene hippolyta, Oregon silverspot butterfly

Strix occidentalis caurina, northern spotted owl

3. Nestucca River Watershed

This area encompasses the entire Nestucca River watershed and the adjacent Sand Lake watershed in southern Tillamook County.

This area contains about a dozen aquatic diversity areas and includes core areas for chum, coho, and spring chinook salmon, as well as winter steelhead. Federal lands in the Nestucca River watershed are designated an "adaptive management area," where managers are expected to explore and test alternative strategies that emphasize restoration of late-successional forests and conservation of fisheries and biological diversity. Most of the Nestucca River watershed burned in the late 1800s and early 1900s and less than one percent (200 acres) is in forests greater than 200 years old (USDA/USDI 1996). The bottomlands along the lower river are primarily dairy pastures.

Immediately north of the Nestucca River watershed, Sand Lake is one of Oregon's least developed estuaries, retaining extensive tidal marshes. The area also includes some of the most extensive sand dunes found on the northern Oregon coast and significant remnants of cedar swamps. The Forest Service maintains two research natural areas, and The Nature Conservancy owns a small preserve. Ownership is a mix of national forest, state park, and private lands. The lowlands around the estuary have so far escaped the residential development pressures found in nearby coastal communities.

At-risk plants

Calypogeia sphagnicola, liverwort

Cardamine pattersonii, Saddle Mountain bittercress

Erythronium elegans, Coast Range fawn-lily

Filipendula occidentalis, queen-of-the-forest

Lophozia laxa, liverwort

Pohlia sphagnicola, moss

Silene douglasii var. *oraria*, Cascade Head catchfly

Sidalcea hendersonii, Henderson sidalcea

Sidalcea hirtipes, bristly-stemmed sidalcea

Sidalcea nelsoniana, Nelson's sidalcea

At-risk animals

Ascaphus truei, tailed frog

Brachyramphus marmoratus, marbled murrelet

Branta canadensis leucopareia, Aleutian Canada goose

Charadrius alexandrinus nivosus, western snowy plover

Clemmys marmorata marmorata, northwest pond turtle

Falco peregrinus anatum, peregrine falcon

Oncorhynchus clarki clarki, coastal cutthroat trout

Oncorhynchus kisutch ssp., coho salmon

Oncorhynchus mykiss ssp., winter steelhead

Rana aurora, northern red-legged frog

Speyeria zerene hippolyta, Oregon silverspot butterfly

Strix occidentalis caurina, northern spotted owl

4. Tillamook Bay Watershed

This area includes the watersheds of the Trask, Wilson, and Kilchis rivers, which converge in Tillamook Bay.

Tillamook State Forest — which occupies the upper watersheds of the Trask, Wilson, and Kilchis rivers — encompasses one of the largest blocks of forest in the Coast Range that has not been fragmented by recent timber harvests. Comprised of lands reforested in the 1950s and 1960s following a series of extensive fires, the 200,000 acres of state lands in the "Tillamook Burn" provide a unique opportunity to design and test landscape-scale strategies for biodiversity conservation in managed forests. The three rivers contain some of the most important habitats for coastal salmon in the state, and they support a half-dozen other at-risk species. The river delta areas of Tillamook Bay are key areas for migrating waterfowl, shorebirds, and a variety of estuarine-dependent species.

The Tillamook Bay National Estuary Project offers an opportunity to link conservation efforts in the estuary and adjacent agricultural lands with forest management in the upper watershed. A community-based planning process is intended to provide a model for other coastal areas.

At-risk plants

Dodecatheon austrofrigidum, frigid shootingstar

Filipendula occidentalis, queen-of-the-forest

Lewisia columbiana var. *rupicola*, rosy lewisia

Saxifraga hitchcockiana, Saddle Mountain saxifrage

Senecio flettii, Flett's groundsel

Sidalcea hirtipes, bristly-stemmed sidalcea

Sidalcea nelsoniana, Nelson's sidalcea

At-risk animals

Brachyramphus marmoratus, marbled murrelet

Gulo gulo, wolverine

Oncorhynchus clarki clarki, coastal cutthroat trout

Oncorhynchus kisutch ssp., coho salmon

Oncorhynchus mykiss ssp., winter steelhead

Pelecanus occidentalis, brown pelican

Strix occidentalis caurina, northern spotted owl

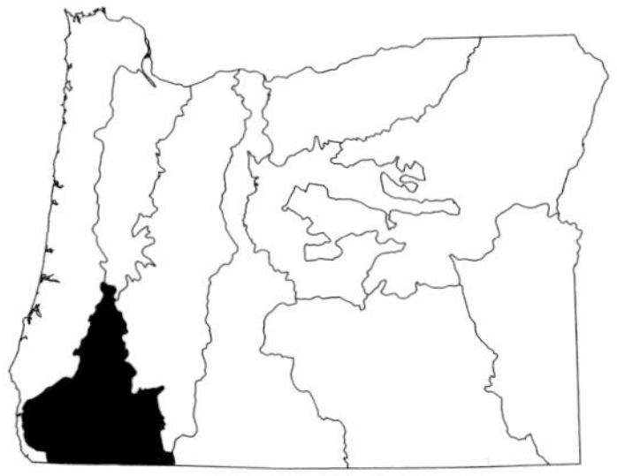

Klamath Mountains Ecoregion

The Klamath Mountains Ecoregion covers most of southwestern Oregon and northwestern California. It includes the Siskiyou Mountains, California's Marble Mountains and Trinity Alps, and the interior valleys and foothills between these mountain ranges. Elevations range from 100 feet to over 7,500 feet. Valley bottoms in the interior generally range between 450 feet elevation in the north around Roseburg to almost 2,000 feet at Ashland near the California border.

The ecoregion has the oldest landscapes in Oregon, and is one of the few parts of the state not shaped largely by volcanism. It also is by far the most geologically diverse, having large areas of metamorphic and sedimentary rocks, as well as granites and basalt. Topography ranges from steep, dissected mountains and canyons to gentle foothills and flat valley bottoms. The ecoregion also has major climatic extremes. Portions far to the west receive more than 120 inches of rain per year, with relatively mild temperatures year-round. The southern interior valleys are much drier, with less than 20 inches of rain per year and summer high temperatures averaging more than 100° F.

The combination of extreme geologic, topographic, and climatic diversity gives this ecoregion the most diverse habitats in Oregon (including, perhaps, the most diverse conifer forests in the world) and makes it a focal point for biodiversity conservation efforts on a national and international scale. The International Union for the Conservation of Nature has declared the Klamath Mountains an "area of global botanical significance," and the

Several large wilderness areas and the network of late-successional reserves established on federal forestlands provide a relatively high level of protection for biodiversity values on almost 20 percent of the ecoregion. These areas include mostly Douglas-fir and Jeffrey pine habitats on the west side of the ecoregion.

The Kalmiopsis and Wild Rogue wilderness areas encompass some of the wildest and most biologically diverse areas in Oregon. Together with adjacent late-successional reserves, these lands comprise one of the largest blocks of relatively undeveloped landscape in the state, a reservoir of regional biodiversity. The late-successional reserves on the west side of the ecoregion include a substantial portion of the region's remaining old growth forests. Forest Service and BLM research natural areas protect examples of many of the region's native plant communities.

The situation is far different in the eastern half of the ecoregion where mid-elevation coniferous forests, ponderosa pine and oak woodlands, and prairie habitats are largely unrepresented in the conservation network.

The Nature Conservancy owns several small preserves that encompass some of the few remaining native habitats in the Rogue and Bear Creek valleys. Other conservation lands are limited to a few small parks and wildlife areas.

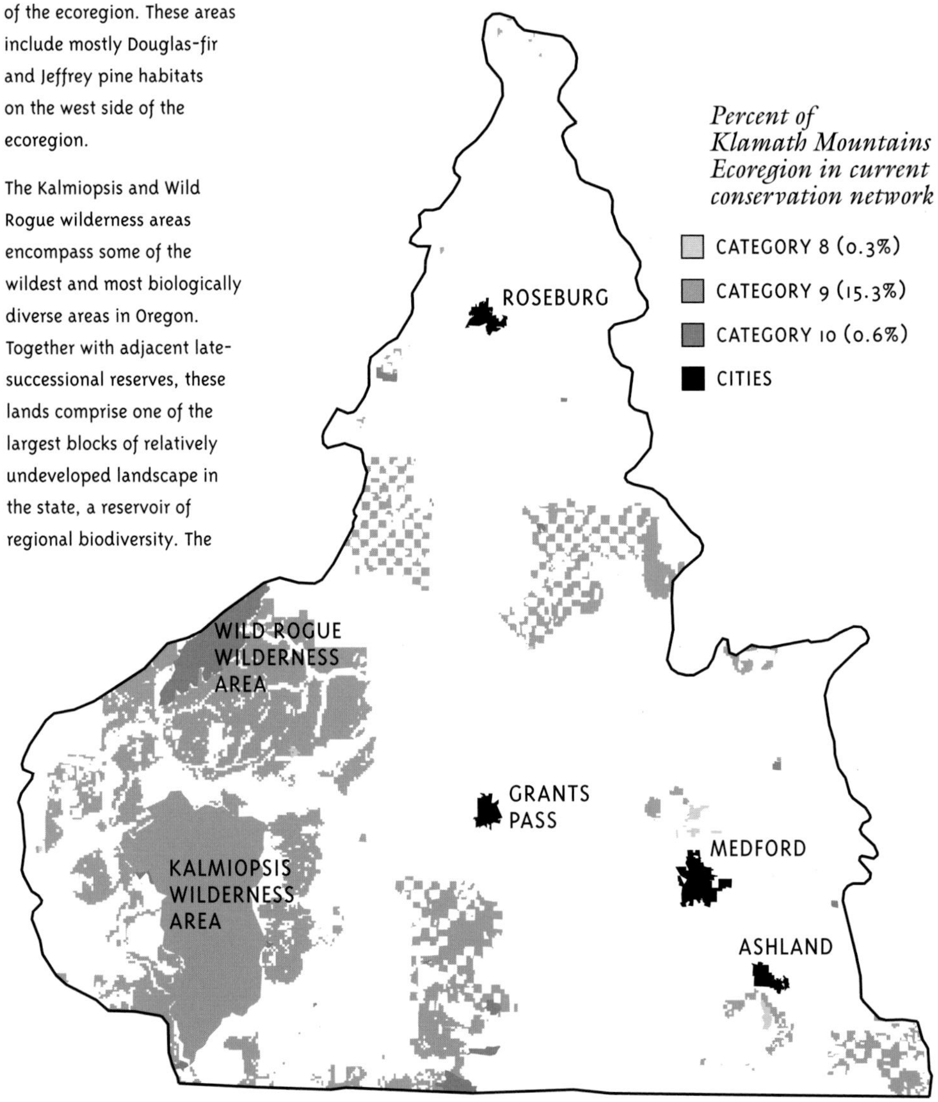

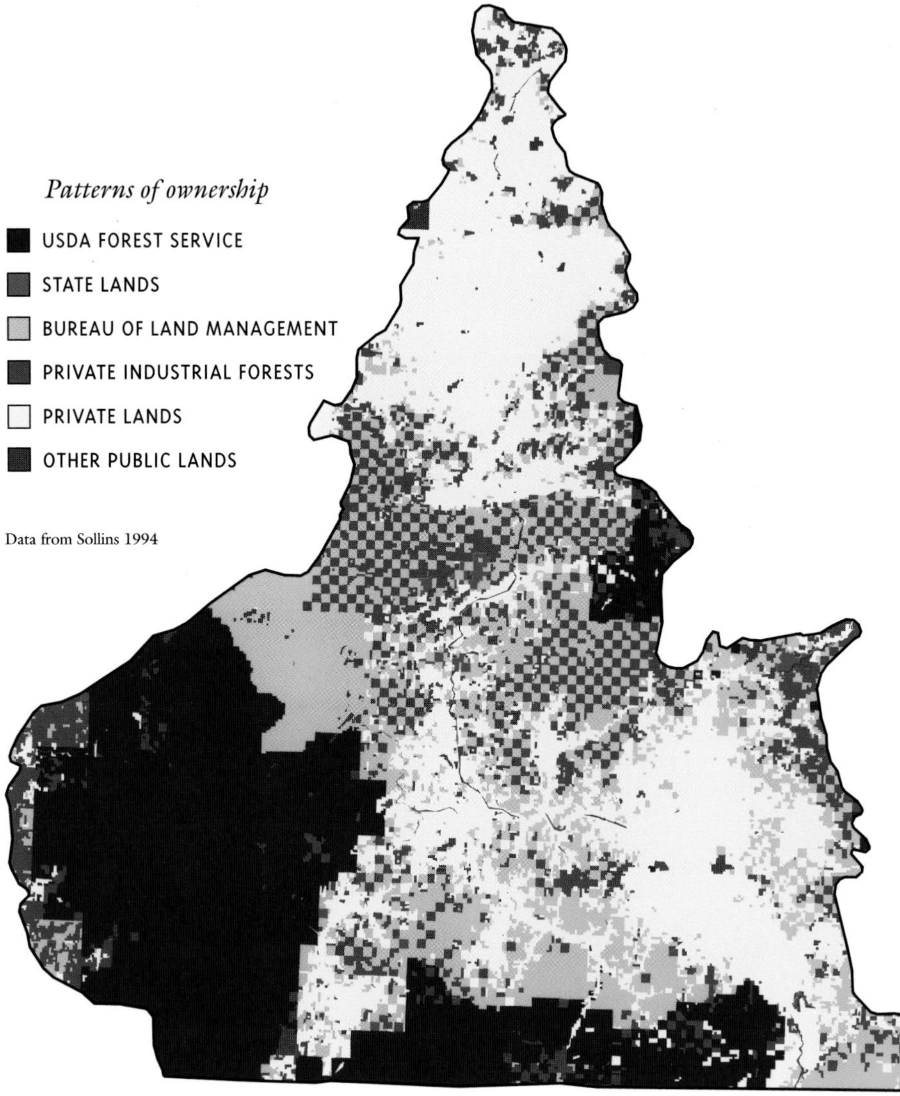

World Wildlife Fund has designated it as "globally outstanding" in richness and distinctiveness of its species, communities, and ecological processes (Ricketts et al. 1997).

In addition to diverse habitats, the ecoregion is a floristic crossroads. Its flora includes elements of the Sierra Nevada Mountains, Sacramento Valley, and Coast Range Mountains of California; the Cascade Mountains of Oregon and Washington; and the Great Basin. Because of its geologic age, stable climate, and many unusual habitats, the ecoregion is a major center of species endemism for vascular plants. Of the 4,000 native plant taxa occurring in Oregon, about half are found in this ecoregion, with about a quarter of these found only here. The region is also known for its diversity of conifers, with 30 different species. (In Oregon, the West Cascades has the second largest number of conifer species, with 18 species).

Human population is concentrated in the valleys along the Interstate 5 corridor. Forest products, agriculture, and tourism are the foundations of the local economy.

Agate Desert, Rogue Valley
Photographer, Alan D. St. John

VEGETATION ANALYSIS

Broad-scale vegetation maps are a blunt tool for analysis in an ecoregion as diverse and complex as the Klamath Mountains. Species composition within the ecoregion's forests changes with elevation, latitude, longitude, and substrate. As a result, the historic and current vegetation maps used in this analysis provide highly simplified views of a very complex landscape. Despite these weaknesses, overall trends and conservation priorities are readily apparent in an analysis of the current and historic vegetation maps.

Prior to European settlement, the landscape was dominated by three major vegetation types — Douglas-fir forests, oak woodlands, and ponderosa pine woodlands. Together, these general types comprised 85 percent of the landscape. All three types are now priorities for conservation in this ecoregion, with old growth Douglas-fir and both woodland types having declined 55 to 60 percent over the past 150 years, largely due to logging, fire suppression, and rural residential development. (Declines among lower-elevation plant communities included within these general types are even greater.) Other priorities include native grasslands, which have been almost completely eliminated, and Port Orford cedar forests, which have been decimated by logging and disease.

Douglas-fir forests (including second growth) appear to be well represented in the current conservation network, with 23 percent found in wilderness areas and late-successional reserves with biodiversity management ratings of 8-10. However, the numbers mask significant concerns for the biological diversity encompassed within these broad vegetation types. Landscape patterns of biodiversity management and timber harvest highlight the uneven nature of existing protection for these forests. In the Siskiyou Mountains of Curry and Josephine counties, wilderness areas, late-successional reserves, and other special management areas contain large blocks of unharvested forests. In the northern part of the ecoregion, many of the late-successional reserves on BLM lands are fragmented by a checkerboard of public and private lands. In the foothills east of Interstate 5, most of the lands mapped as Douglas-fir forests are characterized by recent clearcuts or areas of patchy forest, and few areas are managed with an emphasis on biodiversity values.

Low-elevation **oak and ponderosa pine woodlands** of the ecoregion's valley bottoms and foothills are almost all privately owned and have been heavily impacted by logging, livestock grazing, rural and urban development, and fire suppression. These mixed woodlands of conifer and hardwoods are largely unrepresented in the current network of conservation lands. Recent population growth has increased development pressure in these areas. In the Umpqua Valley, these habitats and their adjacent riparian habitat have also been targeted for conservation to protect the endangered Columbian white-tailed deer *(Odocoileus virginianus leucurus)*.

Native **grasslands,** historically only a small part of the ecoregion, have been almost entirely converted to urban and agricultural development or invaded by non-native annual grasses. Conservation and management of the few remnants has largely been driven by the need to protect the many endemic (and at-risk) plant species found in these habitats.

A number of other globally rare vegetation types have declined significantly in the Klamath Mountains over the past 150 years. **Port Orford cedar forests,** for example, were localized but widespread near the coast and along streams in interior areas with serpentine soils. An introduced root pathogen *(Phytopthera lateralis)* has affected the species over much of its range, decimating stands in areas where the species has shown its best growth potential (USDI/BLM 1994a). Road building for logging and mining spreads this water-borne pathogen. While never abundant, Port Orford cedar communities are endemic to this ecoregion and characterized by unusual plant and animal associations. As such, they are important priorities for conservation.

Virtually all of the Klamath Mountains' habitats were historically shaped by fire. The low- to mid-elevation coniferous forests were a mix of old growth forests and open woodlands, with late-successional conditions typically found on 45-75 percent of the landscape (USDI/BLM 1994a). Fire-tolerant species (Douglas-fir, ponderosa pine, sugar pine, incense cedar, Port Orford cedar) dominated, with shade-tolerant species (western hemlock and white fir) found only in limited areas protected from fire. Woodlands often had understories dominated by grasses or fire-tolerant shrubs, and patches of chaparral. Grasslands were not uncommon in the forest matrix.

The pattern of frequent, low-intensity fires that shaped these habitats has been interrupted by fire detection and suppression techniques that have extended average fire-return intervals from 10-30 years to more than 80 years. After 70 years of fire suppression, woodlands have become forests, understories are often shrubby and dense, and shade-tolerant species (white fir and tan oak) are much more widespread.

Obstacles to restoring more natural patterns of fire are significant. The patchy mosaic of public and private ownerships and the presence of scattered rural residential development throughout much of the ecoregion make it difficult to manage fires on a landscape basis. Fuels accumulated over past decades have increased the intensity of fires and the potential risk of larger fires. Because of these factors, reintroducing fire as prescribed burns or "controlled wildfires" will be difficult in much of the ecoregion, and the historic decline of the Klamath Mountains' woodland types is likely to continue.

AT-RISK SPECIES

Animals. At-risk animal species in the ecoregion reflect the broad habitat changes that have occurred in the forests, woodlands, and grasslands of the Klamath Mountains.

Late-successional forests provide habitat for two at-risk birds, the northern spotted owl *(Strix occidentalis caurina)* and the marbled murrelet *(Brachyramphus marmoratus)*. The spotted owl is found throughout the ecoregion, while the murrelet appears to be limited to areas within 30 miles of the coast (USDI/BLM 1994a). Other at-risk species associated with older forests include the wolverine *(Gulo gulo),* fisher *(Martes pennanti),* and several frogs and salamanders. The fisher was virtually extirpated in southwestern Oregon, but has slowly begun to reappear as a result of reintroduction and protection from trapping (USDI/BLM 1994a). Wolverine reports are scattered and not very recent. The Del Norte salamander *(Plethodon elongatus)* and the Siskiyou Mountains salamander *(P. stormi)* are both found on moist, rocky slopes and may have been strongly affected by removal of old growth Douglas-fir habitat. The tailed frog *(Ascaphus truei)* is associated with clear, cold streams in older forests (USDI/BLM 1994a).

Oak woodlands and grasslands in the northern portion of the ecoregion provide habitat for the Columbian white-tailed deer. The deer tend to stay close to riparian areas. Residential and subdivision development, particularly along the North Umpqua River, is the primary threat to the riparian habitats used by this species (USDI/BLM 1994b).

Other at-risk species include the tricolored blackbird *(Agelaius tricolor)* and the northwestern pond turtle *(Clemmys marmorata marmorata),* both impacted by loss and degradation of valley wetland habitats.

Plants. The ultramafic soils (low in silica, rich in iron and magnesium) that underlie a large portion of southwestern Josephine County have acted as a strong selective force, driving the evolution of about 40 plant species uniquely adapted to these conditions. Seeps that reach the surface provide wetland habitat for the carnivorous California pitcher plant *(Darlingtonia californica)* and five at-risk endemic plant species. Jeffrey pine savannas in drier serpentine soils (low in iron, rich in magnesium and silica) provide habitat for an additional eight species of at-risk plants, most of which are perennial forbs. Mining — especially surface mining of the ultramafic soils for nickel, chromium, and cobalt — is a major threat to all these plant species.

Another group of endemic at-risk plants occurs in vernal pools — seasonal wetlands associated with spring) throughout the Rogue River Valley, particularly in the Agate Desert region of the north Medford Plains. The Umpqua Valley also has a suite of species restricted to the western interior valley bottom wetlands, including hairy popcorn flower *(Plagiobothrys hirtus),* red-root yampah *(Perideridia erythrorhiza)*, and white camas *(Camassia leichtlinii* ssp. *leichtlinii).*

Other concentrations of rare plants are found on the high-elevation granites along the Siskiyou Divide and on varied substrates in the Rogue River Canyon.

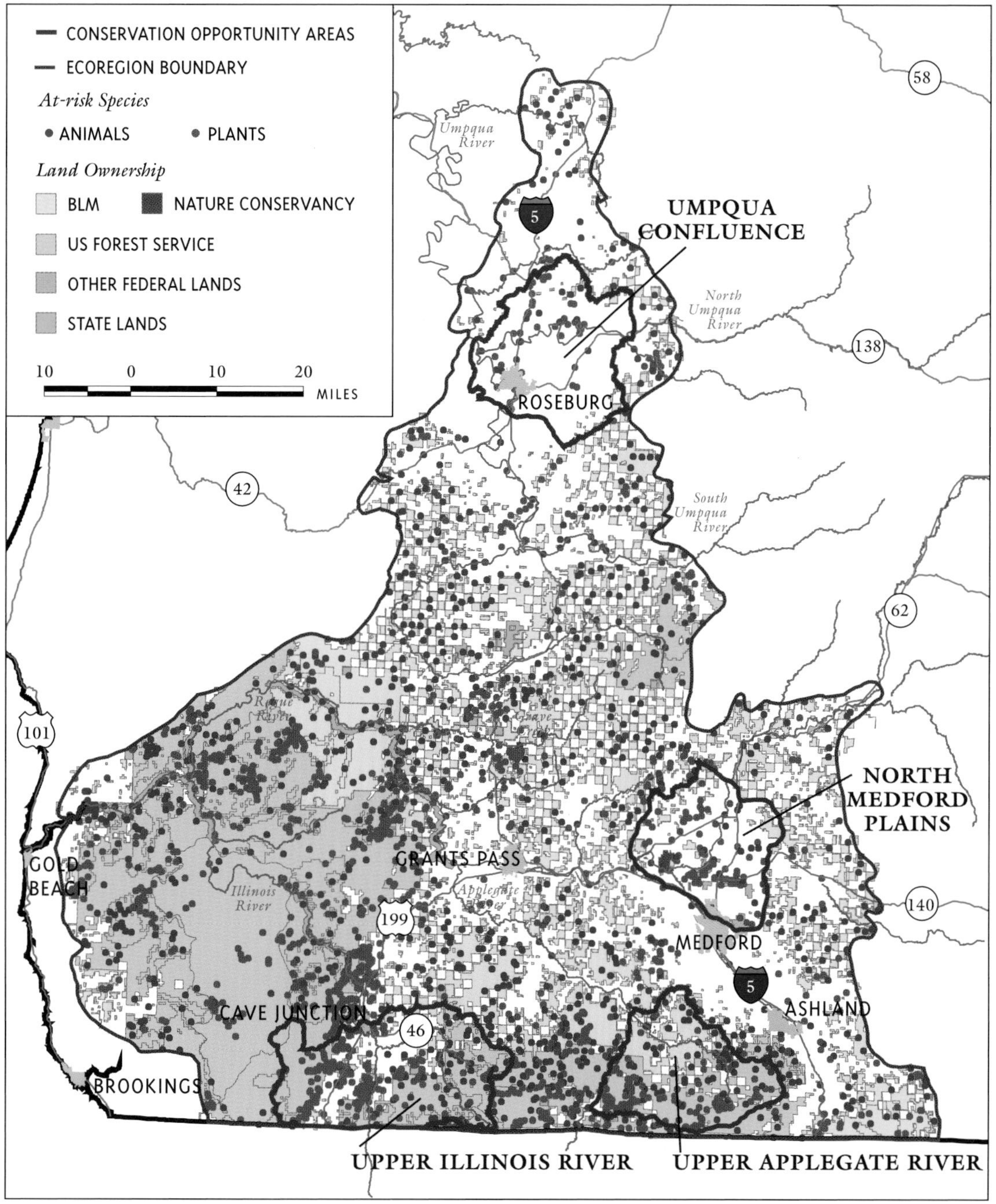

Locations of at-risk plant and animals recorded in the Oregon Natural Heritage Program's data bases are shown in relation to land ownership and the Oregon Biodiversity Project's conservation opportunity areas.

AQUATIC SPECIES ANALYSIS

High-quality aquatic habitats in this ecoregion are primarily limited to the most rugged and inaccessible portions of the Siskiyou Mountains. Aquatic ecosystems at low- and mid-elevations have suffered widespread degradation, affecting a variety of aquatic species, from wide-ranging fish like salmon and steelhead to narrow endemic plants.

Early gold miners in the Applegate watershed found more salmon in their sluice boxes than gold, often selling the fish to finance their mining operations (LaLande 1995). The Rogue and Umpqua rivers became internationally famous for their salmon and steelhead fishing. Today, native stocks of virtually all of the ecoregion's anadromous fish are depressed and declining, and several species have been listed or proposed for listing under the federal Endangered Species Act. Rogue Basin coho salmon, estimated at 60,000 adults in the 1890s based on cannery shipments, still occupy 90 percent of their historic habitats, but wild populations have declined to a few thousand fish (Prevost et al. 1996).

Although salmonids have garnered most of the attention, other aquatic species are experiencing similar declines. Surveys for northwestern pond turtles *(Clemmys marmorata marmorata)* in the Rogue Basin found turtles in less than 10 percent of locations that have historically supported populations (USDI/BLM 1994a). Inventories of streams in the northern half of the ecoregion found aquatic insect communities degraded throughout the area (USDI/BLM 1994b). Beavers *(Castor canadensis)* have been extirpated from many of the Klamath Mountains' basins (Prevost et al. 1996).

Large-scale hydraulic mining for gold caused the earliest and perhaps largest impacts on aquatic habitats in the Rogue River Basin (Prevost et al. 1996), washing away entire hillsides, altering stream courses, and depositing massive quantities of rock and sediments on floodplains. Placer mining for gold continues to be a threat to habitat for fish, wildlife and at-risk plants along many southern Oregon streams. By 1900, water rights for most tributary streams in the Rogue Basin were already over-allocated (Prevost et al. 1996). Diversions of water for irrigation have depleted instream flows at critical times of the year for the past century. Decades of timber harvesting, road building, and land clearing for agriculture and urban development have reduced riparian vegetation, increased erosion, and degraded or destroyed natural wetlands.

Reduced riparian canopy cover and wider, shallower, and less complex stream channels have taken their toll on water quality, with peak water temperatures up to 10° F higher than historic levels in some parts of the Rogue River Basin (Prevost et al. 1996). Similar habitat conditions prevail in the northern part of the ecoregion (USDI/BLM 1994b). In recent years, however, improvements in timber harvest, other land use practices, and habitat restoration efforts have begun to reverse the decline of aquatic ecosystems in many areas. Overall, water quality and riparian habitats are in an upward trend of recovery, according to local salmon restoration planners (Prevost et al. 1996).

The middle reaches of the Rogue and Umpqua rivers, and the headwaters systems of the Siskiyou Mountains are of special significance for aquatic biodiversity in the Klamath Mountains Ecoregion. The middle reaches of the Rogue and Umpqua rivers, although degraded, contain important spawning and rearing areas for some salmonids and provide critical connecting corridors to large blocks of higher quality habitats in the Cascade and Siskiyou mountains. These lower elevation areas contain what were historically probably the most productive habitats for salmon, as well as most of the region's remaining wetlands and many of its at-risk species.

The headwaters systems in the Siskiyou Mountains have been less impacted by human activities. These areas include a group of watersheds on the lower Rogue River and a complex that encompasses the headwaters of the Illinois and North Fork Smith rivers. The upper Illinois River is particularly significant, supporting virtually all of the Rogue Basin's production of wild coho salmon, as well as a high-risk population of winter steelhead (USDI/BLM 1994a). Southeast of Ashland, the Jenny Creek watershed— a tributary of the Klamath River — provides habitat for two species not found anywhere else in the ecoregion: the Jenny Creek sucker *(Catostomus rimiculus),* a local endemic; and redband trout *(Oncorhynchus mykiss* ssp.), which is at the western edge of its range.

SUMMARY OF CONSERVATION ISSUES

Major issues for biodiversity conservation in the Klamath Mountains include:

- The northern and eastern two-thirds of the ecoregion, which were once dominated by grasslands, oak and ponderosa pine woodlands, are essentially unrepresented in the current conservation network.

- Except for forests in the western wilderness areas, a high percentage of conifer forests have been harvested, leaving little old growth and a patchwork of forest and clearcuts in most areas.

- Fire suppression has had a significant effect on forest structure and ecosystem processes. The results have been changes in forest composition, increased stand densities, susceptibility to disease and insect damage, and more intense fires. Patterns of ownership and development complicate the already difficult task of reintroducing fire to restore historic patterns.

- Past mining practices have had profound, and in many cases, irreversible impacts on terrestrial and aquatic habitats in the southern portion of the ecoregion. Mining is ongoing and threats are increasing in some areas.

- Programs to restore coastal salmon populations, a major focus of conservation efforts in this ecoregion, could have broader benefits for aquatic biodiversity.
- Many of the ecoregion's at-risk plant species are found in valley bottom habitats that are in private ownership and vulnerable to development pressures.
- The large number of at-risk endemic plant species in the ecoregion suggests that its unique habitats may support an array of other specialized species, especially invertebrates, that are not well documented or understood, but that may be equally at risk.

CONSERVATION OPPORTUNITY AREAS

The Oregon Biodiversity Project identified four areas in the Klamath Mountains Ecoregion that appear to offer good opportunities to address biodiversity conservation needs.

The Klamath Mountains was one of two ecoregions where the project tested a selection methodology that used computer-based analysis to rank watersheds. (See Blue Mountains for a discussion of a different experimental approach.) In this case, indices were developed for each subwatershed (five-digit HUC) based on its relative ranking for priority vegetation types (percentage of area); at-

Illinois River
Photographer, Larry N. Olson

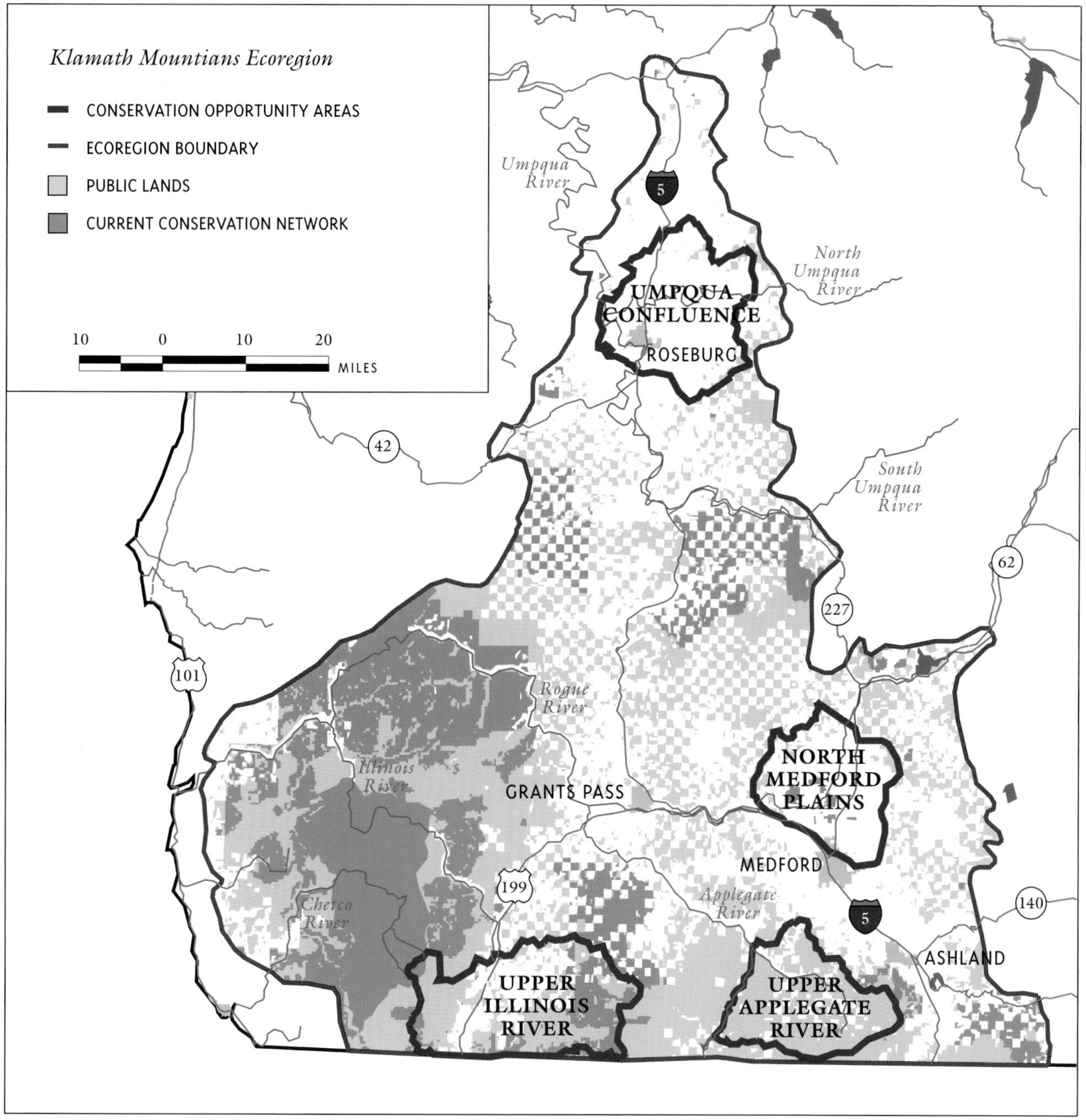

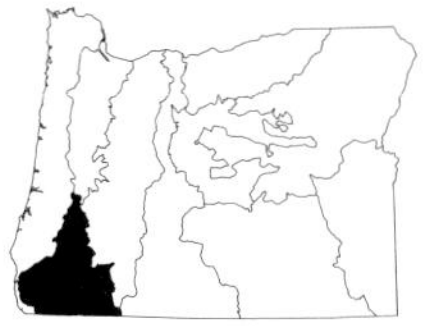

Conservation opportunities for a number of at-risk species and habitat types that are not well represented in the existing conservation network converge in urbanizing areas around two of the ecoregion's largest population centers (Medford and Roseburg). Headwaters areas of two important tributaries to the Rogue River encompass diverse conifer forests, key aquatic diversity areas, and habitat for a broad range of at-risk species.

risk species (overall number); and aquatic habitats (miles of salmonid core area, percentage in aquatic diversity areas). The results highlighted two areas — the Umpqua confluence and north Medford Plains — that are characterized by a convergence of aquatic diversity areas, large numbers of rare species, and valley bottom and mid-elevation habitat types that are not well represented in the existing conservation network.

However, the computer-based selection methodology was inadequate to address the ecoregion's conifer forests, whose diversity and complexity are masked in the coarse scale of the current vegetation map. Further assessment of these habitat types resulted in identification of two other areas with extensive conifer forests — the Upper Illinois River and Upper Applegate — that stand out because of their importance for aquatic diversity and at-risk species and their potential to complement the existing conservation network.

1. Umpqua Confluence

This area encompasses two watersheds — North Umpqua and Deer Creek — in the Roseburg area of the Umpqua Valley.

Two areas in urbanized portions of the ecoregion — this area and the North Medford Plains (see #2, adjacent) — appear to be good targets for more detailed, local-scale, conservation planning and protection efforts. Both areas contain important habitats for at-risk plants, fish, and other aquatic species, as well as significant remnants of vegetation communities not captured in the current conservation network. Management for biodiversity in these areas would complement the current conservation network, which is particularly weak in these parts of the ecoregion.

The area around Roseburg offers a number of conservation opportunities. Current efforts are targeted at slowing the spread of rural residential development, and protecting some of the oak woodlands and mixed hardwood-conifer forests east of town. Habitat conservation efforts along the North Umpqua River could benefit anadromous fish, at-risk plants, the endangered Columbian white-tailed deer, and important oak woodland and ponderosa pine forests.

At-risk plants

Arabis koehleri var. *koehleri*, Koehler's rockcress

Cheilanthes intertexta, coastal lipfern

Limnanthes gracilis var. *gracilis*, slender meadow-foam

Pellaea andromedifolia, coffee fern

Perideridia erythrorhiza, red-root yampah

Plagiobothrys hirtus, hairy popcorn flower

Sisyrinchium hitchcockii, pale blue-eyed grass

Wolffia columbiana, Columbia water-meal

At-risk animals

Bombus franklini, Franklin's bumblebee

Ceraclea vertreesi, Vertrees's ceraclean caddisfly

Clemmys marmorata marmorata, northwestern pond turtle

Lampropeltis getula, common kingsnake

Ochrotrichia vertreesi, Vertrees's ochrotrichian micro caddisfly

Odocoileus virginianus leucurus, Columbian white-tailed deer

Oncorhynchus clarki clarki, coastal cutthroat trout

Oncorhynchus kisutch ssp., coho salmon

Oregonichthys kalawatseti, Umpqua Oregon chub

Rana aurora, northern red-leged frog

Strix occidentalis caurina, northern spotted owl

2. North Medford Plains

This area encompasses the north end of the Medford Plains in the Rogue River drainage.

This area has conservation needs and opportunities similar to those found in the Roseburg area (see #1 above). Its location makes it attractive for industrial development, but the area also has significant biodiversity values. Extensive areas of jurisdictional wetlands and endangered species habitat will require either conservation or mitigation.

Existing conservation lands include Bear Creek Greenway, three Nature Conservancy preserves, the Table Rocks Area of Critical Environmental Concern, Denman Wildlife Area, and Touvelle State Park. A landscape-scale conservation plan could expand and better connect existing conservation areas, protecting the most critical areas for at-risk species.

At-risk plants

Cypripedium fasciculatum, clustered lady's-slipper

Fritillaria gentneri, Gentner's fritillaria

Limnanthes floccosa ssp. *bellingeriana*, Bellinger's meadow-foam

Limnanthes floccosa ssp. *grandiflora*, big-flowered wooly meadow-foam

Limnanthes floccosa ssp. *pumila*, dwarf meadow-foam

Lomatium cookii, Agate Desert lomatium

Microseris laciniata ssp. *detlingii*, Detling's microseris

Navarretia heterandra, Tehama navarretia

Pilularia americana, American pillwort

Plagiobothrys figuratus ssp. *corallicarpus*, coral seeded allocarya

Ranunculus austro-oreganus, southern Oregon buttercup

Wolffia columbiana, Columbia water-meal

At-risk animals

Agelaius tricolor, tricolored blackbird

Clemmys marmorata marmorata, northwestern pond turtle

Lampropeltis getula, common kingsnake

Oncorhynchus kisutch ssp., coho salmon

Oncorhynchus mykiss ssp., winter steelhead

Tadarida brasiliensis, Brazilian free-tailed bat

At-risk plants

Arabis macdonaldiana, Red Mountain rockcress

Arabis modesta, Rogue Canyon rockcress

Arctostaphylos hispidula, hairy manzanita

Calochortus howellii, Howell's mariposa lily

Camassia howellii, Howell's camassia

Carex interior, inland sedge

Cypripedium fasciculatum, clustered lady's-slipper

Epilobium oreganum, Oregon willow-herb

Erythronium howellii, Howell's adder's-tongue

Fritillaria glauca, Siskiyou fritillaria

Gentiana plurisetosa, elegant gentian

Gentiana setigera, Waldo gentian

Hastingsia atropurpurea, purple-flowered rush-lilly

Hastingsia bracteosa, large-flowered rush-lilly

Iliamna latibracteata, California globe-mallow

Lewisia leana, Lee's lewisia

Limnanthes gracilis var. *gracilis*, slender meadow-foam

Lomatium cookii, Agate Desert lomatium

Microseris howellii, Howell's microseris

Monardella glauca, monardella

Pedicularis howellii, Howell's lousewort

Perideridia erythrorhiza, red-root yampah

Salix delnortensis, Del Norte willow

Salix tracyi, Tracy's willow

Senecio hesperius, western senecio

Streptanthus howellii, Howell's streptanthus

Viola primulifolia ssp. *occidentalis*, western bog violet

3. Upper Illinois River area

Bounded on the west by the Kalmiopsis Wilderness, this area includes the upper Illinois River watershed and all or portions of Rough and Ready, Althouse, Succor, and Grayback creeks.

This area supports a number of unique plant community types and late-successional forests, as well as more than 30 at-risk plant and animal species. The area is also important for aquatic biodiversity, with four watersheds containing core areas for coastal salmonids and four aquatic diversity areas identified by the American Fisheries Society. The East Fork Illinois River watershed meets four of five ecological criteria for aquatic diversity areas: high native fish species richness, genetic refuge, reference watershed (highest ecological integrity), and connecting corridor (Bottom et al. 1993).

Ownership in the Upper Illinois River area is mixed, with most of the higher elevation forests in federal ownership. Approximately one-fourth of the federal lands are designated late-successional reserves. The upper end of the Illinois River watershed extends into California and the headwaters of the East Fork are within late-successional reserves and the Siskiyou Wilderness. Private lands in the valley bottoms are primarily pasture, agricultural lands, and small woodlots.

Opportunities exist to consolidate and strengthen the management of sites currently managed for biodiversity. For example, the Rough and Ready Creek watershed contains a state botanical wayside, a BLM area of critical environmental concern, a Forest Service special interest area and wild and scenic river, and a Nature Conservancy preserve. However, management of these sites is not yet coordinated. Cooperation among agencies could provide landscape-scale conservation benefits beyond their current site-specific focus.

At-risk animals

Aneides flavipunctatus, black salamander

Clemmys marmorata marmorata, northwestern pond turtle

Corynorhinus townsendii, Townsend's big-eared bat

Gulo gulo, wolverine

Oncorhynchus kisutch ssp., coho salmon

Oncorhynchus mykiss ssp., winter steelhead

Plethodon elongatus, Del Norte salamander

Plethodon stormi, Siskiyou Mountains salamander

Rhyacophila colonus, O'Brien rhyacophilan caddisfly

Strix occidentalis caurina, northern spotted owl

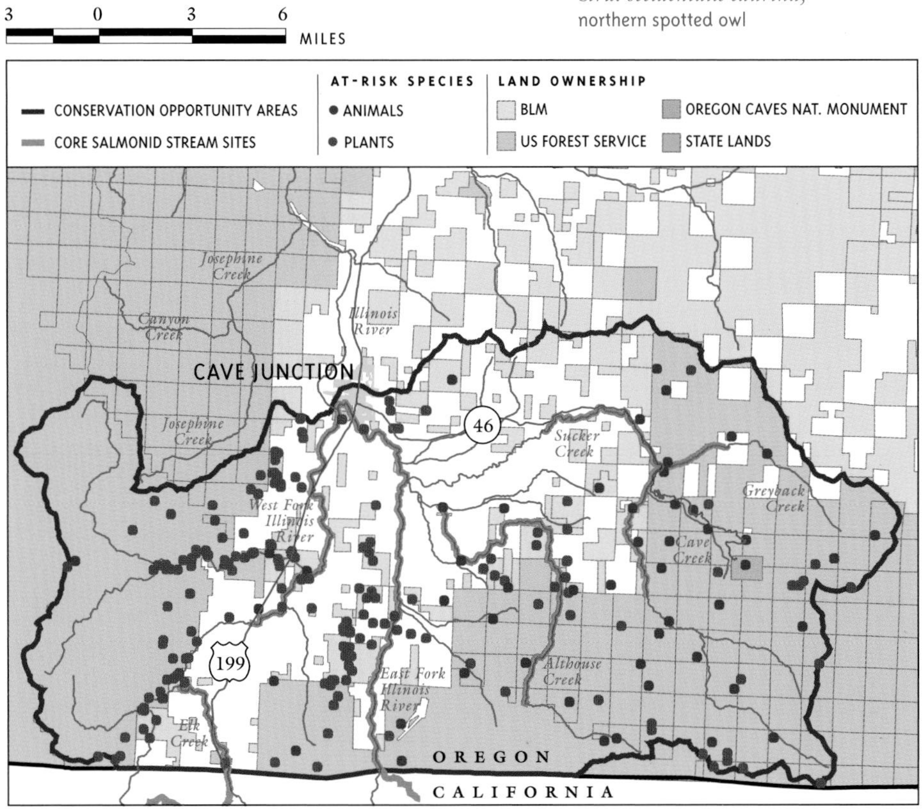

The upper end of the Illimois River watershed is home to numerous at-risk plant species found in unique communities on highly mineralized soils as well as a number of at-risk animals associated with late-successional forest habitats.

4. Upper Applegate area

This area extends from the confluence of the Little Applegate and mainstem Applegate rivers upstream to encompass all of the Little Applegate watershed and the area between Little Grayback Mountain and the mainstem Applegate River to the west.

The area contains some late-successional forests, including some unique Port Orford cedar habitats. Portions of the area have been singled out by the American Fisheries Society and the Northwest Forest Plan for their importance as aquatic habitats. More than two dozen at-risk plant and animal species are found in this area.

Under the Northwest Forest Plan, most federal lands within this area are designated as an adaptive management area, with an emphasis on testing alternative strategies and techniques for sustainable forest management.

The Applegate area has one of the state's most highly developed watershed councils, which brings together public and private stakeholders to collaborate in developing watershed management and restoration strategies.

At-risk plants

Botrychium crenulatum, crenulate grape-fern
Calochortus nudus, Shasta star-tulip
Camissonia graciliflora, slender-flowered evening-primrose
Carex serratodens, saw-tooth sedge
Cimicifuga elata, tall bugbane
Clarkia heterandra, small-fruit clarkia
Cupressus bakeri, Baker's cypress
Cypripedium fasciculatum, clustered lady's-slipper
Delphinium nudicaule, red larkspur
Epilobium siskiyouense, Siskiyou willow-herb
Fritillaria gentneri, Gentner's fritillaria
Horkelia hendersonii, Henderson's horkelia
Isopyrum stipitatum, dwarf isopyrum
Lewisia leana, Lee's lewisia
Lupinus aridus ssp. *ashlandensis*, Mt. Ashland lupine
Mimulus bolanderi, Bolander's monkeyflower
Rhamnus ilicifolia, redberry
Sedum oblanceolatum, Applegate stonecrop
Tauschia howellii, Howell's tauschia

At-risk animals

Aneides flavipunctatus, black salamander
Ascaphus truei, tailed frog
Clemmys marmorata marmorata, northwestern pond turtle
Oncorhynchus kisutch ssp., coho salmon
Oncorhynchus mykiss ssp., winter steelhead
Plethodon stormi, Siskiyou Mountains salamander
Strix occidentalis caurina, northern spotted owl
Tinodes siskiyou, Siskiyou caddisfly

West Cascades Ecoregion

The West Cascades Ecoregion extends from the Columbia River Gorge south almost to the California border. This mountainous, heavily forested ecoregion is bordered on the west by the agricultural lands and woodlands of the Willamette Valley. Further south, are the drier forests and valleys of the Klamath Mountains. To the east, it spills over the crest of the Cascade Mountains to the ponderosa pine forests of the East Cascades Ecoregion.

The western slopes of the Cascade Range feature long ridges with steep sides and wide, glaciated valleys. Most of the rivers draining the northern two-thirds of the ecoregion flow into the Willamette Valley and then to the Columbia River system; the southern third drains to the Pacific Ocean through the Umpqua and Rogue river systems.

Climate varies with elevation and, to a lesser extent, north to south. Higher elevations receive heavy winter snow packs. The drier southern half has a fire regime similar to the Klamath Mountains, with frequent lightning-caused fires. In the northern half, the natural fire regime has historically produced less frequent but more severe fires (USDA/USDI 1994).

The ecoregion is almost entirely forested, and the flora and fauna are similar to those of the Coast Range Ecoregion. Douglas-fir hemlock forests dominate large areas up to elevations of about 3,300 feet. However, most of the previously harvested forests of the lowlands and lower slopes are classified as mixed conifer-deciduous forests, with young Douglas-fir and western hemlock forests found in a mosaic of

Almost 40 percent of the ecoregion is in areas with biodiversity management ratings of 8-10 — the highest percentage of any ecoregion in Oregon.

Most of these lands are within a string of wilderness areas along the crest of the Cascades, Crater Lake National Park, and the federal government's network of late-successional reserves, which are primarily found in mid-elevation forests.

River bottom valleys and low-elevation forests are almost completely absent from the existing network of conservation lands. The major exception is in the Columbia River Gorge, where a national scenic area managed by the U.S. Forest Service includes habitat for high numbers of rare and endemic plant species.

MT. HOOD

DETROIT ▲

MT. JEFFERSON WILDERNESS

THREE SISTERS WILDERNESS

OAKRIDGE

DIAMOND PEAK WILDERNESS

CRATER LAKE NATIONAL PARK

Percent of West Cascades Ecoregion in current conservation network

☐ CATEGORY 8 (1.5%)
▨ CATEGORY 9 (21.9%)
▨ CATEGORY 10 (10.0%)
■ CITIES

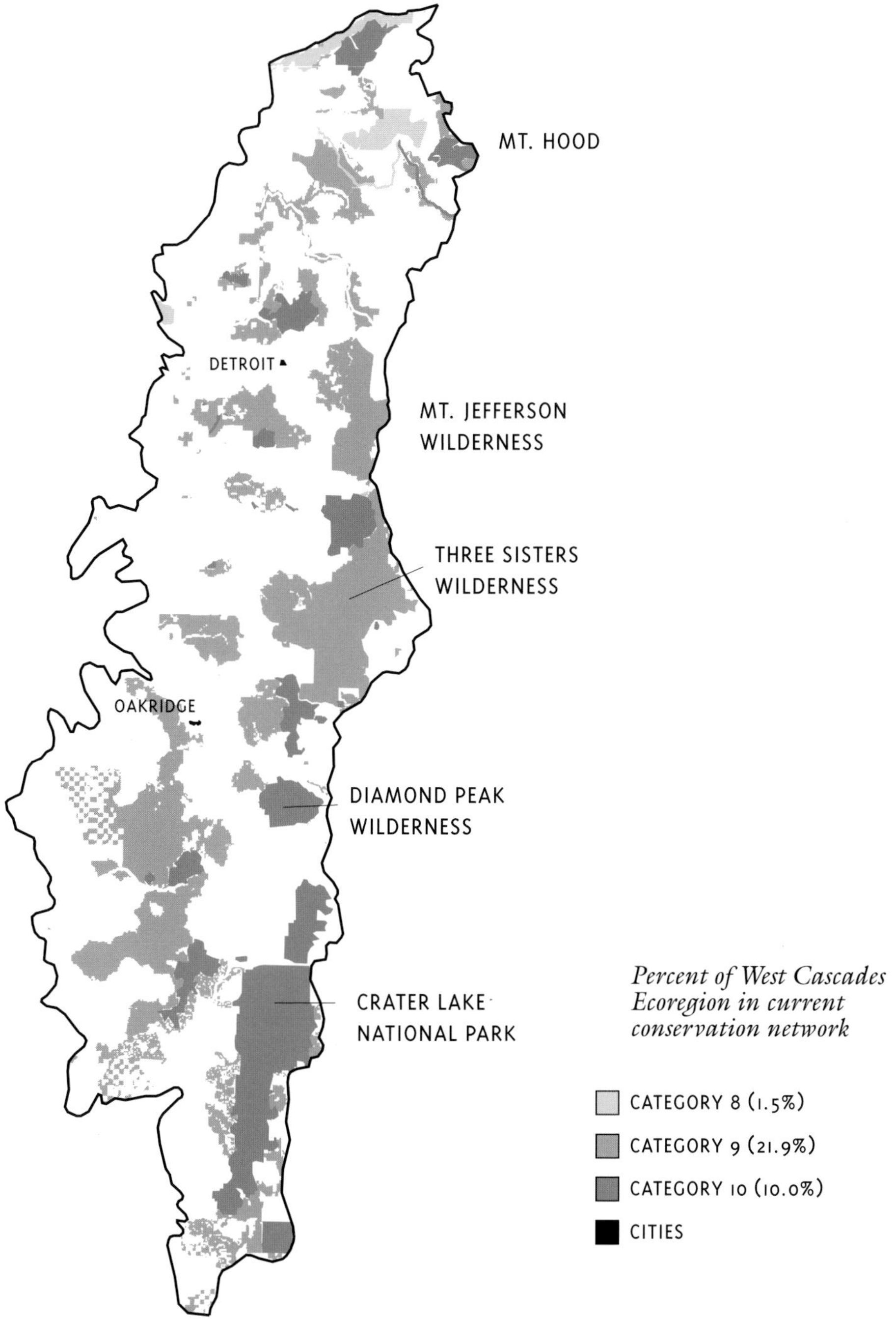

hardwood species such as bigleaf maple and red alder. Silver fir-mountain hemlock forests occur at mid-elevations. At higher elevations, alpine parklands dominate with patches of forest interspersed with shrub and meadow communities. Alpine areas feature a variety of communities ranging from dwarf shrubs, grasses, and forbs to rocks and permanent snowfields.

Conifer forests have long been the foundation of the local economy in the West Cascades, and decades of clearcutting put the ecoregion at the center of controversies over the spotted owl, logging of old growth forests, and management of federal lands. Most of the ecoregion's human population is found in small towns in the river valleys where increasing recreation use supplements the traditional timber-based economy.

VEGETATION ANALYSIS

Unlike the forests of central and eastern Oregon, a century of timber harvests in West Cascades forests has done little to change the overall distribution or abundance of vegetation types. However, the structure and composition of these forests have been altered greatly across much of the ecoregion. More than half the acreage historically classified as Douglas-fir forest shows significant fragmentation by relatively recent timber harvests. Few old growth forests remain in lower elevation areas, which are primarily in private ownership. Federal lands contain substantial acreages of mature and late-successional forests, but almost 95 percent are at elevations higher than 2,000 feet (USDA/USDI 1994) and many are heavily fragmented.

Several of the highest priorities for biodiversity conservation in the West Cascades Ecoregion have been addressed through the Northwest Forest Plan adopted by the Clinton administration for management of federal forest lands within the range of the northern spotted owl. Although focused on the spotted owl, the plan was intended to address the needs of a vast array of species affected by the loss and fragmentation of old growth forests. More than 1,000 species of plants, animals, and fungi closely associated with late-successional and old growth forest ecosystems are analyzed in the plan. The federal plan is expected to provide at least 50 percent probability that populations of most species will stabilize with either good or only moderately limited distributions on public lands. For the majority of species, the probability of stable, well-distributed populations is estimated at 75 percent (USDA/USDI 1994).

Past wilderness designations and the Northwest Forest Plan's late-successional reserves have resulted in almost all of the West Cascades' dominant forest vegetation types being well represented on lands where management emphasizes biodiversity values.

Percentages of major forest types found within areas rated 8-10 on the biodiversity management scale include: Western hemlock-Douglas-fir, 31 percent; mountain hemlock-Shasta fir, 65 percent;

mountain hemlock-Pacific silver fir, 58 percent; Douglas-fir-sugar pine-Ponderosa pine, 20 percent; Pacific silver fir, 45 percent.

As a result, remaining priorities for broad-scale biodiversity conservation in the West Cascades are focused on riparian habitats and several less widely distributed vegetation types historically found along the ecoregion's western edges such as bottomland hardwood forests and oak savannas and woodlands.

Despite major improvements in streamside protections on federal lands under the Northwest Forest Plan, riparian habitats remain a conservation priority because of their importance for a wide range of terrestrial and aquatic species. Almost 40 percent of the perennial stream miles on the Willamette National Forest were adjacent to clearcuts or roads in the early 1980s. As a result, most streams lack adequate large woody debris (USDA/FS 1990b). While riparian habitats in this ecoregion may be more resilient than those east of the Cascades, habitat modifications impact a broad range of species, including resident and anadromous fish, invertebrates, amphibians, birds, and mammals.

North Fork Willamette River
Photographer, Larry N. Olson

Bottomland hardwood forests, formerly found in the lowlands along the ecoregion's rivers, have declined more than 95 percent from pre-European settlement levels, primarily as a result of agricultural development, urbanization, and construction of dams and reservoirs. Very little of what remains is managed for biodiversity values.

Oak savannas and woodlands — found mostly on the margins of the Willamette, Umpqua, and Rogue valleys and the Columbia Gorge — have declined by almost 95 percent. As a result of changes in fire frequency and intensity, Douglas-fir now dominates in many of these areas, and many of the open woodlands have been converted to forests.

AT-RISK SPECIES

Animals. The forested mountain ranges of Oregon and especially the West Cascades have been important to three mammal species that have large home ranges and are sensitive to fragmentation and disturbance: fisher *(Martes pennanti)*, American marten *(Martes americana)*, and wolverine *(Gulo gulo)*. Despite their broad distributions, these species are considered rare throughout much of the coterminous United States. Observations are rare in the West Cascades, but all four species probably persist in some areas of the ecoregion. How they will fare under the Northwest Forest Plan remains to be seen.

Several at-risk frogs and salamanders are associated with older uncut forests, usually those with cold, clear streams and springs and seeps. These species include the tailed frog *(Ascaphus truei)*; northern red-legged frog *(Rana aurora)*; Cascade seep salamander *(Rhyacotriton cascadae)*; Oregon slender salamander *(Batrachoseps wrighti)*; and Cope's giant salamander *(Dicamptodon copei)* (Marshall 1996).

Plants. A number of plant species in the West Cascades are considered rare, including several in the Columbia River Gorge and others that occur in mid- and low-elevation areas. One of the rarest and most specialized forest species in the West Cascades is the fuzzy sandozi *(Oxyporus nobilissimus)*, a fungus that parasitizes noble fir and can grow to four feet in diameter. It is only known to occur at a few sites in the central Cascades of Washington and at just one site in Oregon. Tall bugbane *(Cimicifuga elata)* occurs in forested habitats on north slopes at low to moderate elevations from southern British Columbia to Douglas County, Oregon.

While many species are endemic to a state or ecoregion, it is rare that an entire genus is endemic. Fragrant kalmiopsis *(Kalmiopsis fragrans)*, which occurs in Douglas County on small rocky outcrops within the forest, is one of two species in a genus found only in the West Cascades and the Klamath Mountains. Its limited distribution raises concerns that it could be inadvertently, and perhaps irrevocably, impacted during logging operations.

Pale blue-eyed grass *(Sisyrinchium sarmentosum)* occurs in meadows in southern Washington and in the northern Oregon Cascades at mid-level elevations. In Washington, much of the habitat is on private lands where development is a potential threat. In Oregon, seven populations currently exist on the Mt. Hood National Forest. Grazing and increased recreation uses are potential threats.

AQUATIC SPECIES ANALYSIS

Aquatic habitats have been altered and degraded throughout much of the ecoregion due to logging, road building, and construction of dams and reservoirs.

Native anadromous fish populations in the Willamette Basin portion of the ecoregion have declined dramatically over the past 50 years and have been largely replaced by hatchery fish (USDA/FS 1990b). The strongest native salmonid populations in this part of the ecoregion are the McKenzie River's spring chinook. The river also supports the only bull trout (Salvelinus confluentus) population found west of the Cascades (Marshall 1996).

In the southern half of the ecoregion, the upper portions of the South Umpqua and North Umpqua rivers are among the few remaining strongholds for summer and winter steelhead. These areas also provide important habitat for spring chinook salmon and sea-run cutthroat trout. The Umpqua River system supports the only remaining healthy coastal population of summer steelhead on the entire West Coast (Huntington et al. 1996).

The American Fisheries Society (Bottom et al. 1993) has identified half a dozen clusters of aquatic diversity areas in this ecoregion, most of them headwaters systems subject to a relatively high level of habitat protection under the Northwest Forest Plan and earlier wilderness designations.

SUMMARY OF CONSERVATION ISSUES

Major issues for biodiversity conservation in the West Cascades include:

- Although the Northwest Forest Plan holds considerable promise for stabilization and perhaps recovery for many of the species associated with mature and old growth forests, decades may be required to assess the effectiveness in conserving the region's native biological diversity.
- Ownership of lower elevation forests is fragmented, hindering coordinated management of public and private lands to address conservation needs.
- Opportunities to restore bottomland hardwood forests are limited.
- Oak savannas and woodlands are likely to continue to decline because of the difficulties involved in restoring natural fire regimes.
- Maintenance of current strongholds for native salmonids is critical for aquatic biodiversity.

A botanical treasure chest

Cutting across the uppermost portions of the West and East Cascades ecoregions, the Columbia River Gorge is a botanical treasure chest. Within the gorge's relatively small area — less than a mile from the river's edge to the top of the towering cliffs along most of its 50-mile length — climate and elevation changes create a high diversity of habitat conditions. Glaciation during the last ice age and a series of subsequent floods added to the gorge's diversity.

More than 800 species of native plants are found in the gorge — nearly one-quarter of all plant species found in Oregon. Fifteen plant species are endemic to the gorge and vicinity.

Several of these endemic plant species are also rare. Oregon sullivantia *(Sullivantia oregana)* grows in the spray zone around waterfalls at lower elevations in the west end of the gorge. Howell's daisy *(Erigeron howellii)* also occurs in the west end of the gorge in shady habitats on steep, north-facing slopes. Barrett's penstemon *(Penstemon barrettiae)* grows on both sides of the Columbia River on cliffs and talus slopes near Mosier and Bonneville Dam. Wormskiold sage *(Artemisia campestris* var. *wormskioldii)* once grew on the rocky banks of the Columbia River throughout the east end of the gorge. Most of the plant's suitable habitat was flooded behind Bonneville Dam. The only remaining site in Oregon is on Miller Island, just a few feet above water level. Violet suksdorfia *(Suksdorfia violacea)* occurs on rocky slopes in the central portion of the gorge.

CONSERVATION OPPORTUNITY AREAS

The Oregon Biodiversity Project identified two areas in the West Cascades Ecoregion that appear to offer good opportunities to address biodiversity conservation needs.

The ecoregion's major conifer forest vegetation types are already well represented in the existing conservation network through land management designations under the federal Northwest Forest Plan. As a result, the project's analysis focused most heavily on aquatic diversity areas, salmonid habitats, and areas with concentrations of at-risk species. The two areas selected appear to offer the best opportunities to address these values through broad-scale conservation efforts.

Opal Creek ancient forest
Photographer, Larry N. Olson

Federal land management already emphasizes biodiversity conservation in much of the ecoregion's conifer forests, so conservation opportunity areas in the West Cascades focus primarily on aquatic habitat values and at-risk species found outside the existing conservation network.

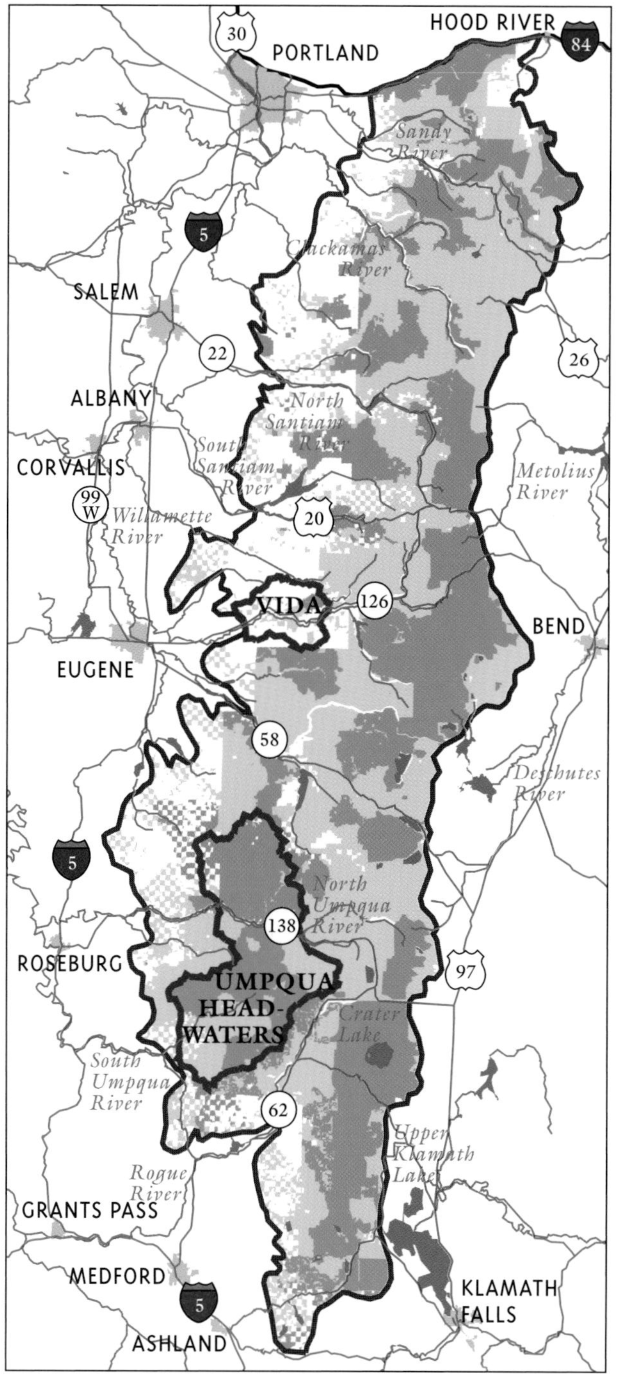

West Cascades Ecoregion

- CONSERVATION OPPORTUNITY AREAS
- ECOREGION BOUNDARY
- PUBLIC LANDS
- CURRENT CONSERVATION NETWORK

10 0 10 20 30 MILES

1. Umpqua Headwaters area

This area includes clusters of aquatic diversity areas in the headwaters of the South Umpqua River and several tributaries of the North Umpqua River below Toketee Falls.

This area encompasses some of the most important salmonid habitat in the West Cascades Ecoregion and also supports a number of at-risk plant and animal species. Substantial portions of the federal lands in this area are within late-successional reserves. The westernmost portions of the North Fork Umpqua area contain a checkerboard of private and BLM lands that may be candidates for land exchanges to consolidate conservation lands in these key watersheds.

Two watersheds in the North Umpqua portion of the area, Steamboat and Canton creeks, have been identified as the most important areas for spawning and rearing habitat for the Umpqua system's summer steelhead (Rahr pers. com. 1997). The Umpqua is one of only two river systems on the entire West Coast that still supports healthy populations of summer steelhead (Huntington et al. 1996). The North Umpqua also includes spring chinook core areas, and supports populations of sea-run cutthroat trout and winter steelhead.

The headwaters systems of the South Umpqua River support healthy stocks of winter steelhead and spring chinook. Most of the streams in this area have been designated as core areas for both species (State of Oregon 1997).

At-risk plants

Asplenium septentrionale, grass-fern

Cimicifuga elata, tall bugbane

Cypripedium fasciculatum, clustered lady's-slipper

Frasera umpquaensis, Umpqua swertia

Fritillaria glauca, Siskiyou fritillaria

Iliamna latibracteata, California globe-mallow

Kalmiopsis fragrans, fragrant kalmiopsis

Limnanthes gracilis var. *gracilis*, slender meadow-foam

Viola primulifolia ssp. *occidentalis*, western bog violet

At-risk animals

Apatania tavala, Cascades apatanian caddisfly

Clemmys marmorata marmorata, northwestern pond turtle

Corynorhintus townsendii, Townsend's big-eared bat

Eobrachycentrus gelidae, Mt. Hood brachycentrid caddisfly

Falco peregrinus, American peregrine falcon

Farula reapiri, Tombstone Prairie farulan caddisfly

Gulo gulo, wolverine

Histrionicus histrionicus, harlequin duck

Martes pennanti, fisher

Oncorhynchus mykiss ssp., winter steelhead

Oncorhynchus clarki clarki, coastal cutthroat trout

Oncorhynchus kisutch ssp., coho salmon

Oregonichthys kalawatseti, Umpqua Oregon chub

Rana aurora, northern red-legged frog

Strix occidentalis caurina, northern spotted owl

2. Vida area

This area includes the lower McKenzie River watershed around Vida, extending from the ecoregion's western boundary upstream nearly to Blue River.

This area encompasses two small aquatic diversity areas and a mixture of old and young forests that support a number of at-risk plant and animal species.

Designated an adaptive management area under the Northwest Forest Plan, the lands around Vida include a mixture of Forest Service, BLM, private industrial, and state ownerships. Management of federal lands within the Blue River Adaptive Management Area is intended to emphasize intensive research on ecosystem and landscape processes and its application to forest management.

Because this area is outside the network of late-successional reserves and includes a mix of public and private lands at relatively low elevations, it presents unique challenges and opportunities for cooperative management to address biodiversity conservation needs across multiple ownerships.

At-risk plants

Cimicifuga elata, tall bugbane

Nephroma occulatum, lichen

At-risk animals

Ascaphus truei, tailed frog

Clemmys marmorata marmorata, northwestern pond turtle

Farula reapiri, Tombstone Prairie farulan caddisfly

Histrionicus histrionicus, harlequin duck

Rhyacotriton cascadae, Cascade seep salamander

Salvelinus confluentus, bull trout

Strix occidentalis caurina, northern spotted owl

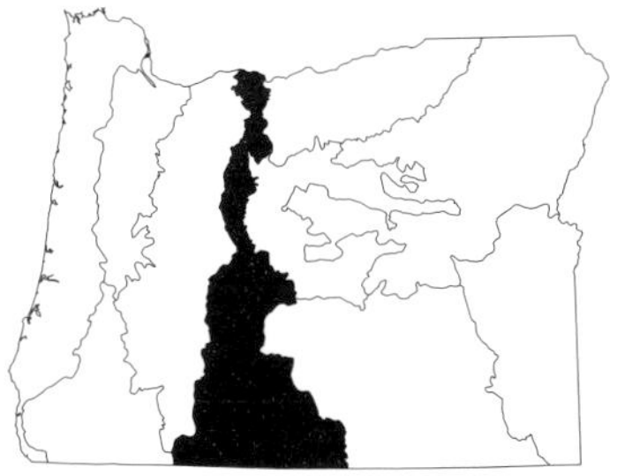

East Cascades Ecoregion

The East Cascades Ecoregion is an ecological transition zone that extends from below the crest of the Cascade Range east to where the ponderosa pine zone meets the sagebrush-juniper steppe. The ecoregion also extends north into Washington and south into California. In Oregon, this ecoregion includes three distinct sections: the eastern slopes of the Cascade Range; the Klamath Basin; and the mountainous area to the southeast, which bulges eastward into the Basin and Range Ecoregion.

The eastern slopes of the Cascades are drier, less steep, and cut by fewer streams than the west side of the mountain range. They are also covered predominantly by conifer forests growing on volcanic soils. Much of the southern half of the ecoregion is covered with a layer of pumice — ranging in depth from a few inches to 50 feet — deposited by the eruption of Mount Mazama. These deep ashes support vast climax forests of lodgepole pine. The northern two-thirds of the East Cascades is drained by the Deschutes River system, which includes a series of large lakes and reservoirs near its headwaters. The southern third is drained by the Klamath River, which flows south and west into California.

The Klamath Basin, which extends into the Modoc Plateau in California, is a broad, relatively flat mid-elevation valley that historically supported a vast expanse of lakes and marshes. Oregon's largest lake, Upper Klamath Lake, is the biggest remnant of this wetland system. Most of the basin's wetlands have been drained and converted to agriculture.

Less than four percent of the ecoregion is in areas with biodiversity management ratings of 8-10. Only a handful of native vegetation types, none of them widespread, have more than five percent of their distribution within areas rated 8-10.

Most of the current conservation network consists of small blocks of native habitat scattered across the ecoregion. Late-successional reserves established under the federal government's Northwest Forest Plan spill over the crest of the Cascades to include some national forest lands within the range of the northern spotted owl.

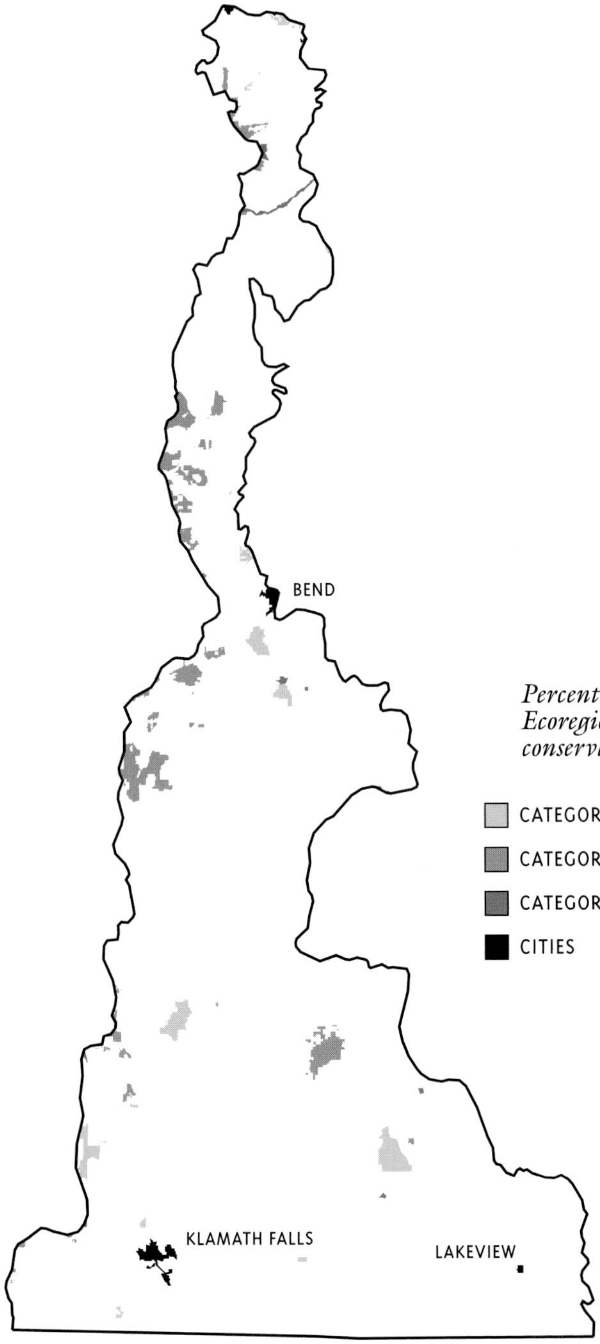

The Gearhart Mountain Wilderness encompasses a block of high-elevation forests on the southeastern edge of ecoregion. Remnants of the Klamath Basin's large historic marshes are found within national wildlife refuges at Upper Klamath Lake and Klamath Marsh, and in The Nature Conservancy's Sycan Marsh Preserve. The Columbia River Gorge National Scenic Area and the Newberry Craters Volcanic National Monument both include relatively intact native habitats that make significant contributions to the ecoregion's biodiversity.

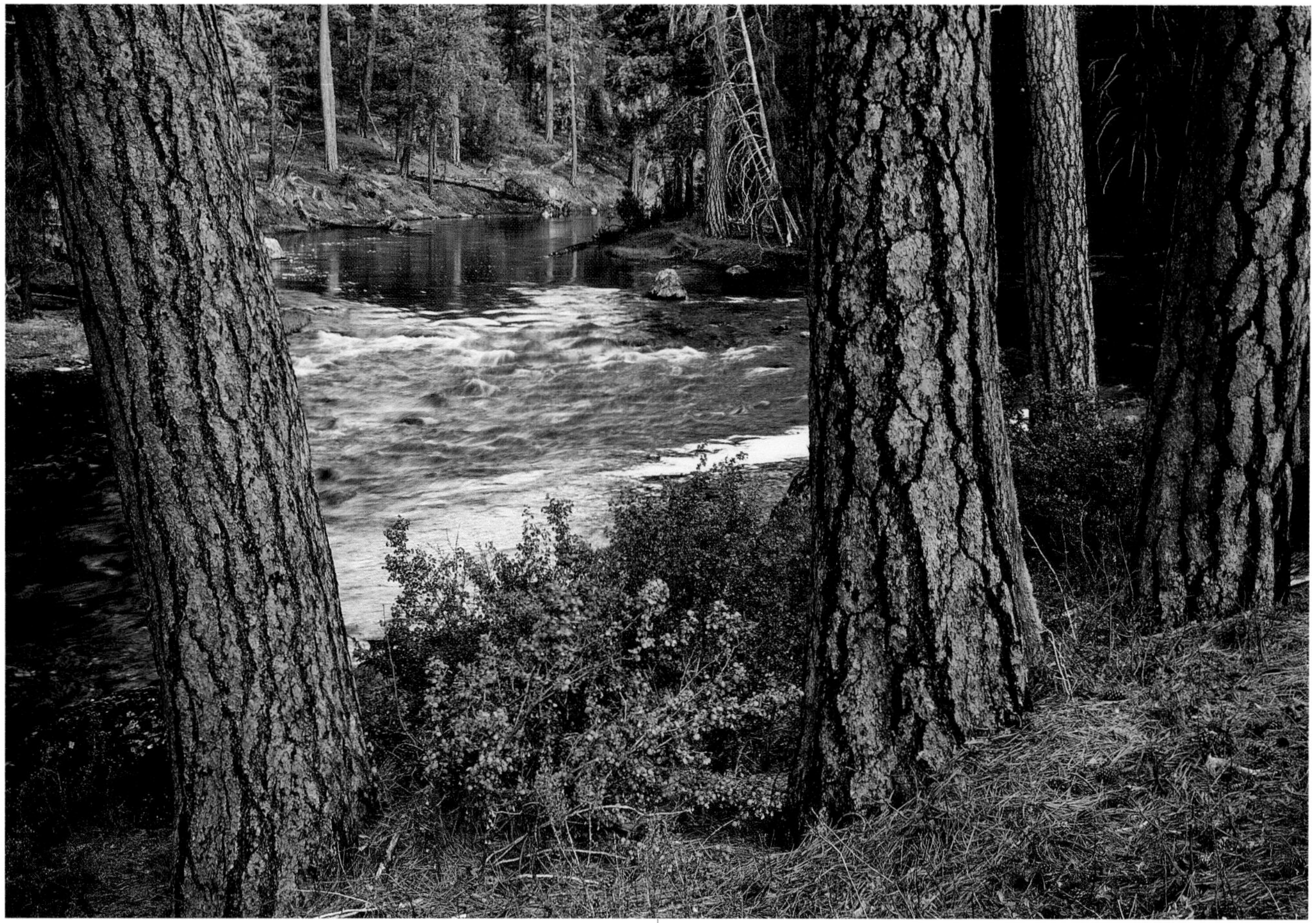

Ponderosa pines along Sycan River
Photographer, Larry N. Olson

The mountainous area to the southeast lacks a generally accepted name, but includes a series of peaks and ridges extending from Paulina Peak near Bend southward through the headwaters of the Williamson, Sprague, and Chewaucan rivers to the Warner Mountains east of Lakeview. These mountains are generally forested, but the valleys and flats between them include large marshes, irrigated meadows and pastures, and arid juniper and sagebrush steppes.

The ecoregion's human population is concentrated in Hood River, Bend, and Klamath Falls. Forest products, agriculture, recreation, and tourism are the biggest contributors to local economies.

VEGETATION ANALYSIS

Three vegetation types — ponderosa pine woodlands, oak woodlands and savannas, and wetlands — stand out as conservation priorities based on an assessment of historic changes and current management status.

Ponderosa pine woodlands have declined by at least two-thirds, according to a comparison of current and historic vegetation maps. Few unharvested areas of old growth remain, and less than five percent of the ecoregion's ponderosa pine-dominated forests and woodlands are found on lands in biodiversity management categories 8-10.

Decades of timber harvest, livestock grazing, and fire suppression have altered the structure of most ponderosa pine forests. The introduction of selective harvesting techniques in the 1940s encouraged the growth of shade-tolerant species (USDA/FS 1990a). In combination with extensive livestock grazing and fire suppression, these practices eventually led to a shift in many areas from ponderosa pine forests and woodlands to mixed conifer forests made up of denser stands of smaller trees, more vulnerable to attack by insects and disease.

Harvest strategies on public lands changed in the mid-1970s, when the U.S. Forest Service shifted to clearcutting. Public outcry led the Deschutes National Forest to shift to uneven-aged management in the mid-1980s (USDA/FS 1990a), but clearcutting continued on other national forests and private lands. By 1988, less than seven percent of the remaining ponderosa pine habitat in the East Cascades was classified in the current vegetation map as having only incidental or no recent timber harvest. More than one-third was classified as forests with patches of clearcuts, and almost 60 percent were classified as clearcuts with patches of remaining forest.

Loss of mature and old growth forests has led to declines among a number of species dependent on these habitats, including small forest carnivores and more than 20 species of birds, ranging from waterfowl and raptors to woodpeckers and songbirds (Puchy and Marshall 1993).

Oak woodlands and savannas, historically found primarily on the north end of the ecoregion, have declined by more than two-thirds as a result of conversion to agriculture, urban development, and fire suppression. As in other ecoregions, these changes have had significant impacts on an entire suite of wildlife species. The oak woodlands east of Mount Hood provide some of the state's last major nesting areas for Lewis' woodpecker *(Melanerpes lewis)*, which depends on habitats with large Oregon white oak trees and large ponderosa pine snags (Puchy and Marshall 1993). Livestock grazing and fire suppression have led to the establishment of conifers in many areas formerly dominated by oak. In other areas fire suppression may have led to expansion of oaks into former shrub steppe habitat.

Wetlands in the great shallow lake and marsh systems of the upper Klamath Basin have been reduced by at least 85-90 percent (USDI/FWS 1988) as a result of drainage and conversion to agriculture and urban uses. Remaining wetlands in the Klamath Basin support one of the largest concentrations of waterfowl in North America, with up to six million ducks and a half-million geese passing through annually and peaks of more than one million birds during fall and spring migration (USDI/FWS 1994). The basin's wetlands also provide important breeding habitat for dozens of species of waterbirds. A number of major wetland restoration projects have begun in the Klamath Basin in recent years, including large-scale projects around Upper Klamath and Agency lakes and at The Nature Conservancy's Sycan Marsh Preserve.

Some of the higher elevation wetlands in the central portion of the ecoregion appear largely intact, but extensive introduction of non-native fish may have substantially altered these ecosystems. Wetland communities dominated by lodgepole pine have experienced significant losses due to residential and commercial development in the LaPine and Chiloquin areas. Substantial loss and degradation of wetlands have also occurred in upper portions of the Deschutes River system due to construction and operation of reservoirs for irrigation storage. The reservoirs flooded some former meadows, and the reversal of the natural hydrologic regime has severely degraded downstream riparian wetlands (USDA/FS 1990a).

AT-RISK SPECIES

The majority of at-risk species in the ecoregion are associated with wetland and riparian habitats. Extensive conversion of wetlands to agriculture and the withdrawal, diversion, and impoundment of water for irrigation and power generation have contributed to species declines.

Animals. At-risk bird species are mostly restricted to wetlands. These include yellow rail *(Coturnicops noveboracensis)*, upland sandpiper *(Bartramia longicauda)*, yellow-billed cuckoo *(Coccyzus americanus)*, greater sandhill crane *(Grus canadensis tabida)*, western grebe *(Aechmophorous occidentalis)*, and red-necked grebe *(Podiceps grisegena)*. The Klamath Basin is also known for the largest concentration of wintering bald eagles *(Haliaeetus leucocephalus)* in the continental United States.

The gray wolf *(Canis lupus)*, which once occurred throughout Oregon, was last seen in the state near Sycan Marsh in 1960. Wolverine *(Gulo gulo)* occurs in the ecoregion at high elevations in relatively undisturbed areas of the Deschutes and Winema national forests and at Crater Lake National Park.

Impacts to the ecoregion's hydrologic regime have had far-reaching effects on aquatic invertebrates and fish. Among fish, the most significant declines have occurred among Lost River and shortnose suckers *(Deltistes luxatus* and *Chasmistes brevirostris)*. Once an important food

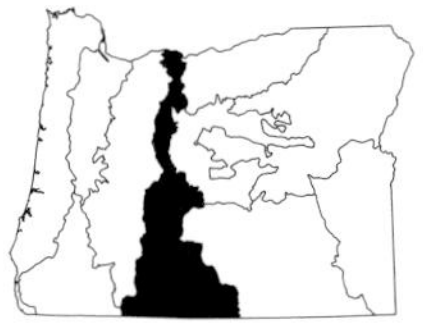

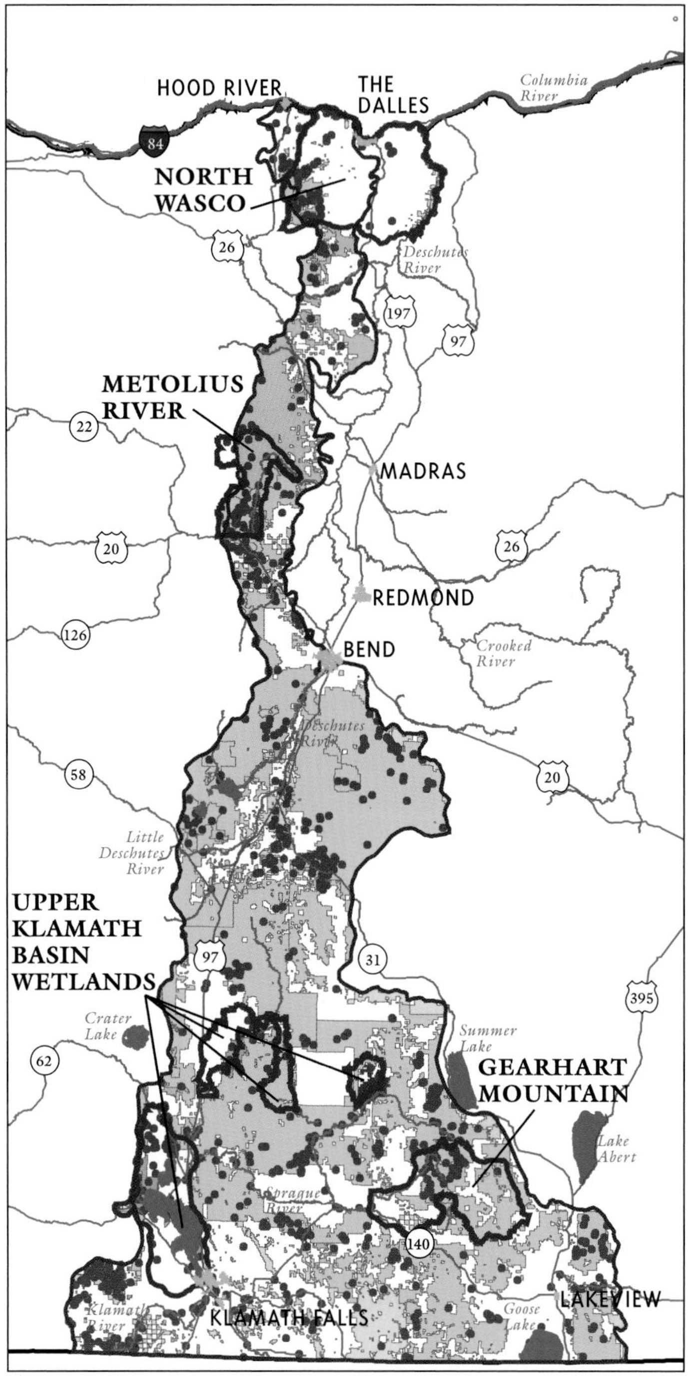

CONSERVATION OPPORTUNITY AREAS

ECOREGION BOUNDARY

At-risk Species

- ANIMALS
- PLANTS

Land Ownership

- BLM
- US FOREST SERVICE
- OTHER FEDERAL LANDS
- STATE LANDS
- TRIBAL LANDS
- NATURE CONSERVANCY

10 0 10 20 MILES

Locations of at-risk plant and animals recorded in the Oregon Natural Heritage Program's data bases are shown in relation to land ownership and the Oregon Biodiversity Project's conservation opportunity areas.

More than a century of logging in the East Cascades has left few large blocks of ponderosa pine forests that have not been impacted by timber harvests.

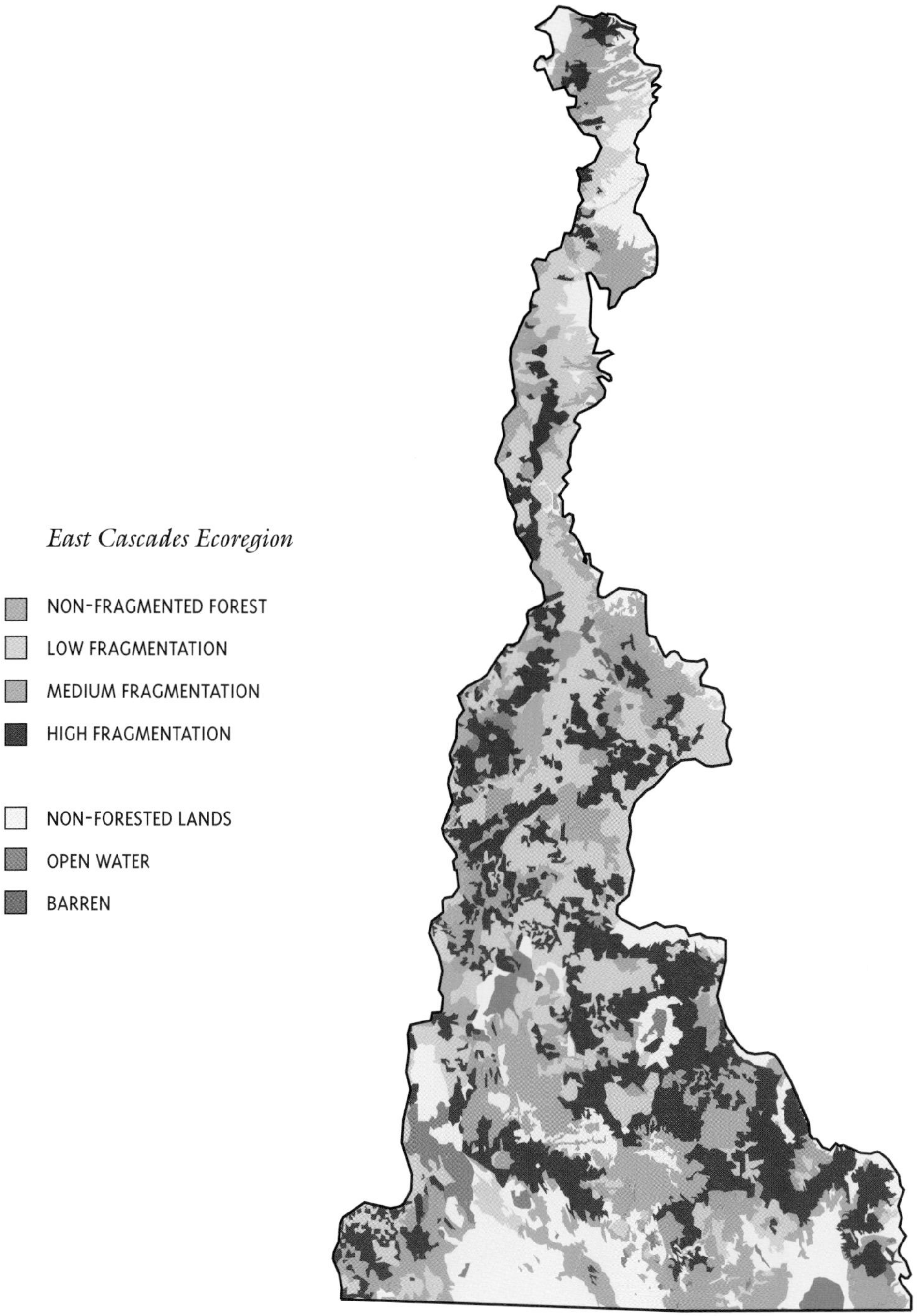

source for the Klamath Tribe, these fish were abundant enough to support a commercial cannery until the 1960s. Today, they are considered at risk throughout their range due primarily to low survival rates among juvenile fish (Marshall 1996). Construction of dams and diversion structures, and reduction of streamside vegetation due to grazing and agricultural conversion, have degraded stream reaches with devastating effects to juvenile fish rearing habitat. The result is that juveniles enter Klamath Lake earlier and smaller than they have historically, making them vulnerable to predators. Moreover, today's lake has higher pH levels due to non-point source pollution runoff from surrounding agricultural lands, which can be toxic to the young fish.

Recent inventories of springs in the area above Upper Klamath Lake have identified at least five species of freshwater snails found nowhere else.

Plants. At-risk plant species in the East Cascades Ecoregion occur in a variety of habitats, from low-elevation riparian areas to alpine habitats. Applegate's milk-vetch *(Astragalus applegatei)*, Peck's penstemon *(Penstemon peckii)*, and pumice grapefern *(Botrychium pumicola)* are endemic to this ecoregion. The Nature Conservancy's Ewauna Flat Preserve, located in Klamath Falls, hosts 99 percent of the remaining Applegate's milk-vetch. Peck's penstemon is found in the central portion of the ecoregion around Sisters and Bend. Pumice grapefern, generally limited to barren pumice at high elevations, has recently been found on dry pumice in lodgepole pine-bitterbrush forests at lower elevations, where it is much more susceptible to human disturbance.

AQUATIC SPECIES ANALYSIS

Aquatic habitats have been degraded across much of this ecoregion. Dams on the mainstem Klamath River block anadromous fish access to the upper Klamath Basin. Impoundment and diversion of stream flows for irrigation have fundamentally altered the hydrology of the Deschutes River system. Normal flows on the Deschutes near Wickiup Reservoir are about 1,500 cubic feet per second, but storage for irrigation limits releases to as little as 20 cubic feet per second during winter and early spring, with major impacts on in-stream and riparian habitats (USDA/FS 1990a).

Timber harvests and grazing have impacted habitats used by native bull trout *(Salvelinus confluentus)*, which spawn and rear primarily in cold and relatively pristine waters in headwaters systems in the Klamath Basin (ICBEMP 1997b). More than a century of livestock grazing has degraded riparian habitats in the ecoregion's mountainous southeastern corner. Within the past decade, almost two-thirds of the Fremont National Forest's riparian areas on intermittent streams were rated as low quality, to the point where many were difficult to distinguish from adjacent uplands (USDA/FS 1989). Loss of wetlands has contributed to the at-risk status of a number of species including Lost River and shortnose suckers.

Despite these impacts, several areas in the East Cascades retain habitat values that make them especially significant for aquatic biodiversity. In the northern half of the ecoregion, the American Fisheries Society has identified three major clusters of aquatic diversity areas: one in northern Wasco County, another that encompasses a large portion of the Warm Springs Indian Reservation, and a third in the Metolius River watershed (Bottom et al. 1993). The Metolius area supports some of the Northwest's strongest remaining populations of bull trout, and White River and Squaw Creek are considered strongholds for redband trout (ICBEMP 1997b).

In the southern half of the ecoregion, aquatic diversity areas identified by the American Fisheries Society are clustered around Upper Klamath Lake, the upper Williamson River, and the headwaters of the Sprague and Chewaucan rivers. The Klamath Basin is a "hot spot" for narrowly endemic fish species (species indigenous to the local area with a very limited distribution), with up to six of these species found in a single watershed (ICBEMP 1997b).

Areas particularly important to other wetland-dependent species include the arc of lakes and marshes that extends from the lower end of the Klamath Basin through Upper Klamath and Agency lakes and up the Williamson River. Goose Lake is an important migratory waterfowl area and supports a number of endemic fish species, and Sycan Marsh provides breeding habitat for an impressive diversity of waterbirds.

SUMMARY OF CONSERVATION ISSUES

Major issues for biodiversity conservation in the East Cascades include:

- Timber harvests, livestock grazing, and fire suppression have fundamentally altered the character and distribution of the region's historic ponderosa pine forests and woodlands. Few significant blocks of old growth ponderosa pine remain in this ecoregion.
- Many oak woodlands in the northern end of the ecoregion have been fragmented and converted to other uses, but remaining oak woodlands represent one of the few opportunities for long-term management to conserve these habitats.
- Riparian habitats have been degraded throughout much of the ecoregion.
- Storage and diversion of water for agricultural uses present serious conflicts with fish, wildlife, and habitat conservation needs in the upper Deschutes and Klamath river basins.
- The vast majority of wetlands have been lost or degraded. Remaining wetland systems provide critical habitat for migratory birds of the Pacific Flyway and support most of the region's at-risk animal species.
- Rapid population growth and increasing recreational uses intensify pressures on sensitive habitats and increase the urgency of habitat conservation efforts.

Big Marsh
Photographer, Larry N. Olson

CONSERVATION OPPORTUNITY AREAS

The Oregon Biodiversity Project identified four areas in the East Cascades Ecoregion that appear to offer good opportunities to address biodiversity conservation needs.

The selection process was more straightforward than some ecoregions for several reasons. The current and historic vegetation maps provide a reasonably good representation of the distribution of major habitat types, and most of the area is relatively well inventoried for at-risk species. As a result, several areas — the large wetlands of the upper Klamath Basin, northern Wasco County's oak woodlands, and the Gearhart Mountain area — emerged as clear choices based on the presence of priority vegetation types, at-risk species, and aquatic diversity areas. The fourth selection, the upper Metolius River area, was identified primarily because of its importance for aquatic diversity.

Although both the Metolius River and Gearhart Mountain areas include some ponderosa pine forests, the project was not able to identify any areas that provide opportunities to conserve large, high-quality blocks of these habitats. Given the historic abundance and biological significance of ponderosa pine habitats in this ecoregion, further investigation of conservation opportunities for these types is clearly warranted.

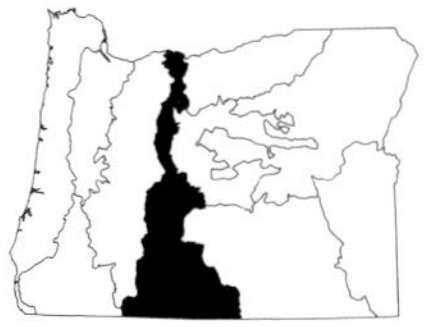

East Cascades Ecoregion

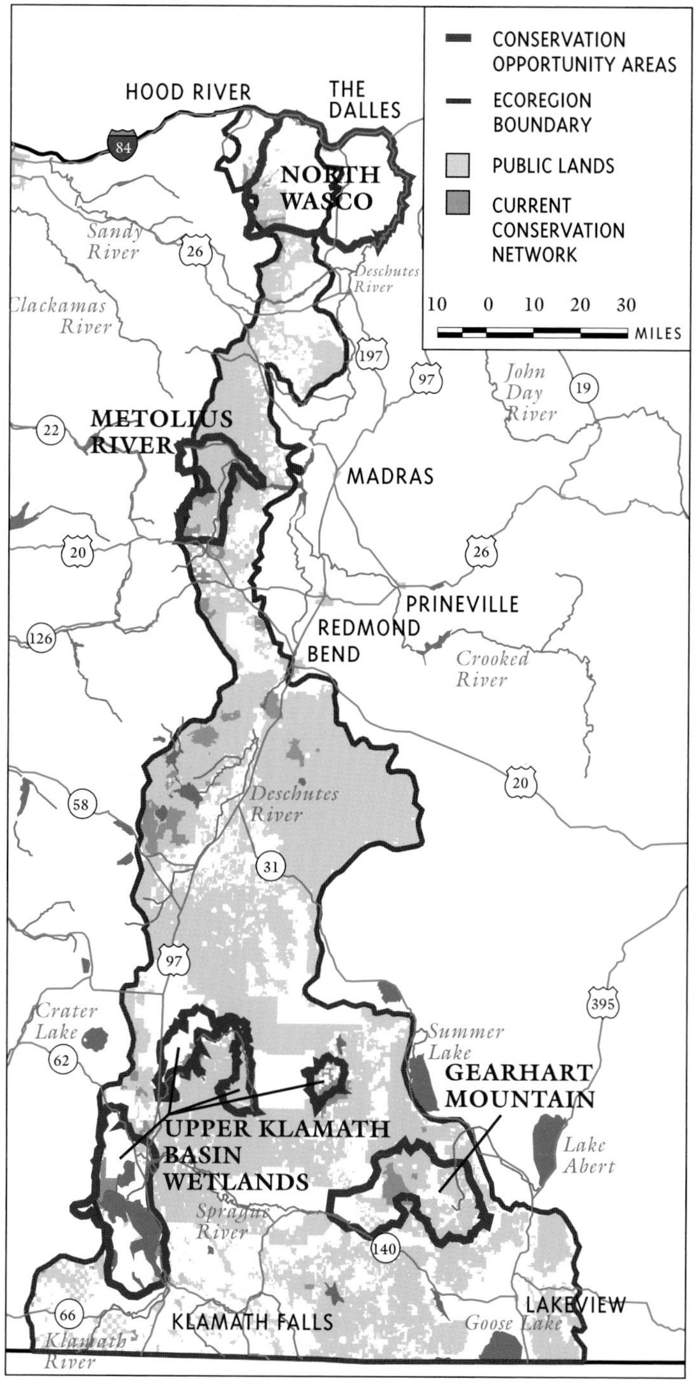

Conservation opportunity areas encompass a variety of East Cascades habitats, ranging from the upper Klamath Basin's wetlands to ponderosa pine, true fir forests, and the oak woodlands found at the edge of the Columbia Basin ecoregion.

At-risk plants

Astragalus appelgatei, Applegate's milk-vetch

Mimulus tricolor, three-colored monkeyflower

Perideridia erythrorhiza, red-root yampah

Plagiobothrys salsus, desert allocarya

Thelypodium brachycarpum, short-podded thelypody

Thelypodium howellii ssp. *howellii*, Howell's thelypody

At-risk animals

Agelaius tricolor, tricolored blackbird

Anodonta californiensis, California floater (mussel)

Athene cunicularia hypugea, western burrowing owl

Bartramia longicauda, upland sandpiper

Catostomus snyderi, Klamath largescale sucker

Chasmistes brevirostris, shortnose sucker

Clemmys marmorata marmorata, Northwestern pond turtle

Coturnicops noveboracensis, yellow rail

Deltistes luxatus, Lost River sucker

Egretta thula, snowy egret

Fluminicola sp. nov., Crooked Creek pebblesnail

Fluminicola sp. nov., Klamath pebblesnail

Fluminicola sp. nov., Odessa pebblesnail

Fluminicola sp. nov., Ouxy Spring pebblesnail

Fluminicola sp. nov., tall pebblesnail

Fluminicola sp. nov., tiger lily pebblesnail

Fluminicola sp. nov., Wood River pebblesnail

Grus canadensis tabida, greater sandhill crane

Ixobrychus exilis hesperis, western least bittern

Lanx alta, highcap lanx (snail)

Lanx klamathensis, scale lanx (snail)

Lyogyrus sp. nov., Klamath duskysnail

Lyogyrus sp. nov., mare's egg duskysnail

Lyogyrus sp. nov., nodose duskysnail

Oncorhynchus mykiss ssp., redband trout

Pelecanus erythrorhynchos, American white pelican

Pisidium ultramontanum, Montane peaclam

Podiceps auritus, horned grebe

Podiceps grisegena, red-necked grebe

Pyrgulopsis archimedes, Archimedes springsnail

Pyrgulopsis, Klamath Lake springsnail

Rana pretiosa, Oregon spotted frog

Strix occidentalis caurina, northern spotted owl

Tympanuchas phasianellus columbianus, Columbian sharp-tailed grouse

Vorticifex effusus dalli, Dall's ramshorn (snail)

Vorticifex effusus diagonalis, lined ramshorn (snail)

Vorticifex klamathensis klamathensis, Klamath ramshorn (snail)

Vorticifex klamathensis sinitsini, Sinitsin ramshorn (snail)

1. Upper Klamath Basin Wetlands

This landscape includes Upper Klamath and Agency Lakes and the Wood River valley; the Williamson River from Solomon Flats upstream through Klamath Marsh to the river's headwaters in northern Klamath County; and Sycan Marsh.

The wetland systems in this area constitute some of Oregon's most important wildlife habitats and are critical to the survival of numerous species, ranging from local endemic fish and invertebrates to continental populations of migratory birds. These wetlands also contribute to the biological diversity of downstream ecosystems in the Klamath Basin in California.

These areas provide habitat for more than 40 at-risk species and include a half-dozen streams and watersheds identified as aquatic diversity areas by the American Fisheries Society (Bottom et al 1993). A portion has also been identified by the Interior Columbia River Basin Ecosystem Management Project as one of nine "hotspots" of species rarity and endemism in eastern Oregon (ICBEMP 1997a).

Portions of this area are already managed primarily for biodiversity values, including the Upper Klamath and Klamath Marsh national wildlife refuges and The Nature Conservancy's Sycan Marsh preserve. Large-scale habitat restoration projects now under way at BLM's Wood River Wetlands, The Nature Conservancy's ownerships at Sycan Marsh and the Williamson River Delta will strengthen the existing conservation network in this area.

Opportunities exist for additional restoration and improvement of wetland and riparian habitats throughout the upper Klamath Basin. The Klamath River Basin Ecosystem Restoration Office is working to coordinate federal agency programs, and a group of local interests is working toward implementation of major restoration projects.

2. Gearhart Mountain area

This area includes Gearhart Wilderness and the headwaters of the Sprague and Chewaucan rivers.

At-risk plants

Castilleja chlorotica, green-tinged paintbrush

Penstemon glaucinus, blue-leaved penstemon

At-risk animals

Gila bicolor oregonensis, Oregon Lakes tui chub

Grus canadensis tabida, greater sandhill crane

Gulo gulo, wolverine

Oncorhynchus mykiss ssp., redband trout

Rana pretiosa, Oregon spotted frog

Salvelinus confluentus, bull trout

Although much of the forest surrounding the Gearhart Wilderness has been harvested, this landscape includes two significant roadless areas (Dead Horse Rim and part of Coleman Rim). Northeast of the wilderness, some relatively intact ponderosa pine woodlands contain populations of two at-risk plant species — blue-leaved penstemon *(Penstemon glaucinus)* and green-tinged paintbrush *(Castilleja chlorotica)*.

Several areas support at-risk animal species, including greater sandhill crane, redband trout *(Oncorhynchus mykiss* ssp.), and bull trout *(Salvelinus confluentus)*.

Aquatic diversity areas in this landscape serve as important genetic refuges. The two southwest of the Gearhart Wilderness are also considered important for ecological function (i.e., important for downstream water quality), while the aquatic diversity area to the southeast qualifies as a reference watershed ("the best of what is left") (Bottom et al. 1993).

3. North Wasco area

(see also #3 in the Columbia Basin Ecoregion, page 189)

This area is bordered to the east by the Deschutes River Canyon, to the south by Tygh Ridge, and to the west by Lookout Mountain. It includes all of the Mill, Fifteenmile, and Mosier creek watersheds.

The southern portions of this area support extensive oak woodlands, and it contains several aquatic diversity areas. The area also provides habitat for more than two dozen at-risk plant and animal species. Increasing development pressures could jeopardize many of these ecological values. Effective land use planning and cooperative efforts with private landowners could reduce some of these threats and provide the basis for a long-term conservation and management strategy.

At-risk plants

Agoseris elata, tall agoseris

Arabis sparsiflora var. *atrorubens*, sickle-pod rockcress

Carex hystericina, porcupine sedge

Juncus torreyi, Torrey's rush

Lomatium farinosum var. *hambleniae*, Hamblen's lomatium

Lomatium suksdorfii, Suksdorf's lomatium

Lomatium watsonii, Watson's desert-parsley

Meconella oregana, white meconella

Mimulus jungermannioides, hepatic monkeyflower

Penstemon barrettiae, Barrett's penstemon

Ranunculus reconditus, Dalles Mt. buttercup

Suksdorfia violacea, violet suksdorfia

At-risk animals

Batrachoseps wrighti, Oregon slender salamander

Clemmys marmorata marmorata, northwestern pond turtle

Cornorhynus townsendii, Townsend's big-eared bat

Falco peregrinus, peregrine falcon

Fisherola nuttalli, shortface lanx

Fluminicola columbiana, Columbia pebblesnail

Gulo gulo, wolverine

Juga hemphilli maupimensis, Deschutes juga (snail)

Monadenia fidelis minor, Oregon snail

Oncorhynchus mykiss ssp., redband trout

Oreohelix variabilis, Dalles mountain snail

Pristinicola hemphilli, pristine springsnail

Strix occidentalis caurina, northern spotted owl

4. Metolius River area

This area includes the upper Metolius River and its tributaries in Deschutes County.

At-risk plants

Agoseris elata, tall agoseris

Lobelia dortmanna, water lobelia

Penstemon peckii, Peck's penstemon

Tritomaria exsecta, liverwort

Tritomaria exsectiformis, liverwort

At-risk animals

Gulo gulo, wolverine

Oncorhynchus mykiss ssp., redband trout

Salvelinus confluentus, bull trout

Strix occidentalis caurina, northern spotted owl

Although rapid population growth and development around nearby Sisters and heavy recreational use throughout the area may pose some long-term threats, this landscape offers significant opportunities to address regional biodiversity conservation needs. Perhaps equally important, this area's high public visibility could make it a showcase for biodiversity management strategies on public lands.

The upper Metolius and its tributaries support a number of at-risk plant and animal species. A stronghold for bull trout, the area includes several aquatic diversity areas highlighted by the American Fisheries Society for their importance as genetic refuges. It is also within one of nine "hotspots" of species rarity and endemism identified by the Interior Columbia River Basin Ecosystem Management Project in eastern Oregon (ICBEMP 1997a).

The Metolius watershed is also the target of a major effort by the Deschutes National Forest to remove dead and dying trees and use prescribed fire to recreate more natural forest conditions in existing mixed conifer forests.

Basin and Range Ecoregion

The Basin and Range Ecoregion includes much of southeastern Oregon's high desert and extends south into California and Nevada. The ecoregion's name reflects its topography and geology, with numerous flat basins separated by isolated, generally north-south mountain ranges. Many of the mountains are fault blocks, with gradual slopes on one side and precipitous basalt rims on the other. Elevations range from 4,100 feet in the lowest basin to more than 9,700 feet on Steens Mountain.

Soils are generally rocky and thin, low in organic matter, and high in minerals. In undisturbed sagebrush and salt desert scrub communities, spaces between plants are occupied by microbiotic crusts, which are composed of free-living, nitrogen-fixing bacteria, lichens, mosses, fungi, and algae. This crust enhances soil stability, improves infiltration of water, provides available nitrogen, and enhances establishment of seedlings. Disturbances such as livestock grazing, off-road vehicles and other human uses have damaged or destroyed this crust in many areas. Frequent fires also retard development of microbiotic crusts. Recovery rates range from a few years for some components up to as much as a century (ICBEMP 1997b).

The ecoregion's climate is arid, with extreme ranges of daily and seasonal temperatures. Runoff from precipitation and mountain snowpacks that doesn't evaporate or soak into the porous mountain soils often flows into low, flat playas where it forms seasonal shallow lakes and marshes. When this water eventually evaporates, it leaves salt and mineral deposits that form alkali flats.

Special management areas on state and federal lands in this ecoregion include a broad range of habitats.

Malheur National Wildlife Refuge encompasses some of the most extensive marshes in the Intermountain West and is internationally significant for migratory birds. Two other large blocks of federal lands that receive special management — Hart Mountain National Antelope Refuge and BLM lands on Steens Mountain — include a variety of habitats, ranging from sagebrush steppe to juniper woodlands and aspen groves.

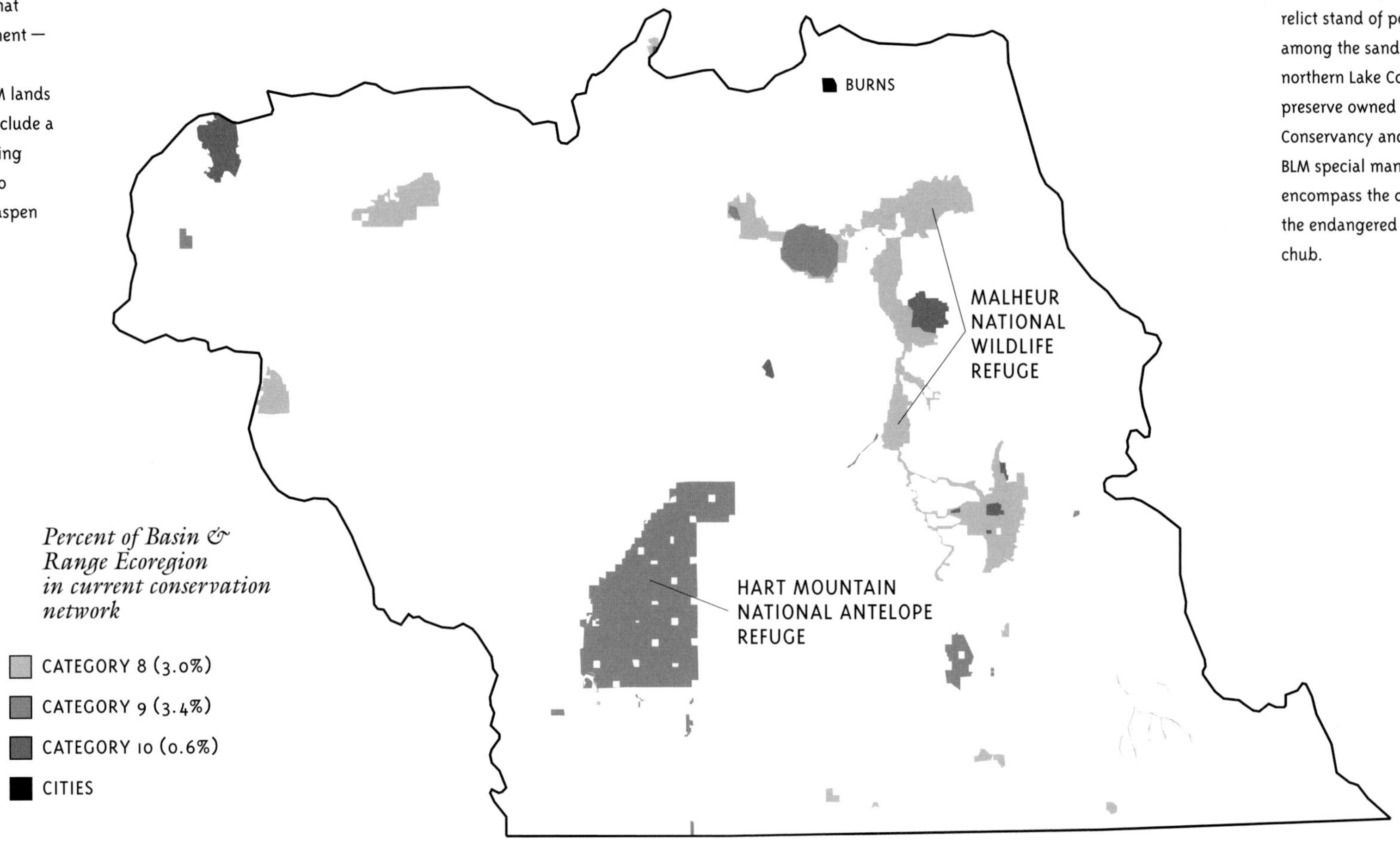

Other conservation lands in the Basin and Range are in smaller, isolated units. The state's Summer Lake Wildlife Area and BLM's Lake Abert and Warner Wetlands areas manage significant remnants of the ecoregion's great historic marshes and saline lakes. The BLM's Lost Forest Research Natural Area protects a unique relict stand of ponderosa pine among the sand dunes of northern Lake County. A small preserve owned by The Nature Conservancy and a surrounding BLM special management area encompass the only habitat for the endangered Borax Lake chub.

Most of the ecoregion is sparsely inhabited. The only communities with more than a few hundred residents are Burns and Lakeview, with populations of about 3,000 each. Livestock, agriculture, and tourism are the foundations of the regional economy. Lumber production, formerly a major source of employment in Burns and Lakeview, has declined with lower harvests on nearby national forests.

VEGETATION ANALYSIS

Uncontrolled livestock grazing before restrictions were first imposed on public lands in the mid-1930s had a profound influence on landscapes throughout the Basin and Range ecoregion, with many areas experiencing serious ecological damage. Conditions on rangelands in general have improved substantially over the past half-century as a result of better livestock management, and most ecosystems are recovering to varying degrees. However, long-term conservation needs for most habitats have not been adequately addressed. Vegetation types that deserve consideration as broad-scale conservation priorities include sagebrush steppe types, salt desert scrub, riparian and wetland types, and mountain mahogany and aspen woodlands.

Sagebrush steppe types cover more than 65 percent of the ecoregion, but few areas contain large, healthy examples of the mosaic patterns historically found in this ecoregion. (A healthy mosaic would include a range of successional stages, from recently burned areas dominated by grasses and forbs to old sagebrush-dominated stands that have not burned for 80 to 100 years.) Less than three percent of the region's big sagebrush types are in biodiversity management categories 8-10.

Within the broad category of sagebrush steppe, communities dominated by basin big sagebrush, which occur on deeper soils, have declined substantially due to agricultural development. Other sagebrush steppe communities (such as those dominated by basin wild rye or needlegrass) have also declined extensively from pre-European settlement levels. Sagebrush steppe ecosystems in general have changed dramatically as a result of livestock grazing and fire suppression. In many areas, they have shifted from mosaics of native perennial grasses, forbs, and shrubs to landscapes heavily dominated by shrubs (mostly sagebrush) and exotic annual forbs and grasses.

Salt desert scrub is found on dry sites with saline soils, often on dry lakebeds. This plant community is dominated by shrubs in the family *Chenopodiaceae* (shadscale, black greasewood, spiny hopsage, saltsage, and winterfat). This low-to-medium shrub habitat can be found on flat desert pavements, low alkaline dunes, around playas, or on gentle slopes above playas. Grasses and annuals (often succulent forbs) grow widely spaced in the understory. Only six percent of the ecoregion's salt desert scrub types are in biodiversity management categories 8-10, mainly on the eastside of the ecoregion. Salt desert scrub is a conservation concern in this ecoregion because entire suites of species (especially reptiles and small mammals) are primarily associated with this vegetation type.

As in other eastside ecoregions, **riparian habitats** of all types are a conservation concern in the Basin and Range. These types include riparian woodlands (dominated by cottonwoods at lower elevations and aspen at higher elevations); riparian shrub thickets (mostly several species of willow, but also birch, alder, and chokecherry); and riparian meadows (native, not mowed or hayed). Riparian meadows include natural spring-seep habitats that are extremely important for a wide variety of species, including butterflies and sage grouse chicks (Dobkin 1995).

Riparian habitats in general are magnets for wildlife and centers of biodiversity in arid landscapes. They are also, arguably, the most heavily impacted and altered habitat type in the Intermountain West (Dobkin 1994), primarily due to livestock grazing and irrigation withdrawals for agriculture (in this region, mostly to grow food for livestock).

Large riparian woodlands were not part of the historic landscape in this ecoregion, and extensive riparian shrublands probably occurred only on the floodplains of the Silvies River near Burns and the Chewaucan River between Paisley and Valley Falls. Most riparian habitats were limited to narrow strips along watercourses, spreading out where topography allowed across modest floodplains with braided channels. Today, remaining riparian habitats have been reduced to fragments along narrow, often entrenched streams. Most of these fragments are too small to show up in the broad-scale map of current vegetation.

Wetlands in this ecoregion range from shallow saline lakes and large permanent deepwater marshes to wet meadows and seasonal playa wetlands. They provide critical habitat for a wide variety of fish and wildlife species, from small populations of narrow endemics to millions of migrating waterfowl and shorebirds. The size and extent of the region's wetlands fluctuate widely from season to season and year to year, depending on precipitation. Malheur Lake, the largest natural freshwater marsh west of the Mississippi, can cover more than 50,000 acres at high water levels. But extended droughts have left the lake completely dry several times in this century (Duebbert 1969).

Significant portions of the ecoregion's major wetland systems are managed for biodiversity values on state and federal wildlife refuges and special management areas in the Warner Valley and at Abert, Summer, Malheur, and Harney lakes. In some areas, flood-irrigation of private hay meadows provides important seasonal habitat for migrating and breeding birds. However, many of the ecoregion's historic wetlands have been converted to agriculture, or have been

Sagebrush stepplands,
Hart Mountain
Photographer, Alan D. St. John

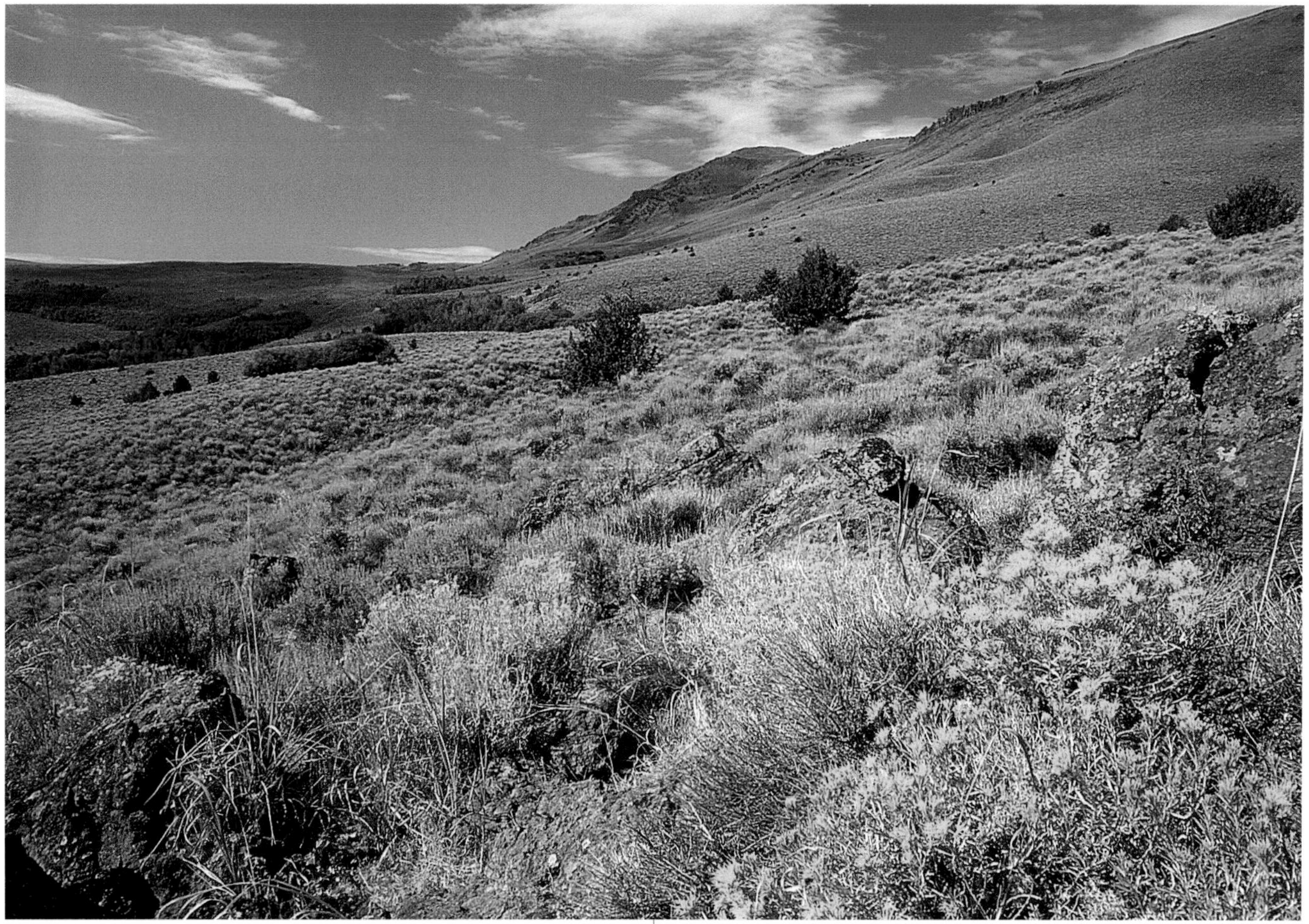

degraded through stream channelization, water diversions, and grazing. Introduced exotic fish have also altered the ecology of wetlands in many basins, with major impacts on water quality and habitat values. Invasive exotic plant species are a growing problem in many areas.

Mountain mahogany and non-riparian **aspen woodlands** are a conservation concern because of the widespread degradation of these habitats, which harbor plant and animals species largely or exclusively linked to these communities. Most of the degradation of these habitats is related to livestock grazing. Fire suppression has significantly expanded the distribution of mountain mahogany from historic levels, but most stands have a degraded understory. The distribution of aspen appears to have changed little from historic levels, but the native grasses among the trees have been replaced by Kentucky bluegrass *(Poa pratensis)* in many stands.

AT-RISK SPECIES

Animals. The ecoregion provides habitat for a number of at-risk animal species. Some are found in typical sagebrush steppe habitats and some occur at ecologically unique sites, such as Borax Lake and Malheur Cave. Borax Lake, an isolated lake fed by hot springs at the southern end of the Alvord Desert, is the only location for the Borax Lake chub *(Gila boraxobius)*. Malheur Cave supports some underground pools with at least two invertebrates — Malheur isopod *(Amerigoniscus malheurensis)* and Malheur pseudoscorpion *(Apochthonius malheuri)* —found nowhere else in the world.

Sagebrush steppe habitats support several at-risk animal species that were formerly much more common. Sage grouse *(Centrocercus urophasianus)* is a widespread gamebird that has suffered from habitat degradation. Kit fox *(Vulpes macrotis)* is at the edge of its range in Oregon, but is found in limited numbers in salt desert scrub communities in the Basin and Range, as well as in the Owyhee Uplands Ecoregion.

While redband trout *(Oncorhynchus mykiss* ssp.) is quite resilient, its range and numbers have been reduced considerably as a result of grazing-related degradation of riparian habitats and competition and hybridization with introduced trout species.

Desert wetland systems are important stopover places for migratory waterfowl and shorebirds, as well as critical nesting habitats for other species. Colonial nesting waterbirds, such as American white pelican *(Pelecanus erythrorynchos)* and white-faced ibis *(Plegadis chihi)*, are particularly dependent on secure nesting habitats afforded by Malheur National Wildlife Refuge and the BLM's Warner Wetlands Area of Critical Environmental Concern.

California bighorn sheep *(Ovis canadensis californiana)*, found at Hart Mountain and on a number of the desert mountain ranges, were largely eradicated in this ecoregion by overhunting and diseases introduced by domestic sheep. Pronghorn *(Antilocapra americana)* is the management focus of Hart Mountain National Antelope Refuge and the Sheldon National Wildlife Refuge. Because of their large home ranges, pronghorn and bighorn sheep may be important indicators of the overall health of Basin and Range ecosystems.

Plants. The Basin and Range Ecoregion provides habitat for numerous at-risk plant species, many of them rare endemics limited to very unusual habitats. Malheur wire lettuce *(Stephanomeria malheurensis)*, for example, is found only at the Narrows, south of Malheur Lake, on an unusual soil type. A nearby fire in the 1970s allowed the spread of cheatgrass into its habitat. Population numbers have since dropped almost to zero, but the plant is also maintained in a research lab.

A number of at-risk species in the buckwheat genus, Eriogonum, are restricted to unusual substrates, often ash or tuff, found in isolated

Locations of at-risk plant and animals recorded in the Oregon Natural Heritage Program's data bases are shown in relation to land ownership and the Oregon Biodiversity Project's conservation opportunity areas.

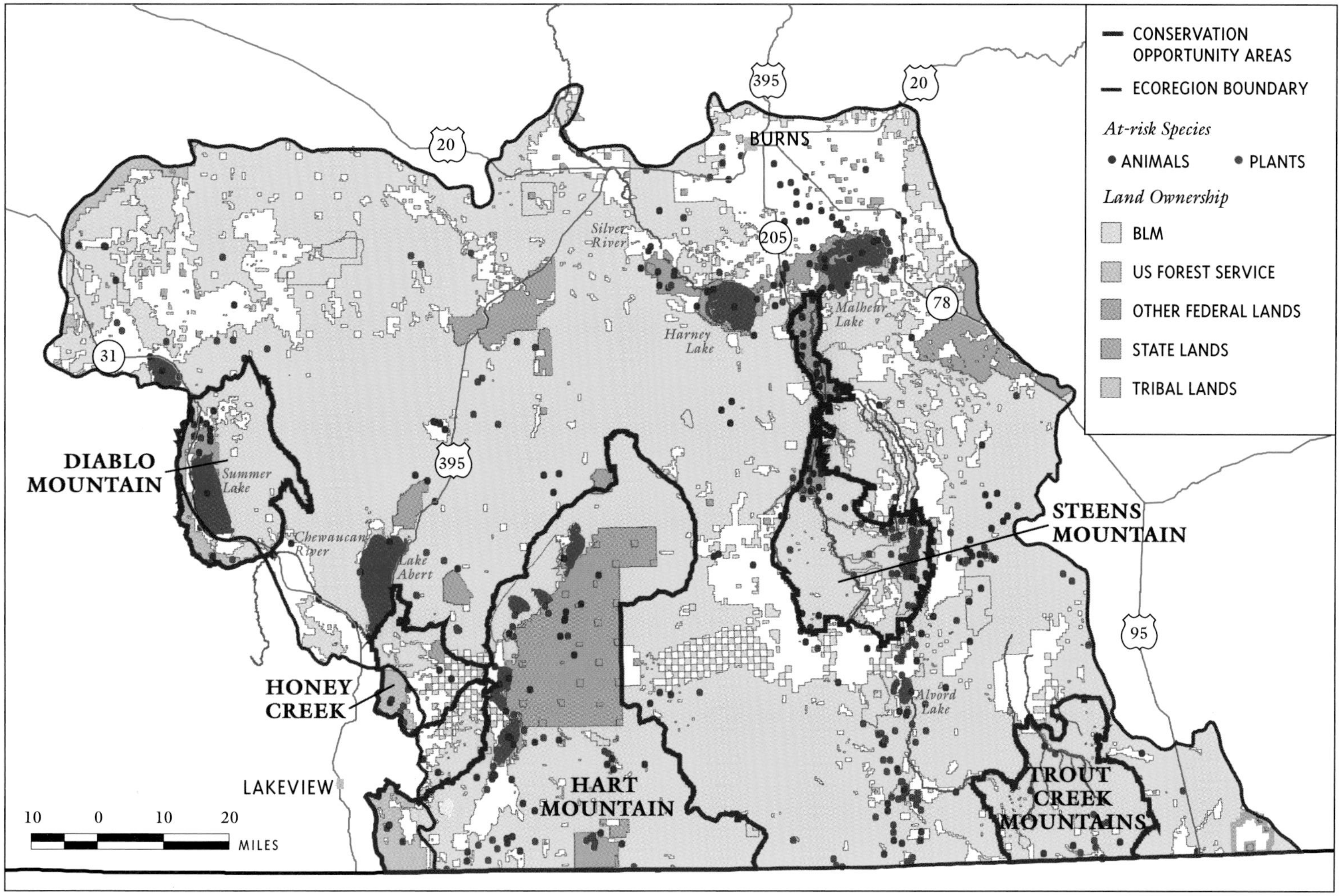

locations in sagebrush steppe. Also found on isolated ash deposits at the eastern and southern ends of the ecoregion are populations of three at-risk plant species that occur in the neighboring Owyhee Uplands Ecoregion: Grimy and Shelly's ivesia *(Ivesia rhypara* var. *rhypara, I. rhypara* var. *shellyii)* and Leiberg's clover *(Trifolium leibergii)*.

Steens Mountain supports a number of at-risk plant species. Most receive some protection, but increasing recreational use and continued livestock grazing may pose greater threats in the future.

Federal land managers are already addressing the conservation needs for the majority of at-risk plant species in this ecoregion. An exception is Cusick's eriogonum *(Eriogonum cusickii)*, which is found largely in unprotected ash deposits within sagebrush steppe. In addition, two at-risk plants — Biddle's lupine *(Lupinus biddlei)* and weak milk-vetch *(Astragalus solitarius)* — are found in more than 40 sites in the ecoregion's big sagebrush steppe habitat, but few are in areas managed for biodiversity.

SUMMARY OF CONSERVATION ISSUES

Major issues for biodiversity conservation in the Basin and Range Ecoregion include:

- Few vegetation types are adequately represented in the existing network of conservation lands, and some are not represented at all.
- Riparian habitats have been degraded throughout the ecoregion, with serious impacts on water quality, fish, and wildlife. These habitats are a high priority for restoration.
- Invasive exotic species pose substantial threats to biodiversity values in a variety of habitats. Shrub steppe exotics, like cheatgrass *(Bromus tectorum)* and yellow star-thistle *(Centaurea solstitialis)*, are displacing native plant communities and reducing forage for livestock. Introduced non-native fish and invasive plants such as perennial pepperweed *(Lepidium latifolium)* and purple loosestrife *(Lythrum salicaria)* have dramatically altered aquatic habitats in marsh and lake ecosystems.
- Increasing recreational use and related development threaten biodiversity values in many areas, including lands that are ostensibly "protected" under special management designations.
- Roadless areas in the region encompass some of the state's largest remaining blocks of undeveloped lands.

CONSERVATION OPPORTUNITY AREAS

The Oregon Biodiversity Project identified five areas in the Basin and Range Ecoregion that appear to offer good opportunities to address biodiversity conservation needs.

BLM wilderness study areas were an important factor in the GIS analysis and selection process for this ecoregion and the adjacent Owyhee Uplands Ecoregion. Formally designated wilderness study areas typically contain large blocks of relatively intact native ecosystems, and their unique management status provides opportunities for policy decisions that could provide for long-term conservation of biodiversity values.

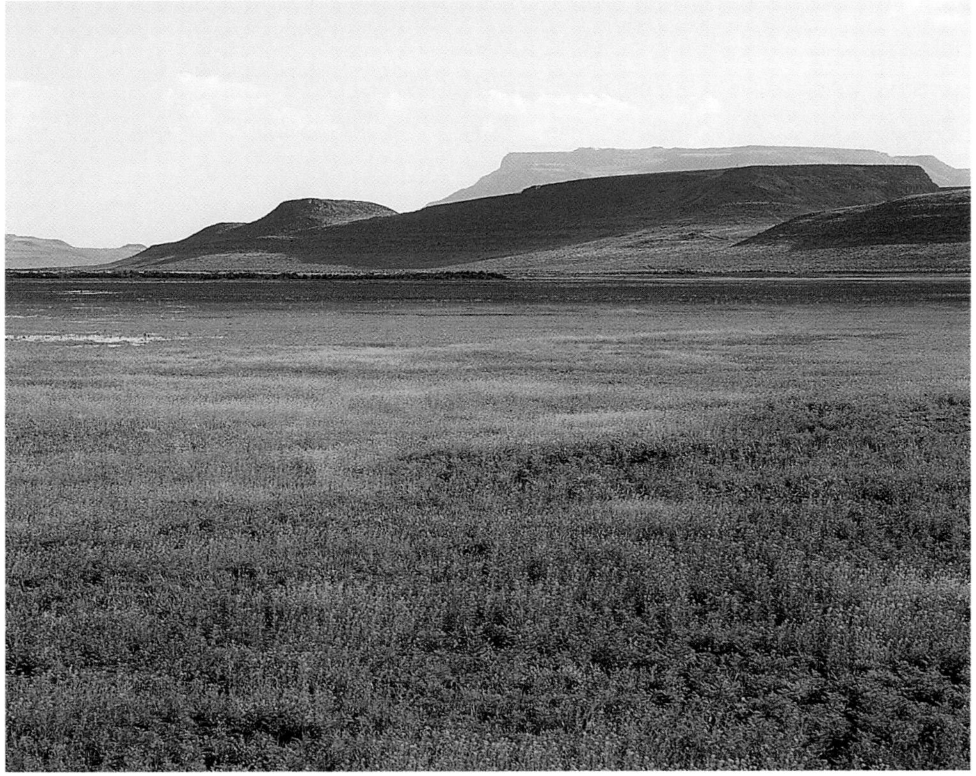

Warner Valley wetlands
Photographer, Harold E. Malde

At-risk species in the Basin and Range are concentrated in several areas that have long been a focus of conservation attention — Hart and Steens mountains, and the wetland and riparian systems associated with the Blitzen and Warner valleys, Summer Lake, and the Trout Creek Mountains. Some of the best large blocks of priority shrub steppe and salt desert scrub vegetation types are found in adjacent complexes of wilderness study areas. Overlays of the priority vegetation and at-risk species maps resulted in identification of some of the largest conservation opportunity areas in the state.

Although conservation opportunity areas are generally intended to complement rather than duplicate the existing conservation network, the Hart Mountain National Antelope Refuge was included because it is an integral component of a much larger area of conservation concern and offers extensive opportunities for biodiversity management. The Steens Mountain conservation opportunity area was expanded to include the Blitzen Valley portion of Malheur National Wildlife Refuge because of the potential to restore more natural ecosystem processes in this highly modified wetland system.

1. Hart Mountain area

Beginning north of Poker Jim Ridge and Bluejoint Lake, this area extends south to the Nevada border, encompassing the entire Hart Mountain National Antelope Refuge, Warner Valley and Guano Creek basins, and portions of the surrounding BLM lands.

This is an extraordinary landscape with high ecological integrity. The Hart Mountain portion includes riparian habitats, aspen woodlands, old growth juniper woodland, and scattered mountain mahogany groves in a big sagebrush-low sagebrush mosaic. The Warner Valley includes a major wetland complex and extensive salt desert scrub. The valley's lakes, springs, and streams provide habitat for a number of rare fish, and its wetlands are among the region's most significant for migratory birds. It is also considered a "hotspot" of species rarity and endemism on a regional scale (ICBEMP 1997a).

This conservation opportunity area is contiguous with the nearly 600,000-acre Sheldon National Wildlife Refuge, which extends across the border into Nevada. This area serves as a critical corridor for a migratory herd of pronghorn that moves annually between wintering grounds on Sheldon National Wildlife Refuge and a summer range on Hart Mountain. The current mandated 15-year exclusion of livestock from the Hart Mountain refuge presents a unique opportunity to explore strategies to restore native plant and animal communities at landscape scales.

At-risk plants

Chaenactis xantiana, desert pincushion
Eriogonum crosbyae, Crosby's buckwheat
Eriogonum prociduum, prostrate buckwheat
Gratiola heterosepala, Boggs Lake hedge-hyssop
Hymenoxys lemmonii, Cooper's goldflower
Ivesia rhypara var. *rhypara*, grimy ivesia
Mimulus latidens, broad-toothed monkeyflower
Plagiobothrys salsus, desert allocarya
Sesuvium verrucosum, Verrucose sea-purslane
Stylocline psilocarphoides, Malheur stylocline

At-risk animals

Brachylagus idahoensis, pygmy rabbit
Catostomus warnerensis, Warner sucker
Centrocercus urophasianus, sage grouse
Charadrius alexandrinus nivosus, western snowy plover
Coccyzus americanus, yellow-billed cuckoo
Egretta thula, snowy egret
Gila bicolor ssp., Catlow tui chub
Gila bicolor eurysoma, Sheldon tui chub
Grus canadensis tabida, greater sandhill crane
Oncorhynchus mykyss ssp. redband trout
Oncorhynchus mykyss ssp., Catlow Valley redband trout
Oncorhynchus mykyss ssp., Warner Valley redband trout
Pelecanus erythrorhynchos, American white pelican
Rhinichthys ocsulus ssp., Fosket speckled dace

2. Honey Creek area

This area encompasses the entire Honey Creek drainage, which extends from the Warner Mountains and Abert Rim on the west downstream to the Warner Valley.

This area complements the much larger Hart Mountain area (see #1 above) to the east. The Honey and Twelvemile creek watersheds contain high-quality streams and high numbers of several at-risk plant and animal species. A portion of the area is within the Abert Rim Wilderness Study Area, but it also includes extensive private lands within a checkerboard of BLM ownership.

None of this area is currently managed for biodiversity values. Because of the interdependent nature of grazing operations on public and private rangelands, conservation needs will have to be addressed through cooperative management.

At-risk plants

Carex limnophila, pond sedge
Galium serpenticum ssp. *warnerense*, Warner Mt. bedstraw
Ivesia shockleyi, Shockley's ivesia
Penstemon glaucinus, blue-leaved penstemon

At-risk animals

Catostomus warnerensis, Warner sucker
Centrocercus urophasianus, sage grouse
Grus canadensis tabida, greater sandhill crane
Oncorhynchus mykiss ssp., Warner Valley redband trout

3. Trout Creek Mountains area

This area in the far southeastern corner of the ecoregion encompasses the Trout Creek Mountains and extends southward to the Nevada border.

This remote area has a number of features that are priorities for conservation: high-quality streams, woody riparian habitats, and significant aspen and mountain mahogany woodlands. The area also supports a half-dozen at-risk plant and animal species.

The complex of wilderness study areas in the Trout Creek Mountains includes some of the most outstanding and diverse high desert wildlife habitat in Oregon. Cutthroat trout populations represent two of the last genetically pure strains of native trout in the Pacific Northwest (USDI/BLM 1991).

At-risk plants

Astragalus calycosus, King's rattleweed

Hymenoxys lemmonii, Cooper's goldflower

At-risk animals

Athene cunicularia hypugea, western burrowing owl

Catostomus tahoensis, Tahoe sucker

Centrocercus urophasianus, sage grouse

Oncorhynchus clarki henshawi, Lahontan cutthroat trout

4. Diablo Mountain area

This area includes all of the Diablo Mountain Wilderness Study Area and the adjacent Summer Lake Basin.

Lying on the western edge of the ecoregion, this area contains one of the largest intact blocks of salt desert scrub habitat in the Oregon portion of the Basin and Range and one of the largest roadless areas in the state.

Summer Lake and the adjacent freshwater wetlands attract a high diversity of migrating and breeding birds, making it a key habitat along the Pacific Flyway. It has also been identified by the Interior Columbia River Basin Ecosystem Management Project as a "hotspot" of species rarity and endemism (ICBEMP 1997a).

At-risk plants

Castilleja chlorotica, green-tinged paintbrush

Penstemon glaucinus, blue-leaved penstemon

Thelypodium brachycarpum, short-podded thelypody

At-risk animals

Brachylagus idahoensis, pygmy rabbit

Centrocercus urophasianus, sage grouse

Charadrius alexandrinus nivosus, western snowy plover

Egretta thula, snowy egret

Falco peregrinus anatum, peregrine falcon

Gila bicolor ssp., Summer Basin tui chub

Grus canadensis tabida, greater sandhill crane

Gulo gulo, wolverine

Pelecanus erythrorhynchos, American white pelican

At- risk plants

Agastache cusickii, Cusick's giant-hyssop

Botrychium lunaria, moonwort

Botrychium minganense, gray moonwort

Camissonia pygmaea, dwarf evening-primrose

Carex backii, Back's sedge

Carex nova, new sedge

Castilleja pilosa var. *steenensis,* Steens Mt. paintbrush

Kobresia bellardii, Bellard's kobresia

Lepidium davisii, Davis' peppergrass

Potamogeton diversifolius, Rafinesque's pondweed

Potamogeton foliosus var. *fibrillosus,* fibrous pondweed

Saxifraga adscendens ssp. *oregonensis,* wedge-leaf saxifrage

At-risk animals

Egretta thula, snowy egret

Gila bicolor ssp., Catlow tui chub

Grus canadensis tabida, greater sandhill crane

Gulo gulo, wolverine

Ixobrychus exilis hesperis, western least bittern

Larus pipixcan, Franklin's gull

Oncorhynchus clarki henshawi, Lahontan cutthroat trout

Oncorhynchus mykyss ssp., redband trout

Oncorhynchus mykyss ssp., Catlow Valley redband trout

Pelecanus erythrorhynchos, American white pelican

Rana luteiventris, Columbia spotted bat

5. Steens Mountain area

This area extends from the edge of the Alvord Basin across the central portion of Steens Mountain and northward down the Blitzen River Valley.

This area encompasses some of the most ecologically diverse landcapes in the Basin and Range Ecoregion. Large portions of the area have barely been touched by development, and the area provides important habitat for a wide variety of wildlife, ranging from migratory birds and big game to rare and endangered mammals and fish. It is also part of an area identified by the Interior Columbia River Basin Ecosystem Management Project as a "hotspot" of species rarity and endemism (ICBEMP 1997a).

Dominated by sagebrush steppe and juniper woodlands, the central portion of Steens Mountain includes high-quality streams and riparian habitats, extensive aspen and mountain mahogany woodlands, and high numbers of at-risk plant and animal species. This area also offers a good opportunity to conserve alpine habitats and the unique and highly diverse ecosystems found in the glacial cirques of the Little Blitzen, and Big and Little Indian gorges.

The Blitzen River Valley wetlands receive a relatively high level of management for biodiversity as part of the Malheur National Wildlife Refuge, but the river is channelized for much of its length through the valley. Restoration of a more naturally functioning river and floodplain would enhance the area's biodiversity values.

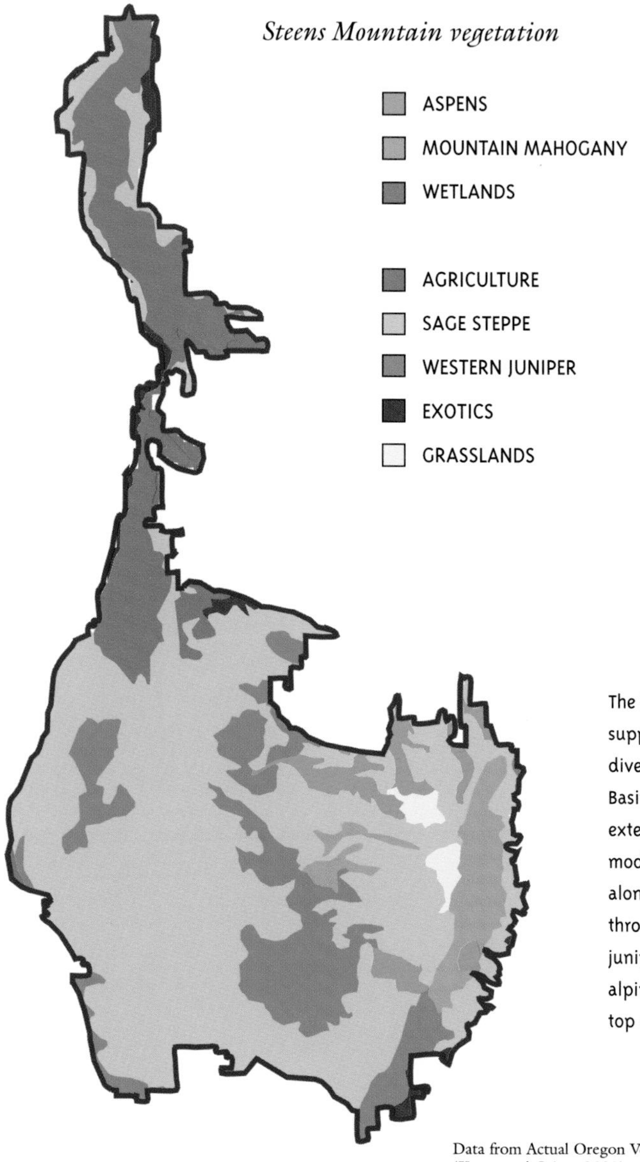

The Steens Mountain area supports some of the most diverse habitats found in the Basin and Range Ecoregion, extending from the highly modified freshwater marshes along the Blitzen River up through sagebrush steppe, juniper and aspen habitats to alpine habitats found near the top of the 9,700-foot mountain.

Data from Actual Oregon Vegetation (Kagan and Caicco 1992)

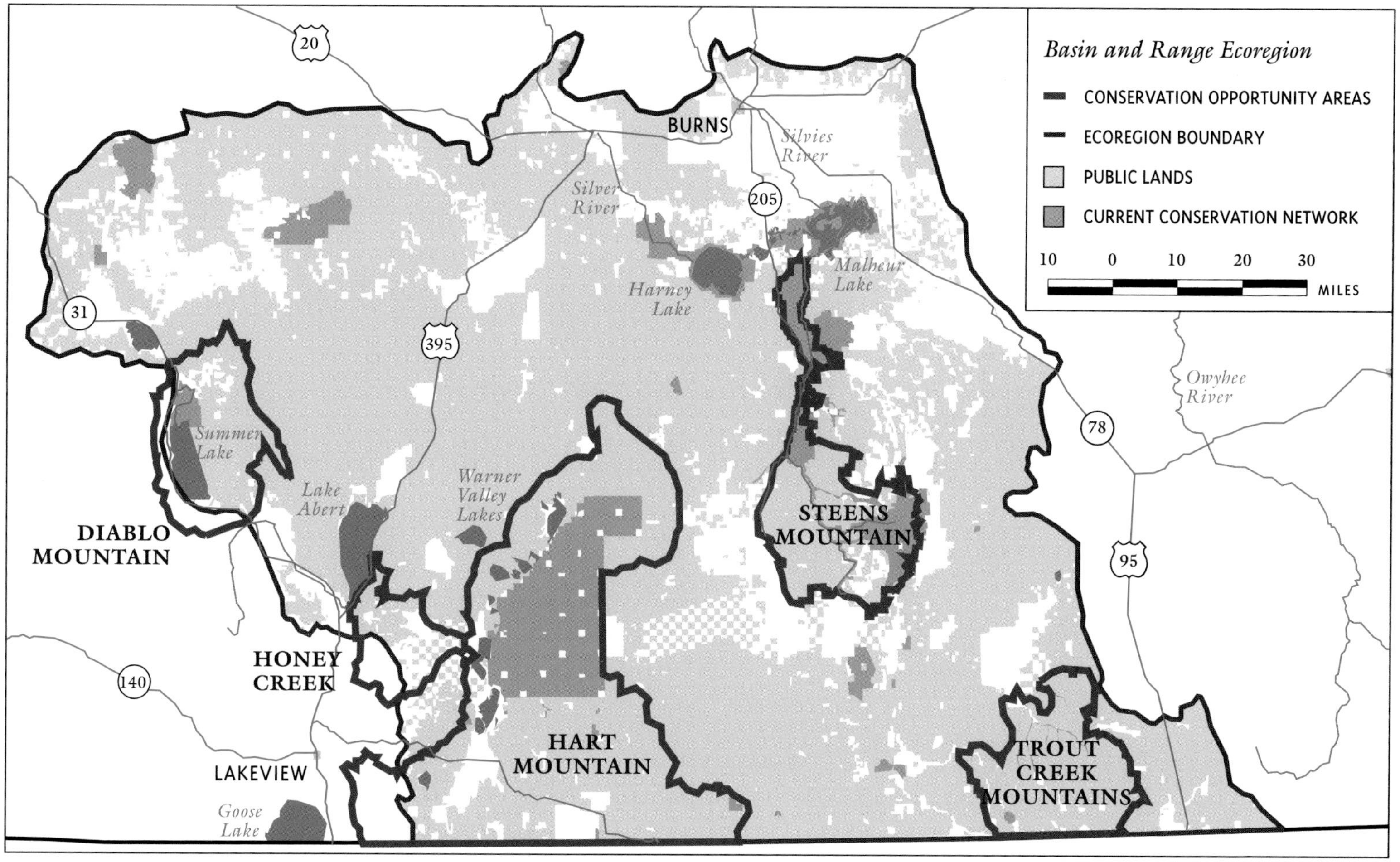

Conservation opportunity areas in the Basin and Range encompass some of the largest blocks of relatively intact native ecosystems in the state. Three of the highlighted areas are anchored by existing wildlife refuges and other special management areas on federal and state lands, and all five areas contain extensive wilderness study areas.

Owyhee Uplands Ecoregion

The Owyhee Uplands Ecoregion covers the extreme southeast corner of Oregon, occupying the entire Owyhee River drainage, as well as the lower end of the Malheur River watershed. The ecoregion extends beyond Oregon's borders, reaching into southwestern Idaho and northern Nevada.

The Owyhee Uplands has vegetation similar to the adjacent Basin and Range Ecoregion, but differs markedly in its terrain. The landscape is basically a broad, undulating plateau cut by deep riverine canyons. Elevations range from 2,100 to 6,500 feet, with the average elevation of the plateau at about 4,000 feet.

The climate is one of extremes, featuring generally wet springs and cold winters with moisture in the form of snow. Annual precipitation is only 8-12 inches. Summers are hot and dry with temperatures regularly exceeding 90° F. Occasional thunderstorms produce more lightning than rain. The climate favors sagebrush steppe vegetation — the dominant vegetation type throughout the cool deserts of the Intermountain West.

Another important influence in the ecoregion is its volcanic geology. Over large portions of the landscape, soils have been derived from underlying layers of basalt and rhyolite. Of particular interest are soils derived from volcanic ash and welded tuffs, which are found in Leslie Gulch and Succor Creek near the Idaho border, at Rome, and throughout the Owyhee canyonlands.

The weathering of exposed volcanic ash has resulted in unique soils with a high clay content and an unusual chemical composition. The adaptational challenge these peculiar soils present for plants has

Less than three percent of the ecoregion is in biodiversity management categories 8-10. Most of these areas are in the southern half, where BLM special management areas and wild and scenic river designations encompass some of the ecoregion's most distinctive landscapes, including some unique assemblages of at-risk and endemic plants. These areas include much of the Owyhee River canyon from Lake Owyhee to the river's upper reaches; the Honeycombs and Leslie Gulch on Owyhee Ridge; state lands on nearby Succor Creek; and a large area around Jordan Craters.

Outside the Owyhee River corridor and canyonlands, management for biodiversity values is almost non-existent. Conservation needs have not been addressed in the region's remote southern plateau, nor in the Malheur, Burnt, and Powder river basins to the north.

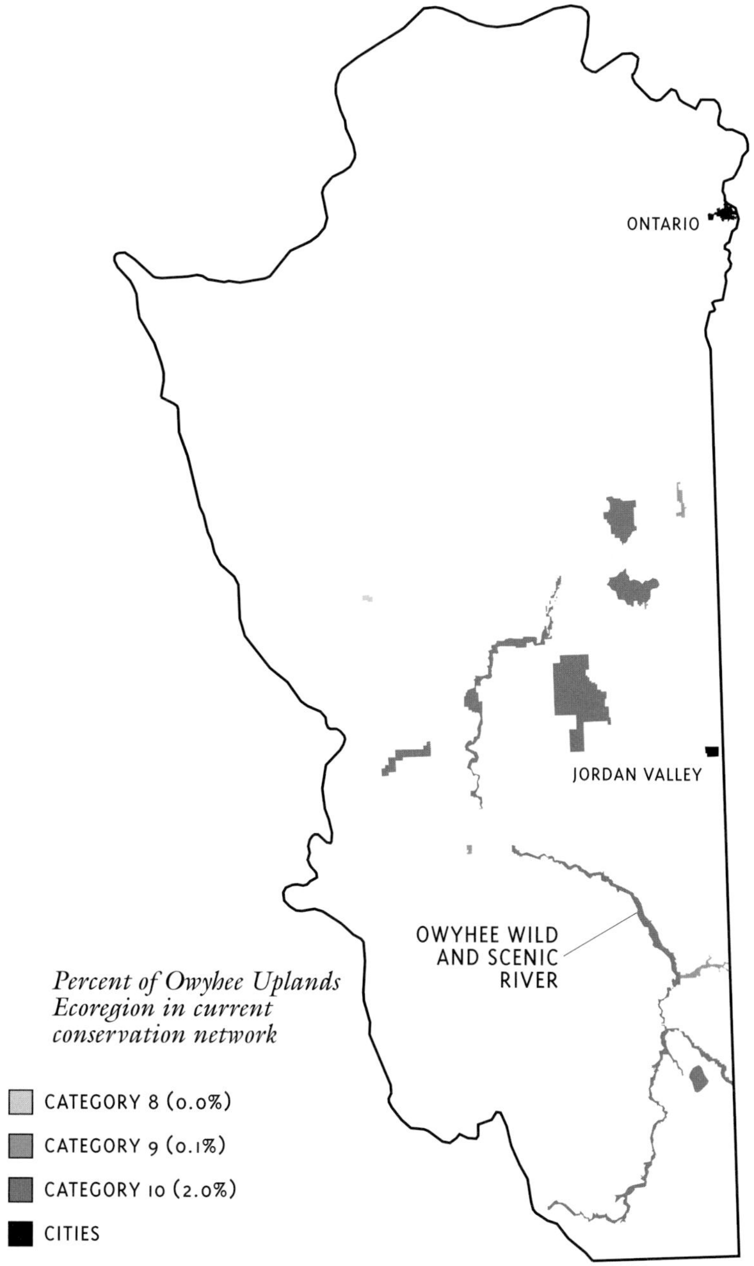

Percent of Owyhee Uplands Ecoregion in current conservation network

Patterns of land ownership

The Owyhee Uplands is one of Oregon's most thinly populated ecoregions, with its scant population concentrated almost exclusively in the Vale-Ontario area. Jordan Valley (population less than 400) is the only other town of any size. Isolated ranches once dotted some of the region's most remote areas (such as the upper reaches of the Owyhee River), but most have either been abandoned or consolidated by owners who now live closer to the ecoregion's population centers.

given rise to a relatively rich flora of endemic species. The welded tuffs in these areas have also produced remarkable rock formations that rival more well known erosional formations in the national parks of Utah's Colorado Plateau country.

Microbiotic crusts are critical to soil productivity and play an important role in salt desert scrub and sagebrush communities. Some believe the absence of these crusts in many areas of the Owyhee Uplands to be related to past heavy livestock grazing (ICBEMP 1997b).

The ecoregion's human population is concentrated in the northeastern corner, where irrigated agriculture in the fertile lowlands along the Snake and Malheur rivers is the foundation of the local economy.

VEGETATION ANALYSIS

Four general vegetation types are priorities for conservation in this ecoregion: big sagebrush, riparian types, salt desert scrub, and mountain mahogany woodlands. Each of these general types includes many different natural communities, some of greater conservation concern than others. Invasive exotic plant species are also a major issue in this region.

Sagebrush plays a critical role in the lifecycles of many of the ecoregion's fauna. High-quality **big sagebrush** communities are of conservation concern because of their declines from historic levels and meager representation within the current network of conservation lands. More than 145 wildlife species in southeastern Oregon depend on tall sagebrush-bunchgrass communities for reproduction or feeding (Puchy and Marshall 1993). Habitat values depend in part on the density of sagebrush relative to bunchgrasses and flowering plants, and the structural diversity provided by sagebrush. Both these attributes are dependent upon natural ecological processes, particularly fire.

As in the adjacent Basin and Range and Blue Mountains ecoregions, uncontrolled livestock grazing in the decades before enactment of the Taylor Grazing Act of 1934 caused serious ecological damage. Rangeland conditions have improved since then in most areas, but livestock grazing and fire suppression, followed by invasion of weedy annual grasses such as cheatgrass *(Bromus tectorum)*, have greatly altered natural fire cycles in sagebrush steppe habitats. Landscapes formerly comprised of mosaics dominated by bunchgrasses and forbs are now heavily and disproportionately dominated by shrubs (mostly sagebrush) and exotic grasses and forbs.

Some areas in the extreme southeast corner of the ecoregion are still relatively intact natural landscapes and support big sagebrush communities that retain much of their ecological integrity. However, basin big sagebrush, which occurs on deeper soils, has been converted to agriculture in the northern part of the ecoregion along the Malheur and Snake rivers. Communities dominated by basin wild rye and needlegrass have virtually disappeared.

Riparian habitats of all types are a conservation concern in the ecoregion. As in the Basin and Range, these types include riparian woodlands (tree-dominated, with cottonwoods at lower elevations), riparian shrub-thicket habitats (mostly willows, but also birch, alder, and chokecherry), and riparian meadows (native, not mowed or hayed).

European settlement and development had its greatest impact on riparian habitats. Early trappers extirpated beaver populations, removing a key component of these ecosystems. Settlers drained and cleared valley wetlands for agriculture, and the introduction of livestock contributed to the hardening of streambanks and

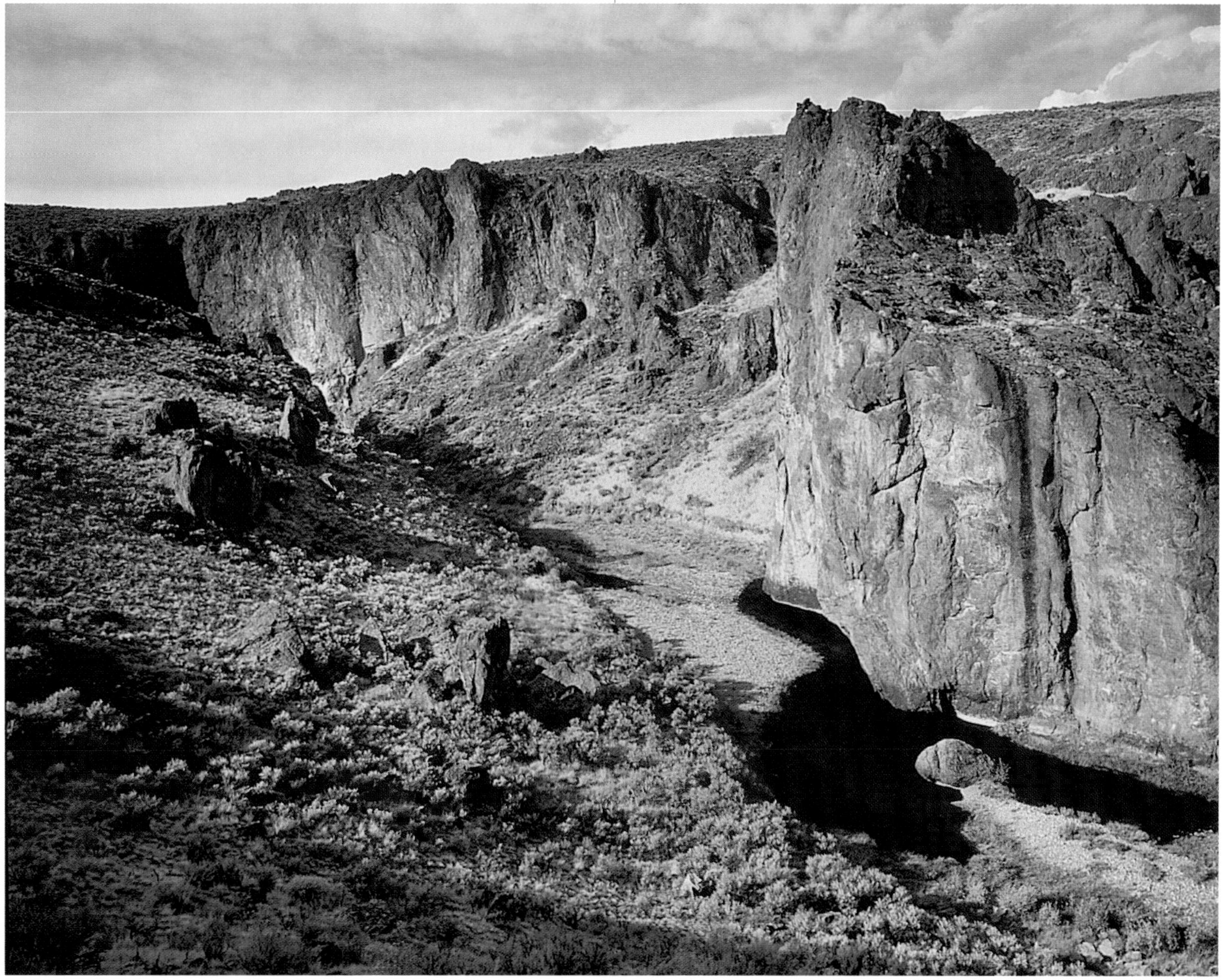

Little West Owyhee River
Photographer, Larry N. Olson

their eventual erosion. As grazing operations expanded to higher elevations, similar ecological declines occurred. Construction of flood control dams and increased stream withdrawals for irrigation and other uses caused further loss and degradation of riparian habitats in low-elevation riverine systems.

Floodplain wetlands dominated by cottonwoods historically occurred along the Malheur, Snake, and lower Owyhee rivers. These long "gallery" forests have been greatly reduced and fragmented, with much of the floodplain developed for agriculture. Along smaller watercourses, streams now are often entrenched and narrow, with much reduced, but nonetheless important, amounts of woody riparian vegetation.

Salt desert scrub is typically found on soils too alkaline to support sagebrush. These alkaline soils tend to accumulate in moist valley bottoms along the larger rivers and around basins and playa lakes that are sinks for runoff from surrounding uplands. Salt desert scrub communities usually have sparse understories and are dominated by one of several species of shadscale *(Atriplex* sp.*)* or black greasewood *(Sarcobatus vermiculatus)*.

Salt desert scrub communities have probably not diminished much from pre-European settlement levels, but they are almost completely unrepresented in the current network of conservation lands. The largest blocks occur within and adjacent to several BLM wilderness study areas. Salt desert scrub is of conservation concern because of the important role played by microphytic crusts, and because it provides habitat for suites of species (especially reptiles and small mammals) that are primarily or exclusively associated with salt desert scrub.

Mountain mahogany woodlands are very diverse and significant in this ecoregion, despite their limited distribution. Under typical conditions, mountain mahogany is found in small groves on ridges and rimrock naturally protected from fire. Understory vegetation may include big sagebrush, mountain snowberry *(Symphoricarpos oreophilus)*, and Idaho fescue *(Festuca idahoensis)*. Stands of mountain mahogany provide important browse and cover for deer and elk, and protection from weather and predators for many small animals. Mountain mahogany has expanded in some areas due to fire suppression, but has been reduced in other areas (such as Mahogany Mountain) as a result of past herbicide spraying.

Introduced **exotic plants** have had a dramatic impact on vegetation communities in this ecoregion. Overgrazing and frequent wildfires have allowed non-native cheatgrass to spread to millions of acres in the Intermountain West, including vast expanses of the ecoregion's sagebrush steppe (Pyke and Borman 1993). Other aggressive invaders of the region's shrub steppe habitat include yellow star-thistle *(Centaurea solstitialis)*, purple star-thistle *(C. calcitrapa)*, and medusahead *(Taeniatherum caput-medusae)*.

Owyhee Salmon: The Lost Connection

The Owyhee Uplands Ecoregion has already lost one of its most remarkable ecological components — the salmon that once ran up the Snake River and then spread throughout the Malheur and Owyhee river basins. The high dams constructed on the lower Snake River during the 1960s brought an end to the Owyhee and Malheur rivers' salmon runs and severed forever the remarkable ecological connection between the Owyhee Uplands and the greater Columbia-Snake basins.

Runs of spring and fall chinook salmon (*Oncorhynchus tshawytscha* ssp.) once traveled up the Owyhee River as far as Nevada. These hardy fish averaged only 10-14 pounds, far smaller than the huge salmon that spawned in the Columbia River system, but they endured a longer and more arduous journey to their spawning grounds.

In some years the vagaries of precipitation in the ecoregion's arid environment left insufficient water for both the salmon's upstream passage and their spawning habitat. But in good years, input of thousands of salmon in the upper reaches of these desert rivers resulted in local abundance for many other species of fish and wildlife. Local Paiute tribes also benefited from the successful fish runs.

These salmon were central to a complex food web of predators and prey, scavengers, and other fish that all depended on the annual salmon runs. With the eradication of the salmon, many of these other species similarly declined or disappeared altogether.

Some exotic plants have been introduced intentionally. For example, the BLM began a massive effort in 1962 to "rehabilitate" degraded rangelands by establishing another non-native grass, crested wheatgrass *(Agropyron cristatum)*, and by eradicating the native sagebrush. Over the course of 10 years, the Vale Rehabilitation Project seeded 250,000 acres to crested wheatgrass and used plowing, chaining, and herbicides to reduce sagebrush on as much as 370,000 acres.

Another exotic plant species, Kentucky bluegrass *(Poa pratensis)*, is now so widespread that it dominates the herbaceous layer of many riparian systems to the exclusion of native grasses. Although Kentucky bluegrass is not noxious and is appreciated for its forage quality, its tenacious and prolific traits have fundamentally altered many natural riparian systems.

AT-RISK SPECIES

Animals. Bighorn sheep *(Ovis canadensis californiana)*, also known as mountain sheep, have been reintroduced following their extirpation from Oregon in the early 1900s and are now found in the Leslie Gulch area and the Owyhee River's canyonlands. Kit fox *(vulpes macrotis)*, which are found in salt desert shrub habitats in the southern end of the Owyhee Uplands and Basin and Range ecoregions, have always been rare in Oregon. Although recent observations are limited, the species' status appears to have changed little in the past 60 years (Marshall 1996). The Mojave black-collared lizard *(Crotaphytus bicinctores)* is also found in the Owyhee River basin, at the northern end of its range. Sage grouse *(Centrocercus urophasianus)* are widely distributed throughout the ecoregion in areas dominated by big sagebrush. Redband trout *(Oncorhyncus mykiss* ssp.) populations survive in some tributaries of the Owyhee and Malheur rivers.

Plants. The Owyhee Uplands are a major source of rare plant endemism in southeastern Oregon. A series of geologically recent volcanic episodes created numerous unique habitats underlain by ash flows. Hills, canyon slopes, and stream terraces in Leslie Gulch, Succor Creek, and other portions of the upper Owyhee River canyonlands are characterized by multi-colored ash flows, each with a unique chemistry.

These ash beds, most found in rhyolitic and welded tuff canyons, provide habitat for more than 10 endemic plant species. These vary from Ertter's senecio *(Senecio ertterae)*, found only in parts of two adjacent gulches on less than 500 acres of habitat, to Owyhee clover *(Trifolium owyheense)*, found at 50 locations, all restricted to local ash deposits. The BLM has designated Leslie Gulch as an area of critical environmental concern, but the conservation needs of the Succor Creek endemics have yet to be addressed.

Other localized plants are found on unusual volcanic substrates throughout the region. Leiberg's clover *(Trifolium leibergii)* is found only on a few

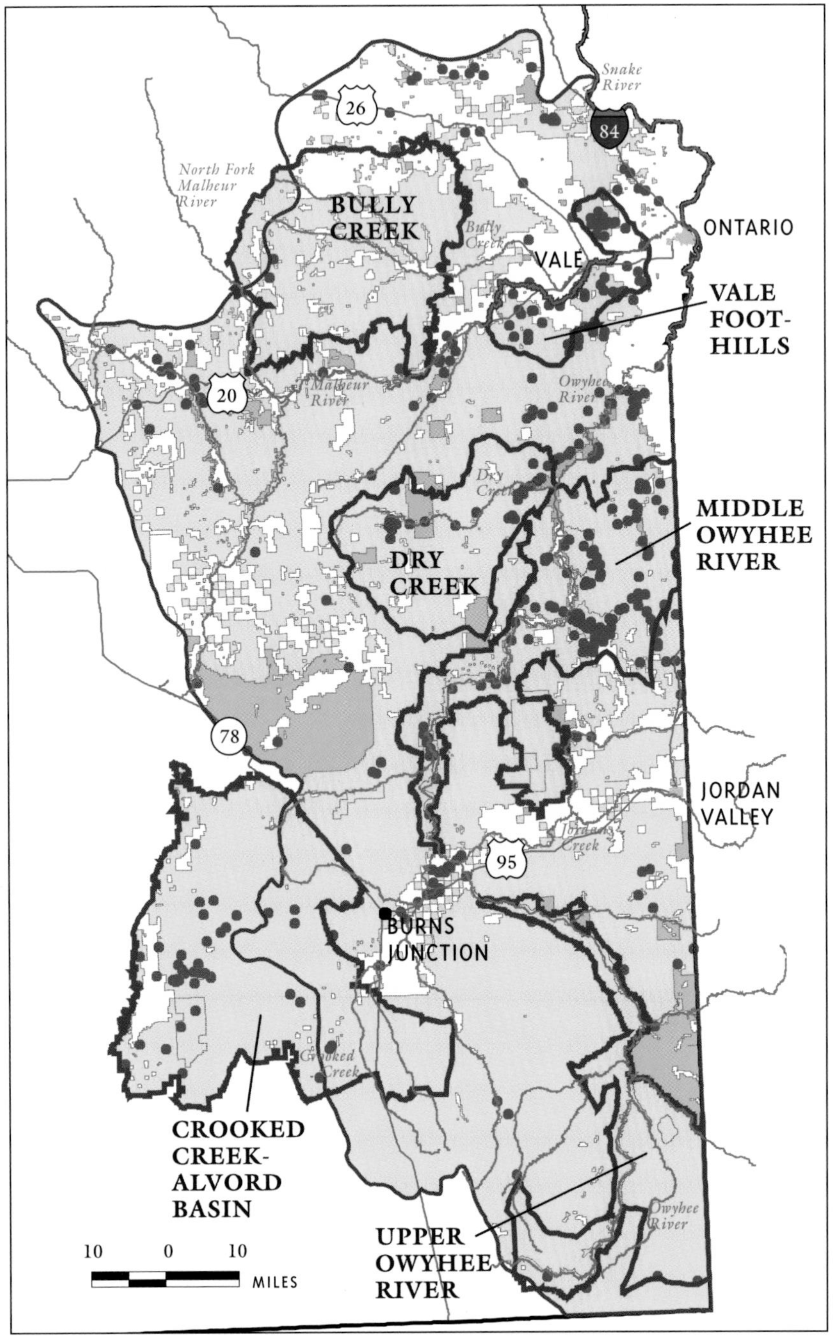

Locations of at-risk plant and animals recorded in the Oregon Natural Heritage Program's data bases are shown in relation to land ownership and the Oregon Biodiversity Project's conservation opportunity areas.

— CONSERVATION OPPORTUNITY AREAS

— ECOREGION BOUNDARY

At-risk Species

● ANIMALS ● PLANTS

Land Ownership

▢ BLM

▨ OTHER FEDERAL LANDS

▨ STATE LANDS

ash beds on private and BLM lands around Drewsey, at the northwestern edge of the ecoregion. The rare and endangered Malheur valley fiddleneck *(Amsinckia carinata)* is found only on a few low volcanic cones at the western edge of the Malheur valley near Harper. Golden buckwheat *(Eriogonum chrysops)* is restricted to four very small rhyolite flows around Skull Creek.

Two other at-risk plant species include Cronquist's stickseed *(Hackelia cronquistii)* and Mulford's milk-vetch *(Astragalus mulfordiae)*, both found in sandy sagebrush steppe along the edges of the Malheur River Valley and the adjacent Snake River Plains in Idaho. A third plant on more widespread habitats is Davis' peppergrass *(Lepidium davisii)*, a local endemic found on the region's sparsely vegetated playas. Conflicts with cattle threaten all three of these species.

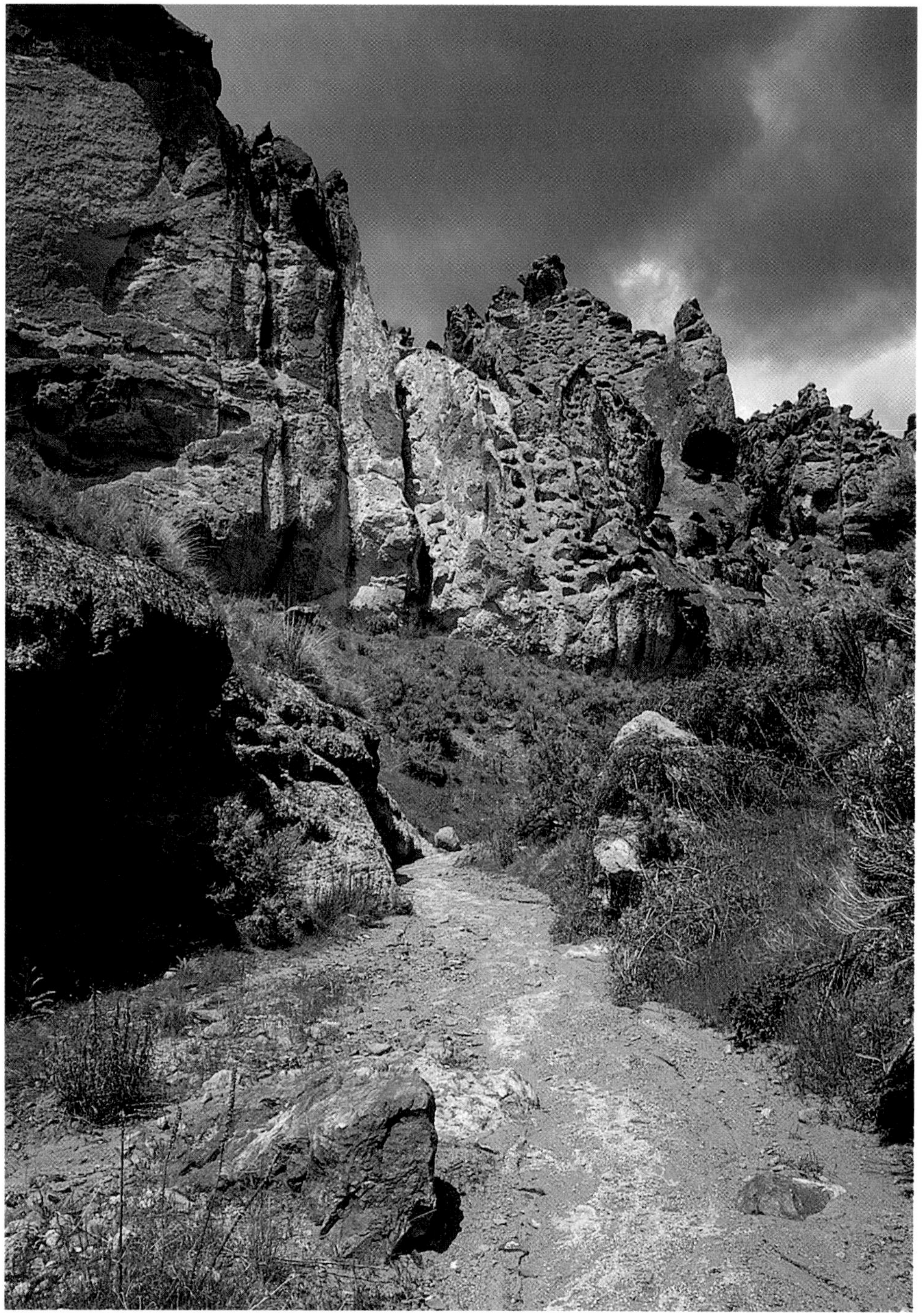

Leslie Gulch

Photographer, George Baetjer

SUMMARY OF CONSERVATION ISSUES

Major issues for biodiversity conservation in the Owyhee Uplands Ecoregion include:

- The existing conservation network is less than three percent of the ecoregion. The few large blocks of conservation lands are primarily limited to canyonlands and big sagebrush lava fields. Sagebrush steppe and riparian habitats are conspicuously absent.
- Few vegetation types are adequately represented in the existing network of conservation lands, and some are not represented at all.
- Past livestock grazing has fundamentally altered the character of sagebrush steppe habitats from mosaics dominated by bunchgrasses and forbs, to sagebrush-dominated landscapes often invaded by exotics.
- Riparian habitats have been seriously degraded, with impacts to water quality, fish, and wildlife. These habitats are a high priority for restoration.
- This ecoregion still contains extensive roadless areas that provide opportunities to conserve large blocks of native habitat. Future policy decisions on the management of BLM wilderness study areas will have major implications for biodiversity conservation.

CONSERVATION OPPORTUNITY AREAS

The Oregon Biodiversity Project identified six areas in the Owyhee Uplands that appear to offer good opportunities to address biodiversity conservation needs.

The selection process was similar in many respects to the Basin and Range Ecoregion, but the existing conservation network provided fewer initial building blocks because of its limited extent and uneven distribution. The current vegetation map was useful in identifying large blocks of big sagebrush and salt desert scrub, but less helpful with two other priority types — riparian and mountain mahogany woodlands. At-risk species and aquatic diversity areas were key factors in the selection process in this ecoregion, and BLM wilderness study areas were used to identify boundaries for some of the conservation opportunity areas.

Most of the areas highlighted in the GIS-based analysis were selected on the basis of a combination of values, but one — the Vale foothills area — was identified primarily because of its importance for at-risk species.

At-risk plants

Argemone munita ssp. *rotundata*, prickly-poppy

Astragalus sterilis, sterile milk-vetch

Carex hystericina, porcupine sedge

Chaenactis cusickii, Cusick's chaenactis

Chaenactis macrantha, large-flowered chaenactis

Chaenactis stevioides, broad-flowered chaenactis

Eriogonum salicornioides, playa buckwheat

Ivesia rhypara var. *rhypara*, grimy ivesia

Lomatium ravenii, Raven's lomatium

Mentzelia mollis, smooth mentzelia

Mentzelia packardiae, Packard's mentzelia

Muhlenbergia minutissima, annual dropseed

Phacelia gymnoclada, naked-stemmed phacelia

Phacelia lutea var. *mackenzieorum*, Mackenzie's phacelia

Senecio ertterae, Ertter's senecio

Trifolium owyheense, Owyhee clover

At-risk animals

Athene cunicularia hypugea, western burrowing owl

Centrocercus urophasianus, sage grouse

Corynorhinus townsendii, Townsend's big-eared bat

Crotaphytus bicinctores, Mojave black-collared lizard

Grus canadensis tabida, greater sandhill crane

Oncorhynchus mykiss ssp., redband trout

Ovis canadensis californiana, California bighorn sheep

Sonora semiannulata, ground snake

1. Middle Owyhee River area

This area includes the Owyhee River Canyon from below Rome downstream to Lake Owyhee and the Leslie Gulch, Succor Creek, and Mahogany Mountain areas.

This area encompasses many of the ecoregion's unique features. The canyonlands downriver from Rome include some of the wildest country in the Owyhee Uplands, and plateau portions include significant blocks of salt desert scrub. Leslie Gulch and Succor Creek harbor a number of rare endemic plant species. Mahogany Mountain supports several of the ecoregion's largest blocks of mountain mahogany woodlands, while the Mahogany Creek watershed functions as a genetic refuge for a number of aquatic species.

Current management of much of this landscape already emphasizes biodiversity values as a result of special designations on some BLM lands. Future management of wilderness study areas, grazing, and protection of rare plants in the Succor Creek area will be key conservation issues for this landscape.

2. Upper Owyhee River area

This area includes three BLM three wilderness study areas in the upper portion of the Owyhee River watershed, extending from Rome south to the headwaters of the West Little Owyhee River and east to the Idaho border.

This landscape encompasses the canyons and uplands along the upper Owyhee River south of Rome. The southwestern-most corner of this area includes a significant portion of the largest block of mountain mahogany woodlands in the ecoregion. The wild and scenic river corridor and associated roadless areas include some of the state's most extensive wildlands. Portions of the Upper West Little Owyhee roadless area have never been grazed and support virtually pristine native vegetation (USDI/BLM 1991).

At-risk plants

Artemisia papposa, Owyhee sagebrush

Hackelia ophiobia, Three Forks stickseed

Lepidium davisii, Davis' peppergrass

At-risk animals

Centrocercus urophasianus, sage grouse

Corynorhinus townsendii, Townsend's big-eared bat

Oncorhynchus mykiss ssp., redband trout

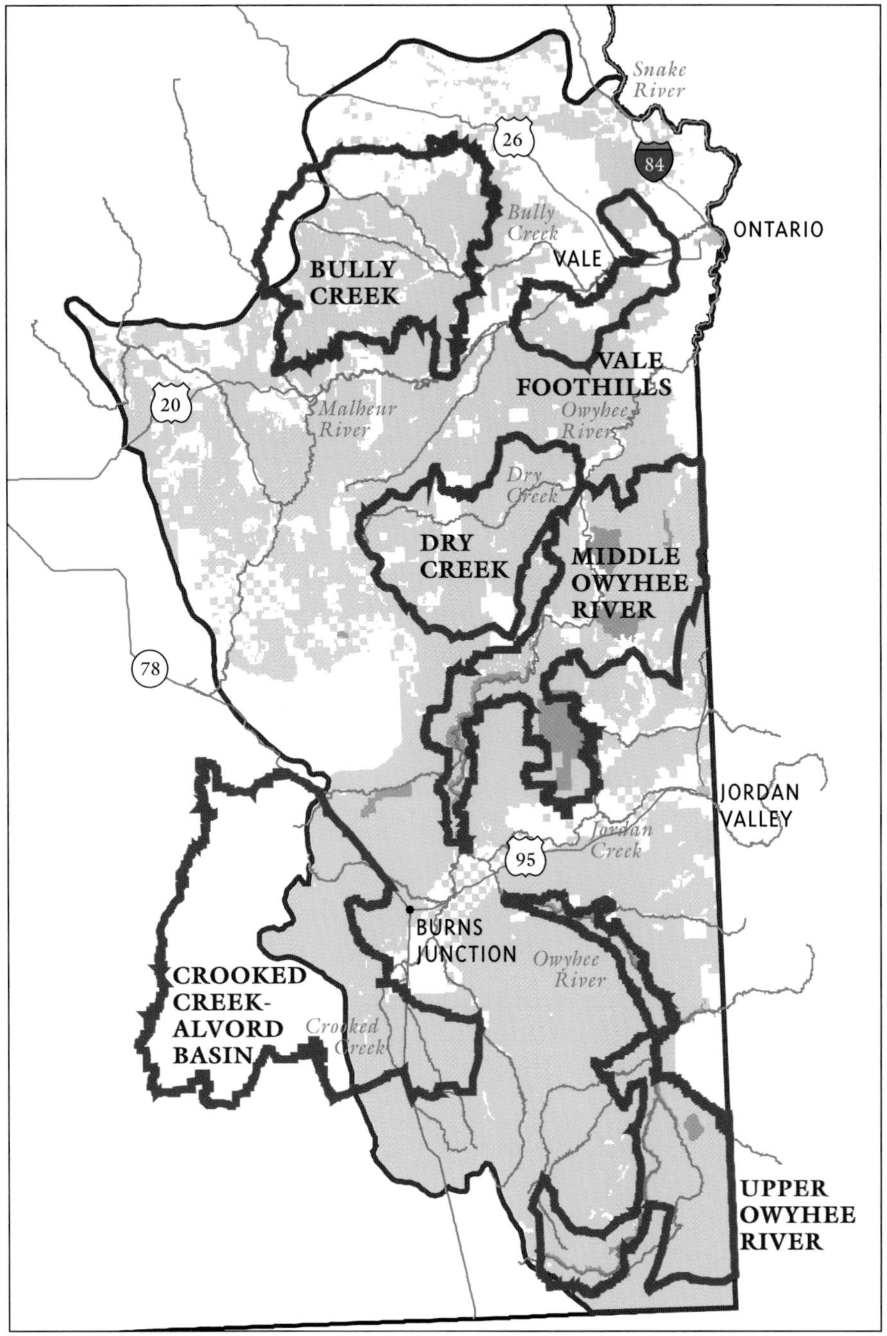

Owyhee Uplands Ecoregion

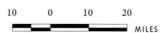

- CONSERVATION OPPORTUNITY AREAS
- ECOREGION BOUNDARY
- PUBLIC LANDS
- CURRENT CONSERVATION NETWORK

10 0 10 20 MILES

Extensive roadless areas on BLM lands in the southern portion of the ecoregion offer opportunities to conserve much of the Owyhee Uplands' native biological diversity. The foothills around Vale are home to some of Oregon's most endangered plant species, while the Bully Creek area encompasses a highly diverse assemblage of habitats in an area where the current conservation network is particularly weak.

At-risk plants

Amsinckia carinata,
Malheur Valley fiddleneck

At-risk animals

Centrocercus urophasianus, sage grouse

Corynorhinus townsendii,
Townsend's big-eared bat

Oncorhynchus mykiss ssp., redband trout

Rana luteiventris, Columbia spotted bat

3. Bully Creek area

This area in northern Malheur County extends from near Juntura northeast across the Bully Creek watershed to Cottonwood Mountain.

Located on the ecoregion's northwestern edge where it transitions to the Blue Mountains, this area contains extensive mosaics of aspen groves scattered among mountain big sagebrush, some western juniper, and ponderosa pine. These aspen habitats range from wet streamside areas to moist mountain slopes. The area also includes significant examples of big sagebrush communities with squaw apple and Thurber's needlegrass. Other features include a block of mountain mahogany woodlands and one of the few streams in the northern part of the ecoregion that retains wild and scenic qualities. The unusually diverse combination of habitats in this area supports species ranging from woodland-nesting goshawks to sage grouse, pronghorn, deer, and elk (USDI/BLM 1991).

Bully Creek vegetation

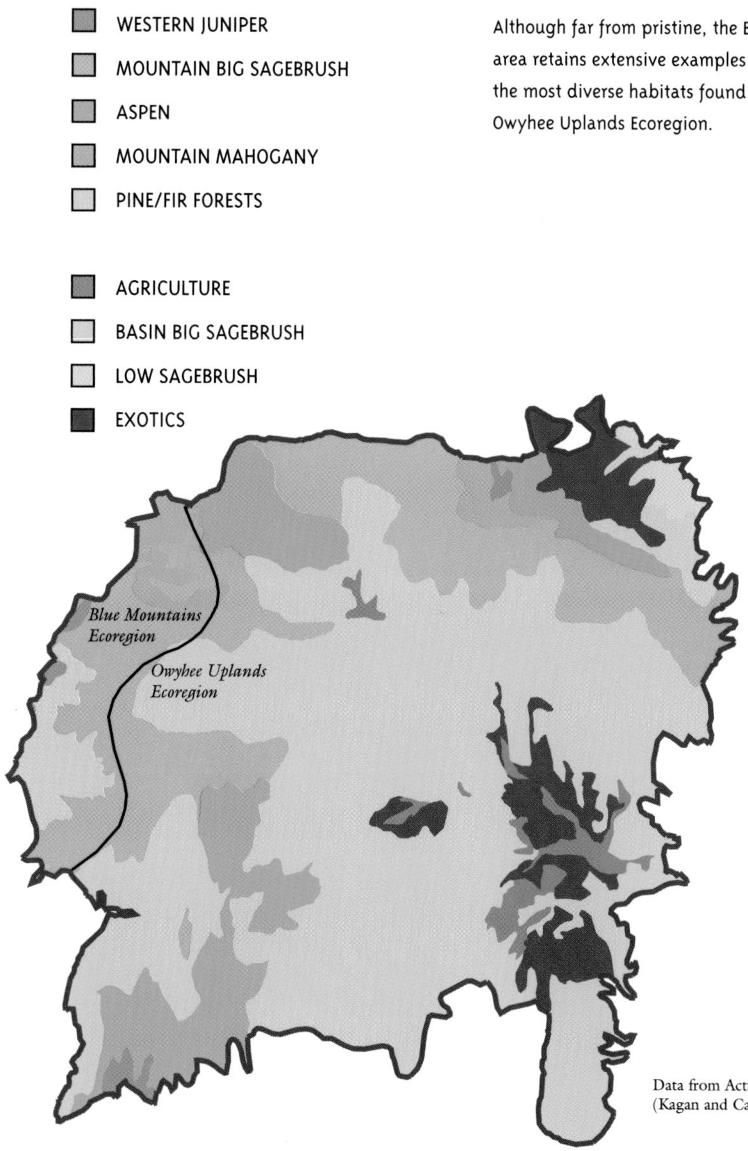

Although far from pristine, the Bully Creek area retains extensive examples of some of the most diverse habitats found in the Owyhee Uplands Ecoregion.

Data from Actual Oregon Vegetation (Kagan and Caicco 1992)

4. Crooked Creek-Alvord Basin area

This area includes parts of three BLM wilderness study areas south and west of Burns Junction in southern Malheur County. The area extends west into the Basin and Range Ecoregion, where it includes the Alvord Basin and Sheepshead Mountains.

At-risk plants

Argemone munita ssp. *rotundata*, prickly-poppy

Chaenactis macrantha, large-flowered chaenactis

Chaenactis xantiana, desert pincushion

Lepidium davisii, Davis' peppergrass

Stipa speciosa, desert needlegrass

Trifolium owyheense, Owyhee clover

At-risk animals

Charadrius alexandrinus nivosus, western snowy plover

Crotaphytus bicinctores, Mojave black-collared lizard

Euderma maculatum, spotted bat

Gila alvordensis, Alvord chub

Oncorhynchus clarki henshawi, Lahontan cutthroat trout

This area is part of a large complex of roadless areas that extends from Highway 95 westward into Alvord Basin, where it abuts the Steens Mountain conservation opportunity area described in the Basin and Range Ecoregion (see #5, page 132).

The Crooked Creek area includes the largest contiguous block of salt desert scrub habitat in the ecoregion and Oregon's best remaining examples of winterfat and black sagebrush vegetation. Exposed ash beds found throughout the area are important habitat for a number of unusual endemic plant species that are a conservation concern but are not currently classified as at-risk.

The Alvord Basin and the areas around the Sheepshead Mountains contain extensive areas of playa, salt desert scrub, and sand dune habitats. They provide habitat for several at-risk endemic fish species and a variety of reptiles, small mammals, and insects (USDI/BLM 1991).

5. Dry Creek area

This area includes most of the Dry Creek watershed, which drains the area west of Owyhee Lake in central Malheur County.

At-risk plants

Astragalus mulfordiae, Mulford's milk-vetch

Astragalus sterilis, sterile milk-vetch

Chaenactis cusickii, Cusick's chaenactis

Eriogonum chrysops, golden buckwheat

At-risk animals

Centrocercus urophasianus, sage grouse

Crotaphytus bicinctores, Mojave black-collared lizard

Pisidium ultramontanum, montane peaclam

Rana luteiventris, Columbia spotted bat

The largest aquatic diversity area identified in this ecoregion, the Dry Creek watershed is recognized by the American Fisheries Society for its importance both as a reference watershed (highest ecological integrity) and a genetic refuge. It also contains high-quality sagebrush and bitterbrush shrub steppe habitats. This landscape is contiguous with the Middle Owyhee River area, described above in #1.

At-risk plants

Astragalus mulfordiae, Mulford's milk-vetch

Hackelia cronquistii, Cronquist's stickseed

At-risk animals

Athene cunicularia hypugea, western burrowing owl

Centrocercus urophasianus, sage grouse

Corynorhinus townsendii, Townsend's big-eared bat

Rana pipiens, northern leopard frog

6. Vale foothills area

This area includes lands around the lower Malheur River Valley near Vale, extending from Sand Hollow Creek on the southwest to Tub Mountain on the north.

The hills around the lower Malheur River valley support small populations of three rare endemic plant species that are among the state's highest risks for extinction, as well as five other imperiled or vulnerable plant and animal species.

None of the three plant species at highest risk — Cronquist's stickseed *(Hackelia cronquistii),* Mulford's milk-vetch *(Astragalus mulfordiae),* and Malheur Valley fiddleneck *(Amsinckia carinata)* — is found in any areas currently managed for biodiversity. Instead, they are found on a mix of public and private ownerships, with most observations on BLM lands. Vulnerable animal species in this area include the yellow-billed cuckoo *(Coccyzus americanus),* which may already have disappeared from Oregon, and sage grouse *(Centrocercus urophasianus).*

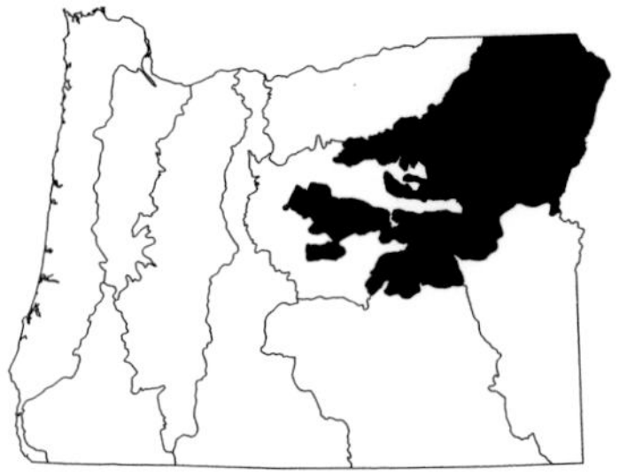

Blue Mountains Ecoregion

The Blue Mountains Ecoregion occupies nearly all of northeastern Oregon and extends into portions of southern Washington and western Idaho.

The region encompasses three major mountain ranges — the Ochoco, Blue, and Wallowa mountains. Its diverse landscapes include deep, rocky-walled canyons, glacially cut gorges, dissected plateaus, broad alluvial river valleys, and numerous mountain lakes, forests, and meadows. Due to sharp elevational differences, the climate varies over broad temperature and precipitation ranges. Overall, the ecoregion is characterized by short, dry summers and long, cold winters.

The flora is intermediate between the east Cascades and the western Rocky Mountains of Idaho and Montana. Species composition changes with altitude. Sagebrush and grassland steppes dominate the entire eastern length of the region, stands of western juniper occur along the southern reaches, ponderosa pine woodlands are characteristic at mid-elevations, and mixed coniferous forests dominate at higher altitudes. More than half the ecoregion is forested, but vast sections at all elevations are treeless due to dry conditions and the harsh climate. Extensive grasslands occur north of the Wallowa Mountains.

The region is thinly populated, with small towns in the major valleys and rural residents scattered throughout the smaller valleys among the mountains. Timber, ranching, agriculture, and tourism provide the foundations for the local economy in most areas.

National forest wilderness areas account for the bulk of the acreage (just under seven percent of the Blue Mountains Ecoregion's total area) with biodiversity management ratings of 8-10.

The largest of these wilderness areas, the Eagle Cap Wilderness in the Wallowa Mountains, contains extensive alpine habitats and high-elevation forests. The Hells Canyon Wilderness includes habitats along the full elevational gradient in one of the most rugged areas in Oregon. The North Fork John Day Wilderness (which received a 7 rating due primarily to the existence of numerous mining claims) encompasses some of the largest blocks of unharvested forest in eastern Oregon and provides one of the most important strongholds for Columbia Basin salmon. Most of the ecoregion's other wilderness areas are relatively small areas along the main spine of the Blue Mountains.

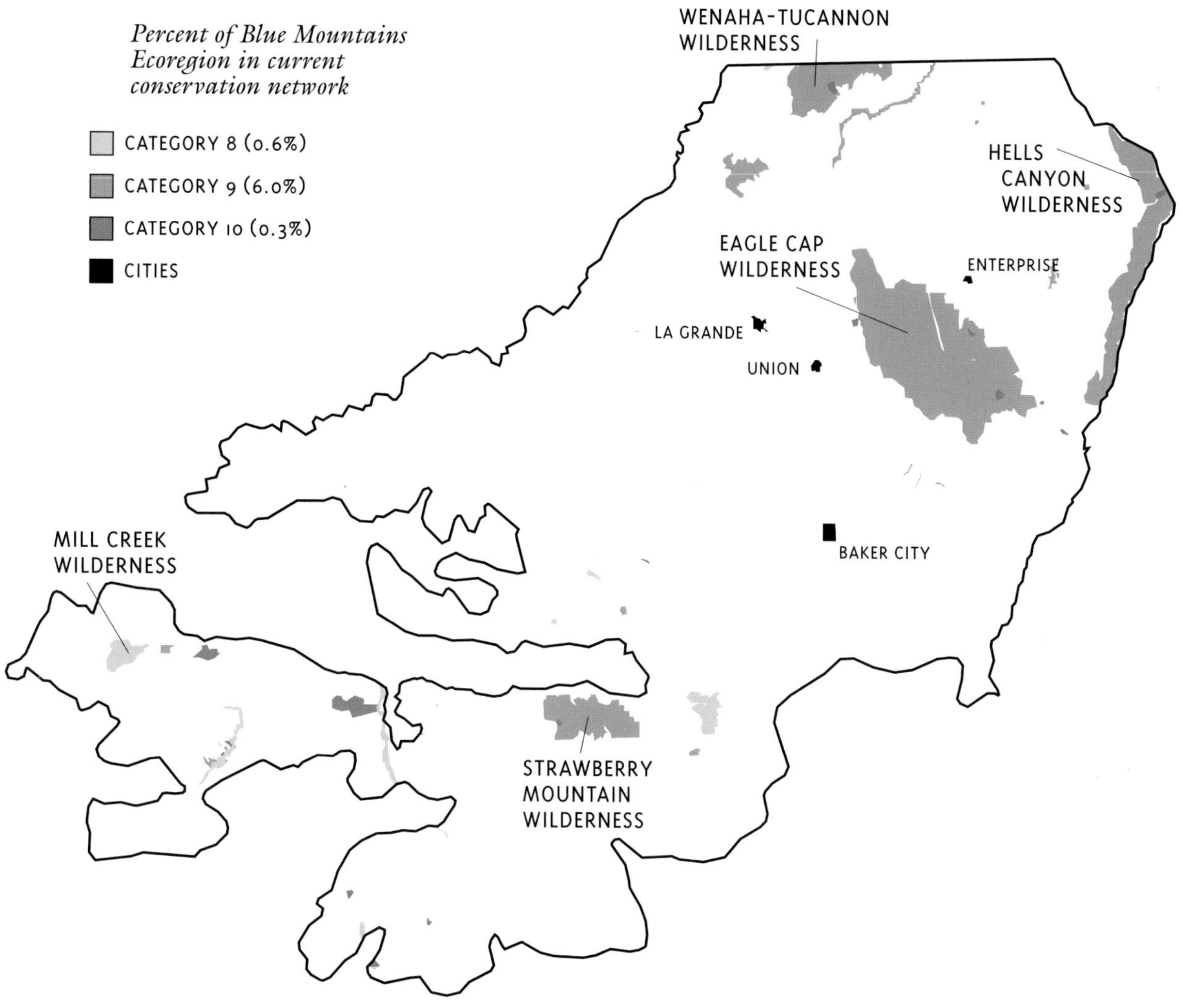

Valley bottomlands and the high-elevation palouse grasslands of the state's northeast corner are almost completely unrepresented in the existing conservation network. The state's Ladd Marsh Wildlife Area includes the last remnants of the Grande Ronde Valley's historic wetlands, and a BLM research natural area in the Keating Valley contains some high-quality riparian habitats. The Nature Conservancy manages 1,222 acres of riparian habitat on the Middle Fork John Day River. The Conservancy's Clear Lake Ridge Preserve includes 3,600 acres of mid-elevation grasslands on the northeast flanks of the Wallowa Mountains.

VEGETATION ANALYSIS

Four vegetation community types are priorities for conservation based on the broad-scale analysis: ponderosa pine woodlands and forests, bottomland hardwoods, fescue grasslands, and wetlands. All show major declines (greater than 50 percent) over the past century.

Ponderosa pine, which historically covered about 40 percent of the ecoregion, has declined dramatically over the past century due to logging, livestock grazing, and fire suppression. A comparison of historic and current vegetation maps shows a decline of more than 60 percent. Forest inventories on national forests further illustrate the changes. According to Langston (1995), ponderosa pine accounted for 57 percent of the Wallowa-Whitman National Forest's timber volume in 1906; by 1991, the figure was less than 20 percent. In 1912, these forests were open stands of ponderosa pines; in 1991, only 10 percent fit this description.

Most of what was historically mapped as ponderosa pine forest is now classified as ponderosa pine-Douglas-fir. The pattern of change is fairly consistent across the ecoregion's forests, where millions of acres have changed over a matter of a few decades from pine to fir, and then from healthy fir to drought-stressed, insect-defoliated fir.

Bottomland hardwoods show a significant decline from historic levels throughout the ecoregion. (For the purpose of this comparison, this category includes cottonwood-hawthorn-willow riparian woodlands and black cottonwood riparian woodlands in the current vegetation map.) These habitats are extremely diverse and important for a wide variety of wildlife. This is particularly true for low-elevation riparian types along the Snake River and in the Grande Ronde Valley and for many high-elevation riparian areas.

Fescue bunchgrasses, formerly the most common grassland types in this ecoregion, have declined by about half, mainly due to agricultural development. Although this general vegetation type is widely distributed, grasslands dominated by Idaho fescue have different species composition in different areas. Fire has probably created conditions that favor plant diversity on these sites (Agee 1994). One large block of these native grasslands remains on a plateau north of the Wallowa Mountains. Known as Zumwalt Prairie, these grasslands cover approximately 123,500 acres. The entire block is in private ownership.

With virtually all of the Grande Ronde and Baker valleys' historic **wetlands** drained and converted to agriculture, most of the region's wetlands are found at higher elevations. These seasonally flooded and sub-irrigated meadows provide important habitat for migrating and breeding birds, including the at-risk upland sandpiper *(Bartramia longicauda)*. The largest remaining blocks of these wetlands — almost all on private lands — are found at Big Summit

Prairie, along the upper Silvies River, and in Bear and Logan valleys.

Grand fir forests, which occur at upper elevations in the Ochoco and Blue mountains, are another type of potential concern. These highly productive forests are being replaced by Douglas-fir as a result of logging and subsequent planting of Douglas-fir. Comparison of the current and historic vegetation maps shows most of these conversions have occurred on national forest lands in the northern Blue and Wallowa mountain ranges. Losses are primarily of old growth grand fir. Large, old grand fir trees infected by Indian Paint fungus provide important prime habitat for pileated woodpeckers *(Dryocopus pileatus)* and vaux swifts *(Chaetura vauxi)*. These forests are also important winter habitat for deer and elk.

ECOSYSTEM CHANGES

Many of the biggest concerns for biodiversity in the Blue Mountains stem from interrelated changes in ecosystem processes and vegetation structure that cannot be seen in a coarse-scale vegetation map.

Fire suppression has dramatically altered forests in the Blue Mountains, resulting in changes in species composition, stand structure, and landscape-scale ecosystem processes. Although the problems associated with fire suppression are fairly well recognized and understood, the solutions are less clear. The scale of the problem is enormous in the Blue Mountains, where high levels of tree mortality caused by insects and disease have dramatically increased the intensity and size of wildfires that do occur. Solutions are costly and are not likely to be the same between forest types or within a particular type (Agee 1993).

Timber harvest and management for timber production has driven most of the changes in the ecoregion's forests. Historically, old growth forests in the Blue Mountains were characterized by very large, old ponderosa pine trees (as well as old growth Douglas-fir and western larch). Old growth pine trees generally have no branches for the lower 70 feet, and have a fire-resistant bark that can be more than six inches thick. Younger trees have lower branches and thinner bark. Logging on public lands has typically removed the largest pine trees, leaving some relatively young, medium-sized trees as part of the "shelterwood" harvest system. While these areas still appear to be forests, they are very different from the historic old growth forests.

Remaining old growth forests provide important nesting habitat for many wildlife species, including species like northern goshawk *(Accipiter gentilis)* that require large areas of intact forests for survival and reproduction (Henjum et al. 1994).

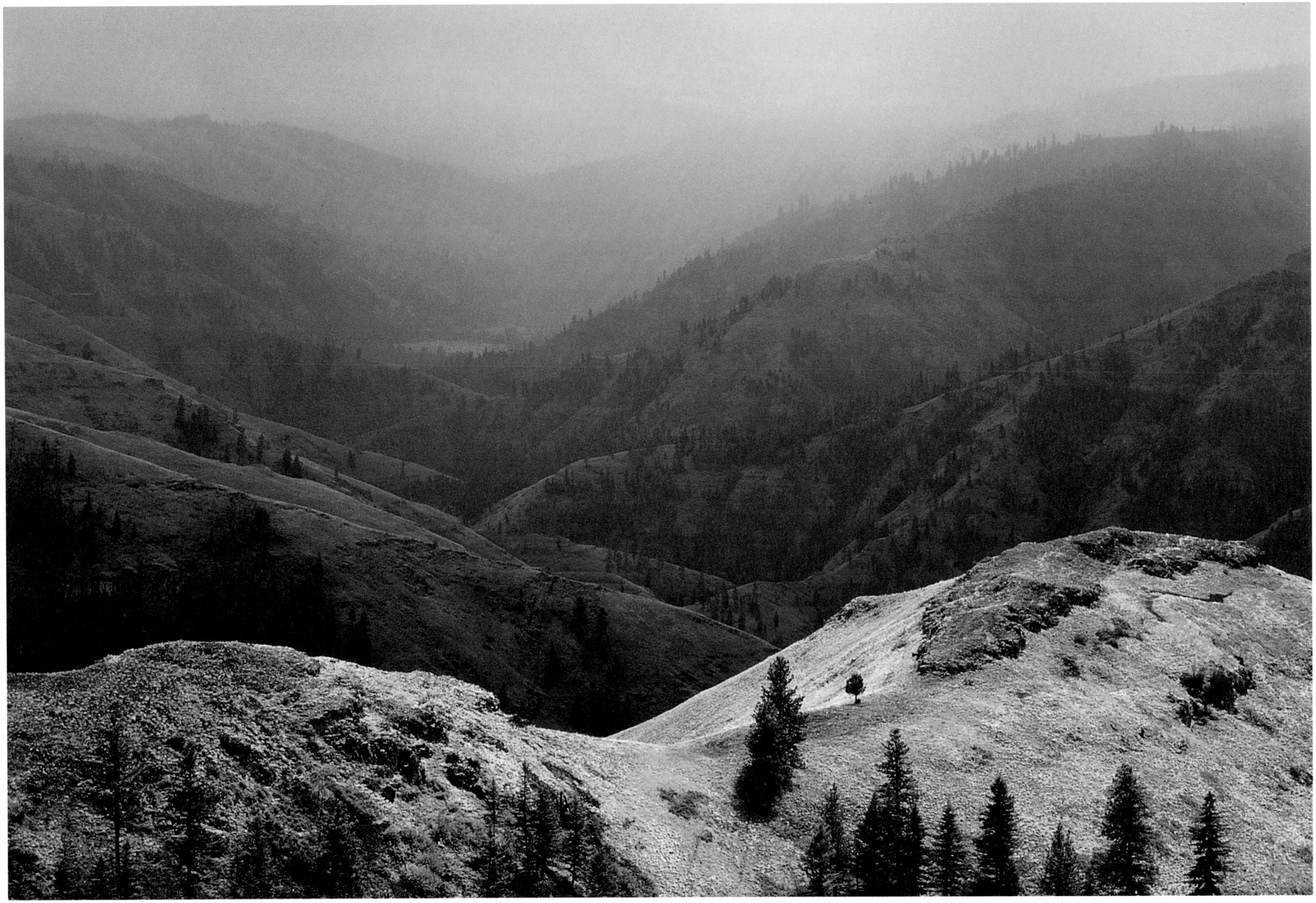

One of the most important differences between old growth and logged forests is their vulnerability to high-intensity fires. The combination of younger trees and fire suppression, which has resulted in the presence of numerous seedlings and saplings, has left most of the managed forests extremely vulnerable to high-intensity canopy fires.

Livestock grazing has also contributed to major ecosystem changes in the Blue Mountains. Beginning in the 1870s, much of this ecoregion experienced intense grazing pressure from immense herds of livestock, especially sheep. Not until the 1930s were controls imposed on livestock numbers and on duration of grazing seasons on public lands. Plant species composition of grasslands, as well as of forest and woodland understories, was greatly affected by livestock grazing pressure, which vastly exceeded the effects of grazing by native ungulates (e.g., deer, elk).

Heavy livestock grazing also contributed to changes in the natural fire regime. Heavy grazing removed the herbaceous "fine fuels" (grasses, sedges, broad-leaved flowering plants) that historically carried fires with great regularity through the ecoregion's grasslands and shrub steppe and low- and mid-elevation woodlands and forests. The result was reduced fire frequency in forests and woodlands, which led to increased density of trees and shrubs — especially relatively fire-intolerant species such as grand and subalpine fir.

Joseph Creek
Photographer, Larry N. Olson

On many grassland and shrub steppe habitats, poor livestock management has had the opposite effect, leading to increased fire frequency on lands where native perennial grasses have been replaced by highly flammable cheatgrass and other exotic annuals as a result of overgrazing (Henson 1982).

In much of the ecoregion, livestock numbers have diminished greatly since the early part of the century, and as a result many areas have shown significant ecological recovery. In general, however, riparian habitats remain degraded

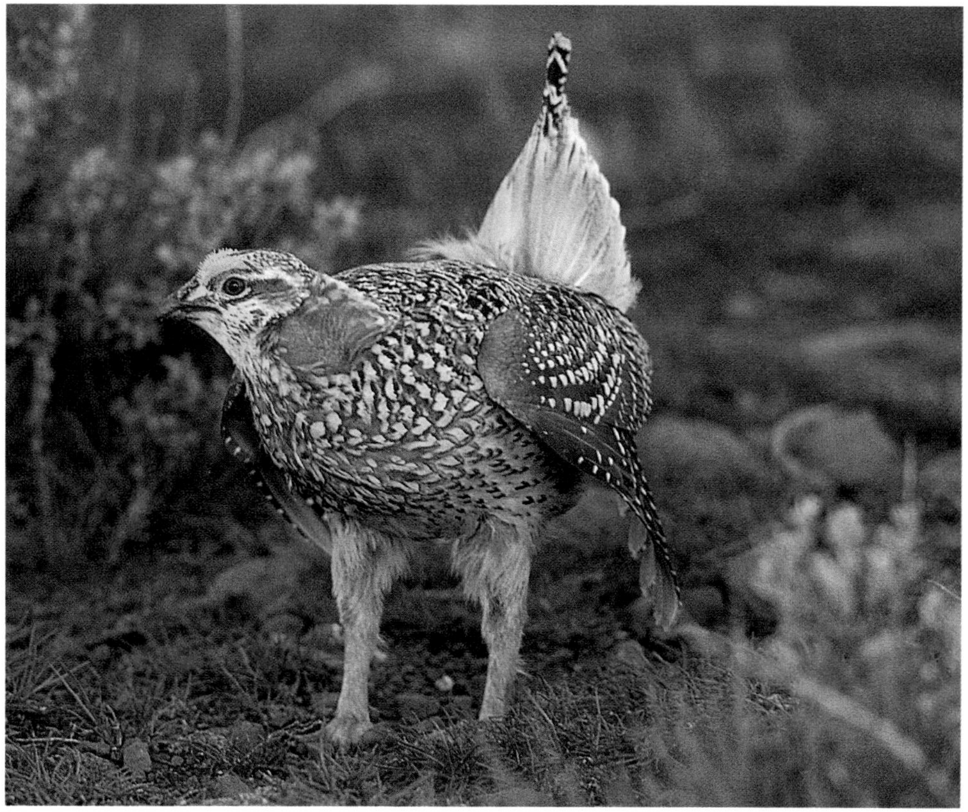

Columbian sharp-tailed grouse
Photographer, Geoff Pampush

from timber harvest practices, road-building in conjunction with logging activities, and livestock grazing. In some areas, intense seasonal grazing pressures from high numbers of deer and elk further retard riparian recovery.

AT-RISK SPECIES

Animals. The upland sandpiper *(Bartramia longicauda)* ranges across much of North America, but the only sizable breeding population west of the Rocky Mountains is found in this ecoregion, where it nests in mountain meadows at mid-elevations. Most are found on private lands in Bear and Logan valleys, but they have also been seen intermittently at Sycan Marsh in the East Cascades.

The Columbian sharp-tailed grouse *(Tympanuchas phasianellus columbianus)* was once common on the ecoregion's prairies, but was extirpated in Oregon by the 1970s. Overhunting and habitat alteration and loss were the main contributing factors. The species was reintroduced in 1991 and early results look promising. But successful restoration will ultimately depend on the continued, combined efforts of managing agencies and local citizens to restore and protect adequate habitat for this symbol of the prairie ecosystem.

Survival of Snake River chinook salmon *(Oncorhynchus tshawytscha)* presents one of the greatest conservation challenges in the Blue Mountains. With one of the longest migration routes in the Pacific Northwest, these fish face near-insurmountable obstacles — dams and impoundments, dramatically changing hydrologic conditions in the mainstem of the Columbia River, loss and degradation of spawning habitat, and overharvest.

Although not currently considered "at-risk" under the definition used in this document, approximately 20 other vertebrate species found in eastside forests have been identified as highly vulnerable due to habitat loss and degradation (Henjum et al. 1994). Included among these species are northern goshawk, three-toed woodpecker *(Picoides tridactylus)*, black-backed woodpecker *(P. arcticus)*, pileated woodpecker *(Dryocopus pileatus)*, flammulated owl *(Otus flammeolus)*, boreal owl *(Aegolius funereus)*, and great gray owl *(Strix nebulosa)*.

Plants. At-risk plant species in the Blue Mountains can be grouped into three types: high-elevation species; Snake River endemics; and valley species (including riparian species) that occur largely on private lands.

The highest diversity of rare species in the ecoregion can be found in the high-elevation habitats of the Wallowa Mountains. At-risk species in these areas are less vulnerable than their lower-elevation counterparts due to the rugged terrain, which tends to discourage intensive human uses, and the protection from development afforded by extensive wilderness designations. However, as recreational pressures increase, these high-elevation species may soon require additional conservation attention. Because of their small numbers and narrow distribution, these species could also be jeopardized by climatic changes if significant warming occurs.

Hell's Canyon of the Snake River is another unique, rugged landscape that hosts its own set of endemic species. Several of these endemics are rare, including the first plant species to be federally listed as endangered in Oregon, Macfarlane's four-o'clock *(Mirabilis macfarlanei)*. This species, first listed in 1979, has since been reclassified as threatened due to the subsequent discovery of additional populations, improved livestock management on public and private lands, and reduced threats to existing populations. Snake River goldenweed *(Pyrrocoma radiata)* inhabits grasslands that are partially protected through the U.S. Forest Service's management of the Hells Canyon National Recreation Area.

Most of the species at highest risk in the region occur largely on private lands in the valleys. Four of these are species of grapefern or "moonwort" *(Botrychium campestre, B. lineare, B. paradoxum, B. pendunculosum)* that occur mainly in the upper portions of the Lostine Valley and are vulnerable to recreational impacts. Two others, Oregon semaphore grass *(Pleuropogon oregonus)* and Howell's spectacular thelypody *(Thelypodium howellii* ssp. *spectabilis)*, occur in the Baker Valley where most of the land has been converted to agricultural use. Two small populations of Howell's spectacular thelypody and one of Oregon semaphore grass are receiving special management through voluntary cooperation of private landowners.

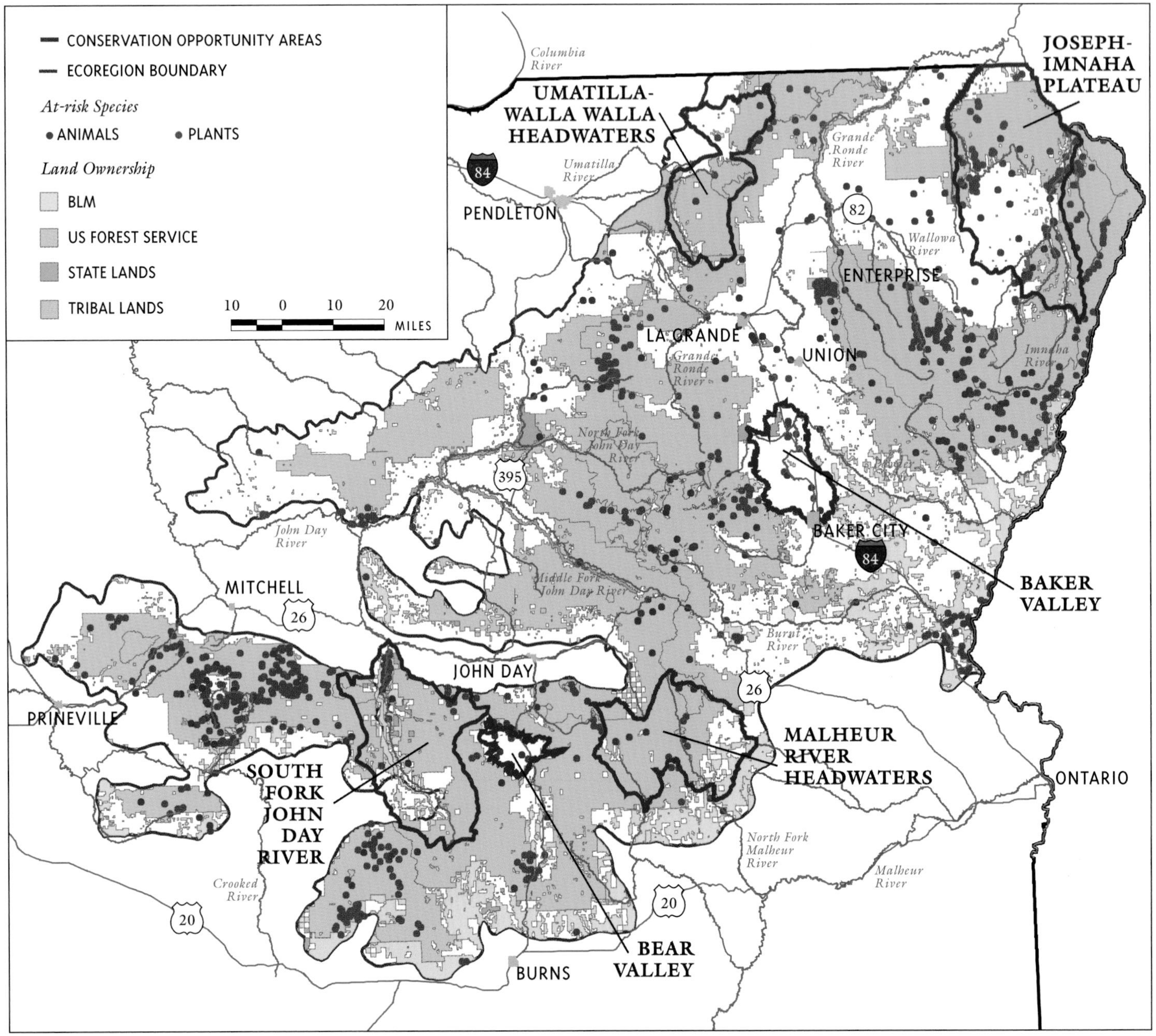

Locations of at-risk plant and animals recorded in the Oregon Natural Heritage Program's data bases are shown in relation to land ownership and the Oregon Biodiversity Project's conservation opportunity areas.

Beaver dam, Middle Fork
John Day River
Photographer, Harold E. Malde

Leave it to Beavers

The American beaver *(Castor canadensis)* is North America's largest rodent, and since 1969, the state animal of Oregon. Beavers were common inhabitants of western landscapes until fur trappers nearly drove them to extinction in the mid-nineteenth century. Their numbers have grown since then, but land managers have traditionally regarded beavers as nuisances. Their dams can block irrigation ditches and flood fields; block culverts and wash out roads; and impound streams and inundate harvestable timber.

Despite these problems, the ecological benefits of beaver activity far outweigh the nuisances. Increasingly, people are coming to appreciate the enormous contribution beavers make to watershed health. In many areas, people are working to restore beavers to areas from which they were extirpated. And in areas where they thrive and sometimes come into conflict with humans, people have found ways to modify beaver activities without removing their dams. Now, instead of viewing beavers as "riparian rats," people see them more and more as "riparian habitat managers" — true keystone species that play a pivotal role in maintaining riparian and watershed health.

Some of the well-documented benefits of beaver activity include:

- raised water tables and related sediment settling, which contributes to the creation of meadows behind beaver dams and to the enhancement of fisheries downstream;
- control of streambank and channel erosion by trapping silt eroding from adjacent lands;
- creation of large carbon-absorbing reservoirs that greatly boost the amount of nitrogen available to plants.
- regeneration of riparian vegetation, which increases food and shelter for numerous invertebrates, other mammals, waterfowl, and songbirds;
- enhancement of fish habitat behind dams by increasing water depth;
- reduction of stream velocity and overall improvement of water quality as riparian vegetation intercepts contamination from agricultural runoff;
- recharging of groundwater reservoirs and stabilization of stream flows throughout the summer and during droughts; and the protection of downstream croplands and urban areas from floods by the beaver's enhancement of upstream water storage (through the creation of meadows and wetlands).

AQUATIC SPECIES ANALYSIS

Blue Mountains salmon and steelhead populations have suffered from the same problems that have led to the decline of anadromous fish throughout the Columbia River basin. A number of the ecoregion's salmon stocks are extinct, several are listed as threatened or endangered under the federal Endangered Species Act, and most others are severely depressed. But many resident salmonid species that spend their entire life cycle within freshwater habitats are also threatened. Native bull trout *(Salvelinus confluentus)* have declined so much that remaining populations have been proposed for listing under the federal Endangered Species Act.

A common thread in the decline of so many different fish taxa is the degradation and simplification of freshwater environments by human land use practices. Different factors contribute to degradation in different places, but in the region as a whole the primary agents have been agriculture and irrigation, timber harvest, road construction, livestock grazing, and mining (McIntosh et al. 1994; Wissmar et al. 1994). Past grazing practices, particularly season-long cattle grazing, are responsible for most of the damage, with logging, road building, and large mammal browsing contributing to lesser degrees.

Despite these problems, the Blue Mountains remain one of the principal strongholds for salmonids in the Columbia River basin (ICBEMP 1997b). More than one-third of the ecoregion is included within the complex of aquatic diversity areas identified by the American Fisheries Society. The large proportion of aquatic diversity areas in northeastern Oregon reflects relatively high-quality habitat associated with several wilderness areas and a diversity of at-risk salmonids, including bull trout, redband trout, summer steelhead, westslope cutthroat trout, and spring and fall chinook (Henjum et al. 1994).

Most of the aquatic diversity areas in the Blue Mountains are found in the higher elevation, forested portions of the ecoregion where upper tributaries provide the last remaining refuge for many native cold-water fish. Historically, many of these smaller tributaries were marginal habitats, particularly for salmonid species, compared with the more productive alluvial valleys of larger streams and rivers (Henjum et al. 1994).

Among the dozen areas the American Fisheries Society identified as aquatic diversity areas, two areas — North Fork John Day and the upper Walla Walla — each meet four out of five ecological criteria for the designation. The John Day River system is particularly critical for aquatic biodiversity because it is the only major river in the Oregon portion of the Columbia River basin where genetic integrity of native salmonid stocks has not been diluted by the introduction of hatchery fish.

SUMMARY OF CONSERVATION ISSUES

Major issues for biodiversity conservation in the Blue Mountains Ecoregion include:

- The current conservation network is largely limited to higher mountain forests and alpine areas. Lower elevation vegetation types such as valley bottom grasslands, dry forests, wetlands, and shrublands are largely unrepresented.
- Outside the existing conservation network, most remnant native habitats occur as scattered patches.
- Few large blocks of intact old growth forest remain; most forests have been heavily fragmented by timber harvest and road development.
- Fire suppression, livestock grazing and silvicultural practices have altered the character and composition of forests, leaving them vulnerable to high-intensity fire, insects, and disease. Although reintroduction of fire would help restore forest structure, improve forest health, and benefit native wildlife, it poses significant challenges to forest managers.
- Aquatic habitats have been widely degraded, particularly in valley bottoms and at lower elevations. Habitats least impacted are found primarily in less productive systems at higher elevations.
- Some of the last remaining strongholds of native Columbia River Basin salmon stocks are found in this ecoregion.
- The spread of exotic species threatens native communities and the economic productivity of resource lands.

CONSERVATION OPPORTUNITY AREAS

The Oregon Biodiversity Project identified six areas in the Blue Mountains Ecoregion that appear to offer good opportunities to address biodiversity conservation needs.

The project experimented with a computer-based selection process in this ecoregion. All six-digit hydrologic units were scored and ranked based on a number of criteria or attributes. Positive attributes included at-risk species, priority habitats, and proximity to the existing conservation. Negative attributes included density of roads and human population, and vegetation types dominated by exotic species. The results identified too many potential areas, requiring expert judgment to sort through the candidates.

As a result, the final selections were made using the same basic process employed in the other ecoregions. Priority vegetation types and aquatic diversity areas converged in several key areas that were obvious choices. The highest concentrations of at-risk species were found in Hells Canyon and the Wallowa Mountains in areas that are already within the existing conservation network. Closer examination of at-risk species that are not well represented in the existing conservation network led to selection of the Baker Valley and South Fork John Day areas.

REFERENCE WATERSHED

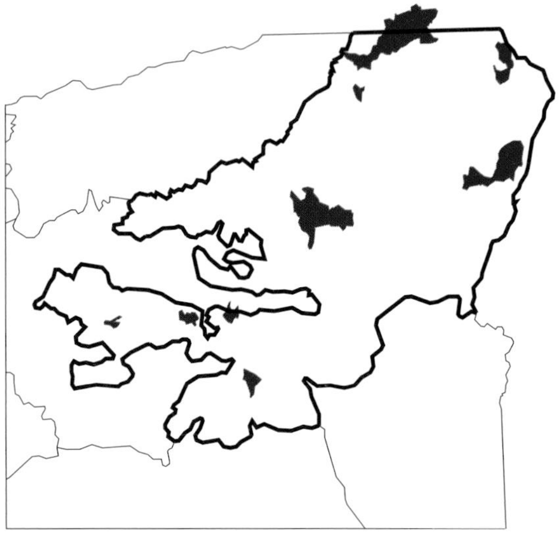

GENETIC REFUGE

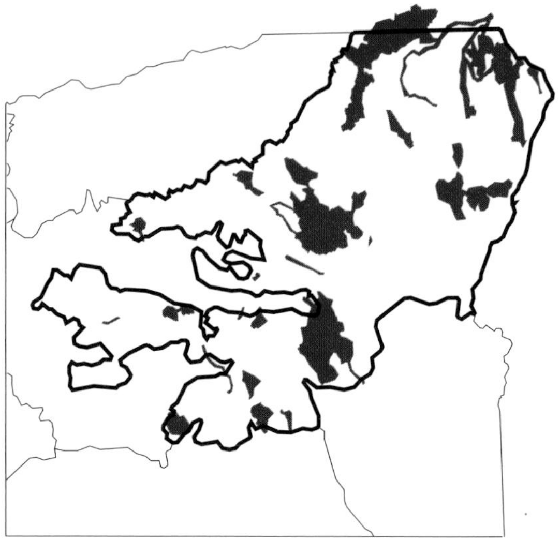

CENTERS OF SPECIES DIVERSITY

ECOLOGICAL FUNCTIONS

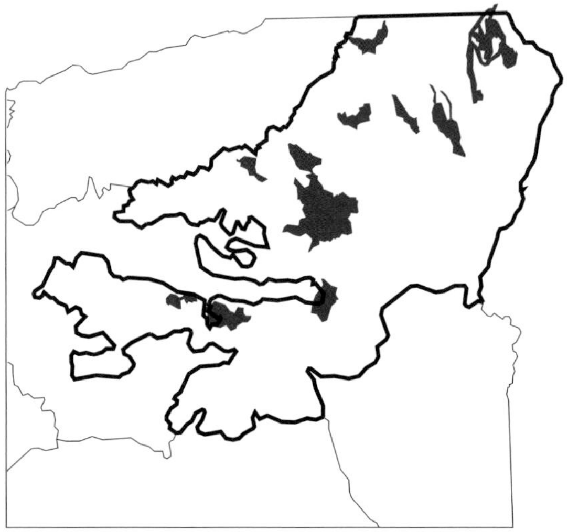

CONNECTING CORRIDOR

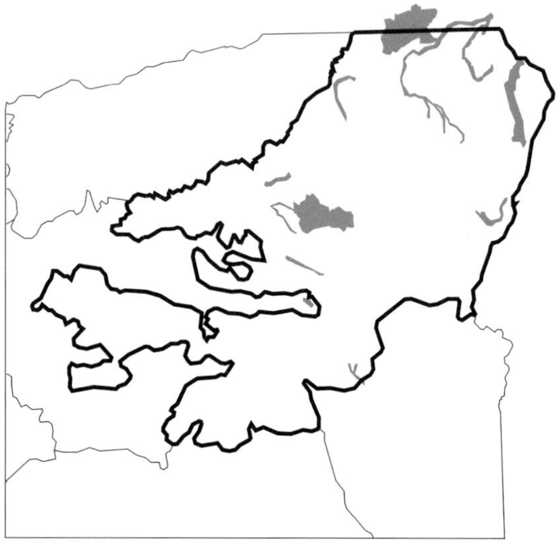

The Blue Mountains are a major stronghold for Columbia Basin slamonids, and more than one-third of the ecoregion is in aquatic diversity areas. Most of the aquatic diversity areas are found at higher elevations where tributary systems provide key refuges for native cold-water fish.

Data from Oregon Critical Watersheds Database (Bottom et al. 1993)

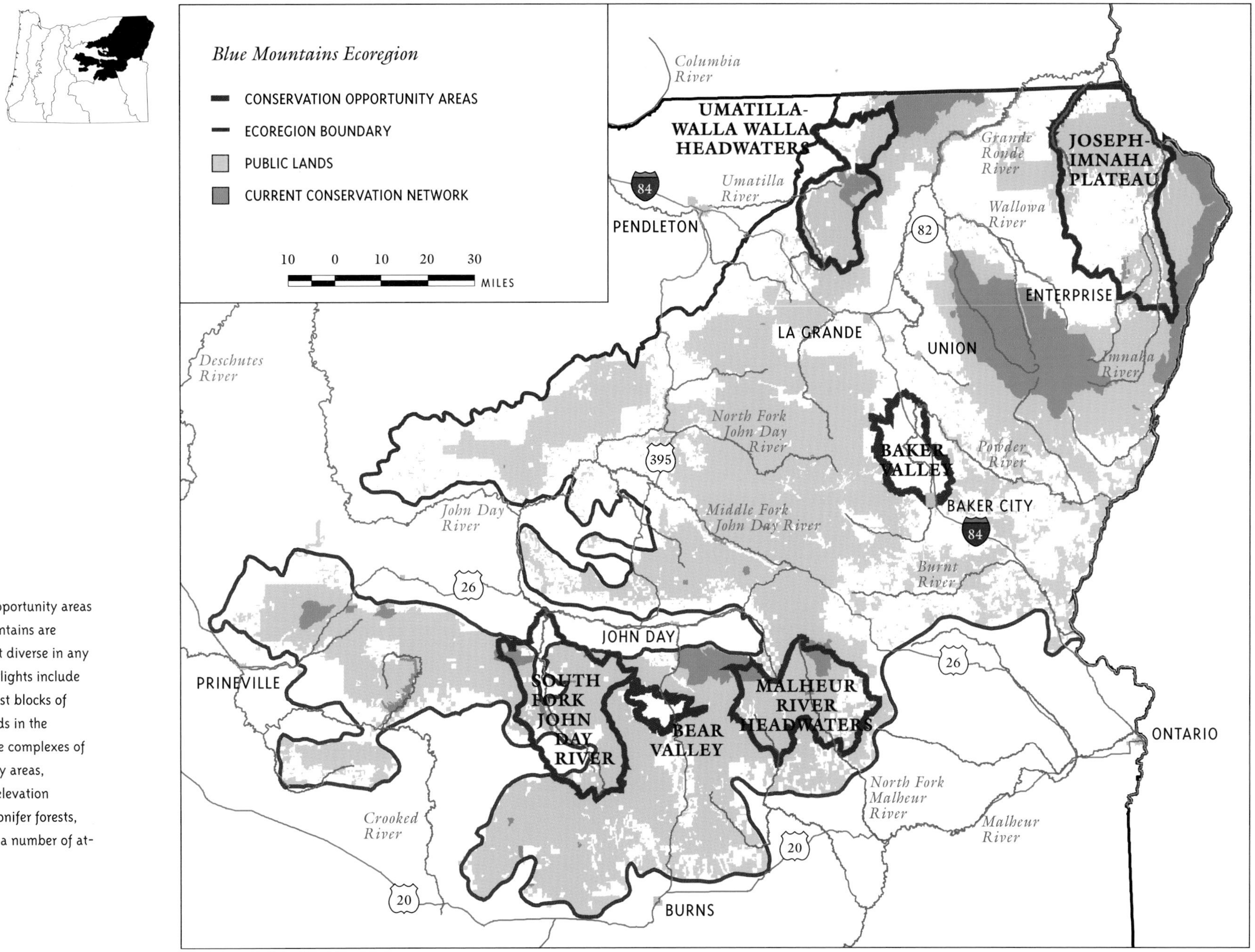

Conservation opportunity areas in the Blue Mountains are among the most diverse in any ecoregion. Highlights include one of the largest blocks of native grasslands in the Northwest, large complexes of aquatic diversity areas, extensive mid-elevation wetlands and conifer forests, and habitat for a number of at-risk species.

At-risk plants

Lomatium ravenii, Raven's lomatium

At-risk animals

Bartramia longicauda, upland sandpiper

Grus canadensis tabida, greater sandhill crane

Gulo gulo, wolverine

Oncorhynchus mykiss ssp., redband trout

Rana luteiventris, Columbia spotted bat

Salvelinus confluentus, bull trout

1. Malheur River headwaters

This area in southern Grant County encompasses the headwaters of the Malheur, North Fork Malheur, and Little Malheur rivers. The area lies between the Monument Rock Wilderness to the east and the Strawberry Mountain Wilderness to the west.

Anchored by two national forest wilderness areas, this area includes three habitat types that are conservation priorities — ponderosa pine woodlands, grand fir forests, and extensive mid-elevation wetlands. The area also includes several at-risk species. With the exception of the portions that lie within the two wilderness areas, current management does not emphasize biodiversity values.

The U.S. Forest Service, through Malheur National Forest, administers most of this area. Some wet meadows on private lands in Logan Valley provide habitat for the at-risk upland sandpiper. The American Fisheries Society has identified aquatic diversity areas in the headwaters of the Malheur, North Fork Malheur, and Little Malheur rivers based on their importance for genetic diversity and overall ecological functioning (Bottom et al. 1993). The upper mainstem Malheur and North Fork Malheur rivers have been designated national wild and scenic rivers.

2. Bear Valley

Located south of John Day in Grant County, this area includes the mosaic of grasslands, wetlands and sagebrush steppe found in Bear Valley.

Surrounded by national forest lands, Bear Valley is predominantly in private ownership. The valley's extensive mid-elevation wetlands support at-risk species ranging from upland sandpiper and greater sandhill crane to redband trout (*Oncorhynchus mykiss* ssp.).

In addition to their habitat values, the valley's wetlands influence downstream water quality and stream flows, which in turn influence biological diversity and agricultural uses in the Silvies River and its floodplain near Burns. Some private landowners in the valley are already incorporating ecosystem management concepts in rangeland stewardship.

At-risk plants

Carex interior, inland sedge

Thelypodium howellii var. *howellii*, Howell's thelypody

At-risk animals

Bartramia longicauda, upland sandpiper

Brachylagus idahoensis, pygmy rabbit

Grus canadensis tabida, greater sandhill crane

Oncorhynchus mykiss ssp., redband trout

Rana luteiventris, Columbia spotted bat

3. South Fork John Day River

This area south of Dayville in Grant County includes most of the South Fork John Day River. It extends down the mainstem of the John Day River into the Picture Gorge conservation opportunity area in the Lava Plains Ecoregion.

This area was selected mainly for its importance for anadromous fish. It includes eight aquatic diversity areas selected by the American Fisheries Society for their ecological function and their value as genetic refuges, reference watersheds (highest ecological integrity), and connecting corridors (Bottom et al. 1993).

At-risk plant species are found throughout the watershed, including the South Fork John Day milk-vetch *(Astragalus diaphanus* var. *diurnus)*, an endemic plant that occurs only in exposed, loose soils and riparian habitats in this drainage.

Hardwood riparian communities still exist along part of the river corridor. Higher elevations include some high quality remnants of ponderosa pine woodland and grand fir forests.

The Black Canyon Wilderness and the national wild and scenic river portion of the South Fork John Day River provide a foundation for broader landscape-level biodiversity management in this area. The state's Murderer's Creek Wildlife Area currently emphasizes management for big game species, but could expand its focus to encompass broader biodiversity values.

At-risk plants

Astragalus diaphanus var. *diurnus*, South Fork John Day milk-vetch

Botrychium ascendens, upward-lobed moonwort

Botrychium crenulatum, crenulate grape-fern

Luina serpentina, colonial luina

At-risk animals

Ovis canadensis californiana, California bighorn sheep

Rana luteiventris, Columbia spotted bat

Oncorhynchus mykiss ssp., redband trout

4. Umatilla-Walla Walla headwaters

This area in Umatilla County includes the upper portions of the Umatilla and Walla Walla river watersheds from Interstate 84 north into Washington.

This area also makes significant contributions to aquatic biodiversity. It contains watersheds that meet all five of the ecological criteria the American Fisheries Society used in identifying aquatic diversity areas (Bottom et al. 1993). It has also been identified by the Interior Columbia River Basin Ecosystem Management Project as a "hotspot" of species rarity and endemism (ICBEMP 1997a).

The forests, streams and grasslands in this area support a number of at-risk species, including wolverine, margined sculpin *(Cottus marginatus)*, redband trout *(Oncorhynchus mykiss* ssp.), and several plant species. Most of the area is within the Umatilla National Forest, and a portion is within the North Fork Umatilla Wilderness. Cooperative efforts between the Forest Service, the Confederated Tribes of the Umatilla Reservation, and other partners could enhance management of this area for a broad range of biodiversity values.

At-risk plants

Botrychium minganense, gray moonwort

Carex backii, Back's sedge

At-risk animals

Cottus marginatus, margined sculpin

Gulo gulo, wolverine

Oncorhynchus mykiss ssp., redband trout

Salvelinus confluentus, bull trout

At-risk plants

Achnatherum wallowaensis, Wallowa ricegrass

Allium geyeri var. *geyeri,* Geyer's onion

Arabis hastatula, Hell's Canyon rockcress

Calochortus macrocarpus var. *maculosus,* green-band mariposa-lily

Calochortus niditus, broad-fruit mariposa-lily

Carex hystericina, porcupine sedge

Erigeron engelmannii var. *davisii,* Englemann's daisy

Leptodactylon pungens ssp. *hazeliae,* Hazel's prickly phlox

Mirabilis macfarlanei, Macfarlane's four-o'clock

Phacelia minutissima, tiny-flower phacelia

Silene spaldingii, Spalding's campion

At-risk animals

Coccyzus americanus, yellow-billed cuckoo

Gulo gulo, wolverine

Fisherola nuttali, shortface lanx

Fluminicola columbiana, Columbia pebblesnail (or spire snail)

Oncorhynchus mykiss ssp., redband trout

Oncorhynchus tshawytscha ssp., Snake River chinook salmon

Polites coras, Peck's skipper butterfly

Salvelinus confluentus, bull trout

Tinodes siskiyou, Siskiyou caddisfly

Tringa melanoleuca, greater yellowlegs

Tympanuchus phasianellus, Columbian sharp-tailed grouse

5. Joseph-Imnaha Plateau

This area in Wallowa County includes most of the Imnaha River and Joseph Creek watersheds. It extends from the upper reaches of the mainstem Imnaha River and the grasslands of Zumwalt Prairie north to the Snake River.

This area stands out for its native grasslands and its contribution to aquatic diversity. Zumwalt Prairie, on the plateau above the Imnaha River and Joseph Creek canyons, is one of the largest remaining native grasslands in the Pacific Northwest. Most of the Idaho fescue bunchgrass habitat in the Blue Mountains Ecoregion has been converted or degraded, making this area a high priority for conservation.

This area's complex of aquatic diversity areas includes watersheds that meet all five ecological criteria used by the American Fisheries Society in its assessment of key aquatic habitats (Bottom et al. 1993).

In addition to its importance to Snake River salmon, this area provides habitat for a number of other at-risk species such as wolverine *(Gulo gulo),* lynx *(Felis lynx),* Columbian sharp-tailed grouse *(Tympanuchus phasianellus),* and 10 at-risk plant species.

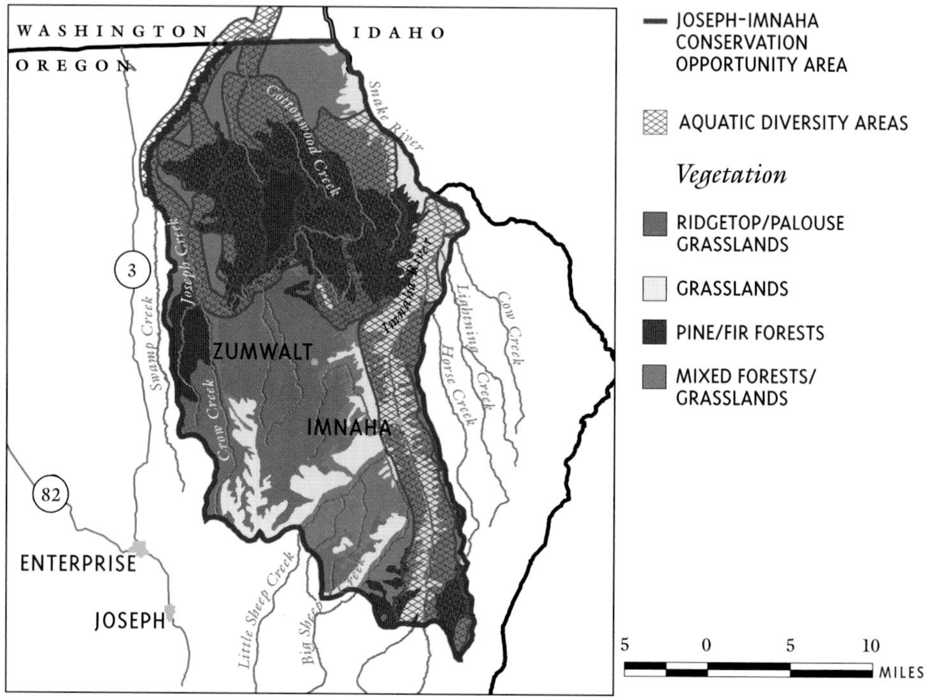

Data from Kagan and Caicco 1992; Bottom et al. 1993

The Joseph-Imnaha area supports some of the Northwest's most extensive remaining native grasslands as well as a number of streams that are key contributors to the ecoregion's aquatic diversity.

At-risk plants

Rorippa columbiae, Columbia cress

Thelypodium howellii ssp. *spectabilis*, Howell's spectacular thelypody

At-risk animals

Brachylagus idahoensis, pygmy rabbit

Chrysemys picta, painted turtle

Dolichonyx oryzivorus, bobolink

Grus canadensis tabida, greater sandhill crane

6. Baker Valley

This area includes the lowlands in the Baker Valley from the North Powder River south to Baker City.

Although most of the Baker Valley's native habitats have been modified or converted for agricultural and urban uses, this area has significant potential for restoration of key habitats. It also supports an at-risk plant species that is among the most vulnerable in Oregon, Howell's spectacular thelypody (*Thelypodium howellii* ssp. *spectabilis*).

Virtually all the valley is in private ownership. Habitat restoration and protection will depend heavily on cooperative efforts with private landowners.

The North Powder River and the northern portions of the mainstem Powder River flow through unplowed bottomlands with potential for restoration, including riparian remnants that could be restored to bottomland hardwood forests. Wetlands, black greasewood flats, and alkaline grasslands can be found in a number of locations, including some high-quality, valley-margin sagebrush vegetation (including the rare three-tipped sagebrush communities).

Wetland and riparian restoration in the valley could improve water quality and late-season stream flows and boost habitat values for a broad range of species. These efforts could be targeted to areas where habitat conservation would also benefit populations of at-risk plant species.

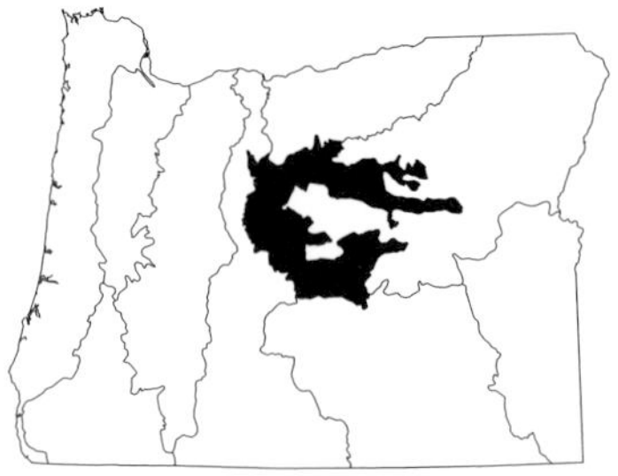

Lava Plains Ecoregion

The Lava Plains Ecoregion is essentially a mid-elevation lava plateau dissected by canyons of the Deschutes, John Day, and Crooked rivers. Elevations range from as low as 1,400 feet in the Deschutes River canyon at Warm Springs to as high as 6,500 feet on higher basalt rims and buttes rising from the plateau.

The climate is arid, with 10-20 inches of precipitation per year. Although some of eastern Oregon's major rivers cross the Lava Plains, most of the water originates in adjoining ecoregions. Before the advent of modern reservoirs and irrigation systems, the plateau had no major lakes and few large wetlands.

Western juniper *(Juniperus occidentalis)* achieves its greatest dominance and diversity in this area, where it occurs in more than 30 plant associations. Before European settlement, basin big sagebrush, native grasslands, and riparian woodlands were widespread in this region. Today, it is more common to find irrigated alfalfa, grains, and mint occupying the region's valley bottoms and plains, while juniper has expanded into many former shrub steppe vegetation types.

The plateau lands along the Deschutes and lower Crooked rivers between Bend and Madras include extensive areas that have been converted to irrigated agriculture and urbanization. Rapid population growth and increasing recreational use have increased development pressures dramatically in the juniper woodlands and sagebrush steppes of this area. Agriculture and recreation are key components of an increasingly diversified economy.

The southeastern arm of the ecoregion is characterized by arid sagebrush steppe. Livestock grazing is the primary land use in this sparsely populated area.

The northeastern arm of the ecoregion extends from the sagebrush steppe and juniper-dominated hills east of the Deschutes plateau to the valleys along the mainstem John Day River and the lower reaches of its north and south forks. Most of the bottomlands along the rivers have been converted to agriculture. Small communities scattered along the John Day River are

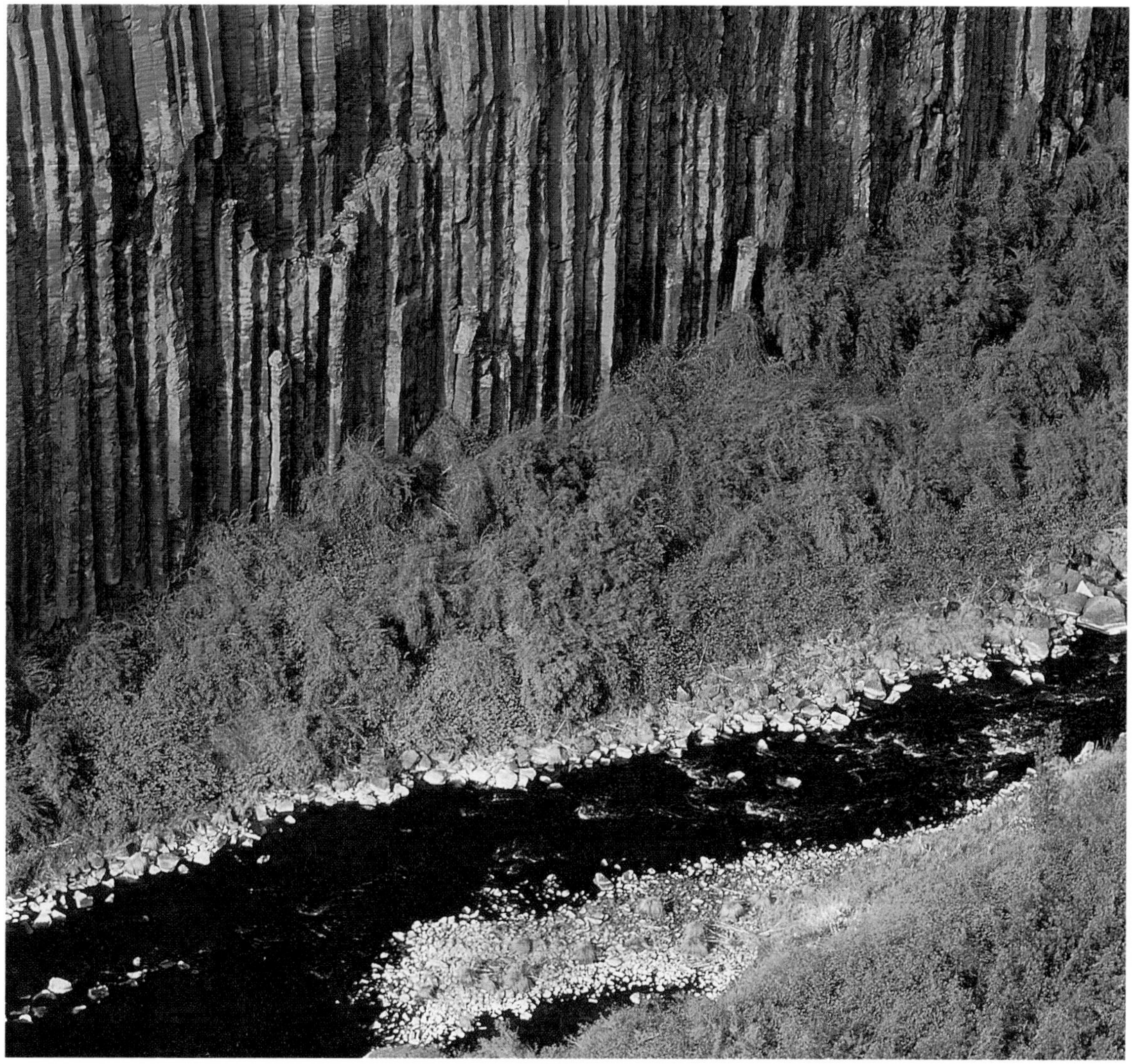

Crooked River
Photographer, Larry N. Olson

Existing management emphasizing biodiversity values is largely limited to a relative handful of BLM special management areas (research natural areas, areas of critical environmental concern, designated wild and scenic rivers) and the John Day Fossil Beds National Monument. Less than two percent of the ecoregion is in areas with biodiversity ratings of 8-10.

Portions of the Crooked, Deschutes, and John Day rivers have received federal protected status through their designation as wild and scenic rivers. These river corridors provide habitat for two of the important at-risk plants in the region (see discussion of at-risk species), and have important implications for the maintenance of fish and wildlife species. They are also a major focus for the region's growing recreation industry.

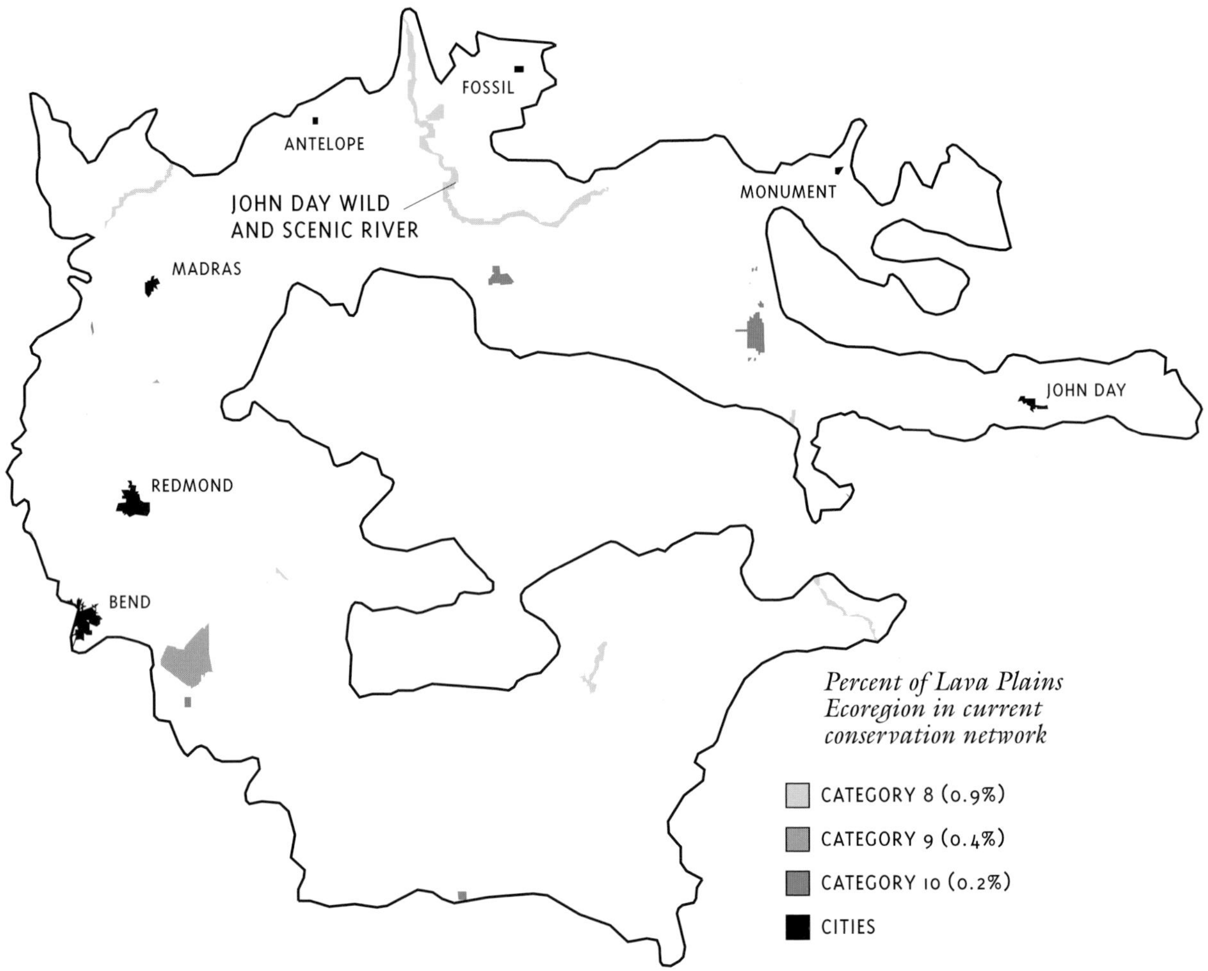

supported by agriculture, grazing, tourism, and processing of timber harvested in the forests of the Ochoco and Blue Mountains.

VEGETATION ANALYSIS

Vegetation types identified as conservation priorities in the Lava Plains include western juniper woodlands, big sagebrush steppe types, native grasslands, and riparian types. Other vegetation types with particular significance for biodiversity include those associated with the ecoregion's unique ash beds.

Healthy western juniper woodlands (with a full complement of native grasses, forbs and shrubs, as well as intact microbiotic crusts) are one of the most diverse plant communities found on the eastside (ICBEMP 1997b), and they support a variety of terrestrial wildlife. Although juniper woodlands are increasing in the Lava Plains (and displacing other native habitat types), examples of healthy juniper woodlands are increasingly rare, and few of these areas are managed for biodiversity values.

Over the past 100 years, juniper has expanded into areas that were formerly sagebrush steppe habitats primarily because of reduced fire frequency (due to fire suppression and livestock grazing) and, perhaps, climate change (ICBEMP 1997b). Overall distribution of western juniper in the Lava Plains has almost doubled from pre-European settlement levels. However, old growth juniper habitats in the valley bottoms have been cleared for grazing, agriculture, residential development, and other uses. Cheatgrass (*Bromus tectorum*) and other noxious weeds have invaded many juniper woodlands. Juniper density has also increased significantly in many areas, with negative impacts on a variety of terrestrial wildlife species.

Only two percent of the Lava Plains' juniper woodlands are in areas with biodiversity management ratings of 8-10. Although the status of juniper in general is not a conservation concern except to the extent that it is displacing other native habitats, conservation of healthy old growth juniper woodlands should be a priority for biodiversity management in this ecoregion.

More than 75 percent of the Lava Plains' big sagebrush steppe types have been converted or modified since European settlement. Some of this loss is a result of conversion to agriculture and other land uses, but most of the decline has resulted from ecosystem changes related to livestock grazing, reduced fire frequency, and invasion by exotic plant species. As in other ecoregions, many of these changes were set in motion by overgrazing before controls were first imposed on livestock on public lands in the mid-1930s. In some areas, fire suppression and heavy grazing that eliminated native grasses allowed expansion of juniper into former sagebrush steppe. Overgrazing of perennial grasses and forbs made sagebrush-steppe more susceptible to invasion by exotic annuals like cheatgrass,

MAJOR VEGETATION TYPES

Data from Actual Oregon Vegetation (Kagan and Caicco 1992)

Russian thistle *(Salsola kali)*, and yellow star-thistle *(Centaurea solstitialis)* (ICBEMP 1997b).

Changes in sagebrush steppe habitats have contributed to declines among a number of terrestrial wildlife species, including birds such as the sage grouse *(Centrocercus urophasianus)*, Brewer's sparrow *(Spizella breweri)*, sage sparrow *(Amphispiza belli)*, and mountain quail *(Oreortyx pictus)*. The changes have also led to declines among small mammals like the pygmy rabbit *(Sylvilagus idahoensis)* that disperse seeds and spores of native plants (ICBEMP 1997b).

Less than two percent of the ecoregion's big sagebrush-bunchgrass communities are in biodiversity management categories 8-10.

Although historically limited in their extent in this ecoregion, **native grasslands** have also experienced major declines (more than 80 percent) from pre-European settlement levels. Losses are have generally occurred as a result of heavy livestock grazing and subsequent invasion by exotics, fire suppression, juniper-sagebrush invasion, conversion to agriculture, and some

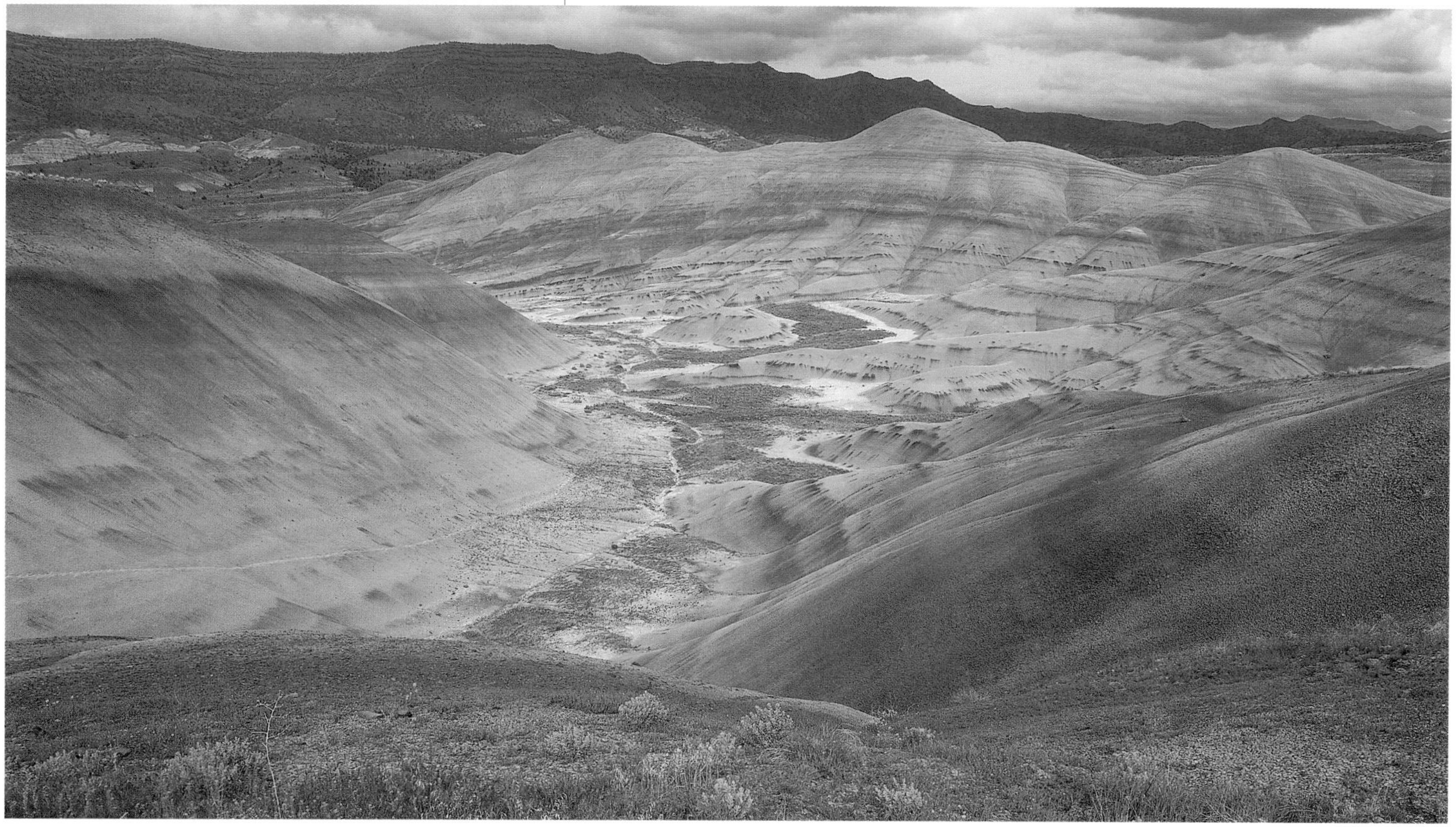

John Day Fossil Beds
National Monument
Photographer, George Baetjer

urbanization. Most remaining grasslands are in private ownership, and less than one percent is in biodiversity management categories 8-10.

As in other ecoregions, **riparian habitats** of all types have suffered significant degradation and losses. While riparian systems have begun to recover in some areas as a result of improved grazing management and active restoration, the losses remain dramatic. For example, the river floodplain along the South Fork John Day above Picture Gorge is currently in irrigated hay meadows, but photos from the late 1800s show the area was dominated by a cottonwood woodland (USDI/BLM and OPRD 1993). Large riparian woodlands have been almost entirely eliminated from the Lava Plains.

The ecoregion's riparian habitats are critical to the health of John Day River anadromous fish runs, which include the largest remaining entirely wild populations of summer steelhead and spring chinook salmon in the Columbia River system. Total runs of sea-run salmonids in the past were estimated at more than 100,000 adults. Spawning populations in recent years have ranged from 1,000-5,000 spring chinook and 7,000-40,000 summer steelhead (USDI/BLM and OPRD 1993).

Some of the best examples of several vegetation types associated with **ash beds** are found within the John Day Fossil Beds National Monument and at the southern end of the ecoregion east of Post. The ash beds themselves provide habitat for a suite of endemic plants that are characteristic of the region. Salt desert scrub types, including shadscale and black greasewood plant communities, are often found adjacent to ash deposits.

AT-RISK SPECIES

Animals. Populations of redband trout *(Oncorhynchus mykiss* ssp.) are found throughout much of the ecoregion, but few are considered "strong populations" (ICBEMP 1997b).

The sagebrush steppe areas south of Highway 20 between Millican and Brothers provide important habitat for the sage grouse *(Centrocercus urophasianus)* (Hanf et al. 1994). Formerly found in all but one of Oregon's counties east of the Cascades, this species is now primarily limited to areas in the Basin and Range and Owyhee Uplands ecoregions. Heavy livestock grazing has contributed to the decline of the sage grouse, and human disturbance is an increasing problem at mating sites (Marshall 1996).

Plants. The at-risk plant species that best characterizes this ecoregion is the arrow-leaf thelypody *(Thelypodium eucosmum)*. Restricted to western juniper habitats, generally in or adjacent to seasonal springs, this tall, showy, purple-flowered mustard is found only in Grant and Wheeler counties, with most of the occurrences clustered near Mitchell and Kimberly. The majority of known sites are on lands managed by BLM's Prineville District. The species remains at risk of serious decline or extirpation due to livestock grazing.

SUMMARY OF CONSERVATION ISSUES

- The broad vegetation types that most characterize the Lava Plains (juniper woodlands, big sagebrush steppe, and native grasslands) are only minimally represented in the current conservation network.
- Less than two percent of this rapidly growing ecoregion is in areas where management emphasizes biodiversity conservation.
- Expansion of urban-related development, off-highway vehicle use, and other recreation activities are likely to further reduce and degrade already fragmented native habitats on the Deschutes plateau and adjacent areas.
- Invasive exotic plant species such as cheatgrass have altered and degraded extensive areas of native habitat in the western and northern portions of the ecoregion.
- Riparian habitats, although widely degraded, play an important role in supporting John Day River system salmon and steelhead populations, which are critical components of Oregon's aquatic biodiversity.

CONSERVATION OPPORTUNITY AREAS

The Oregon Biodiversity Project identified four areas in the Lava Plains Ecoregion that appear to offer good opportunities to address biodiversity conservation needs.

The selection process was constrained by several factors in this ecoregion. The existing conservation network provided little in the way of a framework, and only a few areas contain large blocks of public ownership. Large, high-quality examples of most priority vegetation types were difficult to identify, and most remaining native grasslands are in private ownership. Historic and current distributions of juniper types were overlaid to highlight areas more likely to contain older juniper woodlands. Presence or proximity of invasive exotic vegetation types ruled out consideration of a number of areas. Expansion of urban development and recreational uses could jeopardize biodiversity values in some areas on the west side of the ecoregion.

Concentrations of at-risk plant species and a critical salmonid migration corridor were key factors in selection of one area, Picture Gorge. The other three areas — Clarno, Pine Ridge, and Badlands — were selected primarily because of the presence of priority vegetation types in combination with wilderness study areas or relatively large blocks of public ownership.

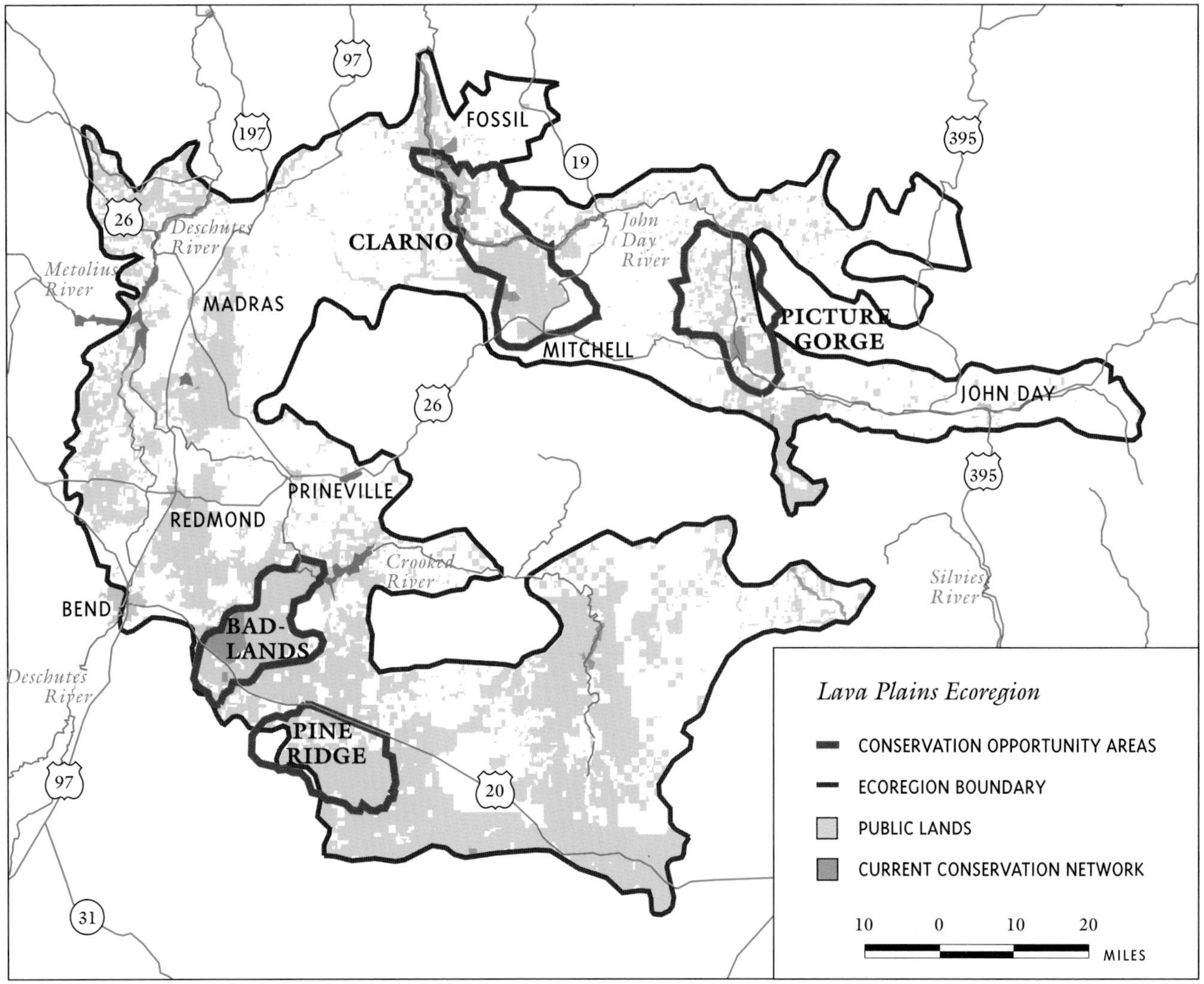

Conservation opportunity areas in this ecoregion focus on several large blocks of relatively intact native habitats and areas that provide critical connections within the John Day River system.

At-risk plants

Carex hystericina, porcupine sedge

Thelypodium eucosmum, arrow-leaf thelypody

At-risk animals

Chrysemys picta, painted turtle

Corynorhinus townsendii, Townsend's big-eared bat

Gulo gulo, wolverine

Oncorhynchus mykiss ssp., redband trout

1. Picture Gorge area

This area in Wheeler and Grant counties includes the mainstem John Day River and watersheds of several tributaries between Kimberly and Dayville. It connects with the South Fork John Day River conservation opportunity area in the Blue Mountains Ecoregion (see #3 on page 163).

This area has been heavily impacted by human uses. A highway borders the river along its entire length, and portions of the river have been channelized with gravel levees. Much of the historic floodplain has been converted to irrigated alfalfa fields and exotic species dominate the adjacent uplands. Sedimentation, low flows, and high water temperatures are key concerns for fish habitat (USDI/BLM and OPRD 1993).

Riparian habitats have begun to recover in some areas due to streamside fencing and other measures, but recovery is likely to be relatively slow and inconsistent along this stretch of river. Nonetheless, the area deserves consideration as a priority for conservation because of its critical role as a connecting corridor for migrating salmonids.

Extensive public ownership and the significant investments that have already been made in riparian restoration could provide a foundation for more biodiversity-oriented management. Cooperative efforts to conserve at-risk plants and restore riparian habitats along the river and its tributaries would help meet biodiversity conservation needs at both the ecoregion and state levels.

2. Clarno area

This area includes lands along the lower John Day River from Clarno south to the Sutton Mountain area north of Mitchell.

This area contains extensive native canyon grasslands and is important for several at-risk species associated with specific habitats, such as arrow-leaf thelypody and spotted bat *(Euderma maculatum)*. It also contains a critical migration corridor for salmonids. Bighorn sheep *(Ovis canadensis californiana)* have been introduced on BLM land on Sutton Mountain.

The area contains some of the few examples of high quality bunchgrass left in this ecoregion. Tributary streams along this portion of the John Day River support anadromous fish runs and some of the ecoregion's best small remnants of riparian habitats. The Spring Basin Wilderness Study Area southeast of Clarno is one of the few remaining roadless areas in this portion of the John Day River basin. However, further upriver, extensive areas have been converted to agriculture or are dominated by exotic plants.

Ownership along the river is a mix of private and BLM lands. The area around Sutton Mountain and lower Bridge Creek is almost entirely public lands, including the unique ash beds of the Painted Hills unit of the John Day Fossil Beds National Monument.

At-risk plants

Camissonia pygmaea, dwarf evening-primrose

Carex hystericina, porcupine sedge

Juncus torreyi, Torrey's rush

Thelypodium eucosmum, arrow-leaf thelypody

At-risk animals

Corynorhinus townsendii, Townsend's big-eared bat

Euderma maculatum, spotted bat

Oncorhynchus mykiss ssp., redband trout

At-risk plants

Castilleja chlorotica, green-tinged paintbrush

At-risk animals

Centrocercus urophasianus, sage grouse

Corynorhinus townsendii, Townsend's big-eared bat

3. Pine Ridge area

This area in southeastern Deschutes County extends eastward from Pine Mountain and includes lands lying south of Highway 20 between Millican Valley and Brothers.

This area encompasses a large block of relatively intact native habitat that includes big sagebrush communities, bluebunch wheatgrass and Idaho fescue grasslands, salt desert scrub, and older juniper woodlands. Bordered on the west by the ponderosa pine woodlands of the East Cascades Ecoregion, this area is in an ecological transition zone at the juncture of three ecoregions. It provides habitat for sage grouse, Townsend's big-eared bat *(Corynorhinus townsendii)* and several at-risk plant species.

Ownership is a mix of BLM and private lands. Coordinated management of these lands to maintain and improve their biodiversity values could help address a number of this ecoregion's conservation needs.

4. Badlands area

This area in southeastern Deschutes County extends from the Horse Ridge area south of Highway 20 north and east to include several BLM wilderness study areas around Alfalfa.

This area includes what is probably the largest block of high-quality old growth western juniper habitat in Oregon, and perhaps anywhere. The area's mosaic of sandy soils, Mt. Mazama ash, windblown loess, silts, and volcanic clays support an impressive diversity of juniper communities, which in turn, provide important habitat for a variety of birds and other wildlife.

The BLM maintains a 600-acre research natural area on Horse Ridge at the south end of this area, and much of the public land north of Highway 20 is in designated wilderness study areas. However, off-road vehicle use is a problem in some areas, and recreational activities could pose a greater threat in the future due to rapid population growth in nearby Bend and Redmond.

At-risk plants

Castilleja chlorotica, green-tinged paintbrush

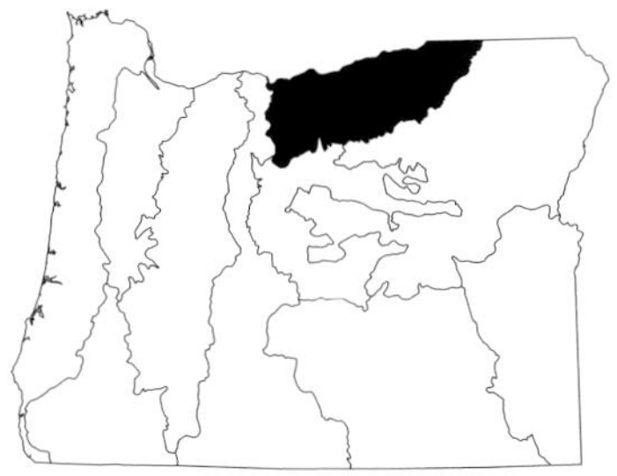

Columbia Basin Ecoregion

The Oregon portion of the Columbia Basin Ecoregion (sometimes referred to as the Umatilla Plateau) extends from the eastern slopes of the Cascades Mountains south and east from the Columbia River to the Blue Mountains. This ecoregion also extends northward to encompass most of eastern Washington.

The Columbia River, with its historic floods and large deposits of loess (wind-borne silt and sand) from the end of the last ice age, has greatly influenced the region. Most of the Oregon portion of the ecoregion is a lava plateau broken by basalt canyons carved by the Deschutes and John Day rivers and other streams that flow into the Columbia River. The climate is arid, with cold winters and hot summers. Most of the ecoregion receives less than 15 inches of precipitation per year (some areas as little as eight inches), much of that in the form of snow.

The majority of the ecoregion's natural vegetation is sagebrush steppe and bunchgrass prairie, often called palouse prairie because of the deep, loess soils. Sandy deposits along the Columbia River support open dunes, bitterbrush steppe, and western juniper. The rivers are generally characterized by intermountain riparian vegetation, with black cottonwood, willows, chokecherry, and aspen dominating riverbanks. Riparian habitats dominated by black hawthorn and white alder are less common.

Prior to European settlement, the region supported vast natural grasslands broken by brushy draws and tree- and rimrock-bordered streams.

Less than two percent of the ecoregion is in biodiversity management categories 8-10. More than 90 percent of the land in this ecoregion is in private ownership. Major public lands are the Department of Defense's Umatilla Army Depot and Boardman Bombing Range and the Boeing State Lease lands.

The Boardman Bombing Range research natural area protects part of one of the Columbia Basin's larger remaining blocks of native grasslands. The Navy is discontinuing use of the bombing range and the status of its lands and research natural area is now in question.

The Boeing State Lease lands were leased to the Boeing Corporation in 1961 for 71 years to allow for the construction of a space industrial park that never materialized. Instead, Boeing has been sub-leasing the property and developing it for agriculture. It contains high-quality examples of sand dunes and sandy steppe habitats, although significant portions have been developed for agriculture. Recent proposals by Boeing to expand agricultural development at the site have met with opposition because of potential additional impacts to wildlife and fish affected by increased withdrawals of Columbia River water.

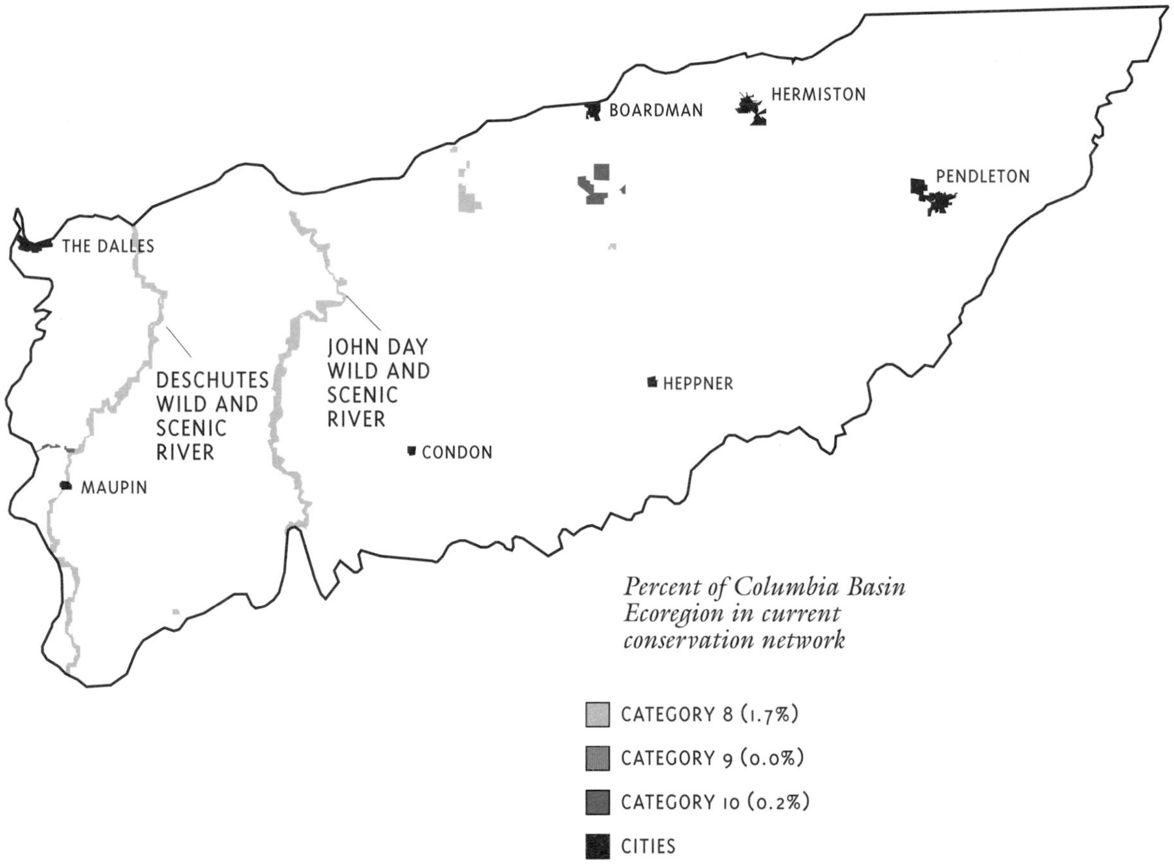

Percent of Columbia Basin Ecoregion in current conservation network

The Army Corps of Engineers manages a large corridor along the Columbia River; much of this is high-quality remnant bunchgrass and steppe vegetation, although Interstate 84 bisects most of this area. The BLM administers lands along the John Day River canyon , which is the only publicly owned corridor from the Blue Mountains to the Columbia River. National wildlife refuges and state wildlife areas near Umatilla and at Willow Creek include some of the few remaining, relatively natural habitats in areas otherwise dominated by agriculture.

The Nature Conservancy maintains several preserves (Lindsey Prairie, Lawrence Memorial Grasslands) that support native grasslands. Canyon grasslands along the Deschutes and John Day rivers are managed by the BLM under federal wild and scenic rivers designation.

The Confederated Tribes of the Umatilla Indian Reservation recently established the Wanaket Wildlife Area on a 2,000-acre former ranch near Umatilla. The project is part of the Bonneville Power Administration's efforts to mitigate for major losses to wildlife caused by construction of the John Day and McNary dams.

Because of the deep loess soils, mild climate (due to low elevations), and the presence of adequate water (either from wells or from the Columbia, Snake, or Umatilla rivers), this ecoregion is well suited for farming. The gentle bunchgrass slopes were farmed by the earliest European settlers, and are still some of the most valuable farmland in the Pacific Northwest.

Human population is concentrated in the northeastern portion of the ecoregion, where Pendleton, Hermiston, and other smaller communities serve as commercial centers for the agricultural economy.

VEGETATION ANALYSIS

The Columbia Basin Ecoregion is second only to the Willamette Valley in the percentage of landscape converted to non-native habitats and human uses. There are no vegetation types adequately represented in lands managed for biodiversity in this ecoregion. The only vegetation types that have not declined dramatically are those occurring on lands that cannot be farmed: canyon grasslands (bluebunch wheatgrass-Idaho fescue canyon grasslands) and scablands (rigid sagebrush steppe and Sandberg bluegrass scabland).

Lawrence Memorial
Grassland Preserve
Photographer, Harold E. Malde

The remaining grasslands in the Oregon portion of this ecoregion represent one of the largest assemblages of these habitats in the Pacific Northwest. Dry grasslands in the Columbia River Basin have declined by more than half from historic levels, and plant and animal species associated with these habitats have declined as much as or more than any other group of species in the region (ICBEMP 1997b).

Vegetation types of greatest conservation concern are those that still have some potential for restoration. Three major groups fit this criterion: palouse grasslands, sandy shrub steppe communities, and basin big sagebrush steppe. Although never widespread in the ecoregion, three other habitat types — riparian and oak woodlands and wetlands — merit consideration as conservation priorities as well.

Palouse grasslands, which once dominated most uplands above 1,000 feet elevation, have been almost entirely replaced by cultivated wheat or invaded by exotic plant species. They occur in a matrix with canyon grasslands, seasonal and perennial riparian habitats, scabland habitats, and mounded prairie (mima mounds). The current conservation network does not include any of these communities. A few good-quality examples remain on private lands.

Sandy shrub steppe communities, which occur along the Columbia River, include bitterbrush/needle-and-thread grass (or any bitterbrush steppe); sandy grasslands dominated by needle-and-thread; and sand dune communities dominated by sagebrush, bitterbrush, and western juniper. These communities have been almost entirely replaced by irrigated agriculture. Some examples can be found on public lands, primarily the Boardman Bombing Range, and the Boeing State Lease Lands.

Basin big sagebrush steppe communities include basin big sagebrush/needle-and-thread grass, and basin big sagebrush/bluebunch wheatgrass, which formerly occupied the low-elevation, loess uplands in the Columbia Basin. Almost all have been converted to agriculture. Some high-quality examples can be found in the Washington portion of the ecoregion. In Oregon, small examples remain on the Boeing State Lease Lands and the Boardman Bombing Range, but these communities are otherwise limited to roadside remnants and scattered fragments along agricultural fields.

As in all the arid ecoregions east of the Cascades, **riparian woodlands** are a critical habitat that have been drastically altered. Habitats along the Columbia River and Willow Creek have been permanently altered by dam construction. Riparian habitats along most of the smaller streams have been converted to agriculture. Small remnants of riparian habitats remain isolated along the mainstem John Day and Deschutes river canyons as they flow through the ecoregion. The Umatilla River is the only river in the ecoregion with a network of remnant riparian habitats, and these are impacted by diversion of stream flows for irrigation.

Oak woodlands, also historically limited in this ecoregion, have increased, probably due to fire suppression. Oak habitats on the western edge of the Columbia Basin extend into the East Cascades; this may be one of the best areas in the state to address conservation needs for this habitat.

Few natural **wetlands** remain in this ecoregion. Historic wetlands along the Columbia River have been inundated by reservoirs, while flood-plain wetlands along the Umatilla and Walla Walla rivers and other tributary streams have largely been developed for agriculture. Most remaining wetlands are artifacts of human development, such as marshes established in the backwater fringes of reservoirs and wetlands created as a result of irrigation practices. The scarcity of wetland habitats has magnified the importance of those that do exist, which provide critical habitat for many migratory birds.

As in all ecoregions, the invasion of **exotic plants** is a major concern. Cheatgrass *(Bromus tectorum)* has long been a widespread weed dominating abandoned farmland. Medusahead *(Taeniatherum caput-medusae)* and Russian thistle *(Salsola kali)* are also now widely distributed throughout the basin. More recent imports, primarily knapweeds and thistles, have been expanding rapidly in the basin, often replacing cheatgrass but sometimes replacing native bunchgrasses. An introduced tree, Russian olive *(Elaeagnus angustifolia)*, is a problem at low elevations in the basin, especially in riparian areas.

AT-RISK SPECIES

Animals. Loss of grassland habitats in the Columbia Basin has led to the decline of many animal species. Washington ground squirrel *(Spermophilus washingtoni)* now occurs in whatever larger remnants of steppe shrub habitat are available (mainly in the area from the Boeing lease lands across to Umatilla).

At-risk birds include grasshopper sparrow *(Ammodramus savannarum)*, which is also a grassland-dependent species; remaining populations in the ecoregion are associated with remnant native grassland. Burrowing owl *(Athene cunicularia hypugea)* has been reduced to a handful of pairs, although previously it was common throughout the palouse grassland region of the Columbia Plateau. Other more widespread species that have been reduced to remnant patches of higher-quality grasslands include the Ferruginous hawk *(Buteo regalis)*, Swainson's hawk *(Buteo swainsoni)*, and long-billed curlew *(Numenius americanus)*.

Plants. Laurences's milk-vetch *(Astragalus collinus* var. *laurentii)* is an endemic variety of milk-vetch restricted to the western portions of Umatilla and Morrow counties. It occurs on deep, loess soils in palouse grasslands (bluebunch wheatgrass-Idaho fescue). None of this plant's populations is found on lands managed for biodiversity values. Most occur along roadsides and unplowed "eyebrows" of cultivated fields.

Most of the ecoregion's remaining native habitats are found in canyonlands and in higher-elevation areas that are unsuitable for intensive agriculture.

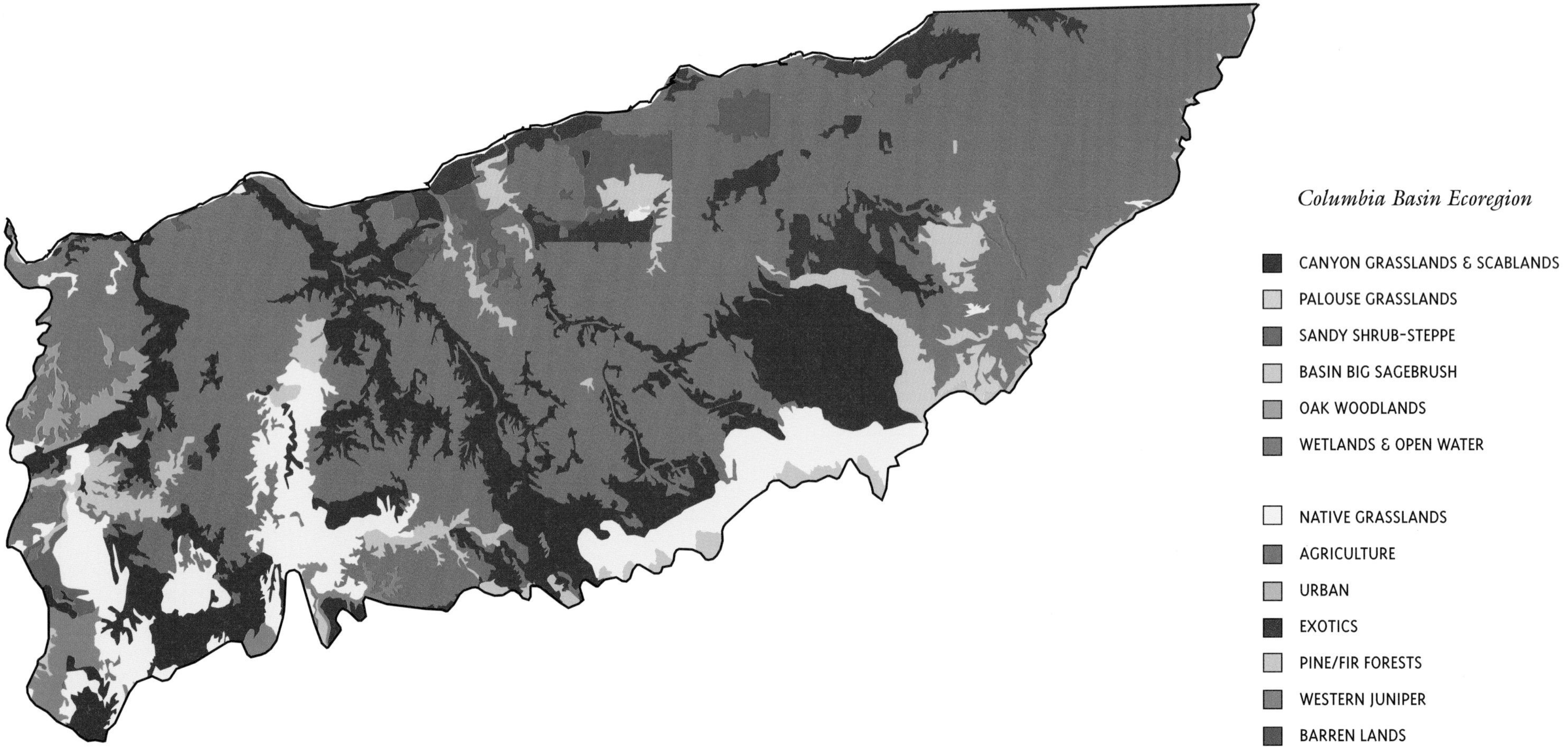

Data from Actual Oregon Vegetation (Kagan and Caicco 1992)

Locations of at-risk plant and animals recorded in the Oregon Natural Heritage Program's data bases are shown in relation to land ownership and the Oregon Biodiversity Project's conservation opportunity areas.

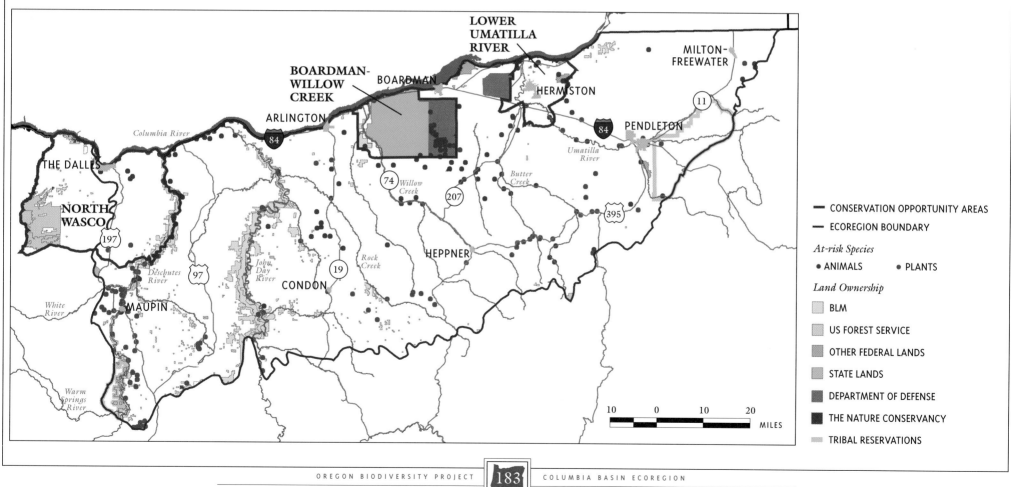

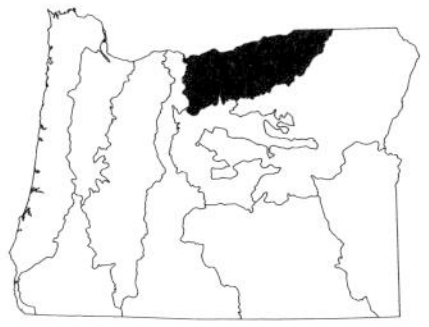

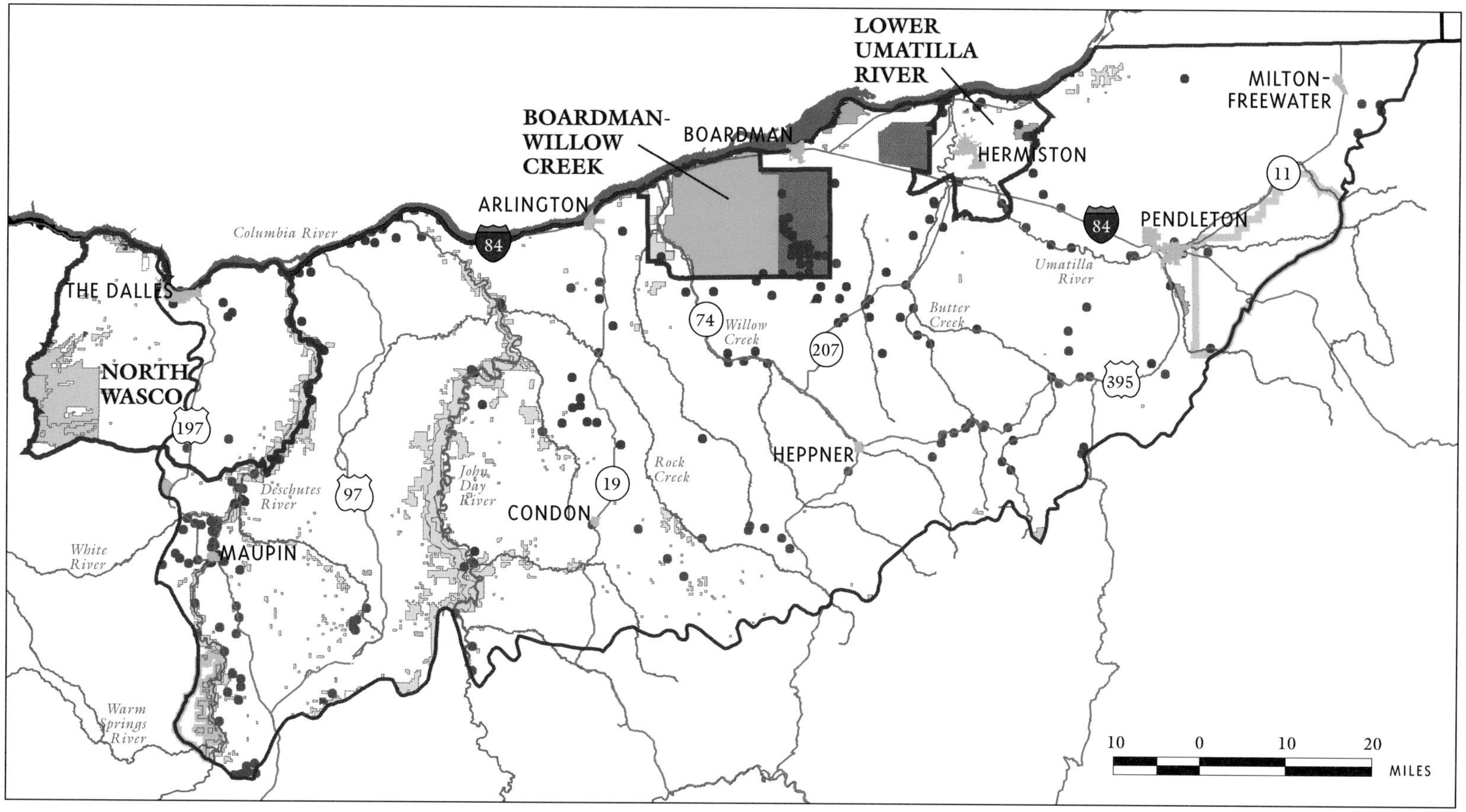

— CONSERVATION OPPORTUNITY AREAS

— ECOREGION BOUNDARY

At-risk Species

- ANIMALS
- PLANTS

Land Ownership

- BLM
- US FOREST SERVICE
- OTHER FEDERAL LANDS
- STATE LANDS
- DEPARTMENT OF DEFENSE
- THE NATURE CONSERVANCY
- TRIBAL RESERVATIONS

Three other milk-vetch species *(A. tweedyi, A. succumbens, and A. sclerocarpus)* occur only in the Columbia Basin. These species are still too common to be considered at-risk, but their distribution is largely outside the current conservation network, mainly on private lands.

Sessile mousetail *(Myosurus sessilis)* is restricted to vernal pools south of Arlington and in the Sacramento Valley of northern California. The Oregon sites are on private lands immediately adjacent to a regional waste disposal site and a toxic waste disposal site.

Hepatic monkeyflower *(Mimulus jungermannioides)*, a perennial plant endemic to moist cliffs in the Columbia Basin, has been extirpated in Washington, but still occurs in a number of sites in Oregon. Threats are limited (due to the cliff habitat), but none of the sites is managed for biodiversity values.

Several other native plant species are either extinct or have been extirpated in the Oregon portion of this ecoregion. Two plants — Thompson's sandwort *(Arenaria franklinii* var. *thompsonii)* and Douglas' milk-vetch *(Astragalus kentrophyta* var. *douglasii)* — are believed to be extinct since neither has been seen in the last half century. Rosy balsamroot *(Balsamorhiza rosea)*, Robinson's onion *(Allium robinsonii)*, gray cryptantha *(Cryptantha leucophaea)* and northern wormwood *(Artemisia campestris* ssp. *wormskioldii)* are considered at-risk plant species in Washington, but extirpated in the Oregon portion of the ecoregion. Columbia cress *(Rorippa columbiae)* occurs in undammed portions of the Columbia River (below Bonneville Dam and in the Hanford reach), but is no longer found in other portions of the Oregon Columbia Basin.

AQUATIC SPECIES ANALYSIS

The pervasive impacts of human development have dramatically reduced the ecoregion's importance for aquatic species. Loss and degradation of riparian habitats and irrigation have been the primary factors behind this decline.

Diversions for irrigation have depleted flows in many of the streams and tributaries associated with the Columbia River. Groundwater pumping has lowered water tables as withdrawals have exceeded annual recharge of aquifers.

The Columbia Basin historically supported diverse and abundant populations of salmonids, but most stocks have been heavily depleted and a number of populations are extinct. The Wilderness Society's data on the status of salmonids (1993) and the Healthy Native Stocks data (Huntington et al. 1994, 1996) are helpful in characterizing the ecoregion.

The only healthy stock is the lower John Day River's summer steelhead. Population extinctions have occurred in all stocks except summer and winter steelhead *(Oncorhynchus mykiss* ssp.) and sockeye salmon *(Oncorhynchus nerka)*.

Winter steelhead populations are considered endangered, while endangered sockeye use this ecoregion only as a migratory corridor.

Redband trout *(Oncorhynchus mykiss* ssp.) have been extirpated from a substantial portion of their historic habitat in the ecoregion. The loss of this species, the most resilient of salmonids, can be viewed as a "strong indication of disruption in the aquatic ecosystem processes" (ICBEMP 1997b).

The American Fisheries Society was unable to identify any aquatic diversity areas in the ecoregion (Bottom et al. 1993). However, both the Umatilla and Walla Walla rivers retain high-quality habitats in their headwaters in the Blue Mountains Ecoregion. Habitat restoration in the lower rivers is critical for conservation of aquatic biodiversity in both ecoregions.

SUMMARY OF CONSERVATION ISSUES

Major issues for biodiversity conservation in the Oregon portion of the Columbia Basin Ecoregion include:

- Much of the native vegetation of the ecoregion has been converted to human land use. Restoration opportunities are limited.
- The current conservation network includes less than two percent of the area of the ecoregion. None of the native vegetation types is adequately represented in the current conservation network.
- Public lands on the Boardman Bombing Range and Boeing State Lease Lands contain some of the largest remaining blocks of high-quality native habitat. Decisions on future management of these lands have critical implications for ecoregional biodiversity.
- Aquatic habitats have been widely degraded. Restoration of flows and riparian habitats on lower rivers is essential to maintain ecological connections to high-quality headwater systems.
- This is one of the few ecoregions that still offers opportunities to conserve oak woodlands.

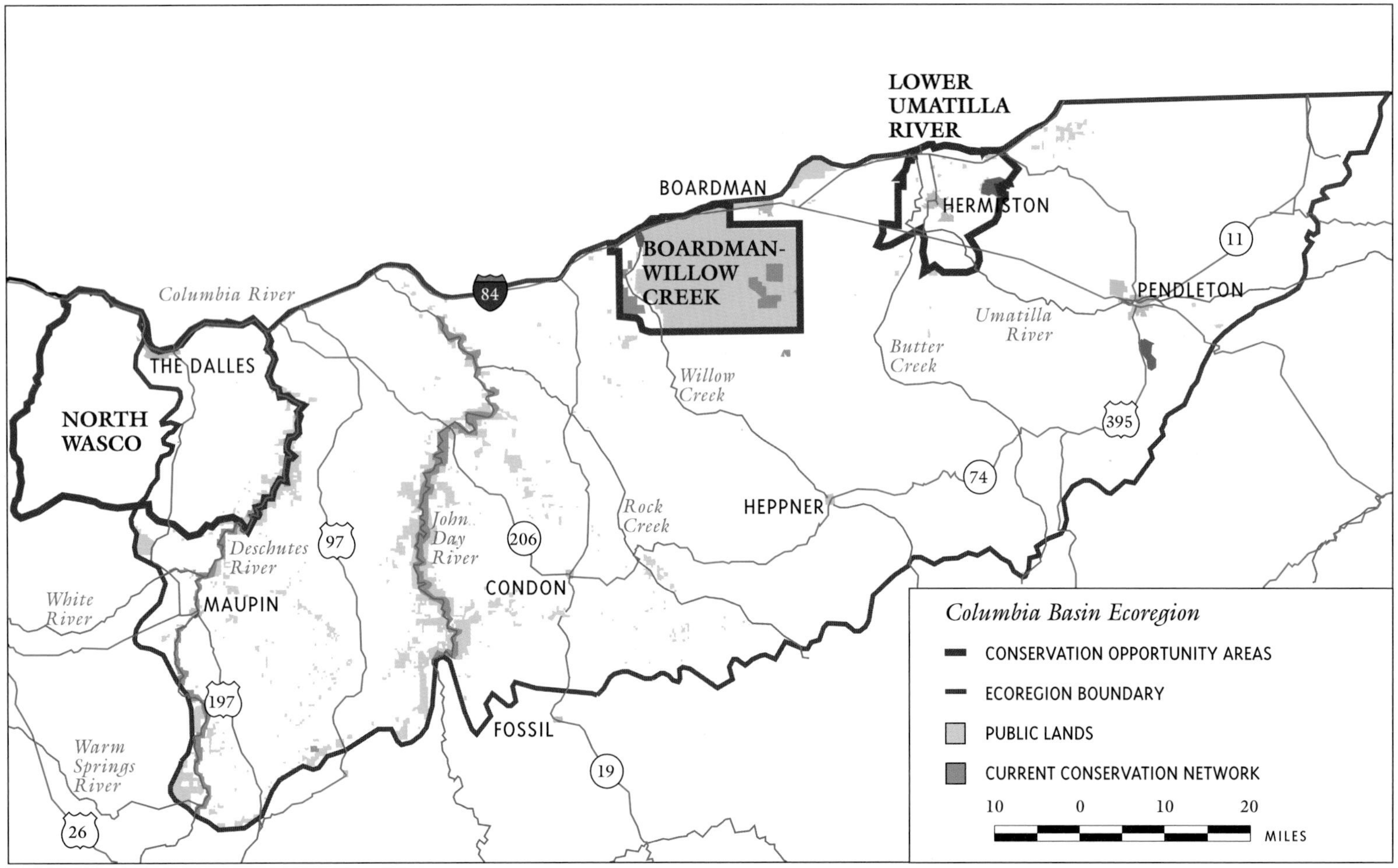

The U.S. Navy's Boardman Bombing Range and adjacent state lands leased to the Boeing Corporation contain some of the largest remnant native habitats in the Oregon portion of the Columbia Basin. Most native habitats in the lower end of the Umatilla River watershed have been converted to agriculture, but targeted restoration efforts could produce major benefits for fish and wildlife.

CONSERVATION OPPORTUNITY AREAS

The Oregon Biodiversity Project identified three areas in the Columbia Basin Ecoregion that appear to offer good opportunities to address biodiversity conservation needs.

Selection of areas was based primarily on the potential to conserve or restore significant remnants of native shrub steppe, grassland, and riparian habitats. Despite weaknesses in the current and historic vegetation maps, the few large blocks of remaining native habitats at low elevation stand out dramatically. Finer-resolution vegetation maps may reveal opportunities to conserve some of the remaining mid-elevation grasslands in the future.

Bunch grass, Lawrence Memorial Grassland Preserve
Photographer, Don Lawrence

At-risk plants

Allium robinsonii, Robinson's onion

Astragalus collinus var. *laurentii*, Laurence's milk-vetch

Cryptantha leucophaea, gray cryptantha

At-risk animals

Ammodramus savannarum, grasshopper sparrow

Athene cunicularia hypugea, western burrowing owl

Spermophilus washingtoni, Washington ground squirrel

1. Boardman/Willow Creek area

This area includes the U.S. Navy's Boardman Bombing Range, the Boeing State Lease lands, the state's Willow Creek Wildlife Area, and adjacent BLM and private lands on the west side of Willow Creek.

The U.S. Navy's Boardman Bombing Range and the adjacent Boeing State Lease lands contain the largest remnants of native grasslands and shrub steppe in public ownership. Long-term protection and management of these native habitats for biodiversity values should be a top conservation priority in this ecoregion.

Sixmile Canyon, an ephemeral stream that bisects the Boeing property, has developed a substantial riparian system over the past decade due to upstream irrigation and impoundments.

Development of a long-term conservation and management strategy for these public lands would address several of the highest priorities for biodiversity conservation in this ecoregion.

2. Lower Umatilla River area

This area includes bottomlands along the Umatilla River from Echo north to the Columbia River and along the plateau east to Cold Springs Canyon.

Restoration of instream flows and floodplain riparian and wetland habitats would help rebuild the Umatilla River's salmon runs and benefit a wide variety of native wildlife. The Confederated Tribes of the Umatilla Indian Reservation's Wanaket Wildlife Area offers opportunities for restoration and long-term management of several types of habitat. Conservation efforts in this area will require close cooperation between the tribes, private landowners, and state and federal agencies.

At-risk animals

Agelaius tricolor, tricolored blackbird

Athene cunicularia hypugea, western burrowing owl

Chrysemys picta, painted turtle

Cottus marginatus, margined sculpin

Oncorhynchus mykiss ssp., redband trout

Pelecanus erythrorhynchos, American white pelican

Spermophilus washingtoni, Washington ground squirrel

3. North Wasco area

(see also conservation opportunity area #3 in the East Cascades Ecoregion, page 119)

This area is bounded by the Deschutes River Canyon to the east; Tygh Ridge to the south; and on the west, the headwaters of the Mill, Fifteenmile, and Mosier creek watersheds.

The higher portions of this area support extensive oak woodlands and it contains several watersheds identified as aquatic diversity areas. It also provides habitat for more than two dozen at-risk plant and animal species. Increasing development pressures could jeopardize many of these ecological values. Effective land use planning and cooperative efforts with private landowners could reduce some of these threats and provide the basis for a long-term conservation and management strategy.

At-risk plants

Agoseris elata, tall agoseris

Arabis sparsiflora var. *atrorubens*, sickle-pod rockcress

Astragalus tyghensis, Tygh Valley milk-vetch

Carex hystericina, porcupine sedge

Juncus torreyi, Torrey's rush

Lomatium farinosum var. *hambleniae*, Hamblen's lomatium

Lomatium suksdorfii, Suksdorf's lomatium

Lomatium watsonii, Watson's desert-parsley

Meconella oregana, white meconella

Mimulus jungermannioides, hepatic monkeyflower

Penstemon barrettiae, Barrett's penstemon

Ranunculus reconditus, Dalles Mt. buttercup

Suksdorfia violacea, violet suksdorfia

At-risk animals

Batrachoseps wrighti, Oregon slender salamander

Clemmys marmorata marmorata, northwestern pond turtle

Corynorhinus townsendii, Townsend's big-eared bat

Falco peregrinus, peregrine falcon

Fisherola nuttalli, shortface lanx

Fluminicola columbiana, Columbia pebblesnail

Gulo gulo, wolverine

Juga hemphilli maupimensis, Deschutes juga (snail)

Monadenia fidelis minor, Oregon snail

Oncorhynchus mykiss ssp., redband trout

Oreohelix variabilis, Dalles mountain snail

Pristinicola hemphilli, pristine springsnail

Strix occidentalis caurina, northern spotted owl

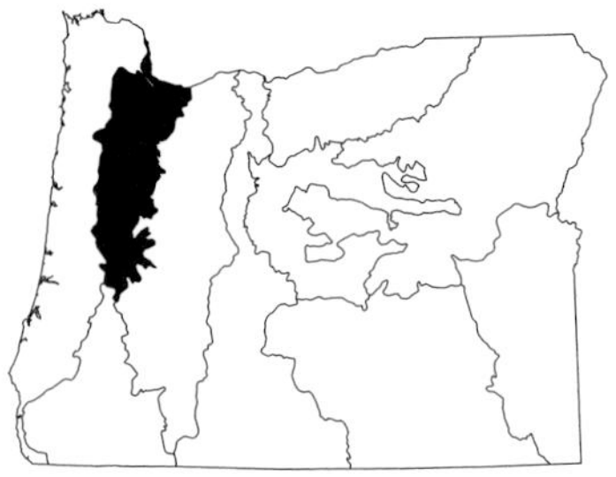

Willamette Valley Ecoregion

Bounded on the west by the Coast Range and on the east by the Cascade Range, this ecoregion encompasses the Willamette Valley and adjacent foothills. Twenty to 40 miles wide and 120 miles long, the valley is a long, level alluvial plain with scattered groups of low, basalt hills. Elevations on the valley floor are about 400 feet at the southern end near Eugene, dropping gently to near sea level at Portland. Average annual precipitation is around 40 inches, most of it falling as rain between November and June. Snow is infrequent at lower elevations and summers are generally warm and dry.

The Willamette Valley is among the state's most altered ecoregions. Development for agriculture, urbanization, fire suppression, construction of dams and impoundments, drainage of marshes and wetlands, commercial forestry, livestock grazing, and introduction of exotic plants and animals have all dramatically reshaped the valley's ecosystems.

Historically a mixture of forest, open savanna, prairie, and riparian woodlands, today's valley floor is a mosaic of farms, suburbs, and cities interspersed with small scattered patches of grasslands, coniferous forests, shrub lands and hardwood communities. In the foothills, conifer forests, primarily Douglas-fir at lower elevations, dominate.

The Willamette Valley is home to more than 70 percent of Oregon's population and is the fastest growing ecoregion in the state. Growth is concentrated around Portland, Salem, and Eugene — the state's three largest urban centers. The valley's human population is expected to double within

The Willamette River: Lifeblood of the Valley

With a watershed of more than 11,200 square miles, the Willamette River is the longest river in Oregon and the primary waterway in the valley. From the junction of the Coast Fork and Middle Fork near Springfield, the Willamette meanders more than 185 miles north to its confluence with the Columbia. Along the way, the river swells with the waters of numerous tributaries flowing out of the Cascades and the Coast Range.

the next 25 years, presenting major challenges to Oregon's statewide land use planning goals.

The valley is home to 16 of the state's top 17 private sector employers (Smith 1997). Manufacturing, high technology, forest products, agriculture, and services all play important roles in the valley's diversified economy.

Fertile soil and abundant rainfall make the valley the most important agricultural region in the state. Major crops include fruits, nuts, berries, greenhouse and nursery crops, grass seed, corn, grains, and hops, with more than half the production marketed overseas (Smith 1997).

Willamette Valley near Corvallis
Photographer, Ed Alverson

Prior to European settlement, the Willamette River system dominated the landscape, occupying braided, shallow channels that moved constantly across a broad floodplain with numerous sloughs and extensive marshlands. The river's flows varied with the seasons, rising slowly from late August through the winter, peaking during spring snowmelt in the Cascades, then falling sharply until the rains returned. During times of peak flow, the river frequently flooded large portions of the valley, at times attaining widths of two to six miles (Benner and Sedell 1997).

Over the past 150 years, the river has been transformed into a deeper, straighter, and narrower channel, and flows have been regulated by a number of dams in the upper watersheds of the Willamette's tributaries. These deliberate modifications resulted in a complex web of unintended secondary changes that have fundamentally altered the river system's natural ecological processes and functions. The end result is that the ecological integrity of the entire system has been severely compromised (Benner and Sedell 1997).

Although analysis of votes on several statewide ballot measures and legislative voting records indicates that Willamette Valley residents demonstrate the highest level of support in the state for conserving natural lands, this ecoregion has the lowest percentage of land managed for biodiversity conservation. Less than one percent of the ecoregion is in biodiversity management categories 8-10. Many of these areas are isolated and under increasing pressure from development in surrounding areas.

Remnant native habitats within the existing network of conservation lands are limited to a relatively few, small, isolated locations managed by The Nature Conservancy and state and federal agencies.

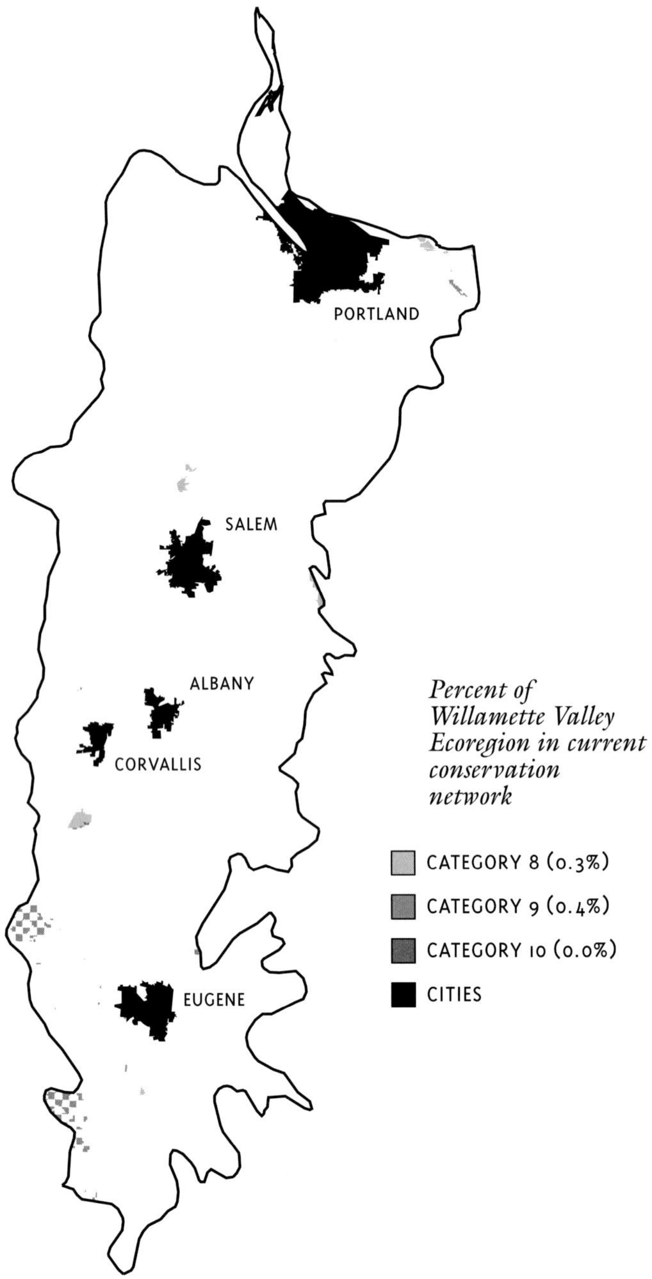

Some of the largest blocks of land where management gives some formal recognition to biodiversity values are within fragments of the Willamette Greenway. Others are found within a half-dozen major parks and wildlife areas, including the state's Sauvie Island and Fern Ridge wildlife areas; Willamette Mission State Park; and the Finley, Baskett Slough, and Ankeny national wildlife refuges. Some areas set aside by local governments for parks and greenspaces maintain smaller fragments of relatively natural habitat. The Nature Conservancy maintains a number of relatively small preserves. Two of these, Willow Creek and Kingston Prairie, encompass some of the largest remaining blocks of native Willamette Valley wet prairie.

VEGETATION ANALYSIS

Three general habitat types — oak savannas and woodlands, wetlands, and bottomland hardwood forests — stand out as broad-scale conservation priorities based on an assessment of historical changes and current management status. A fourth type that was historically abundant, native prairie grasslands, remains a conservation priority, but this type has been reduced to such small fragments that it doesn't even show up in the current vegetation map used in the project's ecoregional analyses.

Little precise information exists on the nature of the valley's original grasslands. However, historical accounts indicate that prior to European settlement, native grasses and forbs, which provide abundant habitat for numerous terrestrial species, covered much of the valley. Native Americans regularly set fires that helped maintain the valley's mosaic of grasslands, oak savannas, riparian and conifer forests, and marshes.

Today, after more than a century of extensive agricultural conversion, urbanization, and fire suppression, less than one percent of the original native Willamette Valley grasslands and savannas remain. Many of the ecoregion's at-risk species occupy these few remaining grassland habitats. Maintenance of these habitats is dependent in part on periodic burning, which poses significant management problems in many areas of the valley.

Oak savannas covered perhaps half the ecoregion before European settlement. The savanna types have been reduced by more than 80 percent, in part due to conversion for agriculture, but also as a result of fire suppression. Fire suppression allowed many of the savannas to develop into **oak woodlands** and eventually forests. More than half the remaining oak woodlands are now dominated by Douglas-fir, and without active management, will eventually become conifer forests.

Remaining oak savannas and woodlands provide some of the ecoregion's most important wildlife habitat. Oregon white oak provides nesting habitat for nearly 200 wildlife species, representing all classes of terrestrial vertebrates (Brown 1985). It is a hardy tree that can tolerate both prolonged drought and extended flooding. With the ecoregion's rapid urbanization, this species has begun to decline sharply during the last 30 years (Thilenius 1968 and Gumtow-Farrior 1992, unpublished paper). This decline, coupled with the tree's slow growth rate and apparent lack of regeneration, will have far-reaching consequences to the many wildlife populations that depend on it.

An estimated 98 percent of remaining Oregon white oak habitats in this ecoregion are in private ownership. Less than one percent of the ecoregion's oak habitats are in biodiversity management categories 8-10. Without active management, including reintroduction of fire or removal of invading conifers, the decline of these ecosystems is likely to continue.

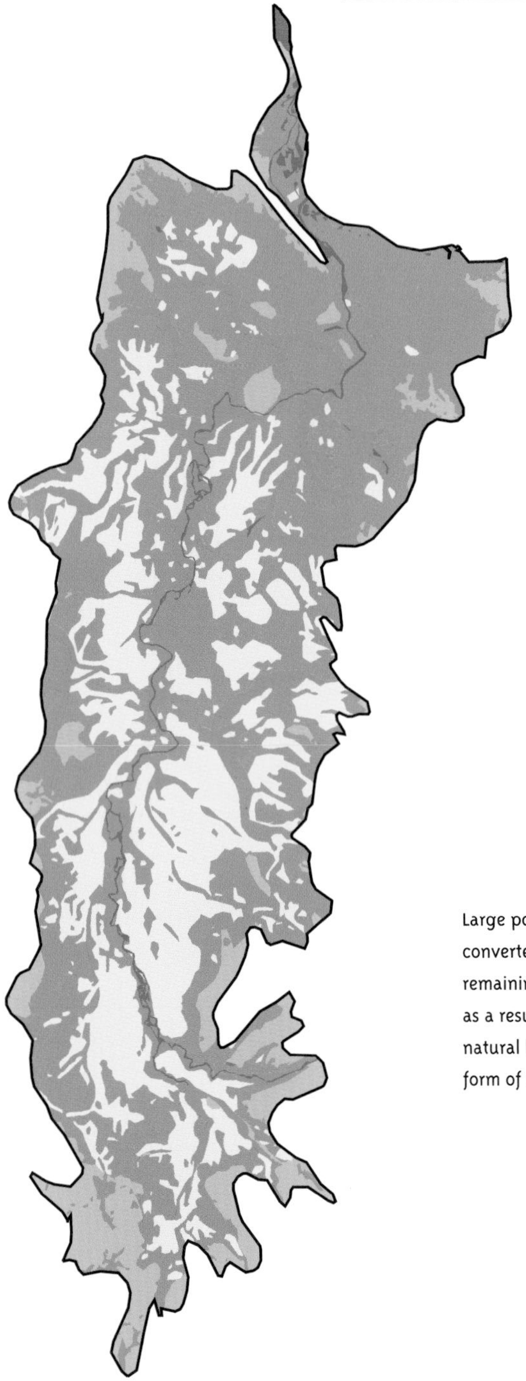

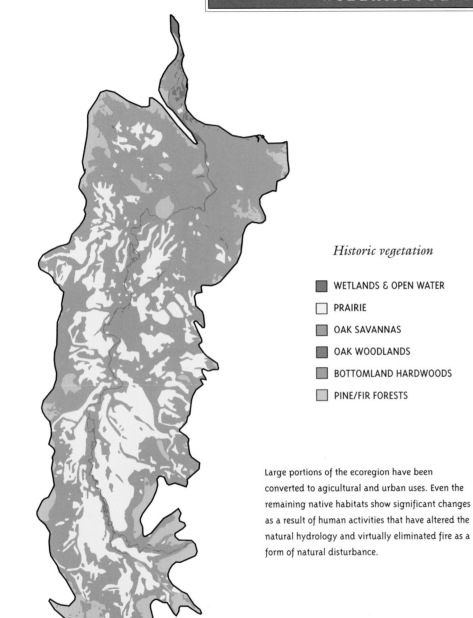

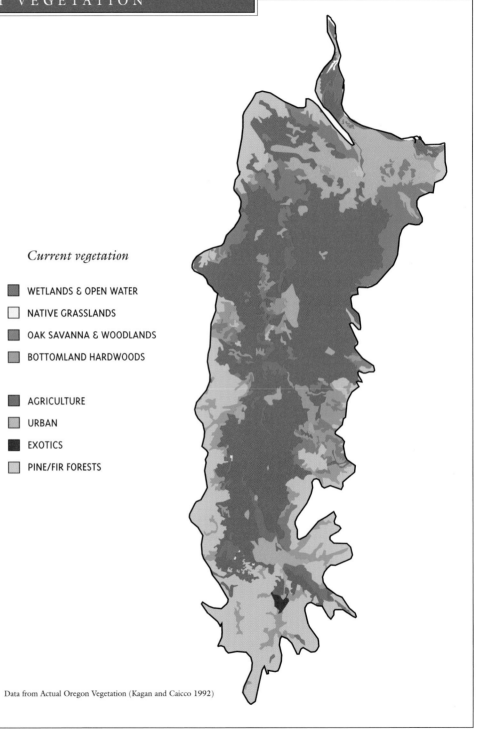

Historic vegetation

- WETLANDS & OPEN WATER
- PRAIRIE
- OAK SAVANNAS
- OAK WOODLANDS
- BOTTOMLAND HARDWOODS
- PINE/FIR FORESTS

Large portions of the ecoregion have been converted to agricultural and urban uses. Even the remaining native habitats show significant changes as a result of human activities that have altered the natural hydrology and virtually eliminated fire as a form of natural disturbance.

Current vegetation

- WETLANDS & OPEN WATER
- NATIVE GRASSLANDS
- OAK SAVANNA & WOODLANDS
- BOTTOMLAND HARDWOODS

- AGRICULTURE
- URBAN
- EXOTICS
- PINE/FIR FORESTS

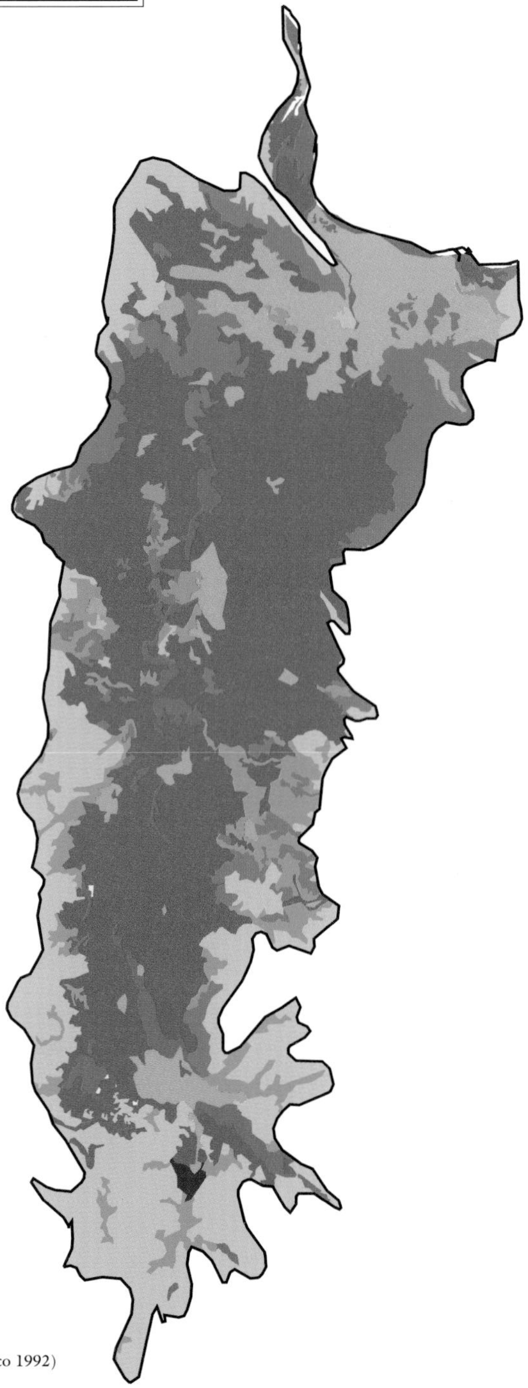

Data from Actual Oregon Vegetation (Kagan and Caicco 1992)

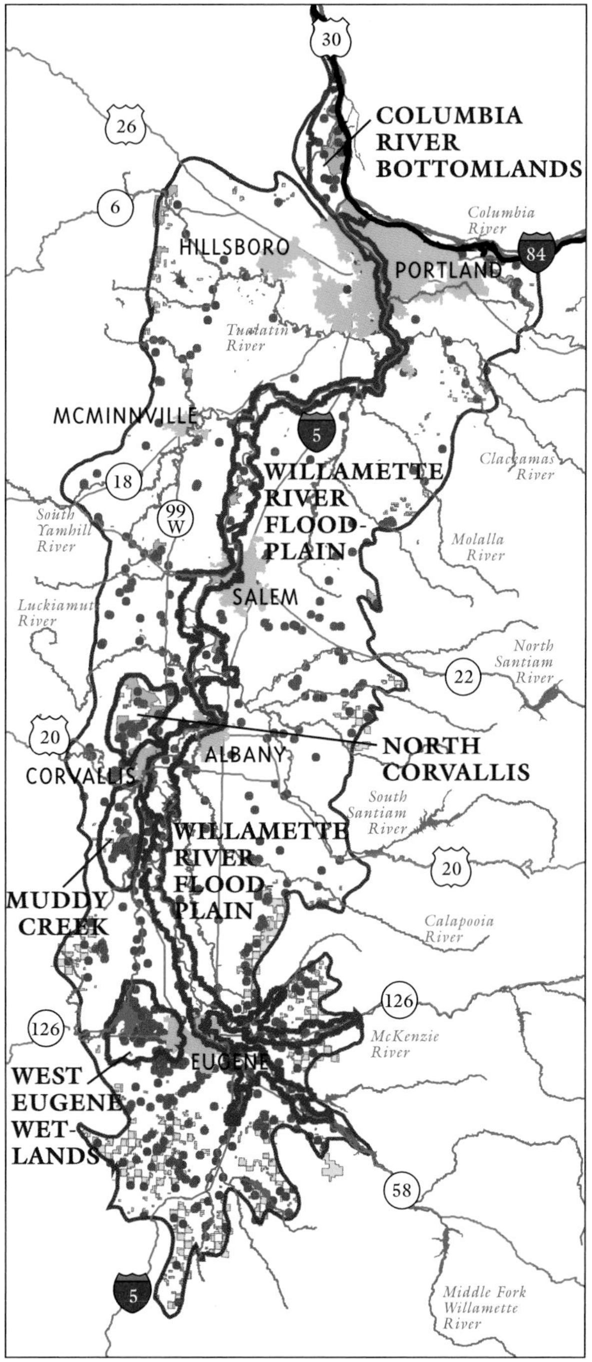

CONSERVATION OPPORTUNITY AREAS

ECOREGION BOUNDARY

At-risk Species

- ANIMALS
- PLANTS

Land Ownership

BLM

US FOREST SERVICE

OTHER FEDERAL LANDS

STATE LANDS

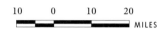

10 0 10 20 MILES

Locations of at-risk plant and animals recorded in the Oregon Natural Heritage Program's data bases are shown in relation to land ownership and the Oregon Biodiversity Project's conservation opportunity areas.

Bottomland hardwood forests formerly dominated much of the Willamette River floodplain and historically occupied about ten percent of the ecoregion's total area. Based on a comparison of current and historic vegetation maps, these habitats have declined by more than 70 percent from historic levels. Where the Willamette River used to be bordered by riparian forests up to seven miles wide, the corridor of bottomland hardwoods has shrunk to only a few hundred feet on average. Many streams now have only a thin strip of riparian vegetation, and some have none. Despite increasing emphasis on protection of riparian habitats and the formal establishment of the Willamette River Greenway, riparian forests continue to decline.

Prior to European settlement, the Willamette Valley contained extensive **wetlands**, ranging from bottomland wet prairies, shrub swamps, and forested wetlands to backwater sloughs, oxbow lakes, and permanent marshes. With settlement, the land was cleared for pasture and drained for agricultural purposes. Many of the wet prairies and bottomland riparian forests survived relatively intact until the 1950s. But with the advent of flood control, irrigation systems, and new farming techniques, farmers were able to develop these areas more intensively (Titus et al. 1996).

Total losses of wetland and riparian habitat since 1850 have been estimated at 87 percent, more than one million acres, based on analysis by the Oregon Natural Heritage Program. Losses among scrub-shrub wetland communities have been particularly severe, and a half-dozen Willamette Valley types are classified by the Heritage Program as imperiled or critically imperiled at the state or global level. Virtually all the valley's remaining wetlands have been degraded by human activities to some degree, and most are dominated by invasive, non-native vegetation.

AT-RISK SPECIES

Animals. Fender's blue butterfly *(Icaricia icarioides fenderi)*, Oregon chub *(Oregonichthys crameri)*, and the western pond turtle *(Clemmys marmorata marmorata)* have received much deserved attention for their at-risk status. Perhaps most emblematic of the ecoregion's animal species declines, however, is the plight of the western meadowlark *(Sturnella neglecta)*, the state bird. This colorful, melodious bird is not considered at-risk under the Oregon Natural Heritage Program ranking system because of its abundance statewide. Nevertheless, it has largely disappeared in recent years from the Willamette Valley (Puchy and Marshall 1993). The species is most at home in open grasslands and was once common throughout the Willamette Valley. In recent years, residential development in the ecoregion's lowland open spaces has contributed to local declines, and the meadowlark is now rare in the ecoregion.

Other at-risk animals include the western gray squirrel *(Sciurus griseus)*, pileated woodpecker

(Dryocopus pileatus), western bluebird *(Sialia mexicana)*, grasshopper sparrow *(Ammodramus savannarum)*, and Oregon vesper sparrow *(Pooecetes gramineus affinis)*. All are associated with the ecoregion's oak and native prairie habitats, which have been reduced to a small fraction of their historic distribution. The dusky Canada goose *(Branta canadensis occidentalis)*, which is threatened primarily by habitat changes in its Alaskan breeding grounds, winters throughout the valley. The Willamette Valley also supports a number of at-risk fish and amphibian species (see aquatic species analysis below). At-risk animals that are now extremely rare or extirpated altogether from the valley include the yellow-billed cuckoo *(Coccyzus americanus)*, Columbian white-tailed deer *(Odocoileus virginianus)*, gray wolf *(Canis lupus)*, and grizzly bear *(Ursus arctos)*.

Plants. Among plants endemic to the valley, at-risk species include Bradshaw's lomatium *(Lomatium bradshawii)*, Willamette Valley daisy *(Erigeron decumbens* var. *decumbens)*, and Nelson's checkermallow *(Sidalcea nelsoniana)*. Kincaid's lupine *(Lupinus sulphureus* ssp. *kincaidii)*, is a larval host plant for an at-risk Valley endemic, Fender's blue butterfly. Other at-risk plants include white rock larkspur *(Delphinium leucophaeum)*, wayside aster *(Aster vialis)*, and tall bugbane *(Cimicifuga elata)*.

Of the 16 plant species in the Willamette Valley considered at-risk, 12 (75 percent) are found in areas with biodiversity management ratings of 8-10.

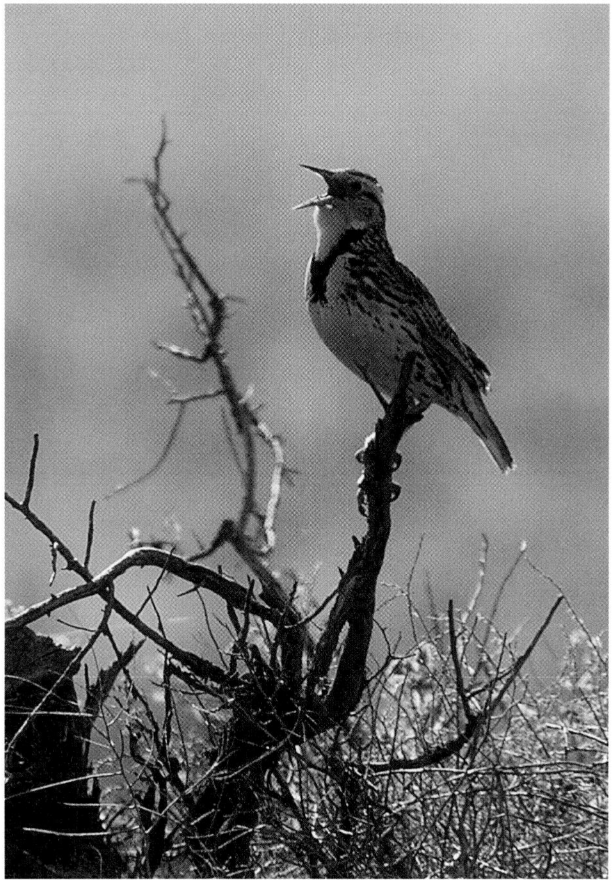

However, less than ten percent of the total occurrences of these species have been recorded within these areas, leaving the majority of known populations outside the current conservation network.

In addition to these at-risk species, the ecoregion is home to a number of more common plants found nowhere else that survive in fence rows and roadsides throughout the Willamette Valley. If present trends continue, at least some of these will join the list of at-risk species in the future.

Western meadowlark
Photographer, Geoff Pampush

AQUATIC SPECIES ANALYSIS

Like the prairie ecosystem, Willamette Valley streams, rivers, and wetlands have changed dramatically since European settlement. The length of the river's channel between Eugene and Albany has been reduced by nearly half, from 190 miles to 100 miles, primarily as a result of development related to navigation and agriculture (Benner and Sedell 1997).

Flood control has reduced natural disturbances that historically helped create new river features (off-channel aquatic habitat, gravel bars, deep channel pools), which in turn created diverse aquatic habitat. Mainstem floodplain lands that were historically flooded every ten years are now flooded only once in 100 years.

Up until the 1960s toxin levels from industrial point-source pollution were so great that major fish kills were periodically recorded in the Willamette River. Ensuing efforts to clean up the river and to conserve and restore riparian habitat have greatly improved the river's water quality. But growing development pressure along the mainstem and increases in non-point source pollution make the river's water quality a continuing concern.

The Willamette Valley is home to a number of at-risk aquatic species, including Oregon chub *(Oregonichthys crameri)*, spring chinook salmon *(Oncorhynchus tshawytscha)*, western pond turtle, painted turtle *(Chrysemys picta)*, clouded salamander *(Aneides ferreus)*, western toad *(Bufo boreas)*, northern red-legged frog *(Rana aurora)*, and foothill yellow-legged frog *(Rana boylii)*. Winter steelhead *(Oncorhynchus mykiss)* have been proposed for listing under the federal Endangered Species Act.

While habitat loss and degradation are clearly central to the decline of these species, the spread of aggressive exotics like the bullfrog *(Rana catesbiana)* and the largemouth bass *(Micropterus salmoides)* has also had devastating effects on native aquatic species.

SUMMARY OF CONSERVATION ISSUES

Major issues for biodiversity conservation in the Willamette Valley Ecoregion include:

- Pressure on valley ecosystems from population growth, economic development, and pollution is likely to increase.
- More than half the ecoregion has been converted to non-native habitats as a result of agricultural or urban development.
- Formerly widespread habitat types have declined dramatically. Oak savanna and prairie have been almost entirely eliminated from the valley. Bottomland hardwoods have declined by more than two-thirds. Remaining Oregon white oak

woodlands have been substantially altered by fire suppression and livestock grazing. Wetlands have been destroyed or degraded throughout the valley.

- Fire has effectively been eliminated as a form of natural disturbance, while the frequency, extent, and intensity of flooding have been significantly altered.
- Non-native plant and animal invasions disrupt native communities and diminish populations of at-risk native species.
- The Willamette River has largely been confined to a single channel and disconnected from its floodplain.
- Habitats for at-risk native plant and animal species are largely confined to small and often isolated fragments such as roadsides and sloughs.
- Ninety-six percent of the ecoregion is privately owned, with few large ownerships.
- Less than one percent of the ecoregion is in areas where management emphasizes conservation of biodiversity values. None of the half-dozen state and federal wildlife areas in the valley contains more than small fragments of native habitat. Most publicly owned lands that support relatively natural habitats are managed for recreational values.
- Opportunities for large-scale protection or restoration of native landscapes are limited. Existing growth and development, high land costs, and the fragmented nature of ownerships and remaining native habitats all present barriers to large-scale ecosystem restoration.
- Broad-scale conservation strategies will need to focus on restoring and maintaining more natural ecosystem processes and functions within a landscape that is managed primarily for other values. This may include an emphasis on more "biodiversity-friendly" management techniques for existing land uses and restoration of some key ecosystem components such as river-floodplain connections and wetland and riparian habitats. "Fine-filter" conservation strategies that focus on needs of individual at-risk species and key sites are particularly critical in this ecoregion.

CONSERVATION OPPORTUNITY AREAS

The Oregon Biodiversity Project identified five areas in the Willamette Valley Ecoregion that appear to offer good opportunities to address biodiversity conservation needs.

Unlike most other ecoregions, the current vegetation map was of little use in selecting conservation opportunity areas in the Willamette Valley. With a minimum mapping unit of 320 acres and a landscape dominated by agriculture and urban uses, most of the remaining upland native habitats are too small to show up. Oak woodlands appear as large blocks in some areas in the current vegetation map. However, a finer-resolution GIS coverage developed by the Oregon Department of Fish and Wildlife reveals these "blocks" to be only collections of small fragments of oak woodlands. The project was unable to identify any obvious opportunities for large-scale conservation of oak woodland habitats with the information available.

Lacking high-resolution, current vegetation data, the analysis focused more heavily on at-risk species. Most at-risk species are found within the Willamette River floodplain and other areas historically dominated by wetland and riparian habitats. Selection of conservation opportunity areas was largely driven by opportunities to restore wetland and floodplain habitats in areas that would help conserve at-risk species and complement the existing conservation network.

1. West Eugene wetlands

This area, west of Eugene, includes the Amazon Creek drainage, Willow Creek Natural Area, and lands around Coyote Creek, Fern Ridge Reservoir, and Long Tom River.

Although the vast majority of this area has been converted to urban and agricultural uses, its fragments of native habitats support the greatest concentration of native prairie remnants and associated at-risk species in the Willamette Valley (The Nature Conservancy 1996).

Development in the urbanized portions of the area is guided by the West Eugene Wetlands Plan, which is eventually intended to restore a more natural system of wetlands and other native habitats along Amazon Creek and its tributaries. The plan is being implemented through the cooperative efforts of local, state, federal, and private partners. The program has the potential to link together a network of habitats extending out to Fern Ridge Reservoir and down the Long Tom River. The reservoir's wetlands are an important habitat for migratory birds, and adjacent uplands support fragments of native habitats.

At-risk plants

Aster curtus, white-topped aster

Aster vialis, wayside aster

Erigeron decumbens var. *decumbens*, Willamette Valley daisy

Horkelia congesta spp. *congesta*, shaggy horkelia

Lomatium bradshawii, Bradshaw's desert parsley

Lupinus sulphureus ssp. *kincaidii*, Kincaid's lupine

Montia howellii, Howell's montia

At-risk animals

Chrysemys picta, painted turtle

Clemmys marmorata marmorata, northwestern pond turtle

Icaricia icarioides fenderi, Fender's blue butterfly

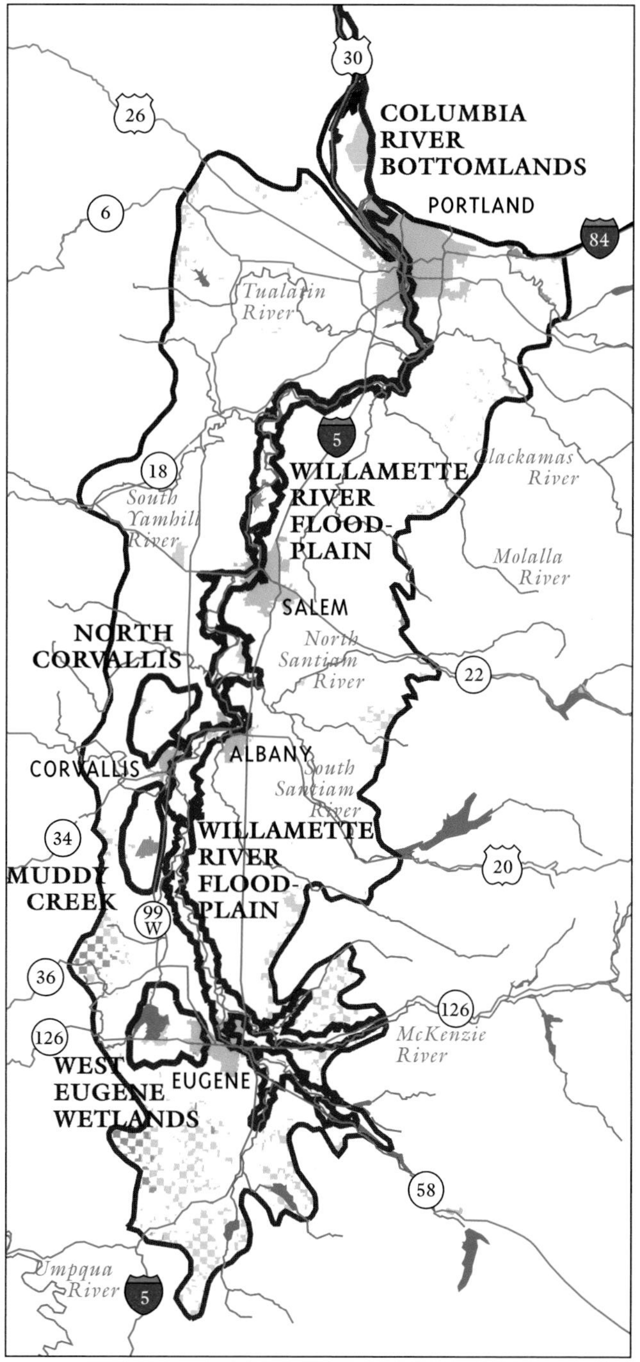

Willamette Valley Ecoregion

- CONSERVATION OPPORTUNITY AREAS
- ECOREGION BOUNDARY
- PUBLIC LANDS
- CURRENT CONSERVATION NETWORK

10 0 10 20 MILES

Wetland and floodplain habitats are the central focus of most of the ecoregion's conservation opportunity area. Unlike most other native habitats in the Willamette Valley, some of these areas still have potential for restoration of more natural ecosystem functions and processes.

At-risk plant species

Aster curtus, white-topped aster

Aster vialis, wayside aster

Carex comosa, bristly sedge

Cimicifuga elata, tall bugbane

Delphinium leucophaeum, white rock larkspur

Delphinium pavonaceum, peacock larkspur

Erigeron decumbens var. *decumbens*, Willamette Valley daisy

Horkelia congesta spp. *congesta*, shaggy horkelia

Howellia aquatilis, Howellia

Hydrocotyle verticillata, whorled marsh pennywort

Lomatium bradshawii, Bradshaw's lomatium

Lupinus sulphureus ssp. *kincaidii*, Kincaid's lupine

Mimulus tricolor, three-colored monkeyflower

Montia howellii, Howell's montia

Pellaea andromedifolia, coffee fern

Sidalcea nelsoniana, Nelson's sidalcea

Sullivantia oregana, Oregon sullivantia

Wolffia columbiana, Columbia water-meal

2. Willamette River floodplain

This broadly defined area includes lands mapped as historic bottomland hardwood forests along the entire length of the Willamette River's floodplain from the confluence of its Coast and Middle forks downstream to the Columbia River.

Growing recognition of the floodplain's potential role in addressing Willamette River flood hazard and water quality issues could provide opportunities for watershed management changes with far-reaching benefits for biodiversity values. Restoration in the historic floodplain would reduce flood hazards and improve water quality, and at the same time, address some of the ecoregion's highest biodiversity conservation priorities — reestablishing the connection between the river and its floodplain, and restoring wetlands and riparian forests.

Opportunities for floodplain habitat restoration exist along much of the Willamette River. However, several areas within and adjacent to the floodplain stand out as being particularly important targets for habitat protection and restoration because of their ecological values and the presence of some existing public ownerships.

The area around the **Coast Fork-Middle Fork confluence** south of Springfield supports a number of at-risk species. The publicly owned lands on and around Mt. Pisgah encompass one of the area's larger blocks of native habitats. The floodplain contains some of the largest populations of western pond turtles in the Willamette Valley with good opportunities for wetland and bottomland restoration. The county park has native bottomland and upland prairie, a large great blue heron rookery and high-quality oak woodlands, with some small remnants of oak savannas. The prairie and oak woodlands provide habitat for a number of at-risk plants *(Lomatium bradshawii, Cimicifuga elata,* and *Aster vialis).*

Near **Buena Vista,** the area around the Santiam and Luckiamute rivers' confluence with the Willamette River retains extensive bottomland hardwood forests and includes several relatively large state-owned properties that are part of the Willamette Greenway. Nearby Ankeny National Wildlife Refuge is mostly agricultural land managed to provide habitat for wintering geese, but the refuge could provide opportunities for extensive restoration of native habitats.

North of Salem, **Willamette Mission State Park** contains the largest intact black cottonwood *(Populus balsamifera* ssp. *trichocarpa)* forest in the Willamette Valley, as well as areas of other bottomland hardwoods. The park includes areas that have high potential for restoration of wetlands and other floodplain habitats. Flood-prone bottomlands in the area could provide opportunities to test large-scale floodplain restoration strategies.

At-risk animal species

Acetropis americana, American acetropis grass bug

Branta canadensis leucopareia, Aleutian Canada goose

Chloealtis aspasma, Siskiyou chloealtis grasshopper

Chrysemys picta, painted turtle

Clemmys marmorata marmorata, northwestern pond turtle

Euphydryas editha taylori, Taylor's checkerspot butterfly

Falco peregrinus, peregrine falcon

Megascolides macelfreshi, Oregon giant earthworm

Oregonichthys crameri, Oregon chub

Rana aurora, northern red-legged frog

Rana boylii, foothill yellow-legged frog

Strix occidentalis caurina, northern spotted owl

3. Muddy Creek area

This area includes the riparian zones and floodplain of Muddy Creek, William L. Finley National Wildlife Refuge, and surrounding oak-fir woodlands in Benton County.

This area contains some of the best Oregon ash-Oregon white oak forest remaining in the valley. Much of Muddy Creek contains high-quality riparian forest with good bottomland prairie remnants adjacent to several reaches of the creek.

Within Finley refuge, the Willamette Floodplain Research Natural Area has one of the highest quality tufted hairgrass bottomland prairies in the valley, which is maintained by an active prescribed burning program. The refuge is an important winter habitat for the dusky Canada goose and hosts thousands of Pacific Flyway migratory waterfowl each year. Refuge marshes contain extensive native emergent vegetation, providing habitat for a wide diversity of mammal and avian species. The oak-dominated uplands on the refuge and surrounding foothills have good habitat values and act as corridors to Coast Range conifer forests.

This area provides opportunities to restore riparian forests, oak-conifer woodlands, and limited amounts of native wet prairie. Several creeks, sloughs, and the confluence of Muddy Creek and Mary's River also have restoration potential. The area is adjacent to other important habitats, including the Long Tom River, the mainstem of the Willamette River, and associated oxbow lakes and sloughs.

At-risk plants

Delphinium pavonaceum, peacock larkspur

Erigeron decumbens var. *decumbens*, Willamette Valley daisy

Lomatium bradshawii, Bradshaw's desert parsley

Lupinus sulphureus ssp. *kincaidii*, Kincaid's lupine

Mimulus tricolor, three-colored monkeyflower

Montia howellii, Howell's montia

Sidalcea nelsoniana, Nelson's checkermallow

At-risk animals

Acetropis americana, American acetropis grass bug

Branta canadensis leucopareia, Aleutian Canada goose

Chrysemys picta, painted turtle

Clemmys marmorata marmorata, western pond turtle

Oregonichthys crameri, Oregon chub

Rana aurora, northern red-legged frog

4. North Corvallis area

This area includes the Adair training area of the Oregon Military Department, the Paul Dunn and McDonald State Forests, some isolated BLM properties (including the Forest Peak Research Natural Area), E.E. Wilson Game Management Area, Jackson Frazier wetlands, Bald Hill Park, and the north Corvallis greenway.

The area includes habitat for a number of Willamette Valley endemic plants; some of the best populations of Fender's blue butterfly; and excellent examples of oak woodlands, conifer forests, and bottomland wetlands. The city of Corvallis is working to expand its system of parks to create an open space corridor north of town, which ties in well with this area.

At-risk plants

Cimicifuga elata, tall bugbane

Lomatium bradshawii, Bradshaw's lomatium

Lupinus sulphureus ssp. *kincaidii*, Kincaid's lupine

Sidalcea nelsoniana, Nelson's sidalcea

At-risk animals

Euphydryas editha taylori, Taylor's checkerspot butterfly

Icaricia icarioides fenderi, Fender's blue butterfly

Rhyacophila fenderi, Fender's rhyacophilan caddisfly

Speyeria zerene bremnerii, Valley silverspot butterfly

At-risk plants

Carex comosa, bristly sedge

Cimicifuga elata, tall bugbane

Howellia aquatilis, Howellia

Montia howellii, Howell's montia

Rorippa columbiae, Columbia cress

Sullivantia oregana, Oregon sullivantia

Wolffia columbiana, Columbia water-meal

At-risk animals

Branta canadensis leucopareia, Aleutian Canada goose

Chrysemys picta, painted turtle

Clemmys marmorata marmorata, western pond turtle

5. Columbia River bottomlands

This area includes the bottomlands along the Columbia River from Smith and Bybee lakes in North Portland northwest through Sauvie Island, the Scappoose lowlands, and Deer Island in Columbia County.

The bottomlands along the Columbia River support an abundance of wildlife, including migrating and wintering waterfowl, songbirds, deer, bear, and other large native mammals, as well as a number of at-risk species. Historically subject to regular flooding, the area retains extensive wetlands, including several with at-risk plant communities.

With more than 14,000 acres in state and local wildlife areas and natural areas, this area offers opportunities to restore and manage wetlands and other floodplain habitats on a scale not easily achieved elsewhere in the ecoregion. (Adjacent areas on the Washington side of the Columbia River include more than 10,000 acres of similar habitats in federal and state wildlife areas and county parks.) Although all of these public ownerships give some recognition to biodiversity values, investments in habitat restoration and changes in management practices could boost biodiversity management ratings into the 8-10 range, with long-term benefits for the ecoregion's biological diversity.

Private lands in the Scappoose and Deer Island areas have high potential for restoration of wetlands and bottomland hardwood forests.

Oak grove at Kingston Prairie
Photographer, Alan D. St. John

Conclusion

This document is a summary of the results of almost four years of inquiry, analysis, discussion, and debate about biodiversity conservation in Oregon. Boiling that all down to a few pages of conclusions requires some generalizations that will inevitably provoke disagreement. Nonetheless, one of the initial purposes of the project was to provide a basis for people to step back and examine biodiversity conservation in Oregon from a big-picture perspective. Having spent several years getting to that point, we would be remiss if we didn't conclude with a few general observations about what we have seen.

Forests

Biodiversity in forest ecosystems has been impacted by loss of old growth forest habitats throughout the state. However, long-term conservation needs for westside forests on federal lands have been fairly well addressed through the Clinton administration's Northwest Forest Plan. To the extent that the plan remains intact and is fully implemented, it clearly shifts much of the concern for forest biodiversity to eastside forests, where no similar large-scale conservation strategy is in place.

It remains to be seen whether the planning process undertaken for the federal government's Interior Columbia Basin Ecosystem Management Project will adequately address biodiversity conservation issues in the forests of the East Cascades and Blue Mountains ecoregions. In any event, it is clear that conservation strategies will need to be tailored to the unique needs of each region. In the westside forests covered by the Northwest Forest Plan, biodiversity conservation goals may in many cases be achieved simply by leaving lands alone. East of the Cascades, where decades of fire suppression, timber harvest, and livestock grazing have fundamentally altered natural processes, active intervention will be required to begin the process of restoring more natural forest ecosystems. However, active management to thin over-stocked stands and use prescribed fire to restore forest structure and species composition is not without risks. Because of the uncertainty involved in applying these practices on a broad scale, land managers should proceed with caution, using the principles of adaptive management to evaluate and refine their strategies. In addition, it seems prudent to minimize human disturbance and let natural processes proceed in the few remaining roadless areas where management activities have not already occurred.

Grasslands

Oregon's remaining native grasslands may present the single most compelling case for action to conserve the state's biological diversity. Largely ignored during the debates over forest issues, the native prairies of the Willamette Valley and the bluebunch wheatgrass and Idaho fescue grasslands in the Columbia Basin and Blue Mountains ecoregions have been reduced to small fragments of their historic distribution. Although most of the native grasslands that were vulnerable to development may have already been converted to other uses, few of those that remain are managed to protect their biodiversity values. Conservation action now, while opportunities still exist, could help prevent endangered species crises in the future.

Sagebrush steppe

To many people, the sagebrush steppes of eastern Oregon seem so vast and untouched that it is hard to conceive of any threats to their biological diversity. In reality, virtually all of the wide open spaces of southeastern Oregon show the impacts of livestock grazing, invasion of exotic plants, fire suppression, and other human influences. Yet these areas have largely escaped the effects of urbanization, intensive agriculture, and other relatively permanent forms of development. As a result, the Basin and Range and Owyhee Uplands ecoregions retain much of their native biodiversity. The current conservation network in these ecoregions falls far short of ensuring the levels of biodiversity management found in westside conifer forests. However, these areas provide an abundance of opportunities to implement broad-scale conservation strategies without major changes in current land uses or negative impacts on local communities. Because the vast majority of these two ecoregions is in federal ownership, the Interior Columbia Basin Ecosystem Management Project could provide a vehicle to address many of the biodiversity issues in these two ecoregions.

Aquatic habitats

The decline of many of Oregon's native salmonids toward endangered species status in recent years reflects a broader decline of aquatic ecosystems that has been occurring throughout the state for more than a century. The impacts of human development have been concentrated most heavily around estuaries, in valley bottoms, and other low elevation areas that historically provided the most productive and diverse aquatic habitats. Most remaining high-quality habitats are found in the upper reaches of forested watersheds. These last remaining "strongholds" of aquatic habitat are critical for the survival of many salmonids. However, recovery of salmon populations will also require long-term efforts to restore estuarine, wetland, riparian, and riverine habitats in lower elevation portions of these watersheds. In addition to their importance for salmonids, these lowland habitats support most of the state's other at-risk aquatic species and play a key role in conservation of aquatic diversity.

Ecosystem processes

Changes in ecosystem processes are intertwined with the loss and degradation of native habitats throughout much of Oregon. Changes in fire frequency have led to dramatic changes in the character of many of the state's forests and much of its sagebrush steppe. Fire suppression has altered the mix of native species in many of these habitats and increased the impact of the infrequent but high-intensity fires that do occur. In some areas, overgrazing and introduction of non-native cheatgrass have combined to feed a cycle of frequent fires followed by expansion of cheatgrass, which has virtually eliminated native plant communities.

Changes in natural hydrologic processes are also widespread and have had similar impacts on native habitats and species. Flood control, irrigation, and navigation projects have fundamentally altered most of the state's streams, rivers, and estuaries, with profound impacts to surrounding terrestrial habitats. As with fire suppression, the changes humans have imposed on Oregon's hydrologic systems have sometimes had the paradoxical effect of increasing the magnitude of impacts from natural disturbances, as victims of seasonal flooding can testify.

In many areas of Oregon, restoration of native ecosystems is simply not feasible. However, restoration of more natural ecological processes, including disturbance and hydrology, can help re-establish basic ecosystem functions that are critical to the state's biological diversity. Although this concept has begun to be embraced in some areas, far more work needs to be done to define how land management practices can best be modified to sustain both ecosystem functions and intensive human uses.

Exotic species

Invasive exotic species present problems in native habitats throughout much of Oregon. Although rangeland exotics have spurred increasing concern and some remedial action in many areas, non-native plants continue to spread unchecked across eastern Oregon's sagebrush steppe to the Coast Range's managed forests. Some exotics, such as cheatgrass, scotch broom, and reed canary grass, have been a part of the landscape for so long that their expansion largely escapes notice. Others, such as the *Spartina* species (cordgrass), green crabs, and other exotic species showing up in Oregon's estuaries, are so new that it is not yet possible to gauge the full extent of their impact. Preventing the introduction of undesirable non-native species is exceedingly difficult, and the eradication of established populations can be next to impossible. Where exotics are firmly established, biological controls and other methods will be critical to limiting their impacts and preventing long-term impairment of natural ecosystem processes and functions.

Development pressures

Although broad-scale conservation efforts could address many of Oregon's biodiversity needs, these strategies may not be practical in some areas. This is particularly true in those areas where native habitats have already been lost or severely fragmented and options are limited by rapid growth and development. Examples include the Willamette Valley, some portions of the Coast Range's coastal strip, and some of the more rapidly urbanizing areas of central and southwestern Oregon. In these areas, conservation strategies may need to focus more on site-specific efforts to protect specialized habitats and individual species. In areas where remnant native communities are highly fragmented, restoration may be necessary to create viable habitats.

POLICY ISSUES

All of the issues discussed above present immense challenges. Most will need to be addressed at a variety of levels, ranging from individual sites to watersheds, counties, and ecoregions. However, some of these challenges revolve around institutional and policy issues of statewide scope.

Cross-boundary planning

One of the most conspicuous deficiencies in Oregon's approach to conservation is the degree of fragmentation among natural resource agencies and organizations. The pattern is not unique to Oregon, and is in fact duplicated in federal agencies, academia, and private interest groups. The result has been the creation of seemingly impenetrable institutional walls that inhibit the efficient flow of information; hinder integration of ecological, economic, and cultural concerns; and hamper development of cost-effective conservation programs. Today, we continue to address pieces of our problems without ever really solving them.

Recent years have seen some significant first steps toward the development of institutional arrangements that transcend these traditional barriers. Watershed councils have become a popular approach to coordinating the activities of agencies and private interests across jurisdictional and organizational boundaries. However, to varying degrees, they all suffer from tenuous funding, insufficient technical support, and a lack of formal authority. They also lack the ecological information needed to plan for biodiversity conservation and have difficulty addressing broader scale issues that transcend watershed boundaries.

One option for addressing the problem is the creation of a statewide stewardship council to tackle major cross-cutting issues not effectively addressed by existing institutions. The purpose of the council would be to facilitate the development of a vision for Oregon's natural resources over the long term through the creation of cooperative, public/private partnerships for conservation. The council could be composed of prominent citizens with interest and expertise in economics, conservation, sustainable development, and resource use. It could be an independent entity with a small administrative staff and would not require any regulatory authority.

Information management

Supporting and sustaining an Oregon biodiversity conservation strategy will require significant changes in the way information about natural resources is compiled, interpreted, managed, and communicated. Much of the research undertaken by agencies and academic institutions is narrowly focused on particular species, crops, sites, or activities. Although most research projects produce worthwhile information, the results are seldom placed in a decision-making context where they can be applied to real-world management problems. Some of the results never reach the intended audience due to inadequate communication systems. Similarly, although environmental monitoring is conducted by many agencies, it is typically done at widely varying scales, using inconsistent methods. The result often is the compilation of voluminous data without much interpretation or direct applicability to conservation and management. What is needed is a system that is scientifically valid, cost-effective, relatively easy to implement without extensive training, and consistent across ownership boundaries. Above all, monitoring should produce information needed by decision-makers. The public can help collect and report data if appropriate systems are established by resource agencies to manage the information and if participants are adequately trained.

Although there have been a number of attempts in Oregon to improve management of natural resource information, the current system suffers from many deficiencies. A model proposed by the United Nations Environment Program, called a "clearinghouse network," may hold some promise for a more comprehensive approach to the problem. In this model, stakeholders pool their data through cooperative information management. Various data "themes" — forestry, wildlife, human population, etc. — are managed by appropriate custodian organizations. A central hub is established to handle coordination, facilitate information generation, promote dialogue among custodian organizations, and help develop standards and access agreements (UNEP 1996). A similar clearinghouse network system could be established in Oregon. The hub could reside either in the Governor's office, the Department of Administrative Services, or the State Library. Alternatively, it could be attached to the statewide stewardship council, mentioned above. Consensus on consistent and compatible methods of collecting and entering data, as well as on appropriate custodians for individual data themes will not come easily. Nevertheless, consensus is essential to the success of long-term efforts to manage for biodiversity.

Conservation funding

The single greatest obstacle to effective conservation in Oregon is the lack of broad-based, stable funding for natural resource conservation programs. Less than two percent of the state's general fund is allocated to natural resources — down from three percent in the 1970s. More than 90 percent of the current allocation goes to activities related to resource production — commercial timber production, fire suppression, operation of fish hatcheries, and game management. Federal funding has also declined, and when it is available, the state is often unable to provide required matching money. Unlike many states, Oregon has failed to establish long-term, dedicated revenue for conservation and outdoor recreation programs. Instead, a series of user and permit fees have been patched together over time to fund existing programs. This has led to the creation and perpetuation of programs linked to direct and narrowly focused revenue sources, and to a general neglect of programs without an identified source of funding.

Other states have successfully employed a variety of approaches to conservation funding, including mitigation banking, fines for environmental violations, real-estate transfer taxes, bonding, and others. As pressure on our natural areas continues to increase, the need for investments in conservation will become more evident, perhaps reaching the critical mass needed to spur political action to identify and adopt a reliable revenue source for conservation programs.

PUTTING BIODIVERSITY MANAGEMENT INTO PRACTICE

Even the best public policies won't guarantee that Oregon will retain its native biological diversity throughout the twenty-first century. Effective biodiversity conservation will require concrete action on the ground, in specific places, to conserve and restore species, habitats, and ecological processes.

As noted in the opening pages of this document, the Oregon Biodiversity Project has been guided since its beginning by a belief that many of these challenges can best be addressed through cooperative, non-adversarial efforts. Much of this work will depend on voluntary actions by public and private landowners and resource managers.

Landowners will participate in these efforts only if they see how it serves their interests. A companion publication of the Oregon Biodiversity Project, *Stewardship Incentives* (Vickerman 1998), explores options and incentives for improving stewardship on lands that are not managed primarily for conservation purposes. Direct economic benefits, in the form of payments for conservation easements or management practices, are the most attractive incentives for many landowners. However, it is also possible to "reward" conservation efforts indirectly by making good stewardship easier (removing bureaucratic obstacles, providing good information that is easily understandable) and reducing regulatory uncertainty, which makes land management less costly.

The magnitude and difficulty of the challenges involved in conserving Oregon's biodiversity may make the tasks ahead seem overwhelmingly complex. But in its simplest form, our strategy for long-term biodiversity conservation can be boiled down to three general principles:

1. Protect and maintain remaining native habitats

Virtually all of Oregon's most productive lands have already been converted to commodity production and other human uses. Short-term economic gains involved in converting remaining grasslands to crops, harvesting old growth forests, or developing existing roadless areas are unlikely to compensate for irreversible long-term losses of biological diversity.

2. Restore native habitats and natural ecological processes where feasible and appropriate

It is neither necessary nor realistic to attempt to roll back history and recreate an idealized version of Oregon's historic landscape. But many species that are currently in decline or already at-risk of extinction will continue their downward slide without some action to restore historic habitat losses. Ecosystem restoration does not come quickly or cheaply, but the alternative may very well entail dramatically greater costs to society in the future, both in short-term economic impacts and loss of biodiversity needed to support sustainable economies.

3. Practice better stewardship

Most Oregonians will never see an endangered species, much less have the opportunity to play a direct role in habitat conservation or restoration. But we can all make some contribution to biodiversity conservation efforts. Farmers and forest managers can take a variety of actions to benefit biodiversity and still realize economic gains producing commodities to meet society's needs. Urban dwellers can take steps to reduce their impacts on the environment and their consumption of Oregon's and the world's natural resources.

Native and newcomer alike, we treasure the idea that there's something unique about being an Oregonian. A big part of that sense of uniqueness derives from the knowledge that we do, indeed, inhabit one of the world's last best places — one corner of what others have called "the geography of hope." We can also take some pride in knowing that Oregon has been a leader in protecting its lands and other natural resources through a series of pioneering laws and programs, including the beach bill, the bottle bill, and statewide land use planning.

However, there is much more work to be done, and it is work of a different sort. We need to roll up our sleeves, put on our boots, and work on restoration projects. We need to drive less, recycle more, and use fewer chemicals on our lawns and our fields. We need to stop thinking in terms of our own agencies and our own land and reach across the street and across the fence. We need to be willing to spend more money on knowledge and stewardship incentives. First, however — and most of all — we need to agree that Oregon's biological diversity is of fundamental importance to our lives and the lives of our children. We then need to commit to do whatever we can, in ways small and large, to help conserve the variety of life across this wonderful living landscape.

*Percent of Vegetation Communities within the Current Conservation Network**

Vegetation Community	Private Lands	1-7	8	9	10	Current Conservation Network 8-10	Total (all lands)	% of Total in CCN
alpine and subalpine wetlands	95	2,890				0	2,985	0.0%
bare ground	520	4,671	2,914	1,940	4,568	9,422	14,614	64.5%
big sage bunchgrass	558,422	1,409,113	10,052	5,369	21,577	36,998	2,004,533	1.8%
big sagebrush lava flows	3,497	31,916	167		24,303	24,470	59,883	40.9%
big sagebrush steppe mixed with open ash beds and salt desert scrub	25,972	38,215		182	3,388	3,570	67,757	5.3%
big sagebrush-bitterbrush/needle-and-thread shrub inland dunes	41,205	27,121	149	328		477	68,803	0.7%
big sagebrush/basin wildrye bottomland steppe	29,255	52,897	1,265	84		1,349	83,501	1.6%
bitterbrush steppe	30,834	45,849	95			95	76,778	0.1%
black cottonwood riparian woodlands	6,919	587	363			363	7,869	4.6%
black greasewood salt desert scrub	93,337	105,394	19,019	838	120	19,977	218,709	9.1%
black sagebrush steppe	232	34,494	16			16	34,741	0.0%
bluebunch wheatgrass-Sandberg bluegrass grasslands	66,811	149,273	507	197	3,009	3,712	219,796	1.7%
buckbrush-manzanita chapparal	1,582	952	15	22		37	2,570	1.4%
bud sage steppe	10	718				0	728	0.0%
coast redwood-Douglas fir forests	467	444		1,200		1,200	2,112	56.8%
common snowberry	18,563	719		3,690		3,690	22,972	16.1%
cottonwood-hawthorn-willow riparian woodlands	15,971	1,508		26		26	17,506	0.2%
Douglas fir-Oregon white oak forests and woodlands	213,994	6,510	338	380		718	221,221	0.3%
Douglas fir-ponderosa pine-incense cedar forests	2,067	195				0	2,262	0.0%
Douglas fir-sugar pine-ponderosa pine forests and woodlands	407,136	461,292	626	259,814	23,381	283,821	1,152,249	24.6%
Douglas fir-tanoak-madrone forests	75,176	33,728		12,786		12,786	121,689	10.5%
eastern Oregon (interior) Douglas fir forests	115,677	324,242		69,706	840	70,547	510,465	13.8%
exotics	512,189	1,148,813	13,442	37,183	3,138	53,764	1,714,766	3.1%
farmland and developed pastures	2,464,800	295,324	8,089	423	1,974	10,486	2,770,610	0.4%
grand fir forests	61,998	203,175	4,468	14,314	4,070	22,853	288,026	7.9%
grand fir-western larch forests	14,969	9,200		3,064		3,064	27,233	11.3%
Idaho fescue palouse and montane grasslands	306,669	43,758	5,566	8,894	902	15,362	365,788	4.2%
Idaho fescue-bluebunch wheatgrass grasslands and canyon slopes	239,071	24,060	11,245	6,113	166	17,524	280,655	6.2%
inland sand dunes	1,836	5,738	6,996		43	7,040	14,613	48.2%
Jeffrey pine serpentine woodlands	5,579	36,249	14	27,177	268	27,459	69,286	39.6%
lodgepole pine pumic forests and woodlands	79,028	202,004	2,673	13,445	1,251	17,368	298,401	5.8%
lodgepole pine-subalpine fir forests	3,059	99,035	3,347	19,385	25,202	47,935	150,029	32.0%
low sage dwarf-shrubland	246,203	647,038	3,749	48,143	2,998	54,890	948,130	5.8%
low sagebrush-mountain big sagebrush steppe	19,279	57,679		3,186		3,186	80,144	4.0%
montane wetlands	45,632	8,468	2,206	7,686		9,892	63,991	15.5%
mountain big sagebrush steppe	60,523	99,945	2,064		358	2,422	162,890	1.5%

Vegetation Community	Private Lands	1-7	8	9	10	Current Conservation Network 8-10	Total (all lands)	% of Total in CCN
mountain hemlock-Pacific silver fir forests	834	92,269	9,154	80,990	26,741	116,884	209,987	55.7%
mountain hemlock-Shasta red fir forests	4,430	86,026		20,051	120,335	140,386	230,841	60.8%
mountain mahogany woodlands and shrublands	10,669	48,718	5,906	409	1,092	7,407	66,794	11.1%
mountain snowberry-mountain sagebrush shrublands	367,972	214,219	3,809	32,039	3,479	39,327	621,517	6.3%
open water	112,562	37,675	26,226	14,042	5,493	45,761	195,998	23.3%
Oregon white oak woodlands	89,779	6,475	35	3,023		3,058	99,312	3.1%
Oregon white oak-Oregon ash bottomland-pasture mosaic	52,684	2,929	719		98	817	56,431	1.4%
Pacific silver fir forests	1,628	86,001	250	54,684	1,6478	71,412	159,041	44.9%
playa (unvegetated saltpan)	2,535	17,460	331	78		409	20,404	2.0%
ponderosa pine woodlands	1,014,579	2,053,188	19,172	93,650	17,723	130,546	3,198,312	4.1%
ponderosa pine-Douglas fir forests	209,230	262,064	462	33,317	333	34,112	505,407	6.7%
ponderosa pine-lodgepole pine forests	27,325	97,402	1,984	1,272	470	3,726	128,454	2.9%
ponds	18,252	26,871	6,560	600		7,160	52,283	13.7%
quaking aspen groves	17,960	22,973	4,145	3,991	101	8,237	49,171	16.8%
red alder-bigleaf maple-Douglas fir forests	561,206	221,105	1,550	57,817	331	59,698	842,009	7.1%
rigid sagebrush steppe and scablands	55,102	43,434	224			224	98,759	0.2%
saltsage salt desert scrub	8,232	5,995				0	14,226	0.0%
serviceberry-cherry mountain brush shrubland	16,810	6,285				0	23,095	0.0%
shadescale salt desert scrub (sheepfat salt desert scrub)	22,209	142,943	688		19	707	165,859	0.4%
Shasta red fir forests	9,197	34,030	305	26,063	8,374	34,742	77,968	44.6%
shorepine woodlands	7,337	9,265	584	138	10	732	17,334	4.2%
silver sagebrush playas	15,691	35,374	380	7,055	841	8,276	59,340	13.9%
Sitka spruce forest	391,701	68,423	5,407	25,519	3,161	34,086	494,210	6.9%
subalpine and alpine meadows	19	3,832	4,097	36,729	796	41,623	45,474	91.5%
subalpine fir-lodgepole pine-Engelman spruce forests	1,558	24,238	1,289	58,119	875	60,283	86,079	70.0%
subalpine fir-whitebark pine subalpine woodlands and parklands		10,457	2,091	13,136	18,895	34,122	44,578	76.5%
threetip sagebrush steppe	3,381	20,635				0	24,016	0.0%
tidal saltmarshes	2,203	4		4		4	2,211	0.2%
tule-cattail marshes	23,702	4,431	17,449	713	18	18,180	46,312	39.3%
urban	174,718	1,344	211	18		228	176,291	0.1%
western hemlock-Douglas fir forests	1,210,700	930,148	27,340	603,513	50,779	681,632	2,822,480	24.2%
western juniper woodlands	1,081,031	870,732	29,242	20,961	15,484	65,688	2,017,451	3.3%
white oak-ponderosa pine woodlands and oak-pine-fir woodland-pasture mosaic	223,731	6,106	1,512	961	105	2,578	232,415	1.1%
winterfat salt desert scrub and playa	2,114	4,911		2,005		2,005	9,030	22.2%
Totals:	**11,509,656**	**11,111,173**	**270,504**	**1,736,474**	**413,589**	**2,420,567**	**25,041,396**	**9.7%**

*The current conservation network is defined by the Oregon Biodiversity Project as lands rated 8-10. All values are in hectares. See page 38-39 for a discussion.

Select Bibliography

Agee, J.K. 1993. Fire ecology of Pacific Northwest forests. Island Press, Washington, D.C.

Agee, J.K. 1994. "Fire and weather disturbances in terrestrial ecosystems of the eastern Cascades." U.S. Department of Agriculture, Forest Service, Pacific Northwest Research Station. *Gen. Tech. Report PNW-GTR-320.* Corvallis, Oregon.

Benner, P.A. and J.R. Sedell. 1997. "Upper Willamette River landscape: A historical perspective." In: A. Laenen and D. A. Dunnette (eds.). River Quality: Dynamics and Restoration. CRC Press, Inc., New York.

Bottom, D., S. Beckwitt, J. Christy, S. Clarke, J. Dambacher, C. Frissell, R. Hughes, H. Li, D. McCullough, A. McGee, K. Moore, R. Nawa, S. Thiele. 1993. Oregon critical watersheds database. Watershed Classification Subcommittee of the Natural Production Committee, Oregon Chapter American Fisheries Society. Corvallis, Oregon.

Brown, E.R. (ed.) 1985. Management of wildlife and fish habitats in forests of western Oregon and Washington. U.S. Department of Agriculture, Forest Service.

Csuti, B., A.J. Kimerling, T.A. O'Neil, M.M. Shaughnesy, E.P. Gaines, and M.M.P. Huso. 1997. Atlas of Oregon wildlife: Distribution, habitat, and natural history. Oregon State University Press, Corvallis, Oregon.

Dobkin, D.S. 1994. Conservation and management of neotropical migrant land birds in the northern Rockies and Great Plains. University of Idaho Press, Moscow, Idaho.

Dobkin, D.S. 1995. Management and conservation of sage grouse, denominative species for the ecological health of shrubsteppe ecosystems. USDI Bureau of Land Management. Portland, Oregon.

Duebbert, H.F. 1969. The ecology of Malheur Lake and management implications. U.S. Department of the Interior, Fish and Wildlife Service.

Franklin, J.F. and C.T. Dyrness. 1973. Natural vegetation of Oregon and Washington. Oregon State University Press, Corvallis, Oregon.

Frissell, C.A. 1993. "Topology of extinction and endangerment of native fishes in the Pacific Northwest and California." *Conservation Biology* 7: 342-354.

Gast, W.R., Jr., D.W. Scott, and C. Schmitt. 1991. Blue Mountains forest health report: New perspectives in forest health. U.S. Department of Agriculture, Forest Service, Pacific Northwest Region. Portland, Oregon.

Grumbine, R.E. 1992. Ghost bears: Exploring the biodiversity crisis. Island Press, Washington, D.C.

Gumtow-Farrior, Daniel L. and Catherine M. Gumtow-Farrior. March 1992. Managing Oregon white oak communities for wildlife in Oregon's Willamette Valley: A problem analysis. Unpublished paper.

Hanf, J.M., P.A. Schmidt, and E.B. Groshens. 1994. Sage grouse in the high desert of central Oregon: Results of a study, 1988-1993. U.S. Department of the Interior, Bureau of Land Management, Prineville District.

Henjum, M.G., J.R. Karr, D.L. Bottom, D.A. Perry, J.C. Bednarz, S.G. Wright, S.A. Beckwitt, and E. Beckwitt. 1994. Interim protection for late-successional forests, fisheries, and watersheds: National forests east of the Cascade crest, Oregon and Washington. The Wildlife Society. Bethesda, Maryland.

Henson D. 1982. A Grazing history of southwestern Idaho with emphasis on the Birds of Prey Study Area, U.S. Department of the Interior, Bureau of Land Management. Boise Idaho.

Hessburg, P.F., R.G. Mitchell, and G.M. Filip. 1993. "Historical and current roles of insects and pathogens in eastern Oregon and Washington forested landscapes." In: Hessburg, P.F. (ed.). Eastside Forest Ecosystem Health Assessment (Volume III). U.S. Department of Agriculture, Forest Service, Pacific Northwest Research Station. Portland, Oregon.

Hicks, B.J., J.D. Hall, P.A. Bisson, and J.R. Sedell. 1991. "Response of salmonids to habitat change." *American Fisheries Society Special Publication* 19: 483-518.

Huntington, C., W. Nehlsen, and J. Bowers. 1996. "A survey of healthy native stocks of anadromous salmonids in the Pacific Northwest and California." *Fisheries* 21(3): 6-14.

Huntington, C. 1997. Aquatic conservation strategy for northwest Oregon (unpublished). Oregon Trout. Portland, Oregon.

Interior Columbia Basin Ecosystem Management Project (ICBEMP). 1996. Status of the Interior Columbia Basin summary of scientific findings. Portland, Oregon.

Interior Columbia Basin Ecosystem Management Project (ICBEMP). 1997a. An assessment of ecosystem components in the interior Columbia Basin and portions of the Klamath and Great basins (volume 3). U.S. Department of Agriculture and U.S. Department of the Interior *Gen. Tech. Report PNW-GTR-405.*

Interior Columbia Basin Ecosystem Management Project (ICBEMP). 1997b. Eastside draft environmental impact statement (volume 1). U.S. Department of Agriculture and U.S. Department of the Interior. Portland, Oregon.

Kagan, J.S. and S. Caicco. 1992. Manual of Oregon actual vegetation. Idaho Fish and Wildlife Research Cooperative Unit, University of Idaho. Moscow, Idaho.

Kauffman, J.B. 1982. "Impacts of grazing on wetlands and riparian habitat: A review of our knowledge." In: Developing Strategies for Rangeland Management: A Report by the Committee on Developing Strategies for Rangeland Management. Westview Press, Boulder, Colorado.

LaLande, J. 1995. An environmental history of the Little Applegate River Watershed. U.S. Department of Agriculture, Forest Service, Rogue River National Forest.

Langston, N. 1995. Forest dreams, forest nightmares: The paradox of old growth in the inland West. University of Washington Press, Seattle, Washington.

Lehmkuhl, J.F., P.F. Hessburg, R.L. Everett, M.H. Huff, and R.D. Ottman. 1994. "Historical and current forest landscapes of Eastern Oregon and Washington. Part I: Vegetation patterns and insect and disease hazards," Gen. Tech. Report PNW-GTR-328. U.S. Department of Agriculture, Forest Service, Pacific Northwest Research Station. Corvallis, Oregon.

Leopold, A. 1949. A Sand County almanac. Ballantine Books, New York.

Marshall. D.B. 1996. Species at risk: Sensitive, threatened, and endangered vertebrates of Oregon. Oregon Department of Fish and Wildlife. Portland, Oregon.

McIntosh, B.A., J.R. Sedell, J.E. Smith, R.C. Wissmar, S.E. Clarke, G.H. Reeves, and L.A. Brown. 1994. "Management history of eastside ecosystems: Changes in fish habitat over 50 years, 1935-1992." *Gen. Tech. Report PNW-GTR-327* U.S. Department of Agriculture, Forest Service, Pacific Northwest Research Station. Portland, Oregon.

Meffe, G.K. and C.R. Carroll. 1997. Principles of conservation biology (second edition). Sinauer Associates, Inc., Publishers, Sunderland, Massachusetts.

Nature Conservancy, The. 1996. Interagency conservation strategy for rare native prairie species in west Eugene. Draft report. Portland, Oregon.

Nature Conservancy, The. 1992. Extinct vertebrate species in North America. Unpublished draft list. Arlington, Virginia.

Nehlsen, W., J.E. Williams, and J.A. Lichatowich. 1991. "Pacific salmon at the crossroads: Stocks at risk from California, Oregon, Idaho, and Washington." *Fisheries* 16 (2): 4-21.

Northwest Power Planning Council. 1986. Council staff compilation of information on salmon and steelhead losses in the Columbia River Basin. Portland, Oregon.

Noss, R.F. 1992. A preliminary biodiversity conservation plan for the Oregon Coast Range. Coast Range Association. Newport, Oregon.

Noss, R.F. and A.Y. Cooperrider. 1994. Saving nature's legacy: Protecting and restoring biodiversity. Island Press, Washington, D.C.

Noss, R.F. and Peters, R.L. 1995. Endangered ecosystems: A status report on America's vanishing habitat and wildlife. Defenders of Wildlife, Washington, D.C.

Noss, R.F., E.T. LaRoe, and J.M. Scott. 1995. "Endangered ecosystems in the United States: A preliminary assessment of loss and degradation." *Biological Report 28.* USDI National Biological Service, Washington, D.C.

Office of Technology Assessment. 1993. Harmful non-indigenous species in the United States. U.S. Government Printing Office, Washington, D.C.

Oliver, C.D., L.L. Irwin, and W.H. Knapp. 1994. "Eastside forest management practices: Historical overview, extent of their applications, and their effects on the sustainability of ecosystems." U.S. Department of Agriculture, Forest Service, Pacific Northwest Research Station. *Gen. Tech. Report PNW-GTR-324.* Portland, Oregon.

Perry, D.A. 1995. "Landscapes, humans, and other system-level considerations: A discourse on ecstasy and laundry." In: 1995 Symposium Proceedings of Ecosystem Management in Western Interior Forests, May 3-5, 1994, Spokane, Washington. Department of Natural Resource Sciences, Washington State University. Pullman, Washington.

Prevost, M., R. Horton, J. Macleod, and R.M. Davis. 1996. Southwest Oregon salmon restoration initiative. Rogue Valley Council of Governments.

Puchy, C.A. and D.B. Marshall. 1993. Oregon Wildlife Diversity Plan, 1993-1998 (Draft). Oregon Department of Fish and Wildlife. Portland, Oregon.

Pyke, D.A. and M.M. Borman. 1993. Problem analysis for the vegetation diversity project. U.S. Department of Interior, Bureau of Land Management Technical Note OR-936-01, Portland, Oregon.

Rahr, Guido. 1997. Personal communication. Fish Refuge Working Group, Oregon Trout. Portland, Oregon.

Ricketts, T., E. Dinerstein, D.M. Olson, C. Loucks, P. Hedao, K. Carney, S. Walters, and P. Hurley. 1997. A conservation assessment of terrestrial ecoregions of North America. World Wildlife Fund, Conservation Science Program. Washington, D.C.

Ripley, J.D. 1983. Description of the plant communities and succession of the Oregon coast grasslands. Ph.D. thesis. Oregon State University. Corvallis, Oregon.

Russell, C. and L. Morse. 1992. Extinct and possibly extinct plant species of the United States and Canada. Unpublished report. Review draft, 13. The Nature Conservancy. Arlington, Virginia.

Schultz, S.T. 1990. The Northwest coast: A natural history. Timber Press, Portland, Oregon.

Scott, J.M., M. Murray, R.G. Wright, B. Csuti, T.C. Edwards, Jr., K. Cassidy, F.W. Davis, R.L. Pressey, T. Merrill, and P. Morgan. 1997. Shortcomings in representation of natural vegetation in protected areas (unpublished manuscript). University of Idaho. Moscow, Idaho.

Skovllin, J.M. 1984. "Impacts of grazing on wetlands and riparian habitat: A review of our knowledge." In: Developing Strategies for Rangeland Management: A Report by the Committee on Developing Strategies for Rangeland Management. Westview Press, Boulder, Colorado.

Skovllin, J.M., R.W. Harris, G.S. Strickler, and G. Garrison. 1976. "Effects of cattle grazing methods on ponderosa pine-bunchgrass range in the Pacific Northwest." *Tech. Bulletin 1531,* 324 U.S. Department of Agriculture, Forest Service.

Smith, D. (ed.). 1997. 1997-1998 Oregon Blue Book. Salem, Oregon.

Sollins, P. 1994. Western Oregon industrial forest land ownership. Forest Sciences Laboratory, Oregon State University. Corvallis, Oregon.

State of Oregon. March 1997. Oregon coastal salmon restoration initiative. Report submitted to the National Marine Fisheries Service.

Svejcar, T. and M. Vavra. 1985. "The influence of several range improvements on estimated carrying capacity and potential beef production." *Journal of Range Management* 38: 395-399.

Thilenius, J.F. 1968. "The Quercus garryana forests of the Willamette Valley, Oregon." *Ecology* 49:1124-1133.

Titus, J.H., J.A. Christy, D. Vander Schaaf, J.S. Kagan, and E.R. Alverson. 1996. Native wetland, riparian, and upland plant communities and their biota in the Willamette Valley, Oregon. Oregon Natural Heritage Program, The Nature Conservancy. Portland, Oregon.

United Nations Environmental Programme, World Conservation Monitoring Centre. 1996. Guide to information management in the context of the convention on biological diversity. Nairobi, Kenya.

U.S. Census Bureau. 1995. *TIGER/Line '95*. U.S. Department of Commerce. Washington, D.C.

U.S. Department of Agriculture, Forest Service, Fremont National Forest. 1989. Land and resources management plan and final environmental impact statement.

U.S. Department of Agriculture, Forest Service, Deschutes National Forest. 1990a. Land and resources management plan and final environmental impact statement.

U.S. Department of Agriculture, Forest Service, Willamette National Forest. 1990b. Land and resource management plan and final environmental impact statement.

U.S. Department of Agriculture and U.S. Department of the Interior. 1994. Final supplemental environmental impact statement on management of habitat for late-successional and old-growth forest related species within the range of the northern spotted owl.

U.S. Department of Agriculture and U.S. Department of the Interior. 1996. Northern Coast Range Adaptive Management Area guide. Draft.

U.S. Department of the Interior, Bureau of Land Management, Oregon State Office. 1991. Wilderness study report.

U.S. Department of the Interior, Bureau of Land Management, Prineville District, and Oregon Parks and Recreation Department. 1993. John Day River management plan and environmental impact statement.

U.S. Department of the Interior, Bureau of Land Management, Medford District. 1994a. Medford District proposed resource management plan and environmental impact statement.

U.S. Department of the Interior, Bureau of Land Management, Roseburg District. 1994b. Roseburg District proposed resource management plan and environmental impact statement.

U.S. Department of the Interior, Fish and Wildlife Service. 1988. Concept plan for waterfowl habitat protection — Klamath Basin. Portland, Oregon.

U.S. Department of the Interior, Fish and Wildlife Service. 1994. *Klamath Basin National Wildlife Refuges* (brochure).

Vickerman, S. 1998. Stewardship incentives: Conservation strategies for Oregon's working landscape. Defenders of Wildlife. Lake Oswego, Oregon.

Wilcove, D.S., M. McMillan, and K.C. Winston. 1993. "What exactly is an endangered species? An analysis of the U.S. Endangered Species list: 1985-1991." *Conservation Biology,* vol. 7.

Wilcox, B.A. and D.D. Murphy. 1985. "Conservation strategy: The effects of fragmentation on extinction." *American Naturalist,* vol. 125.

Wilderness Society, The. 1993. Pacific salmon and federal lands, a regional analysis. The Wilderness Society, Bolle Center for Forest Ecosystem Management. Washington D.C.

Williams, J.E., J.E. Johnson, and D.A. Hendrickson. 1989. "Fishes of North America: Endangered, threatened, or of special concern." *Fisheries* 14 (6): 12-20.

Wilson, E.O. 1992. The diversity of life. The Belknap Press of Harvard University Press, Cambridge, Massachusetts.

Wissmar, R.C., J.E. Smith, B.A. McIntosh, H.W. Li, G.H. Reeves, and J.R. Sedell. 1994. "Ecological health of river basins in forested regions of eastern Washington and Oregon." *Gen. Tech. Report PNW-GTR-326.* U.S. Department of Agriculture, Forest Service, Pacific Northwest Research Station. Portland, Oregon.